THE ENVIRONMENT

ISSN 2332-3825

THE ENVIRONMENT

Kim Masters Evans

INFORMATION PLUS® REFERENCE SERIES
Formerly Published by Information Plus, Wylie, Texas

Farmington Hills, Mich • San Francisco • New York • Waterville, Maine
Meriden, Conn • Mason, Ohio • Chicago

The Environment

Kim Masters Evans

Kepos Media, Inc.: Steven Long and
Janice Jorgensen, Series Editors

Project Editor: Laura Avery

Rights Acquisition and Management:
Ashley Maynard, Carissa Poweleit

Composition: Evi Abou-El-Seoud, Jeff Sumner,
Mary Beth Trimper

Manufacturing: Rita Wimberley

Product Design: Kristin Julien

For product information and technology assistance, contact us at
Gale Customer Support, 1-800-877-4253.
For permission to use material from this text or product,
submit all requests online at **www.cengage.com/permissions.**
Further permissions questions can be emailed to
permissionrequest@cengage.com

Cover photograph: © Yvonne Pijnenburg-Schonewille/Shutterstock.com.

Gale
27500 Drake Rd.
Farmington Hills, MI 48331-3535

ISBN-13: 978-0-7876-5103-9 (set)
ISBN-13: 978-1-4103-2546-4

ISSN 2332-3825

This title is also available as an e-book.
ISBN-13: 978-1-4103-2578-5
Contact your Gale sales representative for ordering information.

Printed in the United States of America
1 2 3 4 5   22 21 20 19 18

TABLE OF CONTENTS

PREFACE vii

CHAPTER 1

The State of the Environment: An Overview 1

Public opinion and knowledge about environmental issues have evolved over time and have led to federal and state laws protecting environmental resources. These laws have been debated on their economic impact and on how well they protect citizens from environmental hazards. Various political factors affect the implementation of such laws. The international community is also concerned about the environment and has, with varying degrees of success, instituted environmental standards of protection.

CHAPTER 2

Air Quality 15

Emissions of chemicals from transportation vehicles, industrial facilities, and power plants are mostly to blame for air pollution, which can make people sick and harm the environment. Government regulation, along with the implementation of new technologies, is designed to promote clean air. Although some people believe these measures are too restrictive, others believe the measures do not go far enough.

CHAPTER 3

Climate Change 39

Scientists generally agree that the earth is getting warmer largely because of anthropogenic (human-caused) emissions of greenhouse gases that can bring about climate change. These gases include carbon dioxide, methane, nitrogen oxide, and engineered gases, and their continued emissions could have severe environmental effects on the earth. Many nations have committed themselves to reducing greenhouse gas emissions, with varying levels of success.

CHAPTER 4

A Hole in the Sky: Ozone Depletion 69

Ozone can be either a health hazard or a health protectant, depending on where in the atmosphere it is located. Human-made chemicals, such as chlorofluorocarbons, can deplete the protective layer of ozone found in the upper atmosphere, which shields humans, plants, and animals from excess ultraviolet radiation exposure. The international community plays an important role in safeguarding environmental health by protecting the ozone layer.

CHAPTER 5

Acid Rain 79

The combustion of fossil fuels emits sulfur oxides and nitrogen oxides into the atmosphere, leading to acid rain. Acid rain can harm human health and damage ecosystems. Politicians and environmental groups in the United States and throughout the world have attempted, through legislation and other measures, to reduce pollution that causes acid rain.

CHAPTER 6

Nonhazardous Waste 89

The vast majority of waste generated by modern society is not inherently hazardous. It includes paper, wood, plastics, glass, and nonhazardous metals and chemicals. Landfilling, incineration, and combustion are the most common disposal methods for nonhazardous waste. Nevertheless, these methods have environmental consequences that must be mitigated through design and control techniques.

CHAPTER 7

Nonhazardous Materials Recovery: Recycling
and Composting 105

Problems associated with the disposal of nonhazardous wastes have created a greater need for the recovery of materials through recycling and composting. These methods save landfill space, conserve energy that would be used for incineration, reduce environmental degradation, and minimize the use of new resources. Their implementation and success, however, depend on public participation, government regulation, and economic factors.

CHAPTER 8

Hazardous and Radioactive Waste 115

The most toxic and dangerous waste materials are those classified by the government as hazardous or radioactive. The storage, transport, and disposal of these wastes require special consideration, subjecting them to strict regulatory control and intense public scrutiny. Federal and state governments try to ensure that these wastes are managed in a way that protects both the environment and public health.

CHAPTER 9

Water Issues 135

Water is an essential resource that is necessary for sustaining all forms of life, but human alteration of the environment and patterns of water usage can have a devastating effect on the water supply. Legislation, including the Clean Water Act, seeks to improve and protect the integrity of US surface water, groundwater, oceans, coastal water, and drinking water. The effectiveness of such laws remains a matter of debate.

CHAPTER 10
Toxins in Everyday Life 155

Many of the substances found naturally in the environment or released by modern, industrialized society are poisonous at certain dosages. Such substances may be found in the home, workplace, or backyard; in the foods people eat and in the water they drink; and in consumer products. Common toxins include metals and other chemicals; radiation, particularly from radon exposure; indoor air pollutants, such as asbestos; and foodborne contaminants, including pathogens. These toxins can have damaging effects on human health and the environment.

CHAPTER 11
Depletion and Conservation of Natural Resources 165

Forests and wetlands are rich and valuable ecosystems that are endangered by the activities of humans. The diversity of life on Earth (biodiversity) is also at risk, with many species facing extinction. Although domestic production of minerals and fossil fuels is important economically, it also has environmental consequences that must be addressed.

IMPORTANT NAMES AND ADDRESSES 179

RESOURCES 181

INDEX 183

PREFACE

The Environment is part of the *Information Plus Reference Series*. The purpose of each volume of the series is to present the latest facts on a topic of pressing concern in modern American life. These topics include the most controversial and studied social issues of the 21st century: abortion, capital punishment, care for senior citizens, crime, health care, immigration, national security, sports, weight, women, youth, and many more. Although this series is written especially for high school and undergraduate students, it is an excellent resource for anyone in need of factual information on current affairs.

By presenting the facts, it is the intention of Gale, a Cengage Company, to provide its readers with everything they need to reach an informed opinion on current issues. To that end, there is a particular emphasis in this series on the presentation of scientific studies, surveys, and statistics. These data are generally presented in the form of tables, charts, and other graphics placed within the text of each book. Every graphic is directly referred to and carefully explained in the text. The source of each graphic is presented within the graphic itself. The data used in these graphics are drawn from the most reputable and reliable sources, such as from the various branches of the US government and from private organizations and associations. Every effort has been made to secure the most recent information available. Readers should bear in mind that many major studies take years to conduct and that additional years often pass before the data from these studies are made available to the public. Therefore, in many cases the most recent information available in 2018 is dated from 2015 or 2016. Older statistics are sometimes presented as well if they are landmark studies or of particular interest and no more-recent information exists.

Although statistics are a major focus of the *Information Plus Reference Series*, they are by no means its only content. Each book also presents the widely held positions and important ideas that shape how the book's subject is discussed in the United States. These positions are explained in detail and, where possible, in the words of their proponents. Some of the other material to be found in these books includes historical background, descriptions of major events related to the subject, relevant laws and court cases, and examples of how these issues play out in American life. Some books also feature primary documents or have pro and con debate sections that provide the words and opinions of prominent Americans on both sides of a controversial topic. All material is presented in an evenhanded and unbiased manner; readers will never be encouraged to accept one view of an issue over another.

HOW TO USE THIS BOOK

The condition of the world's environment is an issue of great concern both to Americans and to other people worldwide. Since the late 19th century, humankind's ability to alter the natural world, both deliberately and unintentionally, has increased. Many people fear that without proper restraint, humankind's actions could forever alter, or even eliminate, life on Earth. There are others, however, who believe that these fears are exaggerated and that the substantial cost to business and industry for environmental protection should be minimized. The conflict between these two positions has serious economic, environmental, and political ramifications, within the United States and worldwide. This book examines the steps that have been taken to protect the earth's natural environment and the controversies that surround them.

The Environment consists of 11 chapters and 3 appendixes. Each chapter is devoted to a particular aspect of the environment. For a summary of the information that is covered in each chapter, please see the synopses that are provided in the Table of Contents. Chapters generally begin with an overview of the basic facts and background information on the chapter's topic, then proceed to examine subtopics of particular interest. For example, Chapter 11: Depletion and Conservation of Natural Resources begins with an examination of some of the nation's most valuable natural resources, such as forests and wetlands, and discusses the stressors that affect them. Biodiversity is also discussed, particularly in terms of species loss and the programs devoted to preventing the extinction of plants and animals. Issues related to the world's fisheries and the growing practice of aquaculture are then described. The chapter ends with an overview of issues related to the extraction of minerals and fossil fuels from the earth. The extraction of oil and natural gas resources in environmentally sensitive areas, such as the Arctic regions of Alaska, is given special attention. Readers can find their way through a chapter by looking for the section and subsection headings, which are clearly set off from the text. They can also refer to the book's extensive Index if they already know what they are looking for.

Statistical Information

The tables and figures featured throughout *The Environment* will be of particular use to readers in learning about this issue. The tables and figures represent an extensive collection of the most recent and important statistics on the environment, as well as related issues—for example, graphics cover the amounts of different kinds of pollutants that are found in the air across the United States; probable sources of impairment to assessed water bodies; the amounts of wetlands that are destroyed or created every year; and public opinion on whether environmental protection or economic considerations should have priority. Gale, a Cengage Company, believes that making this information available to readers is the most important way to fulfill the goal of this book: to help readers understand the issues and controversies surrounding the environment and reach their own conclusions about them.

Each table or figure has a unique identifier appearing above it, for ease of identification and reference. Titles for the tables and figures explain their purpose. At the end of each table or figure, the original source of the data is provided.

To help readers understand these often complicated statistics, all tables and figures are explained in the text. References in the text direct readers to the relevant statistics. Furthermore, the contents of all tables and figures are fully indexed. Please see the opening section of the Index at the back of this volume for a description of how to find tables and figures within it.

Appendixes

Besides the main body text and images, *The Environment* has three appendixes. The first is the Important Names and Addresses directory. Here, readers will find contact information for a number of government and private organizations that can provide further information on aspects of the environment. The second appendix is the Resources section, which can also assist readers in conducting their own research. In this section, the author and editors of *The Environment* describe some of the sources that were most useful during the compilation of this book. The final appendix is the detailed Index. It has been greatly expanded from previous editions and should make it even easier to find specific topics in this book.

COMMENTS AND SUGGESTIONS

The editors of the *Information Plus Reference Series* welcome your feedback on *The Environment*. Please direct all correspondence to:

Editors
Information Plus Reference Series
27500 Drake Rd.
Farmington Hills, MI 48331-3535

CHAPTER 1
THE STATE OF THE ENVIRONMENT: AN OVERVIEW

Photographs from outer space impress on the world that humankind shares one planet, and a small one at that. (See Figure 1.1.) The earth is one ecosystem. There may be differences in race, nationality, religion, and language, but everyone resides on the same orbiting planet.

General concern about the environment is a relatively recent phenomenon. It arose in the United States during the turbulent 1960s and early 1970s, when social activism was a major force for change. Environmentalism was truly a grassroots movement in which public outcry spurred politicians to act. The result was a flurry of government regulations that were aimed at cleaning up the worst excesses of industrialism. Over the following decades the environmental movement continued to wield social and political influence, but the initial zeal for aggressive action faded as Americans turned their attention to other challenges. The economy, energy, and terrorism took precedence in the public consciousness. Around the turn of the millennium, environmental activism experienced a rebirth that was driven by concern about a "new" threat facing the world: climate change. This latest revolution in attitudes unleashed a fresh passion about environmental issues, particularly among young people. Nevertheless, this "green" surge was dampened during the latter half of the first decade of the 21st century by the so-called Great Recession (which lasted from late 2007 to mid-2009). A turbulent public debate emerged over the often conflicting priorities of environmental protection versus economic growth. It remains to be seen how this philosophical and political battle will shape future US environmental policy.

HISTORICAL ATTITUDES TOWARD THE ENVIRONMENT
The Industrial Revolution

Humankind has always altered the environment around itself. For much of human history, however, these changes were fairly limited. The world was too vast and people too few to have more than a minor effect on the environment, especially because they had only primitive tools and technology to aid them. All this began to change during the 1800s. First in Europe and then in the United States, powerful new machines, such as steam engines, were developed and put into use. These new technologies led to great increases in the amount and quality of goods that could be manufactured and the amount of food that could be harvested. As a result, the quality of life rose substantially and the population began to boom. The so-called Industrial Revolution was under way.

Although the Industrial Revolution enabled people to live better in many ways, it also increased pollution. For many years pollution was thought to be an insignificant side effect of growth and progress. In fact, at one time people looked on the smokestacks belching black soot as a healthy sign of economic growth. The reality was that pollution, along with the increased demands for natural resources and living space that resulted from the Industrial Revolution, was beginning to have a significant effect on the environment.

The Environmental Revolution

For much of the early 20th century Americans accepted pollution as an inevitable cost of economic progress. During the 1940s and 1950s, however, more and more incidents involving pollution made people aware of the environmental problems that were caused by human activities. In Los Angeles, California, smog (a smoky haze of pollution that forms like a fog in the city; the word was made by combining the words *smoke* and *fog*) contributed a new word to the English language. According to the South Coast Air Quality Management District, in "The Southland's War on Smog: Fifty Years of Progress toward Clean Air" (May 1997, http://library archives.metro.net/DPGTL/epa/1997-southlands-war-on-smog-aqmd.pdf), "World War II dramatically increased

FIGURE 1.1

Space view of earth, photograph. *US National Aeronautics and Space Administration (NASA).*

the region's industrial base and resulting air pollution. The city's population and motor vehicle fleet grew rapidly as well. As a result, according to weather records, visibility declined rapidly from 1939 to 1943. Angelenos grew increasingly alarmed at the smoke that clouded their vision and the fumes that filled their lungs." In 1947 public pressure spurred local officials to create the country's first air pollution control program. This is an example of grassroots activism—actions by ordinary people that are designed to bring about change.

One influential person in the modern environmental movement was Rachel Carson (1907–1964), a prolific writer and biologist who specialized in raising public awareness about natural resources and conservation. In the book *Silent Spring* (1962), Carson described the environmental toll of the chemical insecticide dichloro-diphenyl-trichloroethane (DDT) and other persistent (long-lasting in the environment) synthetic pesticides. Extensive DDT use had begun during World War II (1939–1945). Its effectiveness at killing insects greatly reduced the number of people who died from diseases such as malaria. However, DDT also had a negative effect on the environment. Carson alleged that the synthetic chemicals and their residues had become persistent and were found widely in rivers, lakes, groundwater, soil, and in the bodies of fish, birds, reptiles, other animals, and even humans.

Carson cited the results of scientific studies indicating the lethal effects of DDT on songbirds, bald eagles, pheasants, ducks, and other fish-eating fowl. She made the case that DDT spreads throughout the food chain and

the environment, poisoning organisms along the way. From a human health standpoint, she argued that the chemicals build up in human tissues and likely cause long-term damage to the liver and kidneys. At the time, the lethal effects of acute exposure (short-term exposure to a large dose) of DDT to humans were well documented. Although a cause-and-effect relationship between long-term, low-level exposure and human illness had not been established, Carson contended that chronic exposure must certainly be detrimental to human health. Her work is considered to be one of the driving forces behind the environmental movement.

According to the US Environmental Protection Agency (EPA), in the press release "DDT Ban Takes Effect" (December 31, 1972, https://archive.epa.gov/ epa/aboutepa/ddt-ban-takes-effect.html), approximately 675,000 tons (612,000 t) of the pesticide were applied in the United States between the 1940s and the 1972 ban, mostly to agricultural crops, such as cotton. The EPA notes, however, that insects began developing resistance to the pesticide. (This happens as naturally resistant individuals survive pesticide applications and pass their resistance on to their offspring. Eventually, resistant individuals outnumber susceptible individuals, and the insecticide is no longer effective.) In addition, the EPA cites growing public and government concern about the toxic effects of the pesticide and the development of effective alternatives as reasons for the US ban in 1972 on almost all domestic uses of DDT.

The United States' environmental problems at the time were not limited to air pollution and chemical toxins. In 1969 the Cuyahoga River near Cleveland, Ohio, burst into flames because of pollutants in the water. Clearly, strong and decisive action was needed.

LAWS AND LAWSUITS. In 1970 Congress passed and President Richard M. Nixon (1913–1994) signed a series of unprecedented laws to protect the environment. Nixon proposed and Congress approved the creation of a new federal agency, the EPA, which combined many smaller federal agencies. The EPA was charged with setting limits on water and air pollutants and investigating the environmental impact of proposed, federally funded projects. In the years that followed, many more environmental laws were passed, setting basic rules for interaction with the environment. Most notable among these laws were the Clean Air Act (CAA) of 1970, the Clean Water Act (CWA) of 1972, the Endangered Species Act of 1973, the Safe Drinking Water Act of 1974, and the Resource Conservation and Recovery Act of 1976.

A significant feature of many of these federal laws was the so-called citizen-suit provision. This provision allows ordinary citizens to file lawsuits in civil court against businesses or federal government agencies for failing to meet standards or follow orders laid out by

Congress in the laws. For example, Section 505 of the CWA (https://www.law.cornell.edu/uscode/text/33/1365#) states that "any citizen may commence a civil action on his own behalf." Of course, there are legal technicalities and expenses involved in filing citizen suits. As a result, they are mostly pursued by environmental organizations with the legal savvy and funds to do so.

The late 1960s and early 1970s witnessed the birth of some influential environmental organizations, such as the Environmental Defense Fund, the Union of Concerned Scientists, Greenpeace, and the Natural Resources Defense Council. These groups and long-standing conservation organizations, such as the Sierra Club and the National Audubon Society, quickly realized the power of citizen suits to further their environmental goals. The Environmental Defense Fund's legal battles against DDT played a major role in the banning of the pesticide. In 1971 the Sierra Club founded a legal defense fund that was later renamed Earthjustice (2018, https://earthjustice .org/about/our_history).

By the 1960s many states had already established agencies that were charged with conserving land or protecting health-related resources, such as drinking water. As environmental awareness grew, so did state laws and protection schemes. Small agencies, often operating under a department of health, were merged, or brand-new agencies were created to focus solely on pollution control. The EPA (December 20, 2017, https://www.epa .gov/home/health-and-environmental-agencies-us-states-and-territories) maintains an online listing with links to the environmental agencies in every state and US territory.

EARTH DAY. There are actually two dates that have been celebrated annually as Earth Day. The better-known date is April 22. The idea for this Earth Day began to evolve during the early 1960s. Nationwide "teach-ins" were being held on university campuses across the country to protest the Vietnam War (1954–1975). The US senator Gaylord Nelson (1916–2005; D-WI), troubled by the apathy of US leaders toward the environment, announced that a grassroots demonstration on behalf of the environment would be held during the spring of 1970, and he invited everyone to participate. On April 22, 1970, 20 million people participated in massive rallies on university campuses and in large cities. Earth Day went on to become an annual event.

A lesser-known Earth Day was initiated in 1970 by John McConnell (1915–2012), a peace activist. It was often called the equinox Earth Day because it was celebrated on the vernal equinox (March 21, the first day of spring in the Northern Hemisphere). The United Nations (UN) traditionally celebrated the equinox Earth Day with the ringing of a peace bell. In April 2009 the UN General Assembly officially declared April 22 of each year to be International Mother Earth Day.

RADICAL ENVIRONMENTALISM. The environmental movement inspired some adherents to engage in acts of civil disobedience, such as by chaining themselves to trees that were going to be cut down. More radical actions including sabotage and the destruction of property have also taken place. These acts are known broadly as ecoterrorism or ecotage. Since the late 1970s several environmental groups have allegedly engaged in ecoterrorism, including the Environmental Life Force, the Sea Shepherd Conservation Society, Earth First, the Earth Liberation Front (ELF), and the Animal Liberation Front (ALF).

The ELF and the ALF are perhaps the most active and well-known of the groups. In February 2002 James F. Jarboe of the Federal Bureau of Investigation (FBI; https://archives.fbi.gov/archives/news/testimony/the-threat-of-eco-terrorism) testified before the US House of Representatives, Resources Committee, Subcommittee on Forests and Forest Health, noting, "During the past several years, special interest extremism, as characterized by the Animal Liberation Front (ALF) and the Earth Liberation Front (ELF), has emerged as a serious terrorist threat." Officials suggest that the ELF and the ALF are not so much organizations as an ideology with which many ecoterrorists claim allegiance. The letters "ELF" are often found spray painted near sites that are suspected of being victimized by ecoterrorists. New luxury housing developments in or near sensitive environments have been a frequent target of such crimes. One of the most famous cases occurred in 1998, when arsonists set fire to the Vail Ski Resort in Vail, Colorado. In "Eco-terror Indictments" (January 20, 2006, https://archives.fbi.gov/archives/news/stories/2006/january/elf012006), the FBI indicates the attack did $12 million in damages. In a May 2004 hearing before the US Senate Committee on the Judiciary, John E. Lewis (https://archives.fbi.gov/archives/news/testimony/animal-rights-extremism-and-ecoterrorism), the deputy assistant director of the FBI, stated, "The FBI estimates that the ALF/ELF and related groups have committed more than 1,100 criminal acts in the United States since 1976, resulting in damages conservatively estimated at approximately $110 million."

In 2004 the FBI launched Operation Backfire, a comprehensive and focused investigation of suspected ecoterrorists. According to the bureau, in "Putting Intel to Work: Against ELF and ALF Terrorists" (June 30, 2008, https://archives.fbi.gov/archives/news/stories/2008/june/ecoterror_063008), by 2008 the FBI had obtained indictments against 30 people. As of January 2018, two people believed to be affiliated with the ELF/ALF were listed on the FBI's "wanted" website (https://www.fbi .gov/wanted/dt) for domestic terrorism: Joseph Mahmoud Dibee and Josephine Sunshine Overaker. Both were accused of various ecoterrorism crimes, including arson.

A Change in Attitude toward Environmentalism

Widespread public concern about the nation's serious (and obvious) environmental problems during the 1960s and 1970s pushed politicians to take decisive action. This resulted in major improvements in the condition of the environment. Many of the most dangerous chemicals that once polluted the air and water were banned or their emissions into the environment were greatly reduced. As the highly visible dangers—belching smokestacks and burning rivers—were improved, the initial zeal for environmental action began to fade.

One factor was money. The US economy was booming during the 1960s and early 1970s, when environmental activism began. By the end of the 1970s, however, the economy was burdened with high unemployment and high inflation rates—problems that lasted well into the 1980s. Americans fearing for their jobs rallied against environmental restrictions, believing that the restrictions threatened their livelihood. This war of attitudes came to a head in 1990, when the northern spotted owl was declared a threatened species in the Pacific Northwest. Millions of acres of forestland were set aside as habitat for the species, and logging was banned on federal lands within the area. Loggers bitterly protested the loss of jobs, an argument that won sympathy from the American public. Although the national economy improved tremendously during the 1990s, it did not eliminate people's concerns about the potential negative effects of environmental regulations on the economy.

The impact of environmental protection on private property rights also played a role in the change in attitudes. The Endangered Species Act and the wetlands provisions of the CWA spurred a grassroots private property rights movement. Many people became concerned that these acts, as well as other legislation, allowed the government to take or devalue properties without compensation. For example, if federal regulations prohibit construction on a plot of land that is protected by law, then the landowner may feel that the government is unfairly limiting the use of his or her property. At the very least, the landowner may want government compensation for decreasing the monetary value of the land.

Partisan Politics

During the 1960s and 1970s political support for environmental issues was largely bipartisan (shared by both major political parties). Nevertheless, this condition was not to last. Over the latter decades of the 20th century the Republican Party adopted a more conservative stance (when compared with the Democratic Party) that embraced limited government as one of its main platforms. This position favors freer economic markets, such as through less regulation of industry and businesses. The nation's environmental policy, however, had long been based on a command-and-control scheme in which the EPA established increasingly stricter regulations on industry. During the 1980s the Republican Party began arguing that this approach was too burdensome on industry because of the high compliance costs involved. It was a message that resonated with some sectors of society.

In 1990 Congress performed a major overhaul of the CAA. As is explained in Chapter 2, lawmakers incorporated new market-based programs that give businesses more options in how they achieve pollution control goals. This approach represents a major departure from the traditional command-and-control regulatory scheme. The chief outcome has been the Acid Rain Program (ARP), which is described in detail in Chapter 5. The ARP features a cap-and-trade program in which a cap or maximum limit is set for total emissions of a particular pollutant across an industry group. Nonetheless, individual emitters operating below emissions limits are allowed to sell credits to other companies that are having trouble meeting the limits. An example is shown in Figure 1.2. Initially, the three plants that make up the regulated industry collectively emitted 30 tons (27.2 t). A new overall cap of 15 tons (13.6 t) was established for the industry, which equated to an average limit of 5 tons (4.5 t) per plant. Plant A reduced its emissions by 5 tons, Plant B by 7 tons (6.4 t), and Plant C by 3 tons (2.7 t). Plant A met the new limit. Plant B was 2 tons (1.8 t) below the new limit and Plant C was 2 tons above the new limit. Under a cap-and-trade system Plant B could sell its 2-ton allowance to Plant C. In this way all three plants would meet the new limit overall. The ARP cap-and-trade system has proven effective at curbing the problems with acid rain that were quite evident during the 1980s.

By the 1990s many of the cheapest and easiest environmental problems to fix had already been resolved. Most of the remaining problems were so large or complicated that it was believed that tremendous amounts of money would have to be spent before even modest improvements would be realized. In a way, the environmental movement was a victim of its own success. Emerging issues, such as atmospheric ozone depletion, were less obvious and more difficult to comprehend than environmental problems of the past and aroused less widespread public passion. Nevertheless, a new era of activism was dawning and would have a profound effect on the environmental movement.

Being Green

During the 1990s new waves of social activism began emerging around the world. The so-called antiglobalism or anticapitalism movement captured headlines with demonstrations, and sometimes violent riots, during meetings of the world's industrialized countries, including a summit of the World Trade Organization in Seattle,

FIGURE 1.2

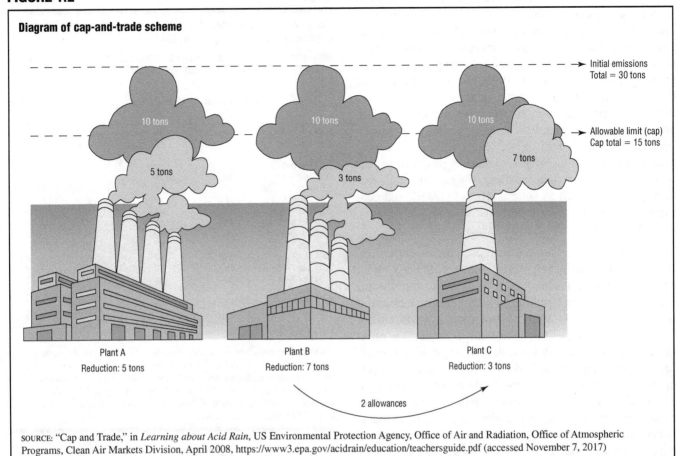

Diagram of cap-and-trade scheme

Initial emissions
Total = 30 tons

Allowable limit (cap)
Cap total = 15 tons

10 tons 10 tons 10 tons

5 tons 3 tons 7 tons

Plant A
Reduction: 5 tons

Plant B
Reduction: 7 tons

Plant C
Reduction: 3 tons

2 allowances

Washington, in 1999. The movement presented a variety of grievances involving environmental, labor, and social issues. At the same time, public awareness was growing about an emerging environmental problem called global warming. As is explained in Chapter 3, a scientific consensus slowly developed that human-related emissions of carbon dioxide and other gases (primarily from the burning of fossil fuels) were causing the atmosphere to hold too much heat and raising the earth's temperature. This phenomenon is called the greenhouse effect because a greenhouse also holds in heat. Concern has risen that continued emissions of greenhouse gases will cause more global warming. This could have climatic consequences, including rising sea levels, stronger storms, and habitat loss and extinction.

In 1997 many countries joined the Kyoto Protocol to the UN Framework on Climate Change (UNFCC), an international agreement brokered by the UN, in which greenhouse gas emissions limits were placed on some countries. The US government refused to enter into the agreement because the emissions from China and India—two of the United States' biggest economic competitors—were not limited. This failure by some countries to hold themselves to higher environmental standards while expecting the United States to do so inflamed antienvironmental

sentiment in the United States. As is explained in Chapter 3, US politicians feared that the international agreement would place an undue economic burden on the United States.

In 2004 the movie *The Day after Tomorrow* dramatized the disastrous consequences of unchecked global warming. Two years later the former vice president Albert Gore Jr. (1948–) released the book *An Inconvenient Truth: The Planetary Emergency of Global Warming and What We Can Do about It*, which reached number one on the *New York Times* best-seller list. A companion documentary film was also highly successful and significantly raised public awareness about the issue.

By that point global warming and climate change had firmly installed some new concepts to the environmental movement:

- Carbon footprint—the amount of carbon that is emitted into the environment by a particular activity

- Carbon offsetting—reducing one's carbon footprint by taking action to reduce carbon emissions, such as by planting trees (growing, healthy trees biologically soak up carbon dioxide from the atmosphere)

- Carbon neutral—a condition in which an activity's carbon footprint is completely offset

Carbon offsetting or reducing one's carbon footprint became a popular activity for many people who were concerned about the consequences of climate change. Companies and organizations sprang up that offered customers opportunities to purchase offsetting options (such as tree plantings). During the 1990s and the first decade of the 21st century, environmentalism at the grassroots level was also expressed through two other means: recycling and buying green (environmentally friendly) products. Examples include recycled-content and energy-saving goods, natural (as opposed to synthetic) products, organically grown foods and clothing fibers, nonfossil fuel energy sources (such as solar and wind power), and ecotourism (vacations that are designed to minimize negative impact on ecologically sensitive areas).

Green consumerism has both champions and critics. Advocates believe it helps raise public awareness about environmental issues and is a good first step toward achieving social and political change. Detractors claim that consumerism in itself is bad for the environment. Economic development is often blamed for causing environmental problems. As a result, there is growing support for sustainability, which is the result of economic development that does not harm the environment (or society). The goal of environmental sustainability is to ensure that natural resources are not irreversibly destroyed, but maintained and even enhanced for the future. The recycling of paper to prevent the destruction of trees is an example of sustainability.

ENVIRONMENTALISM IN THE 21ST CENTURY

Competing national priorities and deeply divisive political partisanship have shaped US policy on multiple issues since the dawn of the 21st century. The terrorist attacks of September 11, 2001, and the subsequent wars in Iraq and Afghanistan greatly heightened security concerns and federal spending on national defense. The Great Recession brought historically high unemployment rates and lingering financial woes. Energy challenges, including high prices and controversy over how best to ensure the nation's energy security, also preoccupied the nation. As is explained in Chapter 11, domestic energy production has environmental consequences. This is true for established technologies, such as offshore drilling, and for newer methods, such as hydraulic fracturing. The reality is that the nation's environmental protection goals continue to come into conflict with economic and energy security goals.

Gallup, Inc., conducts polling to gauge US public opinion on various environmental issues. One question involves the quality of the nation's environment. As shown in Table 1.1, in 2017, 36% of Americans polled in 2017 said the quality of the nation's environment is "getting better," whereas 57% said it is "getting worse." This breakdown is unchanged from 2001, when the question was first asked.

TABLE 1.1

Public opinion on whether the nation's environment as a whole is getting better or getting worse, 2001–17

RIGHT NOW, DO YOU THINK THE QUALITY OF THE ENVIRONMENT IN THE COUNTRY AS A WHOLE IS GETTING BETTER OR GETTING WORSE?

	Getting better	Getting worse	Same (vol.)	No opinion
	%	%	%	%
2017 Mar 1–5	36	57	4	3
2016 Mar 2–6	37	56	5	3
2015 Mar 5–8	41	51	7	1
2014 Mar 6–9	42	50	6	2
2013 Mar 7–10	41	49	7	4
2012 Mar 8–11	42	49	7	2
2011 Mar 3–6	42	48	8	2
2010 Mar 4–7	41	48	8	3
2009 Mar 5–8	41	51	5	2
2008 Mar 6–9	26	68	5	1
2007 Mar 11–14	25	67	7	1
2006 Mar 13–16	25	67	6	2
2005 Mar 7–10	29	63	6	2
2004 Mar 8–11	34	58	6	2
2003 Mar 3–5	33	57	8	2
2002 Mar 4–7	40	54	4	2
2001 Mar 5–7	36	57	5	2

(vol.) = volunteered response

SOURCE: "Right now, do you think the quality of the environment in the country as a whole is getting better or getting worse?" in *In Depth: Topics A to Z: Environment*, Gallup, Inc., 2017, http://news.gallup.com/poll/1615/environment.aspx (accessed November 7, 2017). Copyright © 2017. Republished with permission of Gallup, Inc.; permission conveyed through Copyright Clearance Center, Inc.

In polls dating back to 1984 Gallup has asked respondents to choose whether environmental protection or economic growth should take priority when the two conflict. As shown in Table 1.2, environmental protection was the favorite for more than two decades. Nevertheless, during the latter half of the first decade of the 21st century, public opinion began to shift. In 2009 economic growth was named the preferred objective for the first time. This was also the case during most years through 2013. In 2014 the environment again became the favorite, a position it maintained in 2016 and 2017. During the 2017 poll, 56% of the respondents chose environmental protection, compared with 35% for economic growth.

Since 2001 Gallup pollsters have posed a similar question pitting environmental protection against development of domestic energy supplies, such as oil, gas, and coal. (See Table 1.3.) The results indicate that environmental protection was the favorite (but not by much) until early 2009. Thereafter, public opinion went back and forth between the two objectives. In 2017 environmental protection had the support of 59% of respondents, compared with 34% of respondents who supported development of US energy supplies.

The Political Party Divide

Although Republicans and Democrats differ on many principles, the divide on environmental issues is particularly

TABLE 1.2

Public opinion on whether the environment or the economy should be given priority, 1984–2017

WITH WHICH ONE OF THESE STATEMENTS ABOUT THE ENVIRONMENT AND THE ECONOMY DO YOU MOST AGREE—PROTECTION OF THE ENVIRONMENT SHOULD BE GIVEN PRIORITY, EVEN AT THE RISK OF CURBING ECONOMIC GROWTH (OR) ECONOMIC GROWTH SHOULD BE GIVEN PRIORITY, EVEN IF THE ENVIRONMENT SUFFERS TO SOME EXTENT?

	Environment	Economic growth	Equal priority (vol.)	No opinion
	%	%	%	%
2017 Mar 1–5	56	35	5	4
2016 Mar 2–6	56	37	4	3
2015 Mar 5–8	46	42	6	5
2014 Mar 6–9	50	41	4	5
2013 Mar 7–10	43	48	4	5
2012 Mar 8–11	41	49	6	4
2011 Mar 3–6	36	54	6	4
2010 May 24–25	50	43	4	3
2010 Mar 4–7	38	53	4	5
2009 Mar 5–8	42	51	5	3
2008 Mar 6–9	49	42	5	3
2007 Mar 11–14	55	37	4	4
2006 Mar 13–16	52	37	6	4
2005 Mar 7–10	53	36	7	4
2004 Mar 8–11	49	44	4	3
2003 Mar 3–5	47	42	7	4
2002 Mar 4–7	54	36	5	5
2001 Mar 5–7	57	33	6	4
2000 Apr 3–9	67	28	2	3
2000 Jan 13–16	70	23	—	7
1999 Apr 13–14	67	28	—	5
1999 Mar 12–14	65	30	—	5
1998 Apr 17–19	68	24	—	8
1997 Jul 25–27	66	27	—	7
1995 Apr 17–19	62	32	—	6
1992 Jan 5-Mar 31	58	26	8	8
1991 Apr 11–14	71	20	—	9
1990 Apr 5–8	71	19	—	10
1984 Sep 28-Oct 1	61	28	—	11

(vol) = volunteered response.

SOURCE: "With which one of these statements about the environment and the economy do you most agree—protection of the environment should be given priority, even at the risk of curbing economic growth (or) economic growth should be given priority, even if the environment suffers to some extent?" in *In Depth: Topics A to Z: Environment*, Gallup, Inc., 2017, http://news.gallup.com/poll/1615/environment.aspx (accessed November 7, 2017). Copyright © 2017. Republished with permission of Gallup, Inc.; permission conveyed through Copyright Clearance Center, Inc.

TABLE 1.3

Public opinion on whether the environment or energy production should be given priority, 2001–17

WITH WHICH ONE OF THESE STATEMENTS ABOUT THE ENVIRONMENT AND ENERGY PRODUCTION DO YOU MOST AGREE—[ROTATED: PROTECTION OF THE ENVIRONMENT SHOULD BE GIVEN PRIORITY, EVEN AT THE RISK OF LIMITING THE AMOUNT OF ENERGY SUPPLIES—SUCH AS OIL, GAS AND COAL—WHICH THE UNITED STATES PRODUCES (OR) DEVELOPMENT OF US ENERGY SUPPLIES—SUCH AS OIL, GAS AND COAL—SHOULD BE GIVEN PRIORITY, EVEN IF THE ENVIRONMENT SUFFERS TO SOME EXTENT]?

	Environment	Development of energy supplies	Both equally/neither/ other (vol.)	No opinion
	%	%	%	%
2017 Mar 1–5	59	34	2	4
2016 Mar 2–6	59	34	3	3
2015 Mar 5–8	49	39	6	5
2014 Mar 6–9	51	40	6	3
2013 Mar 7–10	45	46	6	3
2012 Mar 8–11	44	47	5	4
2011 Mar 3–6	41	50	5	4
2010 May 24–25	55	39	4	2
2010 Mar 4–7	43	50	4	3
2009 Mar 5–8	47	46	4	3
2008 Mar 6–9	50	41	6	3
2007 Mar 11–14	58	34	5	3
2006 Mar 13–16	49	42	6	3
2005 Mar 7–10	52	39	6	3
2004 Mar 8–11	48	44	4	4
2003 Mar 3–5	49	40	7	4
2002 Mar 4–7	52	40	5	3
2001 Mar 5–7	52	36	8	4

(vol.) = volunteered response.

SOURCE: "With which one of these statements about the environment and energy production do you most agree—[ROTATED: protection of the environment should be given priority, even at the risk of limiting the amount of energy supplies—such as oil, gas and coal—which the United States produces (or) development of US energy supplies—such as oil, gas and coal—should be given priority, even if the environment suffers to some extent]?" in *In Depth: Topics A to Z: Environment*, Gallup, Inc., 2017, http://news.gallup.com/poll/1615/environment.aspx (accessed November 7, 2017). Copyright © 2017. Republished with permission of Gallup, Inc.; permission conveyed through Copyright Clearance Center, Inc.

wide. As shown in Table 1.3, in 2017 Gallup pollsters found that 59% of Americans favored environmental protection over development of US energy supplies when the two are in conflict. In *Partisan Differences Growing on a Number of Issues* (August 3, 2017, http://news.gallup.com/opinion/polling-matters/215210/partisan-differences-growing-number-issues.aspx), Frank Newport and Andrew Dugan of Gallup note that support for the environment over development of US energy supplies was very high (79%) among Democrats and much lower (35%) among Republicans.

Gallup has asked Americans to rate the overall quality of the US environment as excellent, good, only fair, or poor. As shown in Table 1.4, between 2001 and 2017, 39% to 50% of respondents rated the environment as excellent or good each year. In 2017 the value was 46%.

There were, however, sharp differences between members of differing political parties. According to R. J. Reinhart of Gallup, in *Partisan Gap on Environment Widens after Trump's Election* (March 22, 2017, http://news.gallup.com/poll/206900/partisan-gap-environment-widens-trump-election.aspx), only 37% of Democrats said the US environment was excellent or good in 2017, compared with 64% of Republicans.

Gallup has occasionally gauged public opinion regarding the appropriateness of government action on environmental protection. In 1992, when respondents were first asked about this topic, 68% said the government was doing too little to protect the environment, 26% said government action was about right, and 4% said the government was doing too much. (See Table 1.5.) Over time, lower percentages said the government was doing too little for the environment. For example, in 2017, 59% of the respondents shared this view. Just over a quarter (26%) said the government was doing about the right amount, and 11% said the government was doing too

TABLE 1.4

Public opinion on the quality of the environment, selected years 2001–17

HOW WOULD YOU RATE THE OVERALL QUALITY OF THE ENVIRONMENT IN THIS COUNTRY TODAY—AS EXCELLENT, GOOD, ONLY FAIR OR POOR?

	Excellent	Good	Only fair	Poor	No opinion
	%	%	%	%	%
2017 Mar 1–5	6	40	44	9	1
2016 Mar 2–6	6	37	45	12	1
2015 Mar 5–8	7	43	40	9	1
2014 Mar 6–9	5	39	44	11	*
2013 Mar 7–10	7	41	43	8	*
2012 Mar 8–11	6	38	45	10	1
2011 Mar 3–6	7	38	43	11	*
2010 Mar 4–7	4	42	44	9	1
2009 Mar 5–8	5	34	45	16	*
2008 Mar 6–9	5	35	49	11	*
2007 Mar 11–14	5	35	48	11	1
2006 Mar 13–16	5	35	49	11	*
2005 Mar 7–10	4	37	48	10	1
2004 Mar 8–11	4	39	46	11	*
2003 Mar 3–5	5	36	48	10	1
2002 Mar 4–7	4	43	45	7	1
2001 Mar 5–7	5	41	47	6	1

*Less than 0.5%

SOURCE: "How would you rate the overall quality of the environment in this country today—as excellent, good, only fair or poor?" in *In Depth: Topics A to Z: Environment*, Gallup, Inc., 2017, http://news.gallup.com/poll/1615/environment.aspx (accessed November 7, 2017). Copyright © 2017. Republished with permission of Gallup, Inc.; permission conveyed through Copyright Clearance Center, Inc.

TABLE 1.5

Public opinion on the adequacy of the government's environmental protection measures, selected years 1992–2017

DO YOU THINK THE US GOVERNMENT IS DOING TOO MUCH, TOO LITTLE OR ABOUT THE RIGHT AMOUNT IN TERMS OF PROTECTING THE ENVIRONMENT?

	Too much	Too little	Right amount	No opinion
	%	%	%	%
2017 Mar 1–5	11	59	26	3
2016 Mar 2–6	12	57	29	2
2015 Mar 5–8	16	48	34	1
2014 Mar 6–9	17	48	34	1
2013 Mar 7–10	16	47	35	2
2012 Mar 8–11	17	51	30	2
2011 Mar 3–6	16	49	33	2
2010 Mar 4–7	15	46	35	4
2006 Mar 13–16*	4	62	33	1
2005 Mar 7–10*	5	58	34	3
2004 Mar 8–11*	5	55	37	3
2003 Mar 3–5*	7	51	37	5
2000 Apr 3–9	10	58	30	2
1992 Jan 5–Mar 31	4	68	26	2

*Asked of a half sample

SOURCE: "Do you think the US government is doing too much, too little or about the right amount in terms of protecting the environment?" in *In Depth: Topics A to Z: Environment*, Gallup, Inc., 2017, http://news.gallup.com/poll/1615/environment.aspx (accessed November 7, 2017). Copyright © 2017. Republished with permission of Gallup, Inc.; permission conveyed through Copyright Clearance Center, Inc.

much. Gallup does not provide a breakdown by political party for 2017, but older data show a political divide on this topic. In *About Half in U.S. Say Environmental Protection Falls Short* (April 9, 2015, http://news.gallup.com/poll/182363/half-say-environmental-protection-falls-short.aspx?utm_source=environment&utm_medium=search&utm_campaign=tiles), Justin McCarthy notes that in Gallup's 2015 poll, only 30% of Republicans thought the government was doing too little to protect the environment, compared with 64% of Democrats.

Science and Environmental Protection

US environmental policies and decisions are supposed to be based on science. For example, the CAA states, "Air quality criteria for an air pollutant shall accurately reflect the latest scientific knowledge." Thus, the EPA and other environmental agencies rely on scientific data to craft their approaches to solving environmental problems. In reality, however, science does not always provide black-and-white answers on issues; there can be many caveats, conditions, and levels of uncertainty attached to scientific findings. Thus, the ways in which the findings are interpreted and used to set policy become paramount concerns.

US environmental regulation is based on risk analysis, or more specifically risk-benefit analysis, which at its simplest is a scientific assessment of the risk of something and the benefits that could be achieved by reducing or even eliminating the risk. In theory, the exercise can provide stark choices. For example, the environment would clearly benefit if all pollutant discharges, no matter how small, were outlawed. Numerous benefits to environmental quality and public health would result. However, the regulatory and economic burden to society would be massive. Policy makers seek compromise solutions that are based on sound science and reduce risks and therefore reap benefits, but minimize undesirable consequences. This is a very challenging undertaking. In addition, environmental policy decisions are not made in a political vacuum; political considerations influence which environmental problems receive priority and which do not.

This is particularly true for global warming. As is described in Chapter 3, there is widespread international scientific consensus that global warming is largely caused by human activities, particularly the burning of fossil fuels. As a result, policy makers around the world (particularly in Europe) have focused on reducing greenhouse gas emissions. These decision makers find that the scientific knowledge on the subject convincingly illuminates the risks of the emissions to the world's climate and public health. They believe the benefits of taking aggressive action against global warming outweigh the economic consequences of doing so. US policy makers have been far less likely to share this thinking.

DDT REVISITED. Since the 1962 publication of *Silent Spring*, scientific studies have provided much new (and sometimes conflicting) information on the environmental and human health risks of DDT. For example, some studies indicate that DDT causes thinning of bird eggshells and link it to cancer in humans. Other studies, however, contradict or limit these findings. What is known for certain is that DDT effectively kills the mosquitoes that can carry malaria, a serious and often deadly disease. In "Elimination of Malaria in the United States (1947–1951)" (February 8, 2010, https://www.cdc.gov/malaria/about/history/elimination_us.html), the Centers for Disease Control and Prevention (CDC) notes that malaria once plagued mosquito-ridden areas of the US South and territorial islands. The disease was eliminated in the United States during the late 1940s and early 1950s by widespread use of DDT. Other areas of the world, however, have continued to suffer. According to the CDC (December 20, 2017, http://www.cdc.gov/Malaria), in 2016 an estimated 216 million cases of malaria occurred worldwide, and 445,000 people died from it, mostly children in Africa. The volume of human suffering and the evolving scientific knowledge about DDT have combined to change some opinions about the risk-benefit analysis of the pesticide.

For example, in 2006 the World Health Organization (WHO) and the UN began re-promoting DDT for use in combating malaria after many years of opposing the pesticide. The WHO notes in the press release "Reversing Its Policy, UN Agency Promotes DDT to Combat the Scourge of Malaria" (September 15, 2006, http://www.un.org/apps/news/story.asp?NewsID=19855#.WhRoJUqnHIU) that "extensive research and testing has since demonstrated that well-managed indoor residual spraying programmes using DDT pose no harm to wildlife or to humans."

The Status of Environmental Protection

In subsequent chapters the various factors that shape US policies on environmental protection for specific resources, such as air and water, are examined in depth. Overall, there are three interacting forces that greatly affect policy decisions in the 21st century: legislation, litigation, and political priorities.

Most of the major environmental laws were written many decades ago and have not been substantially changed in years. For example, the last major amendments to the CAA took place in 1990. Thus, the laws reflect the environmental priorities and goals of their times. In some cases the goals have proven difficult to achieve given the political and economic realities that have developed. In *Clean Air Act: EPA Should Improve the Management of Its Air Toxics Program* (June 2006, http://www.gao.gov/new.items/d06669.pdf), the US Government Accountability Office (GAO) describes the ambitious goals laid out in the 1990 CAA amendments for the nation's hazardous air pollutants (or air toxics)

program. Nearly 200 air toxins emitted by tens of thousands of facilities in hundreds of different industries around the country are to be regulated. The GAO notes that the EPA has been very slow at issuing the regulations and meeting the deadlines laid out in the act, in part, because of budget constraints and lack of resources.

The major environmental laws assign many specific tasks to the EPA and lay out deadlines that Congress set for the agency to meet. When the EPA fails to do so, the citizen-suit provisions of the acts allow parties to sue the agency. As a result, litigation has become a major driving factor behind EPA actions. Environmental groups are often the plaintiffs in these cases, but the states also litigate against the EPA when they have competing interests. For example, Chapter 3 describes the long legal battle that California waged against the federal government to set tougher carbon emissions and fuel economy standards than those desired by the EPA. The EPA maintains a website (https://www.epa.gov/noi) that lists the notices the agency has received regarding intents to sue the EPA over alleged failures to perform acts or duties required by law.

Of course, not all litigation against the EPA is driven by the desire for tougher environmental protection. Industry groups and states also sue the agency seeking to prevent control measures from being put into place. Numerous such lawsuits are discussed in subsequent chapters. For example, Chapter 9 describes how several dozen states sued the EPA in 2015 over the Clean Water Rule, a regulation that would expand the types of water bodies that are subject to the CWA. It should be noted that the vast majority of the states that were party to the lawsuit had Republican governors.

As described earlier, environmental policy making is often characterized by political partisanship. Republicans and Democrats have sharply differing views on many environmental issues. As of January 2018, three presidents had served during the 21st century. George W. Bush (1946–), a Republican, was in office from January 2001 through January 2009. He was succeeded by Barack Obama (1961–), a Democrat, who was in office through January 2017. His successor was Donald Trump (1946–), a Republican.

The environmental policies of these presidents represent, in general, the views of their primary voting blocs. For example, Bush's policies reflected the limited government and free-market approach favored by Republicans. As such, the EPA under his administration was subject to extreme criticism by environmental advocates. They had high hopes that Obama would usher in a "green revolution," including aggressive actions against global warming. His policies reflected the traditional command-and-control approach favored by Democrats. However, he made concessions based on the nation's economic conditions. For example, in 2010 the EPA proposed stricter air quality standards for ozone. This proposal elicited fierce political opposition from Republican leaders, who argued it would place a financial burden on industry and lead to layoffs. Such arguments were particularly persuasive as the nation struggled to recover from the lingering effects of the Great Recession. Obama withdrew the proposal, greatly disappointing environmental advocates. In 2015, with the economy improving, the EPA finally implemented the stricter standards, which are described in Chapter 2.

Obama took many actions during his second term (January 2013 to January 2017) to strengthen environmental regulation by the EPA. During the 2016 presidential campaign the Republican candidates complained that regulatory overreach by the agency was stifling US businesses and the economy. Trump, in particular, embraced this position and promised massive reforms and cutbacks at the agency. After taking office in January 2017, he chose Scott Pruitt (1968–) as the new EPA administrator. Pruitt, a Republican, was formerly the attorney general of Oklahoma. In that role he had joined numerous lawsuits during the Obama administration against the EPA over what Pruitt and fellow Republicans viewed as overly burdensome environmental regulations. As head of the EPA, Pruitt has worked to roll back or weaken many such regulations. For example, in October 2017 the EPA formally proposed repealing the Clean Power Plan, an Obama-era rule that imposed greenhouse gas emissions standards on fossil fuel–fired power plants. The contentious political and legal battle over this rule is described in Chapter 3. That chapter also explains measures taken by Trump to disentangle the United States from international obligations to limit emissions of gases widely blamed for global warming. Both Trump and Pruitt have publicly stated they believe that any climate changes that are occurring are natural and not anthropogenic (human-caused). As such, they adamantly oppose any government limits on greenhouse gases.

The EPA's Budget

Trump's goal to limit the EPA's power and reach is also evident in his proposed budget for the agency for fiscal year (FY) 2018. (The federal fiscal year extends from October through September; thus, FY 2018 covers October 2017 through September 2018.) Early each year—usually in February—the president presents to Congress a proposed budget request for the federal government for the upcoming fiscal year. It can take Congress many months and sometimes over a year to approve a budget. Such delays have become common during the early 21st century due to partisan bickering over spending priorities. When Congress fails to pass appropriations (funding) bills by the beginning of October (the start of the fiscal year), it often passes temporary measures called continuing resolutions. A continuing resolution generally keeps funding for an agency around the level it was in the previous year. A continuing resolution remains in effect until a final appropriations bill is passed and enacted.

Figure 1.3 shows the EPA's enacted budgets for FYs 2009 to 2016, the continuing resolution in effect in FY 2017, and Trump's budget request for FY 2018. The latter was $5.7 billion. It is broken down by appropriation in Table 1.6. Overall, the largest chunk of the budget ($2.9 billion) was slated for state and tribal assistance grants. This funding would support environmental protection and environmental programs operated by state and tribal governments.

Trump's requested EPA budget of $5.7 billion for FY 2018 is substantially lower than the amounts allocated to the agency in previous fiscal years. (See Figure 1.3.) The low figure indicates the president's deeply held belief that the EPA has become too powerful. Environmentalists were outraged by the budget proposal. For example, Robinson Meyer complains in "What Does Trump's Budget Mean for the Environment?" (TheAtlantic.com, May 24, 2017), "If he had the power, Donald Trump would allow polluters to spew carbon and chemicals into the air and water, muzzle the science that identifies why that's a problem, and cut off the research and development which is finding a more renewable way of generating power."

As of January 2018, Congress had failed to pass appropriations bills to fund the federal government for FY 2018. The EPA (and other federal agencies) were operating under continuing resolutions. There were signs that Congress would rebuff the deep spending cuts proposed by the president for the EPA's budget. For example, in September 2017 the House of Representatives passed its appropriations bill for the agency that included $7.5 billion in funding. It remained to be seen if the Senate would go along with this funding level or approve a different amount.

THE INTERNATIONAL RESPONSE TO ENVIRONMENTAL PROBLEMS

Environmental issues have never been neatly bound by national borders. Activities taking place in one country often affect the environment of other countries, if not that of the entire planet. In fact, many of the most important aspects of environmental protection involve areas that are not located within any particular country, such as the oceans, or that belong to no one, such as the atmosphere. In an attempt to deal with these issues, the international community has held a number of conferences and developed many declarations, agreements, and treaties.

In 1972 the UN met in Stockholm, Sweden, for a conference on the environment. Delegates from 113 countries gathered, with each reporting the state of his or her nation's environment—forests, water, farmland,

FIGURE 1.3

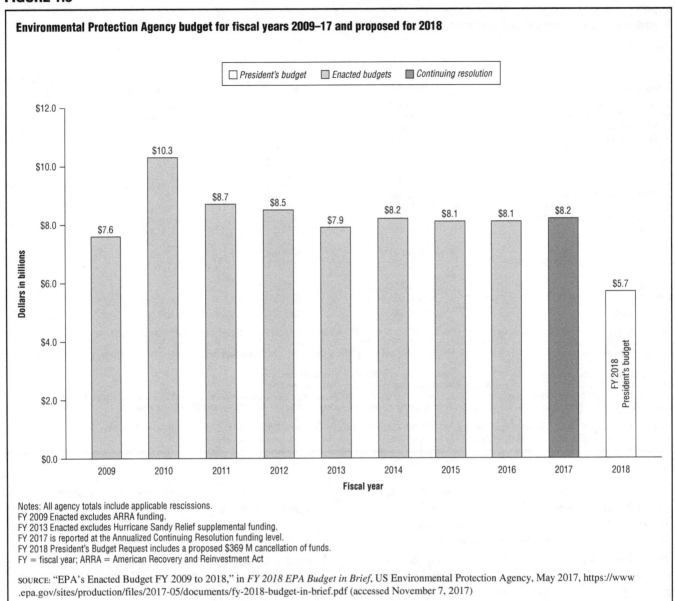

Environmental Protection Agency budget for fiscal years 2009–17 and proposed for 2018

Notes: All agency totals include applicable rescissions.
FY 2009 Enacted excludes ARRA funding.
FY 2013 Enacted excludes Hurricane Sandy Relief supplemental funding.
FY 2017 is reported at the Annualized Continuing Resolution funding level.
FY 2018 President's Budget Request includes a proposed $369 M cancellation of funds.
FY = fiscal year; ARRA = American Recovery and Reinvestment Act

SOURCE: "EPA's Enacted Budget FY 2009 to 2018," in *FY 2018 EPA Budget in Brief*, US Environmental Protection Agency, May 2017, https://www .epa.gov/sites/production/files/2017-05/documents/fy-2018-budget-in-brief.pdf (accessed November 7, 2017)

and other natural resources. The countries that were represented essentially fell into two groups. The industrialized countries were primarily concerned about how to protect the environment by preventing pollution and overpopulation and conserving natural resources. The less developed countries were more concerned about problems of widespread hunger, disease, and poverty that they all faced. They did consider the environment important, however, and were willing to protect it as long as doing so did not have a major negative economic impact on their citizens.

By the end of the two-week meeting, the delegates had agreed that the human environment had to be protected, even as industrialization proceeded in the less developed countries. They established the UN Environment Programme (UNEP), which included Earthwatch, a program to monitor changes in the earth's physical and biological resources. The most important outcome of the conference was awareness of the earth's ecology as a whole. For the first time in global history, the environmental problems of both rich and poor nations were put into perspective. General agreement emerged to protect natural resources, to encourage family planning and population control, and to protect against the negative effects of industrialization.

Since the 1972 conference, hundreds of environmental treaties and agreements have been signed. The United States is a party to most of them. In general, international agreements have had limited success at effecting environmental improvements worldwide. Part of the problem lies in differing opinions about what roles should be played by developed and developing countries. Less developed countries are generally unwilling to alter their laws and economy to end environmentally destructive ways,

TABLE 1.6

Breakdown by appropriation of budgets for the Environmental Protection Agency, fiscal years 2016–18

[Dollars in thousands]

Appropriation	FY 2016 enacted	FY 2017 annualized CR	FY 2018 pres bud	Delta FY 18 PB–FY 17 ACR
Science & Technology (S&T)	$734,648	$733,251	$450,812	($282,439)
Environmental Program & Management (EPM)	$2,635,279	$2,630,269	$1,717,484	($915,785)
Inspector General (IG)	$41,489	$41,410	$37,475	($3,935)
Building and Facilities (B&F)	$42,317	$42,237	$39,553	($2,684)
Inland Oil Spill Programs (Oil)	$18,209	$18,175	$15,717	($2,458)
Hazardous Substance Superfund (SF)	$1,094,169	$1,092,089	$762,063	($330,026)
Superfund program	$1,065,380	$1,063,355	$745,728	($317,627)
Inspector general transfer	$9,939	$9,920	$3,900	($6,020)
Science & technology transfer	$18,850	$18,814	$12,435	($6,379)
Leaking Underground Storage Tanks (LUST)	$91,941	$91,766	$47,429	($44,337)
State and Tribal Assistance Grants (STAG)	$3,518,161	$3,611,473	$2,933,467	($678,006)
Categorical grants	$1,081,041	$1,078,986	$597,347	($481,639)
State revolving funds	$2,257,120	$2,252,829	$2,257,120	$4,291
All Other STAG[a]	$180,000	$279,658	$79,000	($200,658)
Water Infrastructure Finance and Innovation Program (WIFIA)	$0	$20,000	$20,000	$0
E-Manifest	$3,674	$3,667	$0[b]	($3,667)
Cancellations	($40,000)	($40,000)	($369,000)	($329,000)
Agency total	**$8,139,887**	**$8,244,337**	**$5,655,000**	**($2,589,337)**

[a]Section 196 (a) of P.L. 114–254 provided an additional one-time $100 million in FY 2017 to address lead infrastructure in communities with declared emergencies relating to public health threats associated with lead in drinking water. The full amount was allocated to Flint, MI.
[b]The EPA requests an appropriation of $3.67 million that will net to $0 through offsetting collections of E-Manifest system user fees. The appropriation will cover necessary costs to implement and operate the E-Manifest system.
FY = fiscal year. CR = continuing resolution. ACR = annualized continuing resolution. PB = President's budget.
Notes: 1) S&T and IG totals do not include Superfund transfers—see the Superfund line items for annual amounts.
2) As part of the FY 2016 Consolidated Appropriations Act (P.L. 114–113), the EPA received $27 million for cybersecurity activities, of which $5.4 million was allocated to the Superfund Appropriation and $21.6 million was allocated to the Environmental Programs Management Appropriation as part of the agency's FY 2016 Enacted Budget.

SOURCE: "Summary of Agency Resources by Appropriation," in *FY 2018 EPA Budget in Brief*, US Environmental Protection Agency, May 2017, https://www.epa.gov/sites/production/files/2017-05/documents/fy-2018-budget-in-brief.pdf (accessed November 7, 2017)

because a shift to environmentally friendly practices would be too expensive, they claim, for their economies to handle. In contrast, the richer, industrialized countries generally refuse to alter their own behavior unless the less developed countries do so as well. Their reason is not so much the cost of change rather than believing it unfair that the less developed countries want them to carry most of the burden of environmental protection. The less developed countries respond that the industrialized countries became rich via the very practices they now want the less developed countries to stop using. They claim it is unfair to be expected to limit their economic development in ways that the industrialized countries themselves never would have done.

ENVIRONMENTAL JUSTICE: AN EVOLVING ISSUE

The environmental justice issue stems from concerns that poor people and racial minorities are disproportionately subject to environmental hazards. The EPA (November 16, 2017, https://www.epa.gov/environmentaljustice) defines environmental justice as "fair treatment and meaningful involvement of all people regardless of race, color, national origin, or income, with respect to the development, implementation, and enforcement of environmental laws, regulations, and policies."

The environmental justice movement gained national attention in 1982 with a demonstration against the construction of a hazardous waste landfill in Warren County, North Carolina, a county with a predominantly African American population. A resulting congressional study—*Siting of Hazardous Waste Landfills and Their Correlation with Racial and Economic Status of Surrounding Communities* (June 1983, http://archive.gao.gov/d48t13/121648.pdf)—found that, for three out of four landfills surveyed, African Americans made up most of the population living nearby and that at least 26% of the population in those communities was below the poverty level. In 1987 the United Church of Christ published the nationwide study *Toxic Waste and Race in the United States*, reporting that race was the most significant factor among the variables tested in determining locations of hazardous waste facilities.

In June 1992 the EPA concluded in *Environmental Equity: Reducing Risk for All Communities* (https://www.epa.gov/environmentaljustice/epa-environmental-justice-reducing-risk-all-communities-volume-1) that racial minorities and low-income people bore a disproportionate burden of environmental risk. These groups were exposed to lead, air pollutants, hazardous waste facilities, contaminated fish, and agricultural pesticides in far greater frequencies than the general population.

Similar findings were reported by Robert D. Bullard et al. in *Toxic Wastes and Race at Twenty: 1987–2007—Grassroots Struggles to Dismantle Environmental Racism in the United States* (March 2007, http://www.ejnet.org/ej/twart.pdf). The report, which was prepared for the United Church of Christ, found that racial minorities make up the majority of the population in neighborhoods near hazardous waste facilities and that poverty rates in the neighborhoods are 1.5 times greater than the rates in nonhost neighborhoods. Bullard et al. conclude that the evidence supporting environmental racism is strong, noting that "race continues to be an independent predictor of where hazardous wastes are located, and it is a stronger predictor than income, education and other socioeconomic indicators."

According to the EPA (https://www.epa.gov/environmentaljustice), the Office of Environmental Justice was established in 1992 to address environmental impacts that affect minority and low-income communities. In February 1994 President Bill Clinton (1946–) issued Executive Order 12898, Federal Actions to Address Environmental Justice in Minority Populations and Low-Income Populations (https://www.epa.gov/laws-regulations/summary-executive-order-12898-federal-actions-address-environmental-justice), which required federal agencies to develop a comprehensive strategy for including environmental justice in their decision-making. That same year the Office of Environmental Justice established a grants program to provide funds to local groups that address environmental justice issues. In "Environmental Justice Small Grants Program" (December 7, 2017, https://www.epa.gov/environmentaljustice/environmental-justice-small-grants-program), the EPA notes that it has issued more than 1,400 grants since 1994, totaling more than $24 million.

ENVIRONMENTAL EDUCATION

Many states require schools to incorporate environmental concepts, such as ecology, conservation, and environmental law, into many subjects at all grade levels. Some even require special training in environmentalism for teachers. The EPA indicates in "Environmental Education (EE) Grants" (January 18, 2018, https://www.epa.gov/education/environmental-education-ee-grants) that since 1992 it has awarded grants to more than 3,700 projects at a cost of $2 million to $3.5 million per year.

Although the mandating of environmental education pleases environmentalists, some people have concerns. Critics claim that most environmental education in the schools is based on flawed information, biased presentations, and questionable objectives. Critics also say it leads to brainwashing and pushing a regulatory mind-set on students. Some critics contend that, at worst, impressionable children are being trained to believe that the environment is in immediate danger of catastrophe because of consumption, economic growth, and free-market capitalism.

CHAPTER 2
AIR QUALITY

THE AIR PEOPLE BREATHE

According to the US Environmental Protection Agency (EPA), in "Smart City Air Challenge Resource Pages: Air Pollution" (July 5, 2017, https://developer.epa.gov/air-pollution/), the average adult breathes in more than 3,000 gallons (11,400 L) of air each day. Because air is so essential to life, it is important that it be free of pollutants. Poor air quality contributes to disease and premature death, to dying forests and lakes, and to the corrosion of stone buildings and monuments. Air quality is also important to quality of life and recreation because air pollution causes haze that decreases visibility during outdoor activities.

Air pollutants are generated by natural and anthropogenic (human-related) sources. Fossil fuels and chemicals have played a major role in society's pursuit of economic growth and higher standards of living. However, burning fossil fuels and releasing toxic chemicals into the atmosphere can threaten the very air on which life depends.

Air quality plays a major and complex role in public health. Among the factors that must be considered are the levels of pollutants in the air, the levels of individual exposure to these pollutants, individual susceptibility to toxic substances, and the time of exposure that is related to the ill effects from certain substances. Blaming health effects on specific pollutants is also complicated by the health impact of nonenvironmental causes (such as heredity or poor diet).

Scientists do know that air pollution is related to a number of respiratory diseases and other problems, including bronchitis, pulmonary emphysema, lung cancer, bronchial asthma, eye irritation, weakened immune system, kidney disease, and premature lung tissue aging.

THE HISTORY OF AIR POLLUTION LEGISLATION

By the late 1940s smog had become a serious problem in many urban areas of the United States. Extensive industrial growth during World War II (1939–1945), a boom in car ownership, and unregulated outdoor burning were the primary culprits. Los Angeles, California, and other large US cities suffered from smog during hot summer months. In 1952 London, England, experienced an episode of smog so severe that thousands of people prematurely died from respiratory illnesses that were aggravated by poor air quality. The incident was a wake-up call for many governments. Air pollution legislation was quickly passed in England and across Europe.

US Air Pollution Legislation

In the United States concerns about smog led to the passage of the Air Pollution Control Act of 1955. It provided grants to public health agencies to research the threats posed to human health by air pollution. In 1963 the first Clean Air Act (CAA) was passed. It set aside even more grant money for research and data collection and encouraged the development of emissions standards for major sources of pollution. The act was amended several times through the remainder of the decade to expand research priorities and local air pollution control agencies and to set national emissions standards for some sources.

THE CAA OF 1970. In 1970 the CAA received a major overhaul. It required the newly established EPA to establish the National Ambient Air Quality Standards (NAAQS) for major pollutants. These standards are divided into two classes:

- Primary standards are designed to protect public health, with special focus on so-called sensitive populations, including children, the elderly, and people with chronic respiratory problems, such as asthma.

- Secondary standards are designed to protect the overall welfare of the public by reducing air pollution that impairs visibility and damages resources, such as crops, forests, animals, monuments, and buildings.

State environmental agencies have to prepare state implementation plans to show how they intend to achieve compliance with the NAAQS. Counties that consistently meet the NAAQS for a particular pollutant over several years are called attainment areas for that pollutant; counties that consistently do not meet the NAAQS over several years are called nonattainment areas. Nonattainment areas are classified into five categories: marginal, moderate, serious, severe, or extreme, depending on the air quality concentrations. Nonattainment areas can be upgraded to attainment status when air quality data improve and so long as the affected county has an EPA-approved state implementation plan in place. The upgraded areas are called maintenance areas.

The revised CAA also required the setting of National Emissions Standards for Hazardous Air Pollutants and resulted in the New Source Performance Standards. These are technology-based standards that apply when certain types of facilities are first constructed or undergo major modifications. Although the New Source Performance Standards are set by the EPA, state governments are responsible for enforcing them.

In 1977 the CAA was amended again. One major change was expansion of a program called the Prevention of Significant Deterioration. The program is designed to ensure that new facilities built in attainment areas do not significantly degrade the air quality. In addition, the amended law required the formation of an independent technical and scientific committee—the Clean Air Scientific Advisory Committee (CASAC)—to advise the EPA administrator on the setting of the NAAQS. The CAA also mandated that the EPA review the standards for appropriateness every five years.

THE CLEAN AIR ACT AMENDMENTS OF 1990. In 1990 the CAA was substantially revised to better address three issues of growing concern: acid rain, urban air pollution (particularly smog), and emissions of toxic air pollutants. In addition, a national permits program was established and enforcement and compliance procedures were strengthened. The revised law included new and innovative approaches to air pollution legislation. Market-based programs allow businesses more choices in how they achieve pollution control goals. Economic incentives are also included to reduce the reliance on regulations to obtain certain goals. As of January 2018, the CAA consisted of six major sections:

- Title I—Air Pollution Prevention and Control
- Title II—Emission Standards for Moving Sources
- Title III—General
- Title IV—Acid Deposition Control
- Title V—Permits
- Title VI—Stratospheric Ozone Protection

PRIORITY AIR POLLUTANTS

The EPA establishes the NAAQS for six major air pollutants:

- Carbon monoxide
- Lead
- Nitrogen dioxide
- Ozone
- Particulate matter
- Sulfur dioxide

These are called the priority or criteria pollutants and are identified as serious threats to human health. Although the EPA sets the standards for the NAAQS pollutants, it does not have the authority under the CAA to directly regulate individual emitters, such as factories. That authority belongs to the states, which develop state implementation plans to carry out and maintain the standards. The states can have stricter standards than the federal program but not more lenient ones.

The EPA has documented air pollution trends in the United States since 1970. Two kinds of trends are tracked for the priority pollutants: emissions and air quality concentrations. Emissions are calculated estimates of the total tonnage of pollutants that are released into the air annually. All the priority pollutants except ozone are emitted directly into the air. Ozone forms due to atmospheric interactions between other chemicals, mainly volatile organic compounds (VOCs), that are emitted into the air. Thus, VOCs are said to be ozone precursors, and VOC emissions are tracked rather than ozone emissions. The EPA maintains a database called the National Emissions Inventory (https://www.epa.gov/air-emissions-inventories/national-emissions-inventory-nei) that characterizes the emissions of air pollutants in the United States based on data input from state and local agencies. The agency also tracks air quality concentrations based on data collected at thousands of monitoring sites around the country.

Each of the priority pollutants is described in more detail in the following sections.

Carbon Monoxide

Carbon monoxide (CO) is a colorless, odorless gas created when the carbon in certain fuels is not burned completely. These fuels include coal, gasoline, natural gas, oil, and wood.

EMISSIONS AND SOURCES. In *Our Nation's Air* (2017, https://gispub.epa.gov/air/trendsreport/2017), the EPA estimates that carbon monoxide emissions decreased from 143.6 million tons (130.3 million t) in 1990 to 48.7 million tons (44.2 million t) in 2016, a decrease of 66%. (See Table 2.1.) Between 2010 and 2016 carbon monoxide emissions declined 21%.

TABLE 2.1

Percentage change in emissions of air pollutants and their precursors, 1980 vs. 2016, 1990 vs. 2016, 2000 vs. 2016, and 2010 vs. 2016

	1980 vs. 2016	1990 vs. 2016	2000 vs. 2016	2010 vs. 2016
Carbon monoxide	−73	−66	−52	−21
Lead*	−99	−80	−50	−23
Nitrogen oxides (NOₓ)	−62	−59	−54	−30
Volatile organic compounds (VOC)	−55	−42	−21	−10
Direct PM$_{10}$	−57	−18	−15	−4
Direct PM$_{2.5}$	—	−25	−33	−6
Sulfur dioxide	−90	−89	−84	−66

*As a result of the permanent phase-out of leaded gasoline, controls on emissions of lead compounds through EPA's air toxics program, and other national and state regulations, airborne lead concentrations in the US decreased 98 percent between 1980 and 2005. After 2005, the EPA methodology for lead changed and is not comparable to the 2005 and earlier numbers. Since 2008, emissions have continued to decrease by 23 percent from 2008 to 2014. In the 2014 NEI, the highest amounts of Pb emissions are from piston engine aircrafts, and ferrous and non-ferrous metals industrial sources. The 2008 and 2014 estimates were used to approximate the 2010 to 2016 percent change.
NEI = National Emissions Inventory.
PM$_{2.5}$ = particulate matter less than 2.5 micrometers in diameter.
PM$_{10}$ = particulate matter less than 10 micrometers in diameter.

SOURCE: "Percent Change in Emissions," in *Air Quality—National Summary*, US Environmental Protection Agency, July 26, 2017, https://www.epa.gov/air-trends/air-quality-national-summary (accessed November 7, 2017)

Yearly emissions and source data for carbon monoxide are available from the EPA's National Emissions Inventory database (https://www.epa.gov/sites/production/files/2016-12/national_tier1_caps.xlsx). Transportation vehicles have historically been the largest source of the emissions. For 2016 the source breakdown was as follows:

- Highway vehicles—30%
- Off-highway vehicles (e.g., bulldozers)—22%
- Wildfires—18%
- Industrial and other processes—7%
- Stationary fuel combustion (e.g., power plants)—7%
- Miscellaneous—16%

AIR QUALITY. The EPA lists in "NAAQS Table" (December 20, 2016, https://www.epa.gov/criteria-air-pollutants/naaqs-table) two primary standards for carbon monoxide: 35 parts per million (ppm; one-hour average) and 9 ppm (eight-hour average). There are no secondary standards for carbon monoxide.

The national air quality concentrations of carbon monoxide (eight-hour average) between 1990 and 2016 are shown in Figure 2.1, which is based on monitoring data from 100 sites around the country. According to the EPA, in "Carbon Monoxide Trends" (October 23, 2017, https://www.epa.gov/air-trends/carbon-monoxide-trends), the national average declined 77% during this period. In 2016 the measured eight-hour average carbon monoxide concentration at the monitoring sites was 1.4 ppm. This

was well below the national standard of 9 ppm. As shown in Table 2.2, carbon monoxide concentrations declined 14% between 2010 and 2016.

As shown in Figure 2.2, no areas of the country in 2016 had air quality concentrations of carbon monoxide consistently above the NAAQS. Previous nonattainment areas for carbon monoxide have been upgraded to maintenance areas that are classified similarly to nonattainment areas in terms of increasing order of air quality concentrations—marginal, moderate, serious, severe, or extreme. As of December 31, 2017, the EPA (https://www3.epa.gov/airquality/greenbook/cmc.html) listed 43 maintenance areas. None were classified as "extreme." Seven areas were considered "serious" carbon monoxide maintenance areas: Anchorage and Fairbanks, Alaska; Phoenix, Arizona; Los Angeles South Coast Air Basin, California; Denver-Boulder, Colorado; Las Vegas, Nevada; and Spokane, Washington.

As noted earlier, the CAA requires the EPA to review the NAAQS every five years and update them as necessary. These reviews have seldom been completed on time. As of September 2016, the agency (https://www.epa.gov/co-pollution/table-historical-carbon-monoxide-co-national-ambient-air-quality-standards-naaqs) last reviewed the national standards for carbon monoxide in 2011, when it decided to retain them at their previous levels.

ADVERSE EFFECTS. Carbon monoxide emissions have adverse effects on human health and the environment. Carbon monoxide is a dangerous gas that enters a person's bloodstream through the lungs. It reduces the ability of blood to carry oxygen to the body's cells, organs, and tissues. The health danger is highest for people suffering from cardiovascular diseases.

In *Our Nation's Air*, the EPA also notes that carbon monoxide contributes to the formation of two greenhouse gases—carbon dioxide and ozone—in the atmosphere. High levels of greenhouse gases are widely blamed for accelerating global warming and causing climate change.

Lead

Lead (Pb) is a metal that can enter the atmosphere via the combustion or industrial processing of lead-containing materials.

EMISSIONS AND SOURCES. As shown in Table 2.1, the EPA estimates that lead emissions have declined dramatically in recent decades. Between 1980 and 2016 emissions dropped 99%. Before 1985 the major source of lead emissions in the United States was leaded gasoline used in automobiles. Conversion to unleaded gasoline produced a dramatic reduction in lead emissions. As a result, ground transportation has virtually been eliminated as a source of lead emissions in the United States. According to the EPA, in "Basic Information about Lead Air Pollution"

FIGURE 2.1

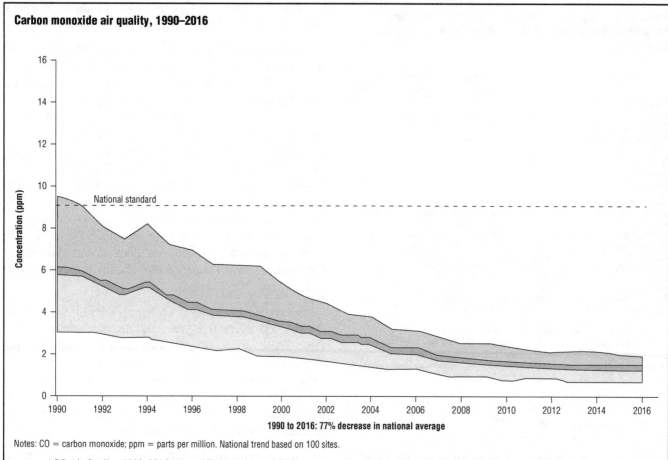

Carbon monoxide air quality, 1990–2016

1990 to 2016: 77% decrease in national average

Notes: CO = carbon monoxide; ppm = parts per million. National trend based on 100 sites.

SOURCE: "CO Air Quality, 1990–2016 (Annual 2nd Maximum 8-Hour Average)," in *Carbon Monoxide Trends*, US Environmental Protection Agency, October 23, 2017, https://www.epa.gov/air-trends/carbon-monoxide-trends (accessed November 7, 2017)

TABLE 2.2

Percentage change in concentrations of air pollutants, 1980 vs. 2016, 1990 vs. 2016, 2000 vs. 2016, and 2010 vs. 2016

	1980 vs. 2016	1990 vs. 2016	2000 vs. 2016	2010 vs. 2016
Carbon monoxide	−85	−77	−61	−14
Lead	−99	−99	−93	−77
Nitrogen dioxide (annual)	−62	−56	−47	−20
Nitrogen dioxide (1-hour)	−61	−50	−33	−15
Ozone (8-hour)	−31	−22	−17	−5
PM$_{10}$ (24-hour)	—	−39	−40	−9
PM$_{2.5}$ (annual)	—	—	−42	−22
PM$_{2.5}$ (24-hour)	—	—	−44	−23
Sulfur dioxide (1-hour)	−87	−85	−72	−56

PM$_{2.5}$ = particulate matter less than 2.5 micrometers in diameter.
PM$_{10}$ = particulate matter less than 10 micrometers in diameter.

SOURCE: "Percent Change in Air Quality," in *Air Quality—National Summary*, US Environmental Protection Agency, July 26, 2017, https://www.epa.gov/air-trends/air-quality-national-summary (accessed November 7, 2017)

(November 29, 2017, https://www.epa.gov/lead-air-pollu tion/basic-information-about-lead-air-pollution), most of the nation's lead emissions are from facilities that process ores or metals (such as lead smelters) and from small aircraft that burn leaded aviation gasoline.

The continued use of lead in aviation gasoline (avgas) in the United States is highly controversial. Rebecca Kessler explains in "Sunset for Leaded Aviation Gasoline?" (*Environmental Health Perspectives*, vol. 121, no. 2, February 2013) that avgas is typically used by small airplanes with piston engines (as opposed to jet engines). Various grades of unleaded and leaded avgas are available. According to Kessler, the "most widely available avgas" at US general aviation airports is 100LL, which contains a small amount of lead to help the fuel burn evenly. (The designation "LL" in avgas grades stands for "low lead.") Since 2003 environmental groups have been petitioning the EPA to ban leaded avgas based on studies that show lead levels are higher than background in the air above and around some airports. A 2011 study conducted by Duke University researchers found higher blood lead levels among children living near airports in North Carolina. As of August 2017, the EPA (https://www.epa.gov/regula tions-emissions-vehicles-and-engines/regulations-lead-emis sions-aircraft) indicated that it would issue a decision on the matter in 2018.

AIR QUALITY. In "NAAQS Table," the EPA lists the primary and secondary standard for lead as 0.15 micrograms

FIGURE 2.2

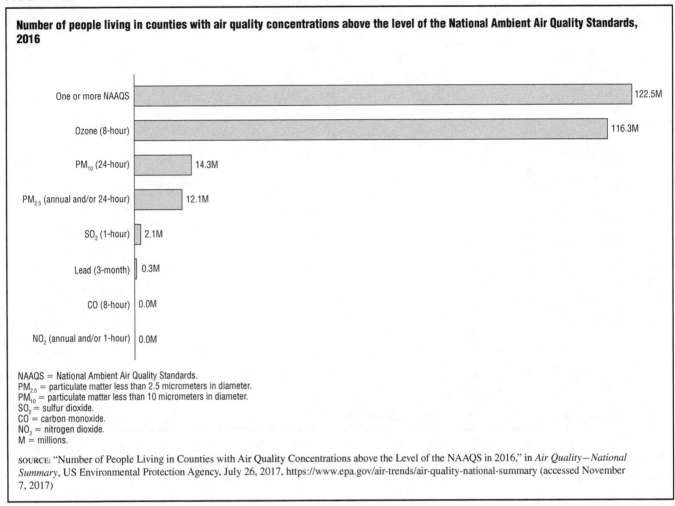

Number of people living in counties with air quality concentrations above the level of the National Ambient Air Quality Standards, 2016

NAAQS = National Ambient Air Quality Standards.
$PM_{2.5}$ = particulate matter less than 2.5 micrometers in diameter.
PM_{10} = particulate matter less than 10 micrometers in diameter.
SO_2 = sulfur dioxide.
CO = carbon monoxide.
NO_2 = nitrogen dioxide.
M = millions.

SOURCE: "Number of People Living in Counties with Air Quality Concentrations above the Level of the NAAQS in 2016," in *Air Quality—National Summary*, US Environmental Protection Agency, July 26, 2017, https://www.epa.gov/air-trends/air-quality-national-summary (accessed November 7, 2017)

per cubic meter ($\mu g/m^3$). This standard was finalized in 2008 and is significantly lower than the previous standard of 1.5 $\mu g/m^3$.

The air quality concentrations of lead based on monitoring data from 18 sites between 1990 and 2016 are shown in Figure 2.3. According to the EPA, in "Lead Trends" (July 18, 2017, https://www.epa.gov/air-trends/lead-trends), the national average declined 99% during this period. As shown in Table 2.2, lead concentrations declined 77% between 2010 and 2016. In 2016 the three-month average lead concentration at the monitoring sites was 0.02 $\mu g/m^3$.

Despite great progress in lead reduction, Figure 2.2 indicates that 300,000 people lived in counties with air quality concentrations consistently above the NAAQS for this pollutant in 2016. The EPA (https://www3.epa.gov/airquality/greenbook/mnc.html) reports that as of December 31, 2017, there were 17 lead nonattainment areas around the country. They included cities or counties in Alabama, Arizona, California, Florida, Illinois, Indiana, Iowa, Kansas, Minnesota, Missouri, Ohio, Pennsylvania, and Puerto Rico.

In October 2016 the EPA published in "Review of the National Ambient Air Quality Standards for Lead" (*Federal Register*, vol. 81, no. 201) its decision to retain the existing NAAQS for lead.

ADVERSE EFFECTS. Lead is a particularly dangerous pollutant because it accumulates in the blood, bones, and soft tissues of the body. It can adversely affect the nervous system, kidneys, liver, and other organs. Excessive concentrations are associated with neurological and mental impairments and behavioral disorders. According to the EPA, in *Our Nation's Air*, prolonged exposure to lead can contribute to cardiovascular problems, such as heart disease and high blood pressure, in adults. Even low doses of lead can damage the brain and nervous system of fetuses and young children. Atmospheric lead that falls onto soil or fresh water bodies can blunt the growth and reproductive capacity of plants and animals and poses an ingestion hazard to humans.

Nitrogen Dioxide

Nitrogen dioxide (NO_2) is a reddish-brown gas that forms in the atmosphere when nitrogen oxide is oxidized. The chemical formula NO_x is used collectively

FIGURE 2.3

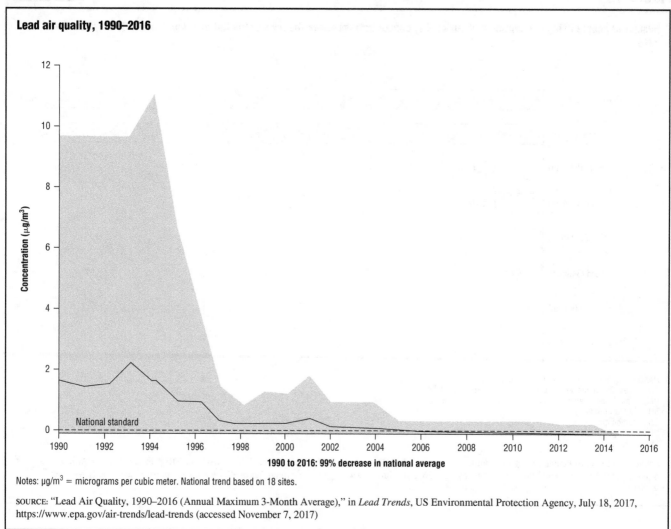

Lead air quality, 1990–2016

Concentration (μg/m³)

National standard

1990   1992   1994   1996   1998   2000   2002   2004   2006   2008   2010   2012   2014   2016

1990 to 2016: 99% decrease in national average

Notes: μg/m³ = micrograms per cubic meter. National trend based on 18 sites.

SOURCE: "Lead Air Quality, 1990–2016 (Annual Maximum 3-Month Average)," in *Lead Trends*, US Environmental Protection Agency, July 18, 2017, https://www.epa.gov/air-trends/lead-trends (accessed November 7, 2017)

to refer to nitrogen oxide, nitrogen dioxide, and other nitrogen oxides.

EMISSIONS AND SOURCES. In *Our Nation's Air*, the EPA estimates that NO_x emissions decreased from 25.2 million tons (22.9 million t) in 1990 to 10.4 million tons (9.4 million t) in 2016, a decrease of 59%. (See Table 2.1.) Between 2010 and 2016 NO_x emissions declined 30%.

Nitrogen oxides primarily come from burning fuels such as coal, gasoline, natural gas, and oil. Yearly emissions and source data are available from the EPA's National Emissions Inventory database. For 2016 the source breakdown for NO_x was as follows:

- Highway vehicles—34%
- Stationary fuel combustion—26%
- Off-highway vehicles—23%
- Industrial and other processes—13%
- Wildfires—1%
- Miscellaneous—3%

AIR QUALITY. The EPA lists in "NAAQS Table" two NAAQS for nitrogen dioxide: a primary standard of 100 parts per billion (ppb; one-hour maximum) and a primary and secondary standard of 53 ppb (annual average). The EPA indicates that the 100 ppb (one-hour) standard was implemented in 2010. The primary and secondary national standard of 53 ppb (annual average) has been in effect since 1971.

Figure 2.4 illustrates the air quality concentrations of nitrogen dioxide (one-hour measure) based on monitoring data from 79 sites around the country between 1990 and 2016. According to the EPA, in "Nitrogen Dioxide Trends" (July 18, 2017, https://www.epa.gov/air-trends/nitrogen-dioxide-trends), the concentration declined 50% during this period. In 2016 the nitrogen dioxide concentration at the monitoring sites was 38.2 ppb. This was well below the national standard of 100 ppb. As shown in Table 2.2, nitrogen dioxide concentrations declined 20% (annual average) and 15% (one-hour measure) between 2010 and 2016.

No areas of the country had air quality concentrations of nitrogen dioxide consistently above the NAAQS in

FIGURE 2.4

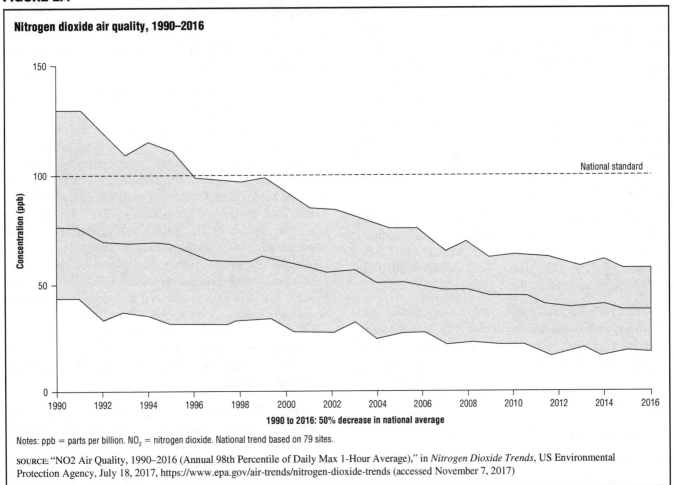

Nitrogen dioxide air quality, 1990–2016

Notes: ppb = parts per billion. NO₂ = nitrogen dioxide. National trend based on 79 sites.

SOURCE: "NO2 Air Quality, 1990–2016 (Annual 98th Percentile of Daily Max 1-Hour Average)," in *Nitrogen Dioxide Trends*, US Environmental Protection Agency, July 18, 2017, https://www.epa.gov/air-trends/nitrogen-dioxide-trends (accessed November 7, 2017)

2016. (See Figure 2.2.) As of December 31, 2017, the EPA (https://www3.epa.gov/airquality/greenbook/nmcs .html) classified the Los Angeles South Coast Air Basin as a nitrogen dioxide maintenance area.

In July 2017 the EPA proposed in "Review of the Primary National Ambient Air Quality Standards for Oxides of Nitrogen" (*Federal Register*, vol. 82, no. 142) to keep the existing nitrogen dioxide standards with no changes. As of January 2018, that decision had not been finalized.

ADVERSE EFFECTS. Nitrogen dioxide reacts with ammonia and water droplets in the atmosphere to form nitric acid and other chemicals that are potentially harmful to human health. Inhalation of these particles can interfere with respiratory processes and damage lung tissue. Particles that are inhaled deeply into the lungs can cause or aggravate respiratory conditions such as bronchitis and emphysema.

Inhalation of even low concentrations of nitrogen dioxide for short periods can be harmful to the human body's breathing functions. Longer exposures are considered damaging to the lungs and may cause people to be more susceptible to certain respiratory problems, such as infections.

Nitrogen dioxide is a major precursor of smog and contributes to acid rain and haze. It can also undergo reactions in the air that lead to the formation of particulate matter and ozone.

Ozone

Ozone is a gas naturally present in the earth's upper atmosphere. The National Oceanic and Atmospheric Administration indicates in "Science: Ozone Basics" (March 20, 2008, http://www.ozonelayer.noaa.gov/sci ence/basics.htm) that approximately 90% of the earth's ozone lies in the stratosphere at altitudes greater than about 9.3 miles (15 km) up to approximately 22.8 miles (35 km). Ozone molecules at this level absorb ultraviolet radiation from the sun and prevent it from reaching the ground. Thus, stratospheric ozone (the ozone layer) is good for the environment. Beneath the stratosphere is the troposphere. Tropospheric (ground-level) ozone is a potent air pollutant with serious health consequences. It is the most complex, pervasive, and difficult to control of the six priority pollutants.

EMISSIONS AND SOURCES. Unlike other air pollutants, ground-level ozone is not emitted directly into the air. It forms mostly on sunny, hot days because of complex chemical reactions that take place when the atmosphere contains other pollutants, primarily VOCs and NO_x. These pollutants are called ozone precursors because their presence in the atmosphere leads to the creation of ozone.

VOCs are carbon-containing chemicals that easily become vapors or gases. Paint thinners, degreasers, and other solvents contain a great number of VOCs, which are also released from burning fuels such as coal, gasoline, natural gas, and wood.

In *Our Nation's Air*, the EPA estimates that VOC emissions decreased from 23.1 million tons (21 million t) in 1990 to 13.4 million tons (12.2 million t) in 2016, a decrease of 42%. (See Table 2.1.) Between 2010 and 2016 VOC emissions declined 10%.

The EPA's National Emissions Inventory database provides yearly emissions and source data. For 2016 the source breakdown for VOCs was as follows (note that the individual percentages do not sum to 100% due to rounding):

- Industrial and other processes—47%
- Wildfires—15%
- Highway vehicles—11%
- Off-highway vehicles—10%
- Stationary fuel combustion—3%
- Miscellaneous—13%

AIR QUALITY. Ozone concentrations can vary greatly from year to year, depending on the emissions of ozone precursors and weather conditions.

The setting of ozone standards has been fraught with controversy. According to the EPA (February 27, 2017, https://www.epa.gov/ozone-pollution/table-historical-ozone-national-ambient-air-quality-standards-naaqs), a one-hour ozone standard was in effect from the 1970s through the 1990s. In 1997 the agency proposed replacing the standard with a new eight-hour standard of 0.08 ppm. This is equivalent to 80 ppb. Industry groups and some states challenged the proposal in court. They argued that the compliance costs necessary to achieve the standard would be too high. The legal battle reached the US Supreme Court, which ruled in *Whitman v. American Trucking Associations Inc.* (531 US 457 [2001]) that the EPA does not have to consider compliance costs when setting ambient air standards.

In 2006 CASAC completed a five-year review and recommended to the EPA that the eight-hour standard be lowered to within the range of 60 to 70 ppb. However, when the EPA published its proposed rule in 2007, the agency called for the standard to be 70 to 75 ppb. This set off another legal battle. Some states and industry groups argued that the proposal was too strict, whereas other states and environmental and health groups criticized it as not being strict enough. A standard of 75 ppb was finalized in March 2008.

A 2013 review resulted in a CASAC recommendation that the standard be set at 60 to 70 ppb. In October 2015 the agency finalized the primary and secondary standards at 70 ppb. This action prompted lawsuits by numerous states and industry groups alleging that the standards were too low. The litigation was still ongoing when newly elected President Donald Trump (1946–), a Republican, entered office in January 2017. He has been intensely critical of the EPA's role under the former administration of President Barack Obama (1961–), a Democrat. President Trump has vowed to reduce the EPA's power and relax the regulatory burden on industry. In June 2017 the EPA announced that enforcement of the new ozone standards would be delayed until 2018. This triggered another flurry of lawsuits from states and environmental groups opposed to the delay. As of January 2018, it was uncertain when and if the new standards would be implemented.

Figure 2.5 illustrates the eight-hour air quality concentrations of ozone based on monitoring data from 436 sites around the country between 1990 and 2016. According to the EPA, in "Ozone Trends" (July 18, 2017, https://www.epa.gov/air-trends/ozone-trends), the national average declined 22% during this period. In 2016 the eight-hour average measured ozone concentration at the monitoring sites was 0.069 ppm (69 ppb), which was below the national standard of 75 ppb. As shown in Table 2.2, ozone concentrations declined 5% between 2010 and 2016.

In 2016, 116.3 million people lived in counties with ozone concentrations above the level of the NAAQS. (See Figure 2.2.) The EPA (https://www3.epa.gov/airquality/greenbook/hnc.html) reports that as of December 31, 2017, there were 38 locations around the country that were designated nonattainment for ozone air quality. Two areas were classified as "extreme" nonattainment for the eight-hour ozone standard: the Los Angeles South Coast Air Basin and the San Joaquin Valley in California. Many other areas in and around major cities were also classified as nonattainment.

ADVERSE EFFECTS. Ground-level ozone is the primary component in smog. It retards crop and tree growth, impairs health, and limits visibility. When temperature inversions occur (the warm air stays near the ground instead of rising) and winds are calm, such as during the summer, smog may hang over a huge area for days at a time. As traffic and other pollution sources add more pollutants to the air, the smog gets worse. Wind often blows smog-forming pollutants away from their sources;

FIGURE 2.5

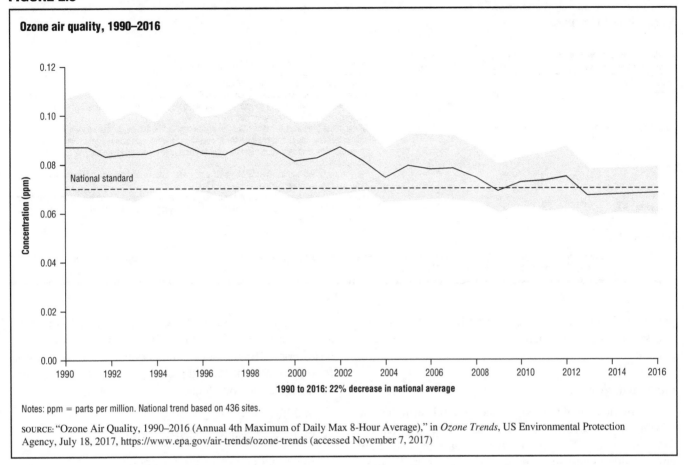

Ozone air quality, 1990–2016

Notes: ppm = parts per million. National trend based on 436 sites.

SOURCE: "Ozone Air Quality, 1990–2016 (Annual 4th Maximum of Daily Max 8-Hour Average)," in *Ozone Trends*, US Environmental Protection Agency, July 18, 2017, https://www.epa.gov/air-trends/ozone-trends (accessed November 7, 2017)

this is why smog can be miles away from where the pollutants were created.

Ozone has different health effects, depending on the concentration and time of exposure. Even the smallest amounts of ozone can cause breathing difficulties. Ozone exposure can cause serious problems with lung functions, leading to infections, chest pain, and coughing. According to the EPA, ozone exposure is linked to increased emergency department visits and hospital admissions because of respiratory problems such as lung inflammation and asthma. Ozone causes or aggravates these problems, particularly in people working outdoors, the elderly, and children. Children are especially susceptible to the harmful effects of ozone because they spend a great deal of time outside and because their lungs are still developing.

The EPA maintains the air quality index (AQI) as a means for warning the public when air pollutants (particularly ozone) exceed unhealthy levels. The AQI values range from 0 to 500. Higher values correspond to greater levels of air pollution and increased risk to human health. An AQI value of 100 is assigned to the concentration of an air pollutant equal to its NAAQS. Table 2.3 shows the ozone AQI. Index values are commonly reported during summertime radio and television newscasts to warn people about the dangers of ozone exposure.

In *State of the Air 2017: Most Polluted Cities* (2017, http://www.lung.org/our-initiatives/healthy-air/sota/city-rankings/most-polluted-cities.html), the American Lung Association ranks metropolitan areas and counties in terms of their ozone pollutant levels. The 10 metropolitan areas with the worst ozone pollution in 2017 were:

- Los Angeles–Long Beach, California
- Bakersfield, California
- Fresno-Madera, California
- Visalia-Porterville-Hanford, California
- Phoenix-Mesa-Scottsdale, Arizona
- Modesto-Merced, California
- San Diego–Carlsbad, California
- Sacramento-Roseville, California
- New York–Newark, New York, New Jersey, Connecticut, Pennsylvania
- Las Vegas–Henderson, Nevada

Overall, cities in California dominated the list of areas of the country with the worst ozone pollution.

Ground-level ozone is also harmful to ecosystems, particularly vegetation. Ozone exposure reduces forest

TABLE 2.3

Air quality index for ozone

Levels of health concern because air quality conditions are:	Air quality index color	Air quality index range	Meaning
Good	Green	0–50	Air quality is considered satisfactory, and air pollution poses little or no risk.
Moderate	Yellow	51–100	Air quality is acceptable; however, for some pollutants there may be a moderate health concern for a very small number of people. For example, people who are unusually sensitive to ozone may experience respiratory symptoms.
Unhealthy for sensitive groups	Orange	101–150	Although the general public is not likely to be affected at this AQI range, people with lung disease, older adults and children are at a greater risk from exposure to ozone, whereas persons with heart and lung disease, older adults and children are at greater risk from the presence of particles in the air.
Unhealthy	Red	151–200	Everyone may begin to experience some adverse health effects, and members of the sensitive groups may experience more serious effects.
Very unhealthy	Purple	201–300	This would trigger a health alert signifying that everyone may experience more serious health effects.
Hazardous	Maroon	301–500	This would trigger a health warning of emergency conditions. The entire population is more likely to be affected.

AQI = air quality index.

SOURCE: Adapted from "Understanding the AQI" and "AQI Colors," in *Air Quality Index (AQI) Basics*, US Environmental Protection Agency, August 31, 2016, https://www.airnow.gov/?action=aqibasics.aqi (accessed November 8, 2017)

yields by stunting the growth of seedlings and increasing stresses on trees. Such damage can take years to become evident.

Particulate Matter

Particulate matter (PM) is the general term for the mixture of solid particles and/or liquid droplets that are found in the air. The primary particles are those that are emitted directly to the atmosphere—for example, dust, dirt, and soot (black carbon). Secondary particles form in the atmosphere because of complex chemical reactions among gaseous emissions and include sulfates, nitrates, ammoniums, and organic carbon compounds. For example, sulfate particulates can form when sulfur dioxide emissions from industrial facilities and power plants undergo chemical reactions in the atmosphere.

The EPA tracks two sizes of PM: PM_{10} and $PM_{2.5}$. PM_{10} particles are those less than or equal to 10 micrometers in diameter. This is roughly one-seventh the diameter of a human hair and small enough to be breathed into the lungs. $PM_{2.5}$ are the smallest of these particles (less than or equal to 2.5 micrometers in diameter). $PM_{2.5}$ is also called fine PM. The particles ranging in size between 2.5 and 10 micrometers in diameter are known as coarse PM. Most coarse PM consists of primary particles, whereas most fine PM consists of secondary particles.

EMISSIONS AND SOURCES. The EPA estimates in *Our Nation's Air* that direct (primary) PM_{10} emissions decreased from 3.2 million tons (2.9 million t) in 1990 to 2.6 million tons (2.4 million t) in 2016, a decline of 18%. (See Table 2.1.) Between 2010 and 2016 direct PM_{10} emissions dropped 4%. Direct $PM_{2.5}$ emissions decreased 25% between 1990 and 2016 and 6% between 2010 and 2016.

Yearly emissions and source data for PM are available from the EPA's National Emissions Inventory database. For 2016 the source breakdown for PM_{10} was as follows (note that the individual percentages do not sum to 100% due to rounding):

- Wildfires—4%
- Stationary fuel combustion—4%
- Industrial and other processes—3%
- Highway vehicles—1%
- Off-highway vehicles—1%
- Miscellaneous—89%

For 2016 the source breakdown for $PM_{2.5}$ was as follows:

- Wildfires—14%
- Stationary fuel combustion—13%
- Industrial and other processes—5%
- Waste disposal and recycling—4%
- Highway vehicles—2%
- Off-highway vehicles—2%
- Metal processing—1%
- Petroleum and relation industries—1%
- Miscellaneous—58%

AIR QUALITY. In "NAAQS Table," the EPA lists multiple primary and secondary standards for PM with various averaging times. For example, there is a primary and secondary standard based on a 24-hour measure for PM_{10} of 150 $\mu g/m^3$.

Figure 2.6 shows the historical trend in PM_{10} air quality between 1990 and 2016 based on data collected

FIGURE 2.6

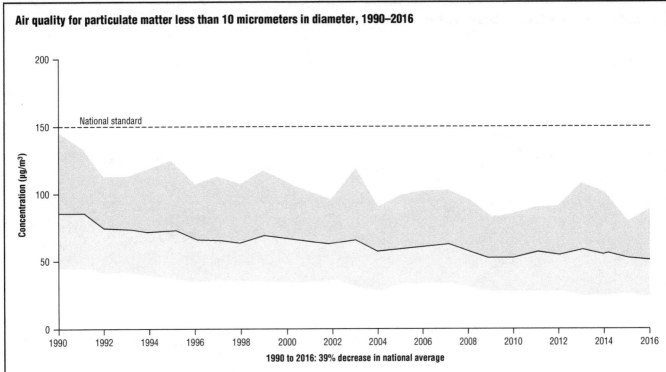

Air quality for particulate matter less than 10 micrometers in diameter, 1990–2016

1990 to 2016: 39% decrease in national average

Notes: μg/m³ = micrograms per cubic meter. National trend based on 149 sites.

SOURCE: "PM10 Air Quality, 1990–2016 (Annual 2nd Maximum 24-Hour Average)," in *Particulate Matter (PM₁₀) Trends*, US Environmental Protection Agency, July 18, 2017, https://www.epa.gov/air-trends/particulate-matter-pm10-trends (accessed November 8, 2017)

by the EPA from 149 monitoring sites. According to the EPA, in "Particulate Matter (PM_{10}) Trends" (July 18, 2017, https://www.epa.gov/air-trends/particulate-matter-pm10-trends), the national average declined 39% between 1990 and 2016. The 24-hour average in 2016 was 51.3 $\mu g/m^3$, well below the national standard of 150 $\mu g/m^3$. As shown in Table 2.2, PM_{10} concentrations decreased by 9% between 2010 and 2016.

Overall, 14.3 million people lived in counties with 24-hour PM_{10} concentrations above the NAAQS in 2016. (See Figure 2.2.) The EPA (https://www3.epa.gov/airquality/greenbook/pnc.html) reports that as of December 31, 2017, 37 areas around the country were nonattainment for PM_{10} concentrations. Areas classified "serious" nonattainment were in Southern California and in parts of Arizona.

In 1999 the EPA began nationwide tracking of $PM_{2.5}$ air quality concentrations. Figure 2.7 shows the historical trend between 2000 and 2016 based on data collected by the EPA from 455 monitoring sites. In 2016 the annual average $PM_{2.5}$ concentration was 7.8 $\mu g/m^3$, less than the standard of 12 $\mu g/m^3$. As shown in Table 2.2, $PM_{2.5}$ concentrations declined 22% (annual average) and 23% (24-hour measure) between 2010 and 2016.

According to the EPA (September 28, 2016, https://www3.epa.gov/ttn/naaqs/standards/pm/s_pm_history.html),

the NAAQS for $PM_{2.5}$ were first issued in 1997 and revised as needed in 2006 and 2012.

In 2016, 12.1 million people lived in counties with $PM_{2.5}$ concentrations above the level of the annual and/or 24-hour NAAQS. (See Figure 2.2.) The EPA (https://www3.epa.gov/airquality/greenbook/rnc.html) notes that as of December 31, 2017, there were 15 locations around the country that were designated nonattainment for $PM_{2.5}$ air quality. Most were major- and medium-sized metropolitan areas.

ADVERSE EFFECTS. PM can irritate the nostrils, throat, and lungs and aggravate respiratory conditions such as bronchitis and asthma. PM exposure can also endanger the circulatory system and is linked to cardiac arrhythmias (episodes of irregular heartbeats) and heart attacks. $PM_{2.5}$ particles are the most damaging because their small size allows them access to deeper regions of the lungs. These tiny particles have been linked to the most serious health effects in humans. Particulates pose the greatest health risk to those with heart or lung problems, the elderly, and especially children, who are particularly susceptible because of the greater amount of time they spend outside and the fact that their lungs are not fully developed. In 2017 researchers announced that fine PM pollution is also harmful to the kidneys. The kidneys, which filter blood, can be damaged by the presence of the

FIGURE 2.7

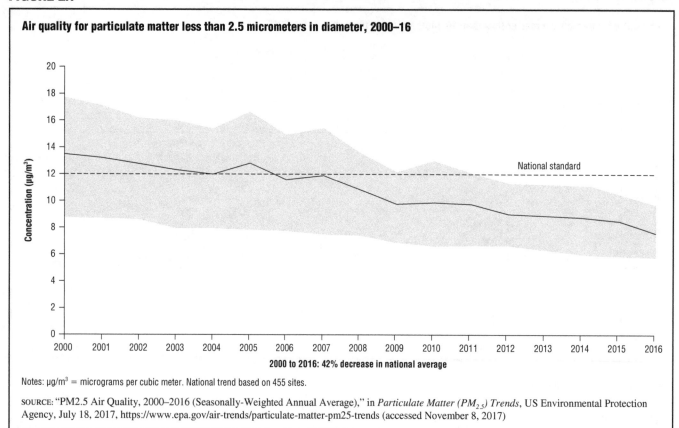

Air quality for particulate matter less than 2.5 micrometers in diameter, 2000–16

2000 to 2016: 42% decrease in national average

Notes: µg/m³ = micrograms per cubic meter. National trend based on 455 sites.

SOURCE: "PM2.5 Air Quality, 2000–2016 (Seasonally-Weighted Annual Average)," in *Particulate Matter (PM₂.₅) Trends*, US Environmental Protection Agency, July 18, 2017, https://www.epa.gov/air-trends/particulate-matter-pm25-trends (accessed November 8, 2017)

tiny particles in the bloodstream. According to Benjamin Bowe et al., in "Particulate Matter Air Pollution and the Risk of Incident CKD and Progression to ESRD" (*Journal of the American Society of Nephrology*, September 21, 2017), $PM_{2.5}$ exposure is strongly associated with an increased risk for chronic kidney disease.

When PM hangs in the air, it creates a haze, limiting visibility. PM is one of the major components of smog and can have adverse effects on vegetation and sensitive ecosystems. Long-term exposure to PM can damage painted surfaces, buildings, and monuments.

Sulfur Dioxide

Sulfur dioxide (SO_2) is a gas composed of sulfur and oxygen. The chemical formula SO_x is used collectively to describe sulfur oxide, sulfur dioxide, and other sulfur oxides.

EMISSIONS AND SOURCES. One of the primary sources of sulfur dioxide is the combustion of fossil fuels that contain sulfur. Coal (particularly high-sulfur coal, which is common to the eastern United States) and oil are the major fuel sources associated with sulfur dioxide. Power plants have historically been the main source of sulfur dioxide emissions. Some industrial processes and metal smelting also cause sulfur dioxide to form.

Sulfur dioxide emissions have decreased since the 1980s because of greater reliance on cleaner fuels with lower sulfur content and the increased use of pollution control devices, such as scrubbers, to clean emissions. The EPA estimates in *Our Nation's Air* that sulfur dioxide emissions declined from 23.1 million tons (21 million t) in 1990 to 2.6 million tons (2.4 million t) in 2016, a decrease of 89%. (See Table 2.1.) Between 2010 and 2016 sulfur dioxide emissions declined 66%.

The EPA's National Emissions Inventory database provides yearly emissions and source data for sulfur dioxide. Fuel combustion in stationary sources (e.g., power plants) has traditionally produced the most sulfur dioxide emissions. For 2016 the source breakdown was as follows (note that the individual percentages do not sum to 100% due to rounding):

- Stationary fuel combustion—73%

- Industrial and other processes—20%

- Wildfires—3%

- Highway vehicles—1%

- Off-highway vehicles—1%

- Miscellaneous—3%

AIR QUALITY. In "NAAQS Table," the EPA lists two NAAQS for sulfur dioxide: a primary standard of 75 ppb (one-hour maximum) and a secondary standard of 0.5 ppm (three-hour average).

Figure 2.8 shows the historical trend in sulfur dioxide air quality between 1990 and 2016 based on data collected by the EPA from 136 monitoring sites. According to the EPA, in "Sulfur Dioxide Trends" (July 18, 2017, https://www.epa.gov/air-trends/sulfur-dioxide-trends), the concentration declined 85% between 1990 and 2016. In 2016 the average one-hour measured concentration at the monitoring sites was 20 ppb. This was well below the national standard of 75 ppb. As shown in Table 2.2, one-hour sulfur dioxide concentrations declined 56% between 2010 and 2016.

In 2016, 2.1 million people lived in nonattainment areas based on the one-hour sulfur dioxide standard. (See Figure 2.2.) The EPA (https://www3.epa.gov/airquality/greenbook/tnc.html) reports that as of December 31, 2017, there were 34 nonattainment areas around the country.

As of January 2018, the agency (https://www.epa.gov/naaqs/sulfur-dioxide-so2-primary-air-quality-standards-federal-register-notices-current-review) was reviewing the existing NAAQS for sulfur dioxide. A final determination was expected sometime in 2018.

ADVERSE EFFECTS. Inhaling sulfur dioxide in polluted air can impair breathing in those with asthma or even in healthy adults who are active outdoors. As with other air pollutants, children, the elderly, and those with preexisting respiratory and cardiovascular diseases and conditions are the most susceptible to adverse effects from breathing this gas.

Sulfur dioxide is a major contributor to acid rain, haze, and PM. Acid rain is of particular concern because of its negative impacts on the environment. Acid rain control measures are described in detail in Chapter 5.

Priority Air Pollutants: Summary

Overall, the United States has achieved significant progress under the CAA at reducing emissions of the priority air pollutants. As shown in Table 2.1, dramatic declines have been realized since 1980. Table 2.2 details the resulting improvements in air quality based on data gathered at monitoring sites around the country. Nevertheless, 122.5 million people lived in counties with air quality concentrations that were consistently above the level of at least one NAAQS in 2016. (See Figure 2.2.) Ozone and PM were the most troublesome pollutants. During the early 21st century the EPA has tightened air quality standards for VOCs (an ozone precursor) and PM. As a result, there has been an improvement in air quality concentrations for these two pollutants. Figure 2.9 shows the number of days classified as "unhealthy for sensitive groups" or higher (more serious) on the AQI for ozone and $PM_{2.5}$ for 35 major US cities. Between 2000 and 2016 the number of days classified at or above this level declined 66%, from 2,076 days in 2000 to 697 days in 2016.

FIGURE 2.8

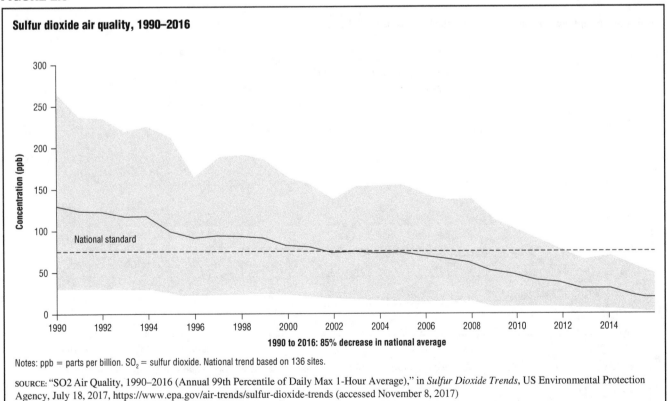

Sulfur dioxide air quality, 1990–2016

1990 to 2016: 85% decrease in national average

Notes: ppb = parts per billion. SO$_2$ = sulfur dioxide. National trend based on 136 sites.

SOURCE: "SO2 Air Quality, 1990–2016 (Annual 99th Percentile of Daily Max 1-Hour Average)," in *Sulfur Dioxide Trends*, US Environmental Protection Agency, July 18, 2017, https://www.epa.gov/air-trends/sulfur-dioxide-trends (accessed November 8, 2017)

In Figure 2.10 the EPA compares aggregate (combined) emissions trends for the six NAAQS air pollutants—carbon monoxide, lead, PM₁₀, PM₂.₅, sulfur dioxide, and VOCs— with other trends between 1970 and 2016. Aggregate emissions declined 73% during this period. This improvement occurred even though there was a sharp rise in both the nation's total vehicle miles traveled and its gross domestic product (the total market value of final goods and services that are produced within an economy in a given year).

CROSS-STATE AIR POLLUTION

One of the difficulties in regulating air pollution is that emissions can travel far from their sources, including across state lines. This can result in a situation in which a state's air quality meets the NAAQS, but emissions from within its borders contribute to another state not meeting the standards. As part of the 1990 amendments to the CAA, Congress added what is called the "Good Neighbor" provision. According to the EPA, in "Interstate Air Pollution Transport" (October 30, 2017, https://www.epa.gov/airmarkets/interstate-air-pollution-transport), the provision "requires EPA and states to address interstate transport of air pollution that affects downwind states' ability to attain and maintain National Ambient Air Quality Standards (NAAQS)." However, finding a suitable solution to cross-state air pollution has proved challenging. Part of the difficulty lies in quantifying the emissions from upwind states that negatively affect downwind states. In addition, as noted earlier, although the EPA has the statutory authority (authority granted by law, in this case the CAA) to set national air quality limits, it cannot tell individual states

FIGURE 2.9

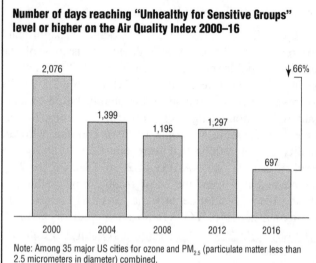

Number of days reaching "Unhealthy for Sensitive Groups" level or higher on the Air Quality Index 2000–16

Note: Among 35 major US cities for ozone and PM₂.₅ (particulate matter less than 2.5 micrometers in diameter) combined.

SOURCE: "Unhealthy Air Quality Days Trending Down," in *Our Nation's Air: Air Quality Improves as America Grows: Status and Trends through 2016*, US Environmental Protection Agency, 2017, https://gispub.epa.gov/air/trendsreport/2017/documentation/AirTrends_Flyer_2017.pdf (accessed November 7, 2017)

FIGURE 2.10

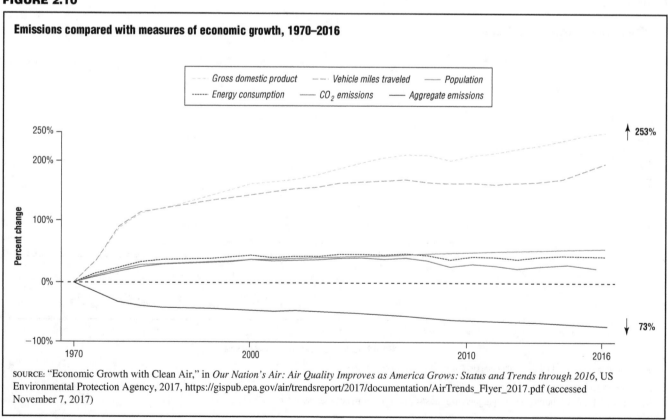

Emissions compared with measures of economic growth, 1970–2016

SOURCE: "Economic Growth with Clean Air," in *Our Nation's Air: Air Quality Improves as America Grows: Status and Trends through 2016*, US Environmental Protection Agency, 2017, https://gispub.epa.gov/air/trendsreport/2017/documentation/AirTrends_Flyer_2017.pdf (accessed November 7, 2017)

how to achieve the limits. Multiple lawsuits have been filed over the decades regarding the complex issues involved.

In 2005 the EPA issued the Clean Air Interstate Rule (CAIR) to tackle problems in the eastern United States with air pollutants that move across state boundaries. The program was to be carried out using a cap-and-trade system, as was already in place for the Acid Rain Program. The CAIR put permanent caps on emissions of sulfur dioxide and nitrogen oxide in 28 eastern states and the District of Columbia. The rule was projected to reduce sulfur dioxide emissions in these states by more than 70% and reduce nitrogen oxide emissions by more than 60% compared with 2003 levels. Control of these pollutants was expected to reduce the formation of fine PM, acid rain, and ground-level ozone across the country.

The CAIR was subjected to legal challenges after its issuance. In July 2008 the US Court of Appeals for the District of Columbia Circuit vacated (revoked) the CAIR in *North Carolina v. EPA* (531 F.3d 896). Later that year the court ordered the EPA to issue a new rule to replace the CAIR. In July 2011 the EPA finalized the Cross-State Air Pollution Rule (CSAPR; https://www.epa.gov/csapr) to replace the CAIR. The CSAPR imposes additional restrictions on the emissions of sulfur dioxide and nitrogen oxide from power plants in many eastern and midwestern states. (See Table 2.4.) These pollutants in particular are prone to cross state lines and contribute to air quality problems, such as ozone, miles away from where they are generated.

The CSAPR was immediately challenged in court. The rule was stayed (temporarily prevented from going into effect) in December 2011 while the legal process played out. In the meantime, the CAIR remained in effect. In August 2012 the US Court of Appeals for the District of Columbia Circuit ruled in *EME Homer City Generation, L.P. v. EPA* (696 F.3d 7) that the EPA had overstepped its authority with the CSAPR. In particular, the court found that the "EPA has used the good neighbor provision to impose massive emissions reduction requirements on upwind States without regard to the limits imposed by the statutory text." The agency appealed the decision, and in April 2014 the US Supreme Court in *EPA v. EME Homer City Generation* (No. 12-1182) ruled in the EPA's favor.

TABLE 2.4

States subject to the Cross-State Air Pollution Rule

State	Required to reduce emissions of NO$_x$ during the ozone season (1997 ozone NAAQS)	Required to reduce emissions of NO$_x$ during the ozone season (2008 ozone NAAQS)	Required to reduce annual emissions of SO$_2$ and NO$_x$ (1997 annual PM$_{2.5}$ NAAQS)	Required to reduce annual emissions of SO$_2$ and NO$_x$ (2006 24-hour PM$_{2.5}$ NAAQS)	SO$_2$ group*
Alabama		X	X	X	2
Arkansas		X			
Georgia	X		X	X	2
Illinois		X	X	X	1
Indiana		X	X	X	1
Iowa		X	X	X	1
Kansas		X		X	2
Kentucky		X	X	X	1
Louisiana		X			
Maryland		X	X	X	1
Michigan		X	X	X	1
Minnesota				X	2
Mississippi		X			
Missouri		X	X	X	1
Nebraska				X	2
New Jersey		X		X	1
New York		X	X	X	1
North Carolina			X	X	1
Ohio		X	X	X	1
Oklahoma		X			
Pennsylvania		X	X	X	1
South Carolina			X		2
Tennessee		X	X	X	1
Texas		X	X		2
Virginia		X		X	1
West Virginia		X	X	X	1
Wisconsin		X	X	X	1
Number of states	**1**	**22**	**18**	**21**	

NO$_x$ = nitrogen oxides; SO$_2$ = sulfur dioxide; NAAQS = National Ambient Air Quality Standards; PM$_{2.5}$ = particulate matter less than 2.5 micrometers in diameter.
*The final CSAPR divides the states required to reduce SO$_2$ into two groups. Both groups must reduce their SO$_2$ emissions beginning in Phase I. Group 1 states must make significant additional reductions in SO$_2$ emissions for Phase II in order to eliminate their significant contribution to air quality problems in downwind areas.

SOURCE: "States That Are Affected by the Cross-State Air Pollution Rule (CSAPR)," in *States That Are Affected by the Cross-State Air Pollution Rule (CSAPR)*, US Environmental Protection Agency, November 7, 2017, https://www.epa.gov/csapr/states-are-affected-cross-state-air-pollution-rule-csapr (accessed November 8, 2017)

The rule includes two phases for sulfur dioxide emissions. All of the covered power plants must reduce their emissions during the first phase. A subset of the covered power plants must then make additional emissions cuts during the second phase. The EPA explains in "Cross-State Air Pollution Rule" (December 14, 2017, https://www.epa.gov/csapr) that it began implementing phase one of the rule in 2015 and phase two in 2017. Overall, the EPA projects that the CSAPR will prevent tens of thousands of premature deaths and illnesses associated with breathing contaminated air.

HAZARDOUS AIR POLLUTANTS

Hazardous air pollutants (HAPs), or air toxics, are pollutants that can cause severe health effects and/or ecosystem damage. Examples of HAPs are arsenic, benzene, beryllium, dioxins, mercury, and vinyl chloride. Serious health risks linked to HAPs include cancer, immune system disorders, neurological problems, reproductive effects, and birth defects. In "What Are Hazardous Air Pollutants" (February 9, 2017, https://www.epa.gov/haps/what-are-hazardous-air-pollutants), the EPA notes that it focuses on 187 HAPs. These chemicals are listed in the CAA and are targeted for regulation under Section 112. As noted earlier, the EPA does not have to consider compliance costs when setting ambient air quality standards. This is not the case for HAP standards. Section 112 specifically directs the agency to set them while "taking into consideration the cost of achieving such emission reduction." This distinction has made the setting of National Emissions Standards for Hazardous Air Pollutants very challenging and fraught with political difficulties.

The major sources of HAP emissions include transportation vehicles, construction equipment, power plants, factories, and refineries. Some air toxics come from common sources. For example, benzene emissions are associated with gasoline. Air toxics are not subject to intensive national monitoring. The EPA, through its National Air Toxics Trends Station Network (https://www3.epa.gov/ttnamti1/natts.html), operated 27 monitoring sites around the country as of 2017.

National Air Toxics Assessments

As of November 2017, the EPA had conducted five National Air Toxics Assessments (https://www.epa.gov/national-air-toxics-assessment): in 1996, 1999, 2002, 2005, and 2011. The results were typically published four to seven years later. In December 2015 the EPA released the 2011 National-Scale Air Toxics Assessment (https://www.epa.gov/national-air-toxics-assessment/2011-national-air-toxics-assessment). It evaluates 180 HAPs plus PM from the burning of diesel fuel. The EPA notes in "Summary of Results for the 2011 National-Scale Assessment" (December 17, 2015, https://www.epa.gov/sites/production/files/2015-12/documents/2011-nata-

summary-results.pdf) that the assessment indicates which of the air toxics pose the greatest potential cancer and noncancer risks to humans. Overall, the EPA concludes:

> NATA estimates that all 285 million people in the U.S. have an increased cancer risk of greater than 10 in one million. Half a million people (less than 1 percent of the total U.S. population based on the 2010 census) have an increased cancer risk of greater than 100 in a million. The average, national, cancer risk for 2011 is 40-in-1 million. This means that, on average, approximately 1 in every 25,000 people have an increased likelihood of contracting cancer as a result of breathing air toxics from outdoor sources if they were exposed to 2011 emission levels over the course of their lifetime.

The agency also includes maps that show the levels of cancer and noncancer risks using census tracts from the 2010 census.

National Emissions Standards for Hazardous Air Pollutants for Power Plants

Section 112 of the CAA singles out electric utility steam generating units for special consideration. The law defines an electric utility steam generating unit as "any fossil fuel fired combustion unit of more than 25 megawatts that serves a generator that produces electricity for sale." Fossil fuels include coal, oil, and natural gas. When the CAA was amended in 1990, Congress directed the EPA to perform a study of emissions from electric utility steam generating units and determine whether the units should be subject to regulation under Section 112. Specifically, the law states: "The [EPA] Administrator shall regulate electric utility steam generating units under this section, if the Administrator finds such regulation is appropriate and necessary after considering the results of the study required by this subparagraph." In December 2000 the agency issued its findings in "Regulatory Finding on the Emissions of Hazardous Air Pollutants from Electric Utility Steam Generating Units" (*Federal Register*, vol. 65, no. 245), which supported the regulation of electric utility steam generating units for air toxics under Section 112. Specifically, the EPA noted that "coal- and oil-fired electric utility steam generating units are significant emitters of HAP, including mercury which is emitted from coal-fired units, and which EPA identified as the HAP of greatest concern to public health from the industry."

Mercury is naturally present in the earth's crust, such as in rocks and fossil fuels, particularly coal. When the fuels are burned, the mercury enters the atmosphere. From there, it can fall into water supplies, where it is absorbed by fish and shellfish. The consumption of contaminated fish and shellfish is the primary source of mercury exposure to humans.

According to the EPA, in *Reducing Toxic Pollution from Power Plants: EPA's Proposed Mercury and Air Toxics Standards* (March 16, 2011, https://www.epa.gov/

sites/production/files/2016-05/documents/proposalpresen tation.pdf), three sources accounted for approximately two-thirds of the nation's total mercury emissions in 1990: power plants, municipal waste combustors, and medical waste incinerators. Emissions from the latter two sources were reduced by more than 96% between 1990 and 2005. However, mercury emissions from power plants declined only 10% during the same period.

In 2005 the EPA issued the Clean Air Mercury Rule (CAMR) to limit and reduce mercury emissions nationwide from coal-fired power plants. The CAMR was immediately unpopular with some state governments, particularly those in the eastern United States, where many coal-fired power plants operate. In February 2008 the US Court of Appeals for the District of Columbia Circuit ruled in *New Jersey v. EPA* (517 F.3d 574) that the CAMR's regulatory approach was invalid.

In March 2011 the EPA (https://www.epa.gov/mats/ epa-proposes-mercury-and-air-toxics-standards-mats-power-plants) proposed mercury and air toxics standards under Section 112. The standards were finalized later that year and cover emissions of mercury and other HAPs from hundreds of power plants around the country. In "Mercury and Air Toxics Standards: Healthier Americans" (December 7, 2017, https://www.epa.gov/mats/healthier-americans), the EPA notes that the new standards are expected to provide numerous health benefits and avoid as many as 11,000 premature deaths annually. (See Table 2.5.) These benefits would come at a significant economic cost. The EPA estimates in *Regulatory Impact Analysis for the Final Mercury and Air Toxics Standards* (December 2011, https://www3.epa.gov/ttnecas1/regdata/ RIAs/matsriafinal.pdf) that compliance with the MATS will cost the power industry around $9.6 billion annually. The economic benefits of the new standards are projected to total up to $90 billion annually. These benefits primarily result from avoided adverse health effects.

TABLE 2.5

Projected annual number of adverse health effects avoided due to implementing the Mercury and Air Toxics Standards Rule

Health effect	Cases avoided
Premature death	4,200–11,000
Chronic bronchitis	2,800
Heart attacks	4,700
Asthma attacks	130,000
Hospital and emergency room visits	5,700
Restricted activity days	3,200,000

MATS = Mercury and Air Toxics Standards.

SOURCE: "Estimated Annual Number of Adverse Health Effects Avoided Due to Implementing the MATS," in *Mercury and Air Toxics Standards: Healthier Americans*, US Environmental Protection Agency, December 7, 2016, https://www.epa.gov/mats/healthier-americans (accessed November 8, 2017)

Multiple industry groups and states sued the EPA over the new standards. In 2015 the case reached the US Supreme Court. In a narrow 5–4 decision, the court ruled in *Michigan v. Environmental Protection Agency* (No. 14-46) that the EPA had failed to correctly follow the CAA because it did not assess the projected costs of the new standards early enough in the rule-making process. However, the Supreme Court did not overturn the MATS; the case was remanded (returned) back to a lower court for reconsideration. As a result, the MATS went into effect in 2015.

In April 2016 the EPA issued "Supplementary Finding That It Is Appropriate and Necessary to Regulate Hazardous Air Pollutants from Coal- and Oil-Fired Electric Utility Steam Generating Units" (*Federal Register*, vol. 81, no. 79). The agency concluded that its cost-benefit analysis supports the new standards under the MATS program. This supplementary finding triggered an additional round of lawsuits against the EPA. By that point the 2016 presidential campaign was well under way. The Republican candidate Donald Trump accused the Obama administration of waging a "war on coal." Trump won the presidency and quickly acted to dismantle or weaken many Obama-era environmental regulations. In April 2017 lawyers for his administration asked a court that was scheduled to hear arguments related to the supplementary finding lawsuits to delay the proceedings. Timothy Cama explains in "Court Delays EPA Mercury Rule Case While Trump Reviews" (TheHill.com, April 27, 2017) that "the case will be on hold while the administration decides whether to repeal the [supplementary finding] or defend it in court." As of January 2018, the Trump administration had not completed its review. Although the MATS remained in effect, its future was uncertain.

THE AUTOMOBILE'S CONTRIBUTION TO AIR POLLUTION

For several decades following the passage of the original CAA in 1970, air pollution from industrial sources was the primary focus of lawmakers and the public. As dramatic achievements in air quality were obtained in this sector, more attention was focused on air pollutants that were associated with transportation vehicles. As noted earlier in this chapter, the EPA estimates that highway vehicles accounted for significant percentages of some of the criteria air pollutant emissions in 2016, including 34% of NO_x, 30% of carbon monoxide, and 11% of VOCs. In addition, highway vehicles are minor sources of other pollutant emissions, including ammonia, PM, and sulfur dioxide.

Exhaust Emissions Limits

The 1990 amendments to the CAA included a program to control air pollution from new motor vehicles. The so-called EPA Tier 1 emissions standards were issued in 1991 and took effect during the mid-1990s. These standards applied to all new light-duty vehicles weighing less than 8,500 pounds (3,900 kg). This included cars, pickup trucks, and sport-utility vehicles. There were different emissions standards by weight class within Tier 1. In 1997 the EPA issued regulations for the National Low Emission Vehicle program, a voluntary program that was modeled after California standards for emissions reductions from motor vehicles.

Because of California's extreme air pollution problems, the 1990 amendments to the CAA allowed states to set stricter emissions standards than those that were required by the amendments, which California did. These included strict new laws on automobile pollution. The California low-emission vehicle (LEV) regulations were originally adopted in 1991 and became applicable in 1994. LEV II regulations were passed in 1998 and became applicable with 2004 model year vehicles. LEV III amendments were adopted in 2012. According to the California Air Resources Board, in *The California Low-Emission Vehicle Regulations* (April 2013, https://www.arb.ca.gov/msprog/levprog/cleandoc/cleancomplete%20lev-ghg%20regs%204-13.pdf), the LEV III regulations will be phased in over the 2015 to 2025 model years.

The remaining 49 states have the option of choosing either the California standards or the standards set under the CAA. Some states have tougher tests for auto emissions than others. In most major metropolitan areas, owners of cars and light trucks are required to pay for exhaust emissions tests. For those that do not pass, repairs must be made to bring them into compliance.

In 1999 the EPA introduced its Tier 2 federal emissions limits for new vehicles. They took effect in 2004 and were completely implemented by 2009. Emissions limits apply to carbon monoxide, formaldehyde, NO_x, nonmethane organic gases, and PM. Manufacturers are allowed the flexibility to certify new vehicles to different sets of exhaust emissions standards called bins. The manufacturers must choose bins for their vehicles that ensure that their corporate sales fleet emits an average of no more than 0.07 grams of NO_x per mile.

In 2014 the EPA (August 17, 2017, https://www.epa.gov/regulations-emissions-vehicles-and-engines/regulations-smog-soot-and-other-air-pollution-passenger) finalized its Tier 3 Vehicle Emission and Fuel Standards Program, which imposes new emissions standards for vehicles and requires lower sulfur content for gasoline. The program became effective in 2017. The agency notes in "EPA Sets Tier 3 Motor Vehicle Emission and Fuel Standards" (March 2014, https://nepis.epa.gov/Exe/ZyPDF.cgi/P100HVZV.PDF?Dockey=P100HVZV.PDF) that the standards will supplement California's LEV III standards and the fuel economy and carbon dioxide emissions standards that were issued jointly in 2010 by the US Department of Transportation's National Highway Traffic Safety Administration (NHTSA) and the EPA. The latter standards are described later in this chapter. Greenhouse gas emissions and standards are discussed in detail in Chapter 3.

DIESEL EMISSIONS SCANDALS. In 2015 a major scandal erupted over allegations that the Volkswagen Group (VW) had deceived regulators about the emissions from some of its diesel-powered vehicles. The article "VW Scandal: Engineer's Testing 'Opened a Can of Worms' for Automaker" (Reuters, September 24, 2015) indicates that from late 2012 through early 2013 researchers at West Virginia University tested the emissions from several different car models with diesel engines. The tests were done while the cars were stationary and under real-life driving conditions. The researchers noticed that two VW models, a Passat and a Jetta, produced much higher emissions during the highway tests than during the stationary tests. They notified the EPA and the California Air Resources Board. According to the article, those two agencies confirmed the test results.

In "Everything We Know about Volkswagen Emissions Scandal" (Freep.com, September 22, 2015), the *Detroit Free Press* notes that the agencies asked VW to explain the discrepancies, and the corporation eventually admitted that it had purposely rigged some of its cars to provide deceptive test results. This was achieved through use of a so-called defeat device. The *Detroit Free Press* explains, "The device would activate the cars' emission controls during testing, but deactivate them in real-world driving." As many as 11 million VW cars worldwide are believed to have been rigged with the defeat devices.

VW's chief executive officer resigned after apologizing for the scandal. In 2016 the corporation reached a $14.7 billion settlement with the US Department of Justice. According to Chris Isidore and David Goldman, in "Volkswagen Agrees to Record $14.7 Billion Settlement over Emissions Cheating" (CNN.com, June 28, 2016), the owners of the 487,000 affected cars in the United States have the option to sell their cars back to the company or have them fixed to meet environmental regulations on auto emissions. In 2017 VW was assessed a $2.8 billion criminal fine by the Department of Justice for its actions. As of January 2018, at least nine company executives had been criminally charged in the scandal, and more arrests were expected.

In May 2017 the Department of Justice filed a civil complaint against Fiat Chrysler Automobiles for alleged violations of the CAA. The EPA explains in the press release "United States Files Complaint against Fiat Chrysler Automobiles for Alleged Clean Air Act Violation" (May 23, 2017, https://www.epa.gov/newsreleases/united-states-files-complaint-against-fiat-chrysler-automobiles-alleged-clean-air-act) that the company is accused of installing manipulative software and defeat devices in approximately 104,000 of its diesel-powered Jeep Grand Cherokee and Ram 1500 vehicles. The EPA claims that the software functions "cause the vehicles' emission control systems to perform differently, and less effectively, during certain normal driving conditions than on federal emission tests, resulting in increased emissions of harmful air pollutants." As of January 2018, the case had not been settled.

In "GM Accused of Cheating on Diesel Emissions" (NBCNews.com, May 26, 2017), Paul A. Eisenstein indicates that other major car companies, including the General Motors Company, have been served with class-action lawsuits by private law firms alleging use of defeat devices on diesel-powered light vehicles. As of January 2018, settlements had not been reached in these cases.

Gasoline Formulations

During the 1980s lead was phased out of gasoline to provide substantial improvements in air quality. A variety of other federal and state standards have gone into effect that dictate particular properties of gasoline, such as volatility (tendency to evaporate) and levels of NO_x, heavy metals, toxic compounds, sulfur, and oxygen. The CAA requires the use of specially blended gasoline in areas of the country that are deemed nonattainment for ozone or carbon monoxide levels. Attainment areas can choose to opt-in to these requirements.

All the varying standards have resulted in the creation of many so-called boutique gasolines that greatly complicate the distribution dynamics for gasoline in the country. Critics complain that a gasoline shortage in one area can often not be relieved by shipping in gasoline from another part of the country because of the highly varying standards.

Corporate Average Fuel Economy Standards

In 1973 some of the nations belonging to the Organization of the Petroleum Exporting Countries imposed an oil embargo that provided a painful reminder to Americans of how dependent the country had become on foreign sources of fuel. Congress passed the 1975 Automobile Fuel Efficiency Act, which set the initial Corporate Average Fuel Economy (CAFE) standards. The NHTSA is responsible for establishing the standards and promulgating the regulations concerning them. The EPA is responsible for calculating the average fuel economy that is achieved by each vehicle manufacturer.

CAFE standards have varied over the decades, but have generally increased with time. In 2010 the NHTSA and the EPA issued a joint rulemaking that established a new program to regulate fuel economy and greenhouse gas emissions, such as carbon dioxide, for model years 2012 to 2016 of cars and light-duty trucks. (See Table 2.6.) Two years later the agencies finalized standards for model years 2017 to 2025. The targets are based on vehicle size or

TABLE 2.6

Fuel economy and carbon dioxide emissions standards for cars and light-duty trucks, model years 2012–25

Year	Cars	Light trucks	Combined cars and light trucks	
		Average required fuel economy (miles per gallon)		
2012	33.3	25.4	29.7	
2013	34.2	26.0	30.5	
2014	34.9	26.6	31.3	
2015	36.2	27.5	32.6	
2016	37.8	28.8	34.1	
2017	40.1	29.4	35.4	
2018	41.6	30.0	36.5	
2019	43.1	30.6	37.7	
2020	44.8	31.2	38.9	
2021	46.8	33.3	41.0	Standards under review
2022	49.0	34.9	43.0	
2023	51.2	36.6	45.1	
2024	53.6	38.5	47.4	
2025	56.2	40.3	49.7	
	Average projected emissions compliance levels under the footprint-based carbon dioxide standards (grams per mile)			
2012	263	346	295	
2013	256	337	286	
2014	247	326	276	
2015	236	312	263	
2016	225	298	250	
2017	212	295	243	
2018	202	285	232	
2019	191	277	222	
2020	182	269	213	
2021	172	249	199	Standards under review
2022	164	237	190	
2023	157	225	180	
2024	150	214	171	
2025	143	203	163	

NHTSA = National Highway Traffic Safety Administration.

Note: The required fuel economy, along with projections of CO_2 emissions, shown here use a model year 2008 baseline. The presented rates of increase in stringency for NHTSA CAFE standards are lower than the Environmental Protection Agency (EPA) rates of increase in stringency for greenhouse gas (GHG) standards. One major difference is that NHTSA's standards, unlike EPA's, do not reflect the inclusion of air conditioning system refrigerant and leakage improvements, but EPA's standards would allow consideration of such improvements which reduce GHGs but generally do not affect fuel economy. The 2025 EPA GHG standard of 163 grams/mile would be equivalent to 54.5 mpg, if the vehicles were to meet this level all through fuel economy improvements. The agencies expect, however, that a portion of these improvements will be made through reductions in air conditioning leakage, which would not contribute to fuel economy.

SOURCE: Stacy C. Davis, Susan E. Williams, and Robert G. Boundy, "Table 4.20. Fuel Economy and Carbon Dioxide Emissions Standards, MY 2012–2025," in *Transportation Energy Data Book, Edition 36*, Oak Ridge National Laboratory, December 2017, http://cta.ornl.gov/data/tedb36/Edition_36_Full_Doc.pdf (accessed December 1, 2017)

footprint (the distance between the axles times the distance between the wheels on the same axle). Table 2.7 shows the emissions and fuel economy targets for model year 2025 for some example cars and light-duty trucks.

The 2012 rule was particularly controversial because it set standards so far into the future (i.e., to 2025). To provide some flexibility, the rule included a provision for a "midterm evaluation" of the standards for the later years of the rule. The NHTSA notes in "Light Duty CAFE Midterm Evaluation" (2018, https://www.nhtsa.gov/corporate-average-fuel-economy/light-duty-cafe-midterm-evaluation) that the midterm evaluation began in

TABLE 2.7

Fuel economy and carbon dioxide emissions targets for cars and light-duty trucks, model year 2025

Vehicle type	Example models	Example model footprint (square feet)	CO_2 emissions target (grams per mile)	Fuel economy target (miles per gallon)
		Example passenger cars		
Compact car	Honda Fit	40	131	61.1
Midsize car	Ford Fusion	46	147	54.9
Fullsize car	Chrysler 300	53	170	48.0
		Example light-duty trucks		
Small SUV	4WD Ford Escape	44	170	47.5
Midsize crossover	Nissan Murano	49	188	43.4
Minivan	Toyota Sienna	55	209	39.2
Large pickup truck	Chevy Silverado	67	252	33.0

CO_2 = carbon dioxide.

Notes: The model year 2025 targets are currently under review. Examples in table use model year 2012 vehicle specifications. The fuel economy from this table will not match the fuel economy listed on the window sticker of a new vehicle. Window sticker fuel economy is calculated by a different methodology than the Corporate Average Fuel Economy.

SOURCE: Stacy C. Davis, Susan E. Williams, and Robert G. Boundy, "Table 4.21. Fuel Economy and Carbon Dioxide Targets for Model Year 2025," in *Transportation Energy Data Book, Edition 36*, Oak Ridge National Laboratory, December 2017, http://cta.ornl.gov/data/tedb36/Edition_36_Full_Doc.pdf (accessed December 1, 2017)

2016 and covered the CAFE fuel economy standards and the greenhouse gas emissions standards for vehicles. In early 2017 the EPA announced that the evaluation was completed and that the greenhouse gas standards would remain in place. Because the greenhouse gas and fuel economy standards are considered linked, the EPA's action suggested that the existing CAFE standards would also remain in place through 2025.

The EPA's decision was announced only days before President Trump took office. His administration soon signaled its intention to reopen the midterm evaluation process. In the press release "EPA to Reexamine Emission Standards for Cars and Light Duty Trucks—Model Years 2022–2025" (March 15, 2017, https://www.epa.gov/newsreleases/epa-reexamine-emission-standards-cars-and-light-duty-trucks-model-years-2022-2025), Scott Pruitt (1968–), the head of the EPA, notes, "These standards are costly for automakers and the American people." Pruitt goes on to say, "We will work with our partners at [the Department of Transportation] to take a fresh look to determine if this approach is realistic. This thorough review will help ensure that this national program is good for consumers and good for the environment." As of January 2018, the midterm evaluation was still in progress. As shown in Table 2.6, the fuel economy and carbon dioxide standards for model years 2021 to 2025 were being reexamined by the agencies.

Alternative Fuels

Early pollution-reducing efforts by vehicle manufacturers focused on reducing tailpipe emissions instead of eliminating their formation in the first place. Automakers introduced lighter engines, fuel injection systems, catalytic converters, and other technological improvements. Since the 1970s concerns about US dependence on foreign oil supplies and environmental issues have focused attention on the development of alternative fuels for transportation vehicles. The Energy Policy Act of 1992 defines alternative fuels as those that are "substantially not petroleum and would yield substantial energy security benefits and substantial environmental benefits." Under the act the following are designated as alternative fuels:

- Coal-derived liquid fuels
- Liquefied petroleum gas (propane)
- Natural gas and liquid fuels domestically produced from natural gas
- Methanol, ethanol, and other alcohols
- Blends of 85% or more of alcohol with gasoline
- Biodiesel and other fuels derived from biological materials
- Electricity
- Hydrogen
- P-series fuels (blends of natural gas liquids, ethanol, and the biomass-derived cosolvent methyltetrahydrofuran)

Although alternative fuels offer energy security advantages over gasoline, their use may substitute one environmental problem for another. Alternative fuels can also have trade-offs in terms of economic and energy effects. This is particularly true for ethanol.

THE ETHANOL DEBATE. Ethanol is an alcohol that can be derived from sugar-containing plants. A variety of plants can be used, but corn is, by far, the sugar source of choice for US-produced ethanol. Ethanol is used as a motor vehicle fuel through two primary means. It can be added to regular gasoline at concentrations of up to 10%

ethanol with 90% gasoline. This mixture is known as E10 and can be used in any regular gasoline-powered vehicle. Another product, E85, is a blend of 85% ethanol with 15% gasoline. E85 can only be used in so-called flex-fuel vehicles that are specially designed to combust either gasoline or gasoline/ethanol mixtures containing up to 85% ethanol. Ethanol has a lower energy content than gasoline. This means that a gallon of E85 gets fewer miles to the gallon than a gallon of gasoline.

Because ethanol is relatively expensive to produce, the federal government has encouraged its production since the 1970s with tax incentives. In addition, the federal government and some state governments have issued mandates (legal requirements) that their fleets of government-owned vehicles increasingly use alternative fuels. At the federal level, the Energy Policy Act of 2005 and the Energy Independence and Security Act of 2007 mandated increased use of biofuels (such as ethanol) through the early 2020s. These mandates have spurred manufacturers to produce more flex-fuel vehicles for government and private customers.

Ethanol is touted by its proponents as an environmentally friendly alternative to gasoline. For example, the Renewable Fuels Association, a national trade association for the ethanol industry, states in "Why Is Ethanol Important?" (2018, http://www.ethanolrfa.org/consumers/why-is-ethanol-important) that "ethanol use reduces greenhouse gas emissions by 43% compared to gasoline. Ethanol also reduces emissions of particulate matter, carbon monoxide, and volatile organic compounds, displacing toxic aromatics such as benzene and toluene." The US Department of Energy's (DOE) Alternative Fuels Data Center notes in "Ethanol Vehicle Emissions" (March 16, 2017, https://www.afdc.energy.gov/vehicles/flexible_fuel_emissions.html) that although ethanol is an alternative fuel, it still produces emissions of "regulated pollutants, toxic chemicals, and greenhouse gases." However, the center points out that "when compared to gasoline, the use of high-level ethanol blends, such as E85, generally result in lower emissions levels."

ALTERNATIVE FUEL VEHICLES AND STATIONS. Alternative fuels cannot become a viable transportation option unless a fuel supply is readily available to consumers. Ideally, the infrastructure for supplying alternative fuels will be developed simultaneously with the vehicles. Table 2.8 estimates the number of alternative fuel highway vehicles that were made available between 2004 and 2015. By far, E85 vehicles were the most common type of alternative fuel vehicle.

As shown in Table 2.9, an estimated 59,926 alternative fuel stations and electric charging outlets were operating around the country as of 2017. The vast majority of them serviced electric vehicles. California (16,932) had the largest number of offerings, followed by Texas

TABLE 2.8

Number of alternative fuel highway vehicles made available, 2004–15

Year	CNG	Electricity	E85	Hydrogen	LNG	LPG
2004	7,752	2,200	674,678	31	136	2,150
2005	3,304	2,281	743,948	74	68	700
2006	3,128	2,715	1,011,399	40	92	473
2007	2,487	3,152	1,115,069	63	26	356
2008	4,440	2,802	1,175,345	63	384	695
2009	3,770	2,255	805,777	26	126	861
2010	4,973	2,229	1,484,945	64	231	747
2011	5,674	25,382	2,116,273	107	137	1,054
2012	7,672	46,624	2,446,966	56	101	1,134
2013	9,454	130,323	2,665,470	10	344	2,700
2014	6,662	92,594	2,433,113	3	535	1,708
2015	8,744	118,560	1,881,500	2	7	2,248

CNG = Compressed Natural Gas.
LNG = Liquefied Natural Gas.
LPG = Liquefied Petroleum Gas.
Note: E85 is a blend of 85% ethanol with 15% gasoline.
Note: "Made available" refers to the supply of warrantied alternative fuel vehicles by manufacturers and aftermarket conversion companies. These do not represent sales.

SOURCE: Stacy C. Davis, Susan E. Williams, and Robert G. Boundy, "Table 6.1. Estimates of Alternative Fuel Highway Vehicles Made Available, 2004–2015," in *Transportation Energy Data Book, Edition 36*, Oak Ridge National Laboratory, December 2017, http://cta.ornl.gov/data/tedb36/Edition_36_Full_Doc.pdf (accessed December 1, 2017)

(3,515), Florida (2,596), Washington (2,241), and Georgia (2,136).

Market success of alternative fuels depends on public acceptance. People are accustomed to using gasoline as their main transportation fuel, and it is readily available. As federal and state requirements for alternative fuels increase, so should the availability of such fuels as well as their acceptance by the general public. Although E85 is heavily marketed by the ethanol industry and supported by government mandates, it is generally not expected to satisfy the United States' long-term need for an environmentally friendly vehicle fuel. In the long run, hydrogen and electricity seem the most promising of the alternative fuels for vehicles.

HYDROGEN-FUELED VEHICLES. As the simplest and most abundant naturally occurring element, hydrogen can be found in materials such as coal, natural gas, and water. For decades advocates of hydrogen have promoted it as the fuel of the future because it is abundant, clean, and cheap. However, challenges with technology, economics, and safety issues have stymied its commercialization potential.

In 2003 President George W. Bush (1946–) announced the creation of the Hydrogen Fuel Initiative (HFI). The goal of this five-year $1.2 billion program was to develop the technology needed for commercially viable hydrogen-powered fuel cells for transportation vehicles and home/business use by 2020. The Energy Policy Act of 2005 extended the HFI beyond the initial five-year program through 2020.

TABLE 2.9

Alternative fuel sites, by state and fuel type, 2017

State	B20 sites	CNG sites	E85 sites	Electric stations	Electric charging outlets	Hydrogen sites	LNG sites	LPG sites	Totals by state*
Alabama	5	32	41	126	252	0	2	97	429
Alaska	0	1	0	6	9	0	0	7	17
Arizona	76	34	26	426	1,055	0	8	93	1,292
Arkansas	5	16	44	56	85	0	1	40	191
California	36	326	137	4,442	16,052	42	45	294	16,932
Colorado	16	44	92	503	1,204	1	1	59	1,417
Connecticut	2	21	4	347	777	2	1	21	828
Delaware	1	1	1	37	97	1	0	9	110
Dist. of Columbia	7	2	3	100	268	1	0	0	281
Florida	14	57	79	1,035	2,301	0	3	142	2,596
Georgia	23	48	55	678	1,905	0	4	101	2,136
Hawaii	8	1	2	271	623	4	0	5	643
Idaho	2	11	6	68	151	0	2	31	203
Illinois	14	48	268	520	1,141	1	2	123	1,597
Indiana	6	35	202	190	384	0	2	186	815
Iowa	9	9	242	109	222	0	0	33	515
Kansas	4	20	21	195	740	0	1	41	827
Kentucky	4	12	73	78	163	0	1	36	289
Louisiana	2	23	11	81	180	0	1	47	264
Maine	3	2	0	116	199	0	0	14	218
Maryland	13	16	36	518	1,255	0	1	34	1,355
Massachusetts	11	16	7	545	1,404	2	1	34	1,475
Michigan	9	23	252	538	1,159	2	0	103	1,548
Minnesota	7	25	355	298	741	0	0	48	1,176
Mississippi	4	7	3	45	69	0	2	91	176
Missouri	3	22	96	356	1,476	0	1	69	1,667
Montana	7	1	2	30	79	0	0	48	137
Nebraska	2	11	86	60	142	0	1	27	269
Nevada	4	5	19	193	553	0	1	34	616
New Hampshire	4	3	0	98	192	0	0	25	224
New Jersey	5	28	5	255	566	0	0	19	623
New Mexico	5	14	12	58	151	0	1	59	242
New York	34	94	69	845	1,724	1	0	71	1,993
North Carolina	116	42	77	543	1,270	0	1	93	1,599
North Dakota	3	1	41	9	13	0	0	24	82
Ohio	14	61	159	346	691	3	6	91	1,025
Oklahoma	5	122	31	54	117	0	1	140	416
Oregon	70	16	10	554	1,343	0	2	56	1,497
Pennsylvania	6	73	56	371	738	0	3	104	980
Rhode Island	5	4	0	88	224	0	0	7	240
South Carolina	24	12	64	221	446	2	1	48	597
South Dakota	2	1	73	23	40	0	0	27	143
Tennessee	29	22	79	445	1,039	0	5	88	1,262
Texas	18	125	215	1,020	2,661	1	19	476	3,515
Utah	1	86	1	138	345	0	6	48	487
Vermont	2	3	0	164	413	0	0	2	420
Virginia	11	20	29	448	1,053	0	2	92	1,207
Washington	39	26	20	779	2,066	0	2	88	2,241
West Virginia	2	4	33	58	151	0	0	13	203
Wisconsin	5	58	153	295	487	0	1	75	779
Wyoming	13	13	13	30	65	0	0	28	132
Totals by fuel	**710**	**1,697**	**3,303**	**18,809**	**50,481**	**63**	**31**	**3,541**	**59,926**

*Totals by state is the total number of fuel types available at stations. Stations are counted once for each type of fuel available. For electric, the number of charging outlets was used.

CNG = Compressed Natural Gas. LNG = Liquefied Natural Gas. LPG = Liquefied Petroleum Gas.

Note: E85 is a blend of 85% ethanol with 15% gasoline. B20 is a blend of 20% biodiesel with 80% petroleum diesel.

This list includes public and private refuel sites; therefore, not all of these sites are available to the public.

SOURCE: Stacy C. Davis, Susan E. Williams, and Robert G. Boundy, "Table 6.11. Number of Alternative Refuel Sites by State and Fuel Type, 2017," in *Transportation Energy Data Book, Edition 36*, Oak Ridge National Laboratory, December 2017, http://cta.ornl.gov/data/tedb36/Edition_36_Full_Doc.pdf (accessed December 1, 2017)

In February 2017 the DOE issued *DOE Hydrogen and Fuel Cells Program: 2016 Annual Progress Report* (https://www.hydrogen.energy.gov/annual_progress16.html). The department notes that the technologies are advancing and that some hydrogen-fueled equipment and vehicles have been adopted commercially. The two prime examples are the Hyundai Tucson (a compact sport-utility vehicle) and the Toyota Mirai (a sedan). Both models are powered by electricity that is generated by on-board fuel cells. In the report, the DOE indicates that BMW, Daimler AG, General Motors, and the Honda Motor Company are expected to introduce fuel cell vehicles to the market "in the near term." As shown in Table 2.9, there were only 63 hydrogen refueling sites around the country in 2017; the majority of them were located in California. The DOE expects that more of the refueling sites will be established across the United States as fuel cell vehicles continue to enter the market.

ALL-ELECTRIC VEHICLES: PROMISE AND REALITY. The all-electric vehicle is not a new invention. Popular during the 1890s, the quiet, clean, and simple vehicle was expected to dominate the automotive market of the 20th century. Instead, it quietly disappeared as automakers chose to invest billions of dollars in the internal combustion engine. It has taken a century, but the all-electric vehicle has returned.

All-electric vehicles run on one or more electric motors that are powered by a battery pack. Because they do not burn or combust a fuel, they have zero tailpipe emissions. However, the production of electricity at utility plants likely generates air pollutants. This is particularly true for coal-fired plants. According to the DOE, in "All-Electric Vehicles" (2018, http://www.fueleconomy.gov/Feg/evtech.shtml), electric cars do have several operational drawbacks. Most of the cars have a range of only about 100 to 200 miles (160 to 320 km) before they need a battery recharge. This is roughly half of the mileage achievable with a gasoline-powered vehicle before it needs refueling. The time required to fully recharge the battery pack of many electric cars ranges from four to eight hours. This is a substantial amount of time to people used to filling their cars with gasoline in a matter of minutes. In addition, the battery packs used in electric cars are large, heavy, and expensive to replace.

According to the DOE (http://www.fueleconomy.gov/), as of January 2018 there were 160 all-electric car models available to consumers covering model years 1984 to 2018. Examples include the Chevrolet Bolt, the Hyundai Ioniq, and the BMW i3 BEV. Tesla Motors also had a few of its models on the list. The company (https://www.tesla.com/supercharger) is notable for its innovative charging technology that allows its cars to be charged to 80% battery capacity in about 30 minutes at special charging stations. Tesla Motors is also known for the luxuriousness of its all-electric cars.

ADVANCED TECHNOLOGY VEHICLES. Many experts believe the most feasible solution in the near future is the use of vehicles that use a combination of gasoline and one of the alternative fuel sources. These are called advanced technology vehicles or hybrid vehicles. Gasoline-electric hybrids have proven to be the most commercially viable option. In fact, the term *hybrid* is now associated almost entirely with the gasoline-electric vehicle. These hybrids rely on a small internal combustion engine and electricity (from batteries). As such, their tailpipe

TABLE 2.10

Sales of hybrid and plug-in vehicles, 1999–2016

Calendar year	Hybrid vehicle sales (thousands)	Plug-in vehicle sales* (thousands)	All light vehicle sales (thousands)	Hybrid share of all light vehicles	Plug-in share of all light vehicles
1999	0.0	0.0	16,711	0.0%	0.0%
2000	9.4	0.0	17,164	0.1%	0.0%
2001	20.3	0.0	16,950	0.1%	0.0%
2002	36.0	0.0	16,675	0.2%	0.0%
2003	47.6	0.0	16,494	0.3%	0.0%
2004	84.2	0.0	16,737	0.5%	0.0%
2005	205.9	0.0	16,774	1.2%	0.0%
2006	251.9	0.0	16,336	1.5%	0.0%
2007	351.1	0.0	15,867	2.2%	0.0%
2008	315.8	0.0	13,015	2.4%	0.0%
2009	290.3	0.0	10,236	2.8%	0.0%
2010	274.6	0.3	11,394	2.4%	0.0%
2011	266.5	17.8	12,542	2.1%	0.1%
2012	434.6	53.2	14,220	3.1%	0.4%
2013	495.5	97.1	15,279	3.2%	0.6%
2014	452.2	118.9	16,192	2.8%	0.7%
2015	384.4	115.3	17,095	2.2%	0.7%
2016	346.9	159.6	17,169	2.0%	0.9%

*Includes plug-in hybrid-electric vehicles and all-electric vehicles.
Note: Plug-in vehicle sales include only those vehicles certified for highway use. Small electric carts and neighborhood electric vehicles are excluded.

SOURCE: Stacy C. Davis, Susan E. Williams, and Robert G. Boundy, "Table 6.2. Hybrid and Plug-In Vehicle Sales, 1999–2016," in *Transportation Energy Data Book, Edition 36*, Oak Ridge National Laboratory, December 2017, http://cta.ornl.gov/data/tedb36/Edition_36_Full_Doc.pdf (accessed December 1, 2017)

emissions are lower than those of comparable vehicles that are powered fully by gasoline.

As shown in Table 2.10, the Oak Ridge National Laboratory estimates that nearly 4.3 million of the vehicles were sold in the United States between 1999 and 2016. All-electric vehicles accounted for 0.9% of all light vehicle sales in 2016.

THE CAA: COSTS AND BENEFITS

In 1970 Congress passed the landmark CAA, proclaiming that it would restore urban air quality. It was no coincidence that the law was passed during a 14-day smog alert in the District of Columbia. The act was amended several times over the following decades, including a massive overhaul in 1990. Although the act has had mixed results, and many goals remain to be met, most experts credit it with making great strides toward cleaning up the air. As of January 2017, the EPA (http://www2.epa.gov/clean-air-act-overview/benefits-and-costs-clean-air-act) had published three comprehensive reports mandated by the CAA on the monetary costs and benefits of controlling air pollution.

In *The Benefits and Costs of the Clean Air Act, 1970 to 1990* (October 1997, https://www.epa.gov/sites/production/files/2015-06/documents/contsetc.pdf), the EPA concludes that the economic value of CAA programs was 42 times greater than the total costs of air pollution control during the 20-year period. The agency finds that many positive consequences occurred in the US economy because of CAA programs and regulations. The CAA affected industrial production, investment, productivity, consumption, employment, and economic growth. In fact, the agency estimates that total agricultural benefits from the CAA were almost $10 billion. The EPA compares benefits with direct costs or expenditures. The total costs of the CAA were $523 billion for the 20-year period, whereas the total benefits equaled $22.2 trillion—a net benefit of approximately $21.7 trillion.

According to the EPA, in *The Benefits and Costs of the Clean Air Act, 1990 to 2010* (November 1999, https://www.epa.gov/sites/production/files/2015-07/documents/fullrept.pdf), the second mandated review of the CAA, the act produced major reductions in pollution that causes illness and disease, smog, acid rain, haze, and damage to the environment. Using a sophisticated array of computer models and the latest cost data, the EPA finds that by 2010 the act had prevented 23,000 Americans from dying prematurely and averted more than 1.7 million asthma attacks. The CAA prevented 47,000 episodes of acute bronchitis, 91,000 occurrences of shortness of breath, 4.1 million lost workdays, and 31 million days in restricted activity because of illness. Another 22,000 respiratory-related hospital admissions were averted, as well as 42,000 admissions for heart disease and 4,800 emergency department visits for asthma.

The EPA estimates that the benefits of CAA programs in the reduction of illness and premature death alone totaled about $110 billion. By contrast, the agency finds that the cost of achieving these benefits was only $27 billion, which was a fraction of the value of the benefits. In addition, the agency reports that there were other benefits that scientists and economists cannot quantify and express in monetary terms, such as controlling cancer-causing air toxins and bringing benefits to crops and ecosystems by reducing pollutants.

At the same time, many cities were still not in compliance with the law. One reason efforts to clean the air were only partly successful was that they focused on specific measures to combat individual pollutants rather than on addressing the underlying social and economic structures that create the problem—for example, the distance between many Americans' residences and their places of work.

In April 2011 the EPA issued *The Benefits and Costs of the Clean Air Act from 1990 to 2020* (https://www.epa.gov/sites/production/files/2015-07/documents/fullreport_rev_a.pdf), the third mandated review of the benefits and costs of the CAA. The agency estimates that by 2020 the CAA as amended will have prevented more than 230,000 early deaths and provided approximately $2 trillion in economic benefits. The vast majority (85%) of these benefits will be attributed to a reduction in premature mortality due to decreased air quality concentrations of PM. Other benefits include decreased premature mortality due to ozone exposure, prevention of health problems (such as myocardial infarctions [heart attacks] and chronic bronchitis), and improved environmental conditions, particularly visibility.

CHAPTER 3
CLIMATE CHANGE

DEFINING CLIMATE AND CLIMATE CHANGE

Climate and weather are not the same thing. Both describe conditions in the lower atmosphere—for example, wet or dry, cold or warm, stormy or fair, and cloudy or clear. Weather is the short-term local state of the atmosphere. Weather conditions can change from moment to moment and can differ in two places that are relatively close together. Climate describes the average pattern of weather conditions that are experienced by a region over a long period. For example, Florida has a warm climate but can experience days and even weeks of cold weather.

The earth's climate as a whole has not changed much over the last several thousand years. In general, most of the planet has been warm enough for humans, animals, and plants to thrive. This was not so in the distant past, when the climate fluctuated between long periods of cold and warmth, each lasting for many thousands of years. Scientists are not sure what triggered these major climate changes. A variety of factors are believed to have been involved, including movement of the tectonic plates, changes in the earth's orbit around the sun, and variations in atmospheric gases.

The earth's temperature depends on a delicate balance of energy inputs and outputs, chemical processes, and physical phenomena. As shown in Figure 3.1, solar radiation passes through the earth's atmosphere and warms the earth. The earth emits infrared radiation. Some outgoing infrared radiation is not allowed to escape into outer space but is trapped beneath the atmosphere. The amount of energy that is trapped depends on many variables. One major factor is atmospheric composition. Some gases, such as water vapor, carbon dioxide, and methane, act to trap heat beneath the atmosphere in the same way that glass panels trap heat in a greenhouse. The panels allow sunlight into the greenhouse, but prevent heat from escaping.

The earth's surface temperature is about 60 degrees Fahrenheit (33 degrees C) warmer than it would be if natural greenhouse gases were not present. Without this natural warming process, the earth would be much colder and could not sustain life as it now exists.

It is necessary, however, to distinguish between the "natural" and the "enhanced" greenhouse effect. The natural greenhouse effect provides a warm atmosphere for the earth that is necessary for life. The theory behind the enhanced greenhouse effect is that human activities have loaded the atmosphere with too much carbon dioxide and other heat-trapping gases. This "global warming" has increased the earth's temperature above that expected from the natural greenhouse effect. Global warming is one aspect of climate change, which poses numerous consequences to the earth's environment and inhabitants. These consequences include rising sea levels, stronger storms, and habitat loss and extinction. (See Figure 3.2.) The primary human activities blamed for inducing climate change are the burning of fossil fuels (mainly coal and oil) and their derivatives (such as gasoline) and the destruction of large amounts of vegetation that normally absorb carbon dioxide.

A GLOBAL PROBLEM

The global nature and consequences of climate change have prompted an international effort to analyze the problem and its possible remedies. In 1988 the World Meteorological Organization (WMO), a nongovernmental agency under the United Nations Environment Programme (UNEP), established the Intergovernmental Panel on Climate Change (IPCC). As of January 2018, the IPCC (http://www.ipcc.ch/publications_and_data/publications_and_data_reports.shtml) had published several assessment reports that provide many data used in this chapter:

- *Climate Change*, which was published in 1990

- *Climate Change 1995*

- *Climate Change 2001*

- *Climate Change 2007*
- *Climate Change 2013: The Physical Science Basis*

FIGURE 3.1

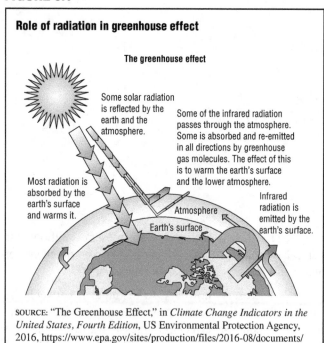

Role of radiation in greenhouse effect

The greenhouse effect

Some solar radiation is reflected by the earth and the atmosphere.

Some of the infrared radiation passes through the atmosphere. Some is absorbed and re-emitted in all directions by greenhouse gas molecules. The effect of this is to warm the earth's surface and the lower atmosphere.

Most radiation is absorbed by the earth's surface and warms it.

Atmosphere

Earth's surface

Infrared radiation is emitted by the earth's surface.

SOURCE: "The Greenhouse Effect," in *Climate Change Indicators in the United States, Fourth Edition*, US Environmental Protection Agency, 2016, https://www.epa.gov/sites/production/files/2016-08/documents/climate_indicators_2016.pdf (accessed November 8, 2017)

GREENHOUSE GASES

Greenhouse gases are gases in the atmosphere that allow shortwave radiation (sunlight) from the sun to pass through to the earth but that absorb and reradiate long-wave infrared radiation (heat) coming from the earth's surface. (See Figure 3.2.) This process serves to warm the lower atmosphere (the troposphere). According to the National Oceanic and Atmospheric Administration (NOAA), in "Science: Regions of the Atmosphere" (March 20, 2008, hhttp://www.ozonelayer.noaa.gov/science/atmosphere.htm), the troposphere extends from the earth's surface up to approximately 5.5 to 7.5 miles (9 to 12 km) above the surface.

Water Vapor

Water vapor is part of the natural water cycle that takes place on and around the earth. Water evaporates from the surface, condenses into clouds, and then returns to the surface as precipitation. The water cycle is also a heat cycle in that it transfers heat around the earth and back and forth between the surface and the atmosphere. Water vapor cycles quickly through the atmosphere, lingering for a few days at most.

Scientists know that water vapor is the most prevalent greenhouse gas in the atmosphere and is responsible for the

FIGURE 3.2

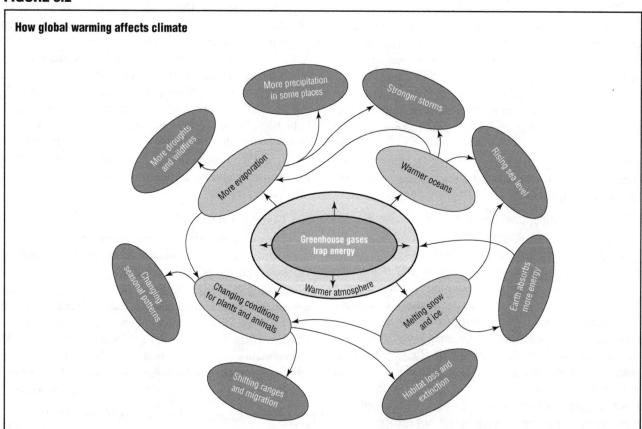

How global warming affects climate

More precipitation in some places

Stronger storms

More droughts and wildfires

More evaporation

Warmer oceans

Rising sea level

Greenhouse gases trap energy

Warmer atmosphere

Earth absorbs more energy

Changing seasonal patterns

Changing conditions for plants and animals

Melting snow and ice

Shifting ranges and migration

Habitat loss and extinction

SOURCE: "Climate Connections," in *A Student's Guide to Global Climate Change: Climate Concepts*, US Environmental Protection Agency, March 3, 2016, https://www3.epa.gov/climatechange//kids/basics/concepts.html (accessed November 8, 2017)

vast majority of the natural greenhouse effect. However, its role in the enhanced greenhouse effect and corresponding climate change has been a matter of debate.

Carbon Dioxide

Carbon dioxide (CO_2) is a heavy colorless gas. It is a respiration product from most living things. It is also released during the decay or combustion of organic materials. Huge amounts of carbon dioxide are cycled back and forth between the oceans and the atmosphere. Likewise, vegetation, algae, and some types of bacteria absorb carbon dioxide from the air. The result of all these processes is a global carbon cycle that maintains carbon dioxide at suitable levels in the atmosphere to sustain the natural greenhouse effect.

Before the 1800s humans had little impact on atmospheric carbon dioxide levels. The Industrial Revolution ushered in widespread use of fossil fuels, primarily coal, oil, and natural gas. Combustion of these carbon-loaded fuels releases large amounts of carbon dioxide. As shown in Figure 3.3 and Table 3.1, the United States emitted 6,587 million metric tons (MMT) of greenhouse gases in 2015. Figure 3.3 provides a breakdown of total emissions by gas. Carbon dioxide accounted for the largest portion of the total.

The burning of fossil fuels by industry and motor vehicles is, by far, the leading source of carbon dioxide emissions in the United States and accounted for 5,411.4 MMT, or 82% of the nation's total greenhouse gas emissions in 2015. (See Table 3.1.) Other anthropogenic (human-caused) sources of carbon dioxide include deforestation, burning of biomass (combustible organic materials, such as wood scraps and crop residues), and certain industrial processes.

The atmospheric lifetime (how long a gas stays in the atmosphere) of carbon dioxide cannot be determined exactly because the gas is continuously cycled back and forth between the atmosphere and the oceans. Mason Inman reports in "Carbon Is Forever" (Nature.com, November 20, 2008) that climate scientists believe that approximately 20% of emitted carbon dioxide can stay in the atmosphere for "many thousands of years." The remainder has an atmospheric lifetime of several decades to several centuries. In "Carbon and Other Biogeochemical Cycles" (*Climate Change 2013: The Physical Science Basis*, http://www.climatechange2013.org/images/report/WG1AR5_ALL_FINAL.pdf), Thomas F. Stocker et al. state, "Involvement of extremely long time scale processes into the removal of a pulse of CO_2 emissions into the atmosphere complicates comparison with the cycling of the other [greenhouse gases]. This is why the concept of a single, characteristic atmospheric lifetime is not applicable to CO_2."

Scientists use the global warming capacity of carbon dioxide as a benchmark against which the global warming capacity of other long-lived gases is compared. The so-called global warming potential (GWP) of carbon dioxide is arbitrarily assigned a value of 1. The GWP of other long-lived greenhouse gases is then calculated based on their relative capacity to trap heat in the atmosphere over the same period. It is important to understand that calculated GWP values are revised by scientists over time as new data become available.

Methane

Methane (CH_4) is a colorless gas found in trace (extremely small) amounts in the atmosphere. It is the primary component of natural gas—the gas trapped beneath the earth's crust that is mined and burned for energy. Human sources of atmospheric methane include landfills, natural gas systems, agricultural activities, coal mining, and wastewater treatment processes.

Methane is an important component of greenhouse gas emissions, second only to carbon dioxide. (See Figure 3.3.) Methane, however, is much more effective at trapping heat in the atmosphere than the same mass of carbon dioxide. For example, in *Inventory of U.S. Greenhouse Gas Emissions and Sinks, 1990–2015* (April 2017, https://www.epa.gov/sites/production/files/2017-02/documents/2017_complete_report.pdf), the US Environmental Protection Agency (EPA) uses a 100-year GWP value of 25 for methane. This means that over 100 years, methane is 25 times more effective at trapping atmospheric heat than the same mass of carbon dioxide. The EPA notes that it uses GWP values from the IPCC's *Climate Change 2007*; newer GWP values are included in *Climate Change 2013: The Physical Science Basis*.

Methane emissions between 1990 and 2015 are listed in Table 3.1 for selected years. Note that the units are million metric tons of CO_2 equivalents. In "Glossary of Climate Change Terms" (August 9, 2016, https://www3.epa.gov/climatechange/glossary.html), the EPA explains that carbon dioxide equivalents are calculated by multiplying the tons of a gas by the GWP of the gas.

Methane emissions in 2015 totaled 655.7 MMT of CO_2 equivalents. (See Table 3.1.) Enteric fermentation, natural gas systems, and landfills were the primary contributors. Enteric fermentation is a natural digestive process that occurs in domestic animals, such as cattle and sheep, that releases methane.

Humans contribute to atmospheric methane levels through activities that concentrate and magnify biological decomposition. This includes landfilling organic materials, raising livestock, cultivating rice in paddies, collecting sewage for treatment, and constructing artificial wetlands. In addition, methane is a by-product of the combustion of biomass and is vented (intentionally and

FIGURE 3.3

US greenhouse gas emissions, by gas, 1990–2015

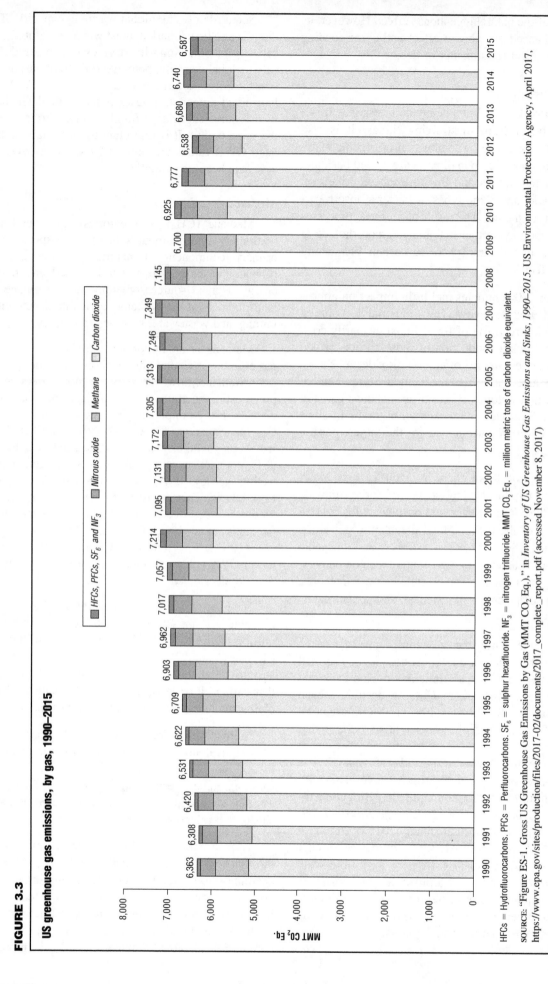

HFCs = Hydrofluorocarbons. PFCs = Perfluorocarbons. SF₆ = sulphur hexafluoride. NF₃ = nitrogen trifluoride. MMT CO₂ Eq. = million metric tons of carbon dioxide equivalent.

SOURCE: "Figure ES-1. Gross US Greenhouse Gas Emissions by Gas (MMT CO₂ Eq.)," in *Inventory of US Greenhouse Gas Emissions and Sinks, 1990–2015,* US Environmental Protection Agency, April 2017, https://www.epa.gov/sites/production/files/2017-02/documents/2017_complete_report.pdf (accessed November 8, 2017)

TABLE 3.1

Trends in US greenhouse gas emissions and sinks, selected years 1990–2015

Gas/source	1990	2005	2011	2012	2013	2014	2015
CO_2	**5,123.0**	**6,131.8**	**5,569.5**	**5,362.1**	**5,514.0**	**5,565.5**	**5,411.4**
Fossil fuel combustion	4,740.3	5,746.9	5,227.1	5,024.6	5,156.5	5,202.3	5,049.8
Electricity generation	1,820.8	2,400.9	2,157.7	2,022.2	2,038.1	2,038.0	1,900.7
Transportation[a]	1,493.8	1,887.0	1,707.6	1,696.8	1,713.0	1,742.8	1,736.4
Industrial[a]	842.5	828.0	775.0	782.9	812.2	806.1	805.5
Residential	338.3	357.8	325.5	282.5	329.7	345.4	319.6
Commercial[a]	217.4	223.5	220.4	196.7	221.0	228.7	246.2
US territories	27.6	49.7	40.9	43.5	42.5	41.4	41.4
Non-energy use of fuels	117.6	138.9	109.8	106.7	123.6	119.0	125.5
Iron and steel production & metallurgical coke production	101.5	68.0	61.1	55.4	53.3	58.6	48.9
Natural gas systems	37.7	30.1	35.7	35.2	38.5	42.4	42.4
Cement production	33.5	46.2	32.2	35.3	36.4	39.4	39.9
Petrochemical production	21.3	27.0	26.3	26.5	26.4	26.5	28.1
Lime production	11.7	14.6	14.0	13.8	14.0	14.2	13.3
Other process uses of carbonates	4.9	6.3	9.3	8.0	10.4	11.8	11.2
Ammonia production	13.0	9.2	9.3	9.4	10.0	9.6	10.8
Incineration of waste	8.0	12.5	10.6	10.4	10.4	10.6	10.7
Urea fertilization	2.4	3.5	4.1	4.3	4.5	4.8	5.0
Carbon dioxide consumption	1.5	1.4	4.1	4.0	4.2	4.5	4.3
Liming	4.7	4.3	3.9	6.0	3.9	3.6	3.8
Petroleum systems	3.6	3.9	4.2	3.9	3.7	3.6	3.6
Soda ash production and consumption	2.8	3.0	2.7	2.8	2.8	2.8	2.8
Aluminum production	6.8	4.1	3.3	3.4	3.3	2.8	2.8
Ferroalloy production	2.2	1.4	1.7	1.9	1.8	1.9	2.0
Titanium dioxide production	1.2	1.8	1.7	1.5	1.7	1.7	1.6
Glass production	1.5	1.9	1.3	1.2	1.3	1.3	1.3
Urea consumption for non-agricultural purposes	3.8	3.7	4.0	4.4	4.0	1.4	1.1
Phosphoric acid production	1.5	1.3	1.2	1.1	1.1	1.0	1.0
Zinc production	0.6	1.0	1.3	1.5	1.4	1.0	0.9
Lead production	0.5	0.6	0.5	0.5	0.5	0.5	0.5
Silicon carbide production and consumption	0.4	0.2	0.2	0.2	0.2	0.2	0.2
Magnesium production and processing	+	+	+	+	+	+	+
Wood biomass, ethanol, and biodiesel consumption[b]	219.4	230.7	276.4	276.2	299.8	307.1	291.7
International bunker fuels[c]	103.5	113.1	111.7	105.8	99.8	103.2	110.8
CH_4	**780.8**	**680.9**	**672.1**	**666.1**	**658.8**	**659.1**	**655.7**
Enteric fermentation	164.2	168.9	168.9	166.7	165.5	164.2	166.5
Natural gas systems	194.1	159.7	154.5	156.2	159.2	162.5	162.4
Landfills	179.6	134.3	119.0	120.8	116.7	116.6	115.7
Manure management	37.2	56.3	63.0	65.6	63.3	62.9	66.3
Coal mining	96.5	64.1	71.2	66.5	64.6	64.8	60.9
Petroleum systems	55.5	46.0	48.0	46.4	44.5	43.0	39.9
Wastewater treatment	15.7	16.0	15.3	15.1	14.9	14.8	14.8
Rice cultivation	16.0	16.7	14.1	11.3	11.3	11.4	11.2
Stationary combustion	8.5	7.4	7.1	6.6	8.0	8.1	7.0
Abandoned underground coal mines	7.2	6.6	6.4	6.2	6.2	6.3	6.4
Composting	0.4	1.9	1.9	1.9	2.0	2.1	2.1
Mobile combustion[a]	5.6	2.8	2.3	2.2	2.1	2.1	2.0
Field burning of agricultural residues	0.2	0.2	0.3	0.3	0.3	0.3	0.3
Petrochemical production	0.2	0.1	+	0.1	0.1	0.1	0.2
Ferroalloy production	+	+	+	+	+	+	+
Silicon carbide production and consumption	+	+	+	+	+	+	+
Iron and steel production & metallurgical coke production	+	+	+	+	+	+	+
Incineration of waste	+	+	+	+	+	+	+
International bunker fuels[c]	0.2	0.1	0.1	0.1	0.1	0.1	0.1
N_2O	**359.5**	**361.6**	**364.0**	**340.7**	**335.5**	**335.5**	**334.8**
Agricultural soil management	256.6	259.8	270.1	254.1	250.5	250.0	251.3
Stationary combustion	11.9	20.2	21.3	21.4	22.9	23.4	23.1
Manure management	14.0	16.5	17.4	17.5	17.5	17.5	17.7
Mobile combustion[a]	41.2	35.7	22.8	20.4	18.5	16.6	15.1
Nitric acid production	12.1	11.3	10.9	10.5	10.7	10.9	11.6
Wastewater treatment	3.4	4.4	4.8	4.8	4.9	4.9	5.0
Adipic acid production	15.2	7.1	10.2	5.5	3.9	5.4	4.3
N_2O from product uses	4.2	4.2	4.2	4.2	4.2	4.2	4.2
Composting	0.3	1.7	1.7	1.7	1.8	1.9	1.9

unintentionally) during the extraction and processing of fossil fuels. It also results from incomplete combustion of fossil fuels. The IPCC notes in "Anthropogenic and Natural Radiative Forcing" (*Climate Change 2013: The*

TABLE 3.1

Trends in US greenhouse gas emissions and sinks, selected years 1990–2015 [CONTINUED]

Gas/source	1990	2005	2011	2012	2013	2014	2015
Incineration of waste	0.5	0.4	0.3	0.3	0.3	0.3	0.3
Semiconductor manufacture	+	0.1	0.2	0.2	0.2	0.2	0.2
Field burning of agricultural residues	0.1	0.1	0.1	0.1	0.1	0.1	0.1
International bunker fuels[c]	0.9	1.0	1.0	0.9	0.9	0.9	0.9
HFCs	**46.6**	**120.0**	**154.3**	**155.9**	**159.0**	**166.7**	**173.2**
Substitution of ozone depleting substances[d]	0.3	99.7	145.3	150.2	154.6	161.3	168.5
HCFC-22 production	46.1	20.0	8.8	5.5	4.1	5.0	4.3
Semiconductor manufacture	0.2	0.2	0.2	0.2	0.2	0.3	0.3
Magnesium production and processing	0.0	0.0	+	+	0.1	0.1	0.1
PFCs	**24.3**	**6.7**	**6.9**	**6.0**	**5.8**	**5.8**	**5.2**
Semiconductor manufacture	2.8	3.2	3.4	3.0	2.8	3.2	3.2
Aluminum production	21.5	3.4	3.5	2.9	3.0	2.5	2.0
Substitution of ozone depleting substances	0.0	+	+	+	+	+	+
SF$_6$	**28.8**	**11.7**	**9.2**	**6.8**	**6.4**	**6.6**	**5.8**
Electrical transmission and distribution	23.1	8.3	6.0	4.8	4.6	4.8	4.2
Magnesium production and processing	5.2	2.7	2.8	1.6	1.5	1.0	0.9
Semiconductor manufacture	0.5	0.7	0.4	0.4	0.4	0.7	0.7
NF$_3$	**1**	**0.5**	**0.7**	**0.6**	**0.6**	**0.5**	**0.6**
Semiconductor manufacture	+	0.5	0.7	0.6	0.6	0.5	0.6
Total emissions	**6,363.1**	**7,313.3**	**6,776.7**	**6,538.3**	**6,680.1**	**6,739.7**	**6,586.7**
LULUCF emissions[e]	10.6	23.0	19.9	26.1	19.2	19.7	19.7
LULUCF carbon stock change[f]	(830.2)	(754.0)	(769.1)	(779.8)	(782.2)	(781.1)	(778.7)
LULUCF sector net total[g]	(819.6)	(731.0)	(749.2)	(753.8)	(763.0)	(761.4)	(758.9)
Net emissions (sources and sinks)	**5,543.5**	**6,582.3**	**6,027.6**	**5,784.5**	**5,917.1**	**5,978.3**	**5,827.7**

+Does not exceed 0.05 MMT CO$_2$ Eq.

[a]There was a method update in this inventory for estimating the share of gasoline used in on-road and non-road applications. The change does not impact total US gasoline consumption. It mainly results in a shift in gasoline consumption from the transportation sector to industrial and commercial sectors for 2015, creating a break in the time series.

[b]Emissions from wood biomass and biofuel consumption are not included specifically in summing energy sector totals. Net carbon fluxes from changes in biogenic carbon reservoirs are accounted for in the estimates for land use, land-use change, and forestry.

[c]Emissions from international bunker fuels are not included in totals.

[d]Small amounts of PFC emissions also result from this source.

[e]LULUCF emissions include the CH$_4$ and N$_2$O emissions reported for *peatlands remaining peatlands*, forest fires, drained organic soils, grassland fires, and *coastal wetlands remaining coastal wetlands*; CH$_4$ emissions from *land converted to coastal wetlands*; and N$_2$O emissions from forest soils and settlement soils.

[f]LULUCF carbon stock change is the net C stock change from the following categories: *forest land remaining forest land, land converted to forest land, cropland remaining cropland, land converted to cropland, grassland remaining grassland, land converted to grassland, wetlands remaining wetlands, land converted to wetlands, settlements remaining settlements, and land converted to settlements.*

[g]The LULUCF sector net total is the net sum of all CH$_4$ and N$_2$O emissions to the atmosphere plus net carbon stock changes.

Notes: Totals may not sum due to independent rounding. Parentheses indicate negative values or sequestration. MMT CO$_2$ Eq. = million metric tons of carbon dioxide equivalent. CO$_2$ = carbon dioxide. CH$_4$ = methane. N$_2$O = nitrous oxide. HFCs = hydrofluorocarbons. PFCs = perfluorocarbons. SF$_6$ = sulfur hexafluoride. NF$_3$ = nitrogen trifluoride. LULUCF = Land Use, Land-use Change, and Forestry.
Total emissions presented without LULUCF. Net emissions presented with LULUCF.

SOURCE: "Table ES-2. Recent Trends in US Greenhouse Gas Emissions and Sinks (MMT CO$_2$ Eq.)," in *Inventory of US Greenhouse Gas Emissions and Sinks, 1990–2015*, US Environmental Protection Agency, April 2017, https://www.epa.gov/sites/production/files/2017-02/documents/2017_complete_report.pdf (accessed November 8, 2017)

Physical Science Basis) that methane is believed to break down in the atmosphere after approximately 12 years.

Ozone

Ozone (O$_3$) is a blue-tinted gas naturally found in the earth's atmosphere. In "Science: Ozone Basics" (March 20, 2008, http://www.ozonelayer.noaa.gov/science/basics.htm), NOAA indicates that approximately 90% of the earth's ozone lies in the stratosphere, the atmospheric layer lying above the troposphere. The so-called ozone layer absorbs harmful ultraviolet radiation from the sun, preventing it from reaching the ground. Scientists believe stratospheric ozone is being depleted by the introduction of certain industrial chemicals, primarily chlorine and bromine. (See Chapter 4.) This depletion has serious consequences in terms of ultraviolet radiation effects and probably lessens the warmth-trapping capability of ozone at this level.

Tropospheric ozone is believed to be a potent greenhouse gas and is the primary component in smog, a key air pollutant. The gas is not emitted directly into the air but forms because of complex reactions that occur when other air pollutants, primarily volatile organic compounds and nitrogen oxides, are present. The primary sources of these ozone precursors are industrial chemical processes and fossil fuel combustion. The atmospheric lifetime of ozone ranges from weeks to months.

Nitrous Oxide

Nitrous oxide (N$_2$O) is a colorless gas found in trace amounts in the atmosphere. Soils naturally release the gas as a result of bacterial processes called nitrification and denitrification. Soils found in tropical areas and moist forests are believed to be the largest contributors. Oxygen-poor waters and sediments in oceans and estuaries are also natural sources. Although nitrous oxide makes up a much smaller portion of greenhouse gases than carbon dioxide, it is much more powerful than carbon dioxide at trapping heat. The IPCC indicates in *Climate Change 2013: The Physical Science Basis* that nitrous oxide has an atmospheric lifetime of 121 years. In *Inventory of U.S. Greenhouse Gas Emissions and Sinks, 1990–2015*, the EPA notes that nitrous oxide has an atmospheric lifetime of 114 years and a 100-year GWP of 298.

Agriculture has been the major source of nitrous oxide emissions in the United States, followed by energy and industrial sources. As shown in Table 3.1, agricultural soil management accounted for 251.3 MMT of CO_2 equivalents of the total 334.8 MMT of CO_2 equivalents of nitrous oxide emissions in 2015, or 75% of the total.

Humans have significantly increased the release of nitrous oxide from soils through the use of nitrogen-rich fertilizers. Other anthropogenic sources include combustion of fossil fuels and biomass, wastewater treatment, and certain manufacturing processes, particularly the production of nylon and nitric acid.

Engineered Gases

Engineered gases are synthetic gases specially designed for modern industrial and commercial purposes. They are also known as "high GWP gases" because they have a high GWP when compared with carbon dioxide. They include hydrofluorocarbons (HFCs), perfluorocarbons (PFCs), and sulfur hexafluoride.

HFCs are chemicals that contain hydrogen, fluorine, and carbon. They are popular substitutes in industrial applications for chlorofluorocarbons (CFCs). CFCs are commonly used in cooling equipment and fire extinguishers. They are one of the culprits blamed for the depletion of stratospheric ozone. PFCs are a class of chemicals that contain fluorine and carbon. They are also increasingly being used by industry as substitutes for ozone-depleting CFCs. Sulfur hexafluoride is a colorless, odorless gas commonly used as an insulating medium in electrical equipment and as an etchant (an etching agent) in the semiconductor industry.

Although emissions of these chemicals are small in comparison to other greenhouse gases, they are of particular concern because of their long life in the atmosphere. The IPCC indicates in *Climate Change 2013: The Physical Science Basis* that many PFCs and sulfur hexafluoride are actually far more potent greenhouse gases than carbon dioxide, with GWP values in the thousands.

Indirect Greenhouse Gases

There are several gases that are considered to be indirect greenhouse gases because of their effects on the chemical environment of the atmosphere. These gases include reactive nitrogen oxides, carbon monoxide, and volatile organic compounds. Most of their emissions are from anthropogenic sources, primarily combustion and industrial processes.

US Greenhouse Gases and Sources

Figure 3.4 shows the annual percentage change in US greenhouse gas emissions between 1991 and 2015. Emissions generally increased on a year-to-year basis through

FIGURE 3.4

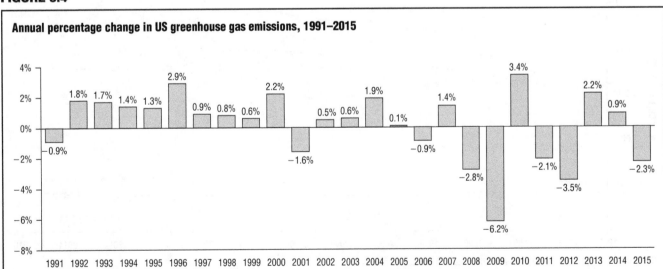

Annual percentage change in US greenhouse gas emissions, 1991–2015

SOURCE: "Figure ES-2. Annual Percent Change in Gross US Greenhouse Gas Emissions Relative to the Previous Year," in *Inventory of US Greenhouse Gas Emissions and Sinks, 1990–2015*, US Environmental Protection Agency, April 2017, https://www.epa.gov/sites/production/files/2017-02/documents/2017_complete_report.pdf (accessed November 8, 2017)

2007. There were sharp declines in 2008 (down 2.8%) and 2009 (down 6.2%). These declines resulted from the so-called Great Recession that occurred during these years. There was significantly reduced demand for fossil fuel–derived energy due to the economic slowdown and high gasoline prices. As shown in Figure 3.4, US greenhouse gas emissions have varied significantly since that time, with some up years and some down years. In 2015 emissions dropped 2.3% compared with 2014. In *Inventory of U.S. Greenhouse Gas Emissions and Sinks, 1990–2015*, the EPA explains that the decline was mostly due to lower carbon dioxide emissions from fossil fuel combustion. This decrease was driven by several factors. The electric power sector relied less on coal and more on cleaner-burning natural gas in 2015. There was also a slight decrease in electricity demand during the year. In addition, the winter was unusually warm, which decreased use of heating fuel (and hence lowered emissions).

Figure 3.5 shows trends in the emissions of greenhouse gases between 1990 and 2016 by the major economic sectors in the United States. The electricity generating sector was the largest emitter, followed by the transportation and industry sectors. The agricultural, commercial, and residential sectors were much smaller contributors. Figure 3.6 provides a different view of emissions trends by economic sector and also shows the net sink due to land use,

land-use change, and forestry. Sinks basically absorb carbon dioxide from the atmosphere. The net sink is the difference between the emissions effect and the sink effect. For example, forest fires produce carbon emissions, whereas growing new forests remove carbon from the atmosphere. The difference between these two effects during a year could be an increase in emissions or a decrease in emissions (i.e., a net sink). Figure 3.7 shows emissions and removals associated with land use, land-use change, and forestry over time. In general, both have remained at relatively constant levels since 1990. Other trends are much more noticeable, particularly the decline in overall emissions from around 2007 to 2015. This decrease is overwhelmingly due to a drop in energy-related emissions during this period.

International Emissions of Greenhouse Gases

The US Department of Energy's US Energy Information Administration (EIA) presents in "International Energy Statistics" (2017, https://www.eia.gov/beta/international/data/browser/#/?c=41000000020000600000000000000g000 20000000000000000001&vs=INTL.44-1-AFRC-QBTU .A&vo=0&v=H&end=2014) data collected on carbon dioxide emissions related to energy consumption around the world. As shown in Table 3.2, Asia and Oceania (46.9%) were responsible for the largest portion of such

FIGURE 3.5

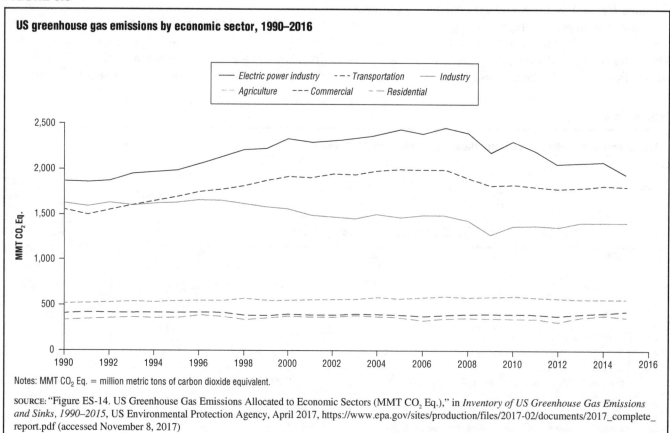

US greenhouse gas emissions by economic sector, 1990–2016

Notes: MMT CO_2 Eq. = million metric tons of carbon dioxide equivalent.

SOURCE: "Figure ES-14. US Greenhouse Gas Emissions Allocated to Economic Sectors (MMT CO_2 Eq.)," in *Inventory of US Greenhouse Gas Emissions and Sinks, 1990–2015*, US Environmental Protection Agency, April 2017, https://www.epa.gov/sites/production/files/2017-02/documents/2017_complete_report.pdf (accessed November 8, 2017)

FIGURE 3.6

US greenhouse gas emissions and sinks by economic sector, 1990–2014

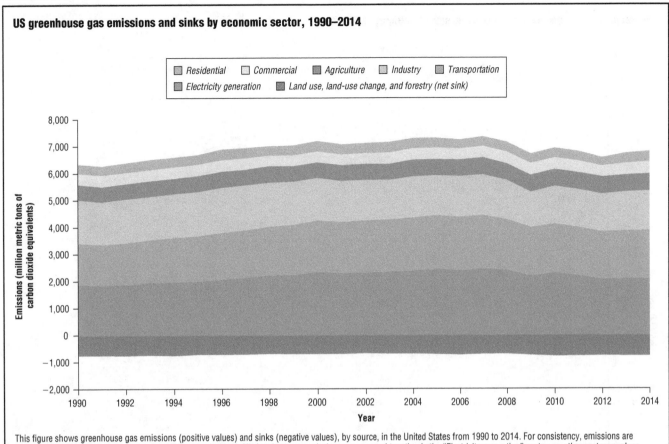

This figure shows greenhouse gas emissions (positive values) and sinks (negative values), by source, in the United States from 1990 to 2014. For consistency, emissions are expressed in million metric tons of carbon dioxide equivalents. All electric power emissions are grouped together in the "Electricity generation" sector, so other sectors such as "Residential" and "Commercial" show only non-electric sources, such as burning oil or gas for heating. The economic sectors shown here do not include emissions from US territories outside the 50 states.

SOURCE: "US Greenhouse Gas Emissions and Sinks by Economic Sector, 1990–2014," in *Climate Change Indicators in the United States, Fourth Edition,* US Environmental Protection Agency, 2016, https://www.epa.gov/sites/production/files/2016-08/documents/climate_indicators_2016.pdf (accessed November 8, 2017)

emissions in 2014, followed by North America (19.4%) and Europe (11.8%). The 20 countries with the largest carbon dioxide emissions in 2014 are listed in Table 3.3. The top-five emitters were China, the United States, India, Russia, and Japan.

In its energy and emissions analyses, the EIA assesses countries based on whether they are members of the Organisation for Economic Co-operation and Development (OECD). The OECD was founded in 1961 and is an international organization of democratic countries with free-market economies (such as the United States). OECD countries are developed countries that are characterized by mature economies and industries and relatively slow rates of growth in population and fuel usage. Non-OECD countries include developing countries in which population, industrial base, and fuel usage are growing quickly. Examples include China, India, Russia, and most other areas of Central and South America, Asia, the Middle East, and Africa.

As shown in Figure 3.8, non-OECD countries are expected to greatly outpace OECD countries in terms of

energy-related carbon dioxide emissions to 2040. China and other developing countries are heavily reliant on coal to fuel their industrial development and electricity production, whereas developed countries, such as the United States, rely more on cleaner-burning fuels such as natural gas. Environmentalism as a social and political force is also much more mature in developed countries.

CHANGES IN THE ATMOSPHERE

The earth's atmosphere was first compared to a glass vessel in 1827 by the French mathematician Jean-Baptiste-Joseph Fourier (1768–1830). During the 1850s the British physicist John Tyndall (1820–1893) tried to measure the heat-trapping properties of various components of the atmosphere. By the 1890s scientists had concluded that the great increase in combustion during the Industrial Revolution had the potential to change the atmosphere's load of carbon dioxide. In 1896 the Swedish chemist Svante August Arrhenius (1859–1927) made the revolutionary suggestion that human activities could actually disrupt this delicate balance. He theorized that the rapid

FIGURE 3.7

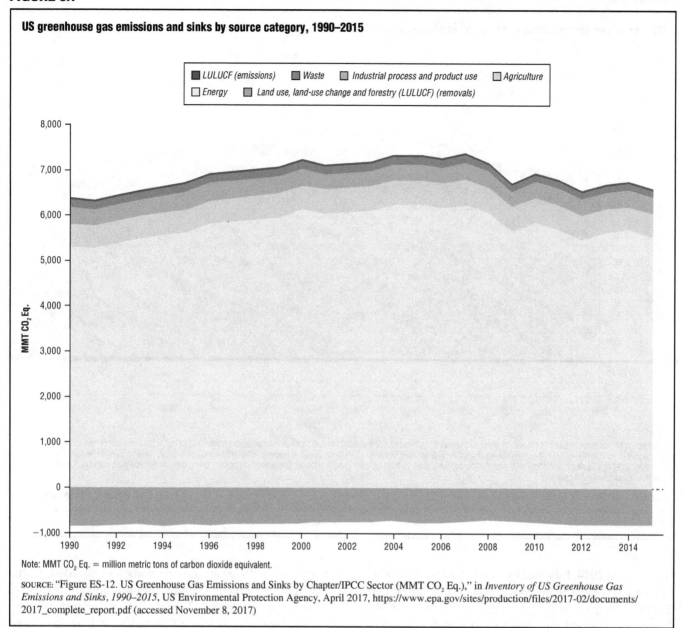

US greenhouse gas emissions and sinks by source category, 1990–2015

Legend:
- LULUCF (emissions)
- Waste
- Industrial process and product use
- Agriculture
- Energy
- Land use, land-use change and forestry (LULUCF) (removals)

Note: MMT CO_2 Eq. = million metric tons of carbon dioxide equivalent.

SOURCE: "Figure ES-12. US Greenhouse Gas Emissions and Sinks by Chapter/IPCC Sector (MMT CO_2 Eq.)," in *Inventory of US Greenhouse Gas Emissions and Sinks, 1990–2015*, US Environmental Protection Agency, April 2017, https://www.epa.gov/sites/production/files/2017-02/documents/2017_complete_report.pdf (accessed November 8, 2017)

increase in the use of coal as a result of the Industrial Revolution could increase carbon dioxide concentrations and cause a gradual rise in temperatures. For almost six decades his theory stirred little interest.

In 1957 studies at the Scripps Institute of Oceanography in California suggested that half the carbon dioxide released by industry was being permanently trapped in the atmosphere. The studies showed that atmospheric concentrations of carbon dioxide in the previous 30 years were greater than in the previous two centuries and that the gas had reached its highest level in 160,000 years. Scientists can estimate the makeup of the earth's atmosphere dating back several hundred thousand years by testing air pockets in ice sheets that are believed to have formed around the same time.

Findings during the 1980s and 1990s provided more disturbing evidence of atmospheric changes. Scientists detected increases in other, even more potent gases that contribute to the greenhouse effect, notably CFC-11 and CFC-12, methane, nitrous oxide, and halocarbons (CFCs, methyl chloroform, and hydrochlorofluorocarbons).

T. J. Blasing of the Carbon Dioxide Information Analysis Center estimates in "Recent Greenhouse Gas Concentrations" (April 2016, http://cdiac.ess-dive.lbl.gov/pns/current_ghg.html) that the average "natural" background atmospheric concentration of carbon dioxide immediately before 1750 was 280 parts per million. Likewise, the average methane level immediately before 1750 was around 722 parts per billion. Increases in these gases are shown in Figure 3.9 and Figure 3.10. These data were collected by NOAA, which compiles long-term records on air quality and solar radiation data. As shown in Figure 3.9, global monthly mean (average) carbon dioxide concentrations grew from around 340 parts per million in 1980 to more than 400 parts per million in 2017. Likewise, global monthly mean methane

TABLE 3.2

World carbon dioxide emissions due to energy consumption, by region, 2014

[Million metric tons of carbon dioxide]

	2014	Percentage of world total
Primary energy CO$_2$ emissions		
Africa	1,268.538	3.8%
Asia & Oceania	15,831.97	46.9%
Central & South America	1,458.379	4.3%
Eurasia	2,550.783	7.6%
Europe	3,982.167	11.8%
Middle East	2,088.482	6.2%
North America	6,552.501	19.4%
Total	**33,732.83**	**100.0%**

SOURCE: Adapted from "International Data: Primary Energy: CO$_2$ Emissions," in *International Energy Statistics*, US Department of Energy, US Energy Information Administration, 2017, https://www.eia.gov/beta/international/data/browser/#/?c=4100000002000060000000000000g00020000000000000 0001&vs=INTL.44-1-AFRC-QBTU.A&vo=0&v=H&end=2014 (accessed November 8, 2017)

TABLE 3.3

Top-20 countries in terms of carbon dioxide emissions due to energy consumption, 2014

[Million metric tons of carbon dioxide]

		2014	
Rank	Nation	Emissions (million metric tons)	Percentage of world total
1	China	9,376.7	27.8%
2	United States	5,507.8	16.3%
3	India	1,895.4	5.6%
4	Russia	1,756.0	5.2%
5	Japan	1,177.1	3.5%
6	Germany	756.2	2.2%
7	Iran	646.1	1.9%
8	Korea, South	643.5	1.9%
9	Canada	607.4	1.8%
10	Saudi Arabia	575.8	1.7%
11	Indonesia	547.5	1.6%
12	Brazil	546.9	1.6%
13	South Africa	472.4	1.4%
14	United Kingdom	446.3	1.3%
15	Mexico	435.8	1.3%
16	Australia	377.8	1.1%
17	Italy	342.7	1.0%
18	France	329.2	1.0%
19	Thailand	324.8	1.0%
20	Turkey	317.0	0.9%

SOURCE: Adapted from "International Data: Primary Energy: CO$_2$ Emissions," in *International Energy Statistics*, US Department of Energy, US Energy Information Administration, 2017, https://www.eia.gov/beta/international/data/browser/#/?c=4100000002000060000000000000g00020000000000000 0001&vs=INTL.44-1-AFRC-QBTU.A&vo=0&v=H&end=2014 (accessed November 8, 2017)

FIGURE 3.8

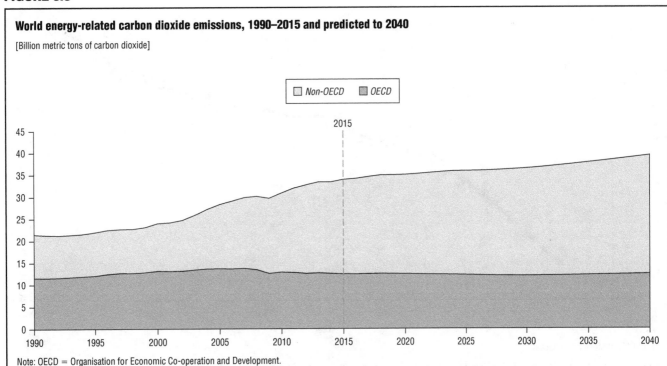

World energy-related carbon dioxide emissions, 1990–2015 and predicted to 2040

[Billion metric tons of carbon dioxide]

Note: OECD = Organisation for Economic Co-operation and Development.

SOURCE: "Energy-related Carbon Dioxide Emissions," in *International Energy Outlook 2017*, US Department of Energy, US Energy Information Administration, September 17, 2017, https://www.eia.gov/outlooks/ieo/pdf/0484(2017).pdf (accessed November 9, 2017)

FIGURE 3.9

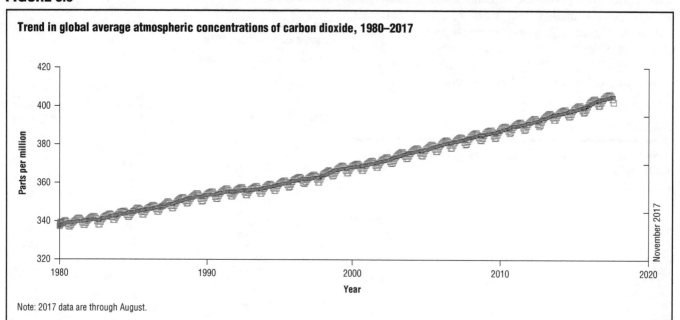

Trend in global average atmospheric concentrations of carbon dioxide, 1980–2017

Note: 2017 data are through August.

SOURCE: "Global Monthly Mean CO₂," in *Trends in Atmospheric Carbon Dioxide*, US Department of Commerce, National Oceanic and Atmospheric Administration, Earth System Research Laboratory, November 2017, https://www.esrl.noaa.gov/gmd/webdata/ccgg/trends/co2_trend_all_gl.pdf (accessed November 9, 2017)

FIGURE 3.10

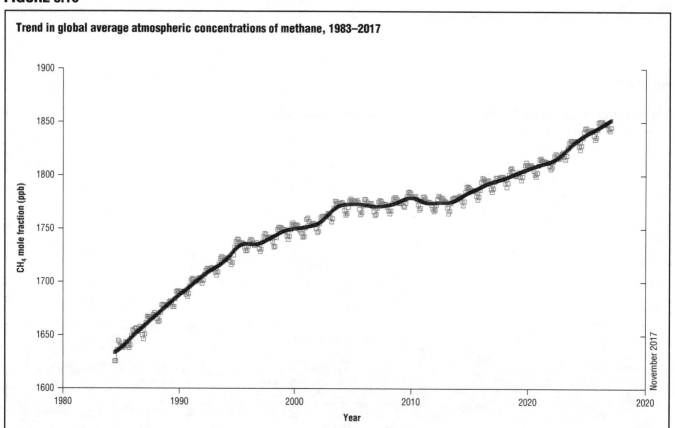

Trend in global average atmospheric concentrations of methane, 1983–2017

Note: 2017 data are through August.

SOURCE: "Global Monthly Mean CH₄," in *Trends in Atmospheric Methane*, US Department of Commerce, National Oceanic and Atmospheric Administration, Earth System Research Laboratory, November 2017, https://www.esrl.-noaa.gov/gmd/webdata/ccgg/trends/ch4_trend_all_gl.pdf (accessed November 9, 2017)

concentrations grew from around 1,630 parts per billion during the mid-1980s to around 1,850 parts per billion in 2017. (See Figure 3.10.)

Scientists agree that atmospheric concentrations of gases known to play a role in the natural greenhouse effect are increasing. There is scientific consensus that this increase is driving up the earth's temperature.

A RECENT WARMING TREND

Scientists do not know how much the global temperature has varied on its own in the last 1,000 years. Temperature records based on thermometers go back only about 150 years. Therefore, investigators have turned to proxy (indirect) means of measuring past temperatures. These methods include chemical evidence of climatic change contained in fossils, corals, ancient ice, and growth rings in trees.

During the late 1990s Michael E. Mann, Raymond S. Bradley, and Malcolm K. Hughes published two reports based on their survey of proxy evidence of temperatures over the previous millennium. The reports were "Global-Scale Temperature Patterns and Climate Forcing over the Past Six Centuries" (*Nature*, vol. 392, April 23, 1998) and "Northern Hemisphere Temperatures during the Past Millennium: Inferences, Uncertainties, and Limitations" (*Geophysical Research Letters*, vol. 26, no. 6, 1999). They concluded that in the Northern Hemisphere the 20th century was the warmest century of the millennium and that 1998 was the warmest year of the millennium. They also noted that the warming trend seems to be closely connected to the emissions of greenhouse gases by humans.

However, some experts questioned the validity of the proxy evidence that was cited in the reports, particularly for the oldest portion of the historical record. In response, Congress asked the National Research Council (NRC) of the National Academy of Sciences to analyze and report on available scientific data regarding historical surface temperatures. The resulting report, *Surface Temperature Reconstructions for the Last 2,000 Years* (https://www.nap.edu/catalog/11676/surface-temperature-reconstructions-for-the-last-2000-years), was published in 2006. The NRC concluded "with a high level of confidence" that the scientific evidence indicates that in the Northern Hemisphere the last few decades of the 20th century were warmer than any comparable period over the last four centuries.

In "Why So Many Global Temperature Records?" (January 21, 2015, https://www.giss.nasa.gov/research/features/201501_gistemp/), Adam Voiland of the National Aeronautics and Space Administration (NASA) notes that four agencies around the world are considered keepers of the "major global temperature record":

- Japanese Meteorological Agency in Tokyo, Japan
- Met Office's Hadley Centre/Climatic Research Unit in Exeter, England
- NOAA's National Climatic Data Center in Asheville, North Carolina
- NASA's Goddard Institute for Space Studies in New York City

According to Voiland, the agencies rely on data from weather stations around the world. However, some areas of the planet (particularly the oceans) have relatively few weather stations. The agencies use slightly different analytical methods to account for missing information. Consequently, they do not always agree on their rankings of the hottest years on record. Even so, Voiland explains that "despite some differences in the year-to-year rankings, the trends observed by all the groups are roughly the same. They all show warming. They all find the most recent decade to be warmer than previous decades."

Since 2000 the planet has experienced multiple years during which it set and then broke high temperature records. Jessica Blunden of NOAA indicates in "International Report Confirms 2016 Was Third Consecutive Year of Record Global Warmth" (August 10, 2017, https://www.climate.gov/news-features/understanding-climate/international-report-confirms-2016-was-third-consecutive-year) that 2016 was the hottest year on record based on 137 years of meteorological data. It was the third year in a row that the planet had climbed to a new high temperature.

Scientists believe the oceans have absorbed much of the excess heat from a warming world. Figure 3.11 shows the anomaly (deviation from the normal) for the average global sea surface temperature between 1880 and 2015, compared with the average between 1971 and 2000. Overall, the temperature increased steadily through the latter part of the 20th century and continued to rise into the early 21st century. Figure 3.12 shows the anomaly for global mean surface (land and ocean) temperatures between 1880 and 2016. There was a strong warming trend from around 1910 through 1940 and then a relatively level period through the mid-1970s. Warming was dramatic through 2002 and then flattened somewhat over the following decade. The temperature anomaly grew steeply over subsequent years through 2016.

INTERNATIONAL ANALYSES

At the 1972 Stockholm Conference, the world's first ecological summit, climate change was not even listed among the threats to the environment. However, many scientists and meteorologists were becoming alarmed about the growing evidence supporting the

FIGURE 3.11

Average global sea surface temperature anomaly, 1880–2015

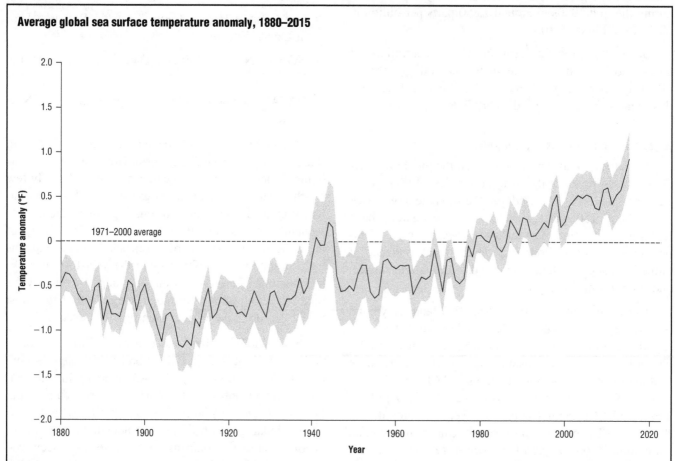

This graph shows how the average surface temperature of the world's oceans has changed since 1880. This graph uses the 1971 to 2000 average as a baseline for depicting change. *Choosing a different baseline period would not change the shape of the data over time.* The shaded band shows the range of uncertainty in the data, based on the number of measurements collected and the precision of the methods used.
°F = degrees Fahrenheit.

SOURCE: "Average Global Sea Surface Temperature, 1880–2015," in *Climate Change Indicators in the United States, Fourth Edition*, US Environmental Protection Agency, 2016, https://www.epa.gov/sites/production/files/2016-08/documents/climate_indicators_2016.pdf (accessed November 8, 2017)

notion of an enhanced greenhouse effect. Data collection and research efforts intensified through the late 1970s and into the 1980s. In 1988 the WMO and the UNEP established the IPCC, which created three working groups to assess available scientific information on climate change, estimate the expected impacts of climate change, and formulate strategies for responding to the problem.

The IPCC's First Assessment Report

The first IPCC assessment report, *Climate Change*, was issued in 1990. Several signs of climate change were noted by the IPCC:

- The average warm-season temperature in Alaska had risen nearly 3 degrees Fahrenheit (1.7 degrees C) in the previous 50 years.

- Glaciers had generally receded and become thinner on average by about 30 feet (9.1 m) in the previous 40 years.

- There was approximately 5% less sea ice in the Bering Sea than during the 1950s.

- Permafrost was thawing, causing the ground to subside (sink), opening holes in roads, producing landslides and erosion, threatening roads and bridges, and causing local floods.

- Ice cellars in northern villages had thawed and become useless.

- More precipitation was falling as rain than as snow in northern areas, and the snow was melting faster, causing more running and standing water.

Using computer models, IPCC researchers predicted that the global mean temperature would increase by 0.5 degrees Fahrenheit (0.3 degrees C) each decade during the 21st century. They also predicted that the global mean sea level would rise by 2.4 inches (6.1 cm) per decade. However, the scientists noted that there were a number of uncertainties in their assumptions due to a lack of data.

FIGURE 3.12

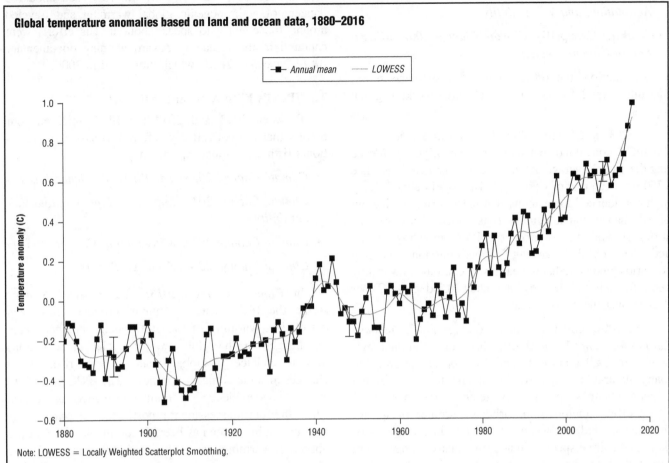

Global temperature anomalies based on land and ocean data, 1880–2016

Note: LOWESS = Locally Weighted Scatterplot Smoothing.

SOURCE: "Global Mean Estimates Based on Land and Ocean Data," in *GISS Surface Temperature Analysis*, National Aeronautics and Space Administration, Goddard Institute for Space Studies, October 13, 2017, https://data.giss.nasa.gov/gistemp/graphs/graph_data/Global_Mean_Estimates_based_on_Land_and_Ocean_Data/graph.pdf (accessed November 9, 2017)

The IPCC's Second Assessment Report

In 1995 the IPCC reassessed the state of knowledge about climate change and published its findings in its second assessment report, *Climate Change 1995*. The IPCC reaffirmed its earlier conclusions and updated its forecasts, predicting that, if no further action is taken to curb emissions of greenhouse gases, temperatures will increase between 1.4 degrees and 6.3 degrees Fahrenheit (0.8 degrees and 3.5 degrees C) by 2100. The panel concluded that the evidence suggests a human influence on global climate. The cautiously worded statement was a compromise following intense discussions. Nonetheless, it was a landmark conclusion because the panel, until then, had maintained that global warming and climate changes could be the result of natural variability.

The IPCC's Third Assessment Report

In 2001 the IPCC released its third assessment report, *Climate Change 2001*, which actually consisted of four reports that addressed various aspects of climate change and its impacts. The IPCC's assessment covered the adaptability and vulnerability of North America to climate change impacts likely to occur from global warming. Among the suggested possible effects of global warming were:

• Expansion of some diseases in North America

• Increased erosion, flooding, and loss of wetlands in coastal areas

• Risk to "unique natural ecosystems"

• Changes in seasonal snowmelts, which would have effects on water users and aquatic ecosystems

• Some initial benefits for agriculture, but those benefits would decline over time and possibly "become a net loss"

The IPCC's Fourth Assessment Report

In 2007 the IPCC released its fourth assessment report, *Climate Change 2007*. Actually, the three working groups of the IPCC each released a report, as follows:

• Working Group I—*Climate Change 2007: The Physical Science Basis*

- Working Group II—*Climate Change 2007: Impacts, Adaptation, and Vulnerability*

- Working Group III—*Climate Change 2007: Mitigation of Climate Change*

In addition, the IPCC published a synthesis report that integrates information from all three working group reports.

In *Climate Change 2007: The Physical Science Basis*, the IPCC concluded that there is "*very high confidence* that the global average net effect of human activities since 1750 has been one of warming." The panel defined "very high confidence" as meaning that there is over a nine out of 10 chance that a hypothesis is correct. This was the strongest wording yet from the IPCC indicting human activities for global warming. Various emissions modeling scenarios predicted that the earth will continue to warm by approximately 0.4 degrees Fahrenheit (0.2 degrees C) per decade over the next 20 years.

The IPCC noted in *Climate Change 2007: Impacts, Adaptation, and Vulnerability* that "observational evidence from all continents and most oceans shows that many natural systems are being affected by regional climate changes, particularly temperature increases." These effects included an earlier occurrence of springtime events and a poleward movement in the ranges of plant and animal species. In addition, many changes were reported in ice and snow ecosystems near the earth's poles. Warming water body temperatures were linked to range changes for algae, plankton, and fish species.

Estimated future impacts of global warming included the loss of freshwater store because of melting glaciers, greater extent of drought areas coupled with more frequent "heavy precipitation" events that tend to cause flooding, and acidification of the earth's oceans because of greater carbon take-up. The latter effect is particularly troubling for ocean coral, which is sensitive to acidity changes. An estimated 20% to 30% of plant and animal species were deemed to be at increased risk of extinction if the global average temperature increases by more than 2.7 degrees to 4.5 degrees Fahrenheit (1.5 degrees to 2.5 degrees C).

Sea level rises were expected to expose millions of people to increased risk of flooding, exacerbate coastal erosion, and endanger coastal ecosystems. Although increasing temperatures would help lower the number of deaths caused by cold exposure in far northern and southern regions, this benefit was expected to be more than offset by higher death rates in the temperate regions of the earth, particularly in developing countries.

The 2007 Nobel Peace Prize

In 2007 the IPCC and Albert Gore Jr. (1948–), the former US vice president, were jointly awarded the Nobel Peace Prize for their work on climate change. During his time in office (1993–2001), Gore was very vocal about the dangers of anthropogenic global warming and traveled around the country to speak about it. His efforts were captured in the Academy Award–winning documentary *An Inconvenient Truth*, which premiered in 2006.

The IPCC's Fifth Assessment Report

Between 2013 and 2014 the IPCC released four reports that are collectively referred to as the organization's fifth assessment report. They are:

- *Climate Change 2013: The Physical Science Basis*

- *Climate Change 2014: Impacts, Adaptation, and Vulnerability*

- *Climate Change 2014: Mitigation of Climate Change*

- *Climate Change 2014: Synthesis Report*

In *Climate Change 2013: The Physical Science Basis*, the IPCC states, "Human influence has been detected in warming of the atmosphere and the ocean, in changes in the global water cycle, in reductions in snow and ice, in global mean sea level rise, and in changes in some climate extremes." The IPCC goes on to state, "This evidence for human influence has grown since [the fourth assessment report]. It is *extremely likely* that human influence has been the dominant cause of the observed warming since the mid-20th century." The organization indicates that the phrase "extremely likely" corresponds with 95% to 100% probability.

The IPCC uses five nonnumeric qualifiers (very low, low, medium, high, and very high) to indicate its level of confidence in various statements in the report. It notes that it has medium confidence that over the period 2016–35 the global mean surface temperature change relative to 1986–2005 will "likely" be in the range of 0.5 to 1.3 degrees Fahrenheit (0.3 to 0.7 degrees C). The organization indicates that the phrase "likely" corresponds with 66% to 100% probability.

The IPCC provides in *Climate Change 2014: Impacts, Adaptation, and Vulnerability* an overview of the major environmental impacts that are associated with global warming, including melting ice and snow, sea level rise and associated flooding, ocean acidification, and extreme weather events (such as droughts). The threats to human health and livelihoods, food security, and plant and animal ecosystems are examined. For North America, the IPCC lists risks that it has high confidence will occur due to specific climate-related drivers:

- Warming and drying trend—threats to human health and well-being and to ecosystems; property damage and losses associated with wildfires

- Extreme temperature events—increased risk of human deaths due to high heat

- Extreme precipitation, damaging hurricanes, and rising sea levels—public health risks; impaired water quality; property and infrastructure damage due to flooding; disruption of ecosystems, supply chains, and social systems

In *Climate Change 2014: Mitigation of Climate Change*, the IPCC defines mitigation as "human intervention to reduce the sources or enhance the sinks of greenhouse gases." The panel calls on governments to work together to achieve mitigation, noting that "climate change has the characteristics of a collective action problem at the global scale, because most greenhouse gases (GHGs) accumulate over time and mix globally, and emissions by any agent (e.g., individual, community, company, country) affect other agents. International cooperation is therefore required to effectively mitigate GHG emissions and address other climate change issues."

INTERNATIONAL AGREEMENTS

In 1992 the United Nations (UN) adopted the UN Framework Convention on Climate Change (UNFCCC; July 18, 2000, http://unfccc.int/cop3/fccc/climate/fact18.htm). The UNFCCC was an international agreement that was presented for signatures at the 1992 Earth Summit in Rio de Janeiro, Brazil. The stated objective of the agreement was: "Stabilization of greenhouse gas concentrations in the atmosphere at a level that would prevent dangerous anthropogenic (man-made) interference with the climate system. Such a level should be achieved within a time-frame sufficient to allow ecosystems to adapt naturally to climate change, to ensure that food production is not threatened and to enable economic development to proceed in a sustainable manner."

The agreement set specific goals for developed countries to track and publish detailed inventories of their greenhouse gas emissions. However, it did not include specific emissions targets that countries had to meet. The UNFCCC (2017, http://unfccc.int/parties_and_observers/items/2704.php) categorized countries based on their level of economic development as follows:

- Annex 1—developed countries that were members of the OECD as of 1992 and countries with economies in transition (EIT), such as Russia and other members of the former Soviet Union

- Annex 2—the OECD members listed under Annex 1 but not the EIT countries

- Non-Annex 1—developing countries, such as China and India

The UNFCCC was signed by more than 100 countries, including the United States. Many environmentalists criticized the treaty as being too weak because it did not establish specific emissions targets that countries had to meet. The treaty did not include specific emissions targets mainly because the United States refused to accept them. The US Senate ratified (formally approved into law) the UNFCCC. The treaty went into effect in 1994.

In 1995, 120 parties to the UNFCCC met in Berlin, Germany, in what became known as the Berlin Mandate, to determine the success of existing treaties and to embark on discussions of emissions after 2000. Differences persisted along North-South lines, with developing countries making essentially a moral argument for requiring more of the richer countries. They pointed out that the richer countries are responsible for most of the pollution. The Berlin talks essentially failed to endorse binding timetables for reductions in greenhouse gases.

The Kyoto Protocol

In 1997 delegates from 166 countries met in Kyoto, Japan, at the UN Climate Change Conference to negotiate actions to reduce global warming. Some developed countries, including the United States, wanted to require all countries to reduce their emissions. Developing countries, however, felt the industrialized countries had caused, and were still causing, most global warming and therefore should bear the brunt of economic sacrifices to clean up the environment. The conference developed an agreement known as the Kyoto Protocol to the UNFCCC. Countries listed in Annex B to the Kyoto Protocol were those listed under Annex 1 to the UNFCCC; they agreed to meet specific greenhouse gas emissions reduction targets by 2008–12 (the first commitment period) as compared with a base year, which was 1990 for most countries.

The treaty went into effect in February 2005. At the time, Australia and the United States were the major holdouts; however, Australia ratified the Kyoto Protocol in 2007. The UNFCCC indicates in "Status of Ratification of the Kyoto Protocol" (http://unfccc.int/kyoto_protocol/background/status_of_ratification/items/2613.php) that 192 parties (191 countries and the European Union [EU], a confederation of European nations) ultimately ratified the treaty. The notable exception was the United States.

Overall, the Kyoto Protocol was expected to effect a total reduction in greenhouse gas emissions by the Annex B parties of at least 5% by 2012, compared with 1990 levels. Although China and India were not required to commit to specific limits, they did have to pledge to develop national programs for dealing with climate change.

THE UNITED STATES' POSITION ON THE KYOTO PROTOCOL. The US Constitution grants the president the power to make treaties with foreign powers, but only with the consent of two-thirds of the Senate. In other words, the president or a designee (such as the vice president) can sign treaties, but they do not become binding under US law until they are approved by the Senate.

The administration of George H. W. Bush (1924–) supported and signed the UNFCCC, which was ratified by the Senate, but opposed precise deadlines for carbon dioxide limits, arguing that the extent of the problem was too uncertain to justify painful economic measures.

In 1998 Vice President Gore signed the Kyoto Protocol on behalf of the United States, but this was a symbolic gesture. President Bill Clinton (1946–) never submitted it to the Senate for ratification. The political climate at the time was unfavorable for a treaty that bound the United States to specific emissions limits but did not set limits on developing countries, such as China and India.

When George W. Bush (1946–) took office in 2001, he affirmed his administration's steadfast opposition to the Kyoto Protocol. His successor was President Barack Obama (1961–). In December 2009 President Obama attended the UN's Copenhagen Summit in Denmark. Environmentalists were hopeful that he would broker a deal with China and the other major developing countries for a new post-Kyoto agreement on greenhouse gas emissions. Negotiations proved fruitless, however, and the main outcome of the conference was a nonbinding agreement called the Copenhagen Accord, in which countries pledged to voluntarily meet target emissions reductions by 2020.

The political realities of Obama's time in office, including the Great Recession and its lingering aftereffects, were not conducive to Senate approval of the Kyoto Protocol. He focused his efforts on domestic regulations and legislation related to global warming. Nonetheless, an emissions target limit of minus 7% was listed for the United States under the Kyoto Protocol. This value was a suggested target because it was not actually binding.

CANADA'S POSITION ON THE KYOTO PROTOCOL. Canada was active in the negotiations that produced the Kyoto Protocol and ratified the agreement in 2002, agreeing to a 6% reduction in greenhouse gas emissions for the first commitment period. However, over the first decade of the 21st century the nation elected more conservative leaders and experienced an oil boom due to the extraction of large-scale deposits of crude oil in the midwestern part of the country. A combination of political and economic factors prevented the nation from making significant progress toward its emissions target goal. In 2011 Canada officially notified the UN that it was withdrawing from the Kyoto Protocol.

MARKET-BASED MECHANISMS. The Kyoto Protocol established market-based mechanisms through which Annex B parties could reduce their emissions. The key component was an emissions trading scheme in which Annex B parties that reduced their emissions by more than their target could sell their extra emissions units (expressed in metric tons of carbon dioxide equivalent) to other Annex B parties. This mechanism is broadly known as carbon trading; however, it was not limited to emissions units. The UN explains in "Emissions Trading" (2014, http://unfccc.int/kyoto_protocol/background/items/2880.php) that parties could also buy and sell removal units (units achieved through planting or expanding forests). In addition, certain approved projects and programs also counted toward carbon trading.

At the time the Kyoto Protocol went into effect, the EU already had a program called the Emissions Trading System, which became part of the international agreement's carbon market program.

KYOTO PROTOCOL RESULTS. Determining the success (or lack thereof) of the Annex B countries at meeting their Kyoto Protocol emissions targets proved to be a slow process. It was not simply a matter of calculating the difference between greenhouse gas emissions between 1990 and 2012 because the various debits and credits under the carbon trading mechanisms also had to be taken into account. The UN (http://unfccc.int/kyoto_protocol/reporting/true-up_period_reports_under_the_kyoto_protocol/items/9049.php) maintains a database of the final true-up reports completed by each protocol party. The vast majority of the reports were submitted in 2015.

Igor Shishlov, Romain Morel, and Valentin Bellassen conclude in "Compliance of the Parties to the Kyoto Protocol in the First Commitment Period" (*Climate Policy*, vol. 16, no. 6, 2016) that all the Annex B parties achieved compliance with the protocol during the first commitment period (through 2012). They note that nine countries actually exceeded their emissions targets but met their commitments through other mechanisms, such as carbon trading credits.

A SECOND COMMITMENT PERIOD. Even before the first commitment period of the Kyoto Protocol ended, international negotiations took place to establish a second commitment period. Delegates at the Copenhagen Summit in 2009 were unsuccessful in their efforts. Media reports indicated deep divisions at the conference between developed and developing countries over each side's level of responsibility in future target agreements. Another round of talks in Bonn, Germany, in June 2011 proved equally divisive.

A second commitment period lasting to 2020 was officially adapted as part of an amendment to the Kyoto Protocol that was passed during a meeting held in Doha, Qatar, in December 2012. However, as of January 2018 the UN (http://unfccc.int/kyoto_protocol/doha_amendment/items/7362.php) indicates that the amendment had not gone into effect due to lack of participation by many major countries. For example, Canada, Japan, Russia, and the United States all declined to participate.

THE LEGACY OF THE KYOTO PROTOCOL. Overall, it is widely agreed that the Kyoto Protocol failed to significantly lessen global emissions of greenhouse gases. In 2011 the PBL Netherlands Environmental Assessment Agency and the European Commission's Joint Research Centre commissioned the report *Long-Term Trend in Global CO₂ Emissions: 2011 Report* (September 2011, http://www.pbl.nl/sites/default/files/cms/publicaties/C02%20Mondiaal_%20webdef_19sept.pdf), which was written by Jos G. J. Olivier et al. The researchers indicate that global carbon dioxide emissions grew from 25 billion tons (22.7 billion t) in 1990 to 36.4 billion tons (33 billion t) in 2010, an increase of 45%. China accounted for nearly 9.9 billion tons (9 billion t), or just over a quarter of the 2010 total. Carbon dioxide emissions doubled in China between 2003 and 2010.

Quirin Schiermeier acknowledges in "The Kyoto Protocol: Hot Air" (*Nature*, vol. 491, no. 7426, November 28, 2012) the success of European nations at meeting their Kyoto Protocol targets, but notes the factors that helped them to do so. He states, "Overall, they met their target with room to spare, cutting their collective emissions by around 16%. But most of those cuts came with little or no effort, because of the collapse of greenhouse-gas producing industries in eastern Europe and, more recently, the global economic crisis." Schiermeier believes the best legacy of the Kyoto Protocol may be the market-based mechanisms, such as the carbon trading schemes, that it helped foster. These mechanisms are expected to play a major role in future greenhouse gas agreements that are reached by the international community.

The Paris Agreement

At a 2011 summit in Durban, South Africa, many nations agreed to a plan of action called the Durban Platform, which lays out the general problems and challenges associated with climate change. The parties agreed to devise a new international agreement regarding climate change by 2015 that would take effect in 2020. Negotiations proved difficult, but during a 2015 summit in Paris a new climate agreement was forged. The Paris Agreement (http://unfccc.int/files/essential_background/convention/application/pdf/english_paris_agreement.pdf) states that the parties' intent is to limit the future increase in the global average temperature to less than 3.6 degrees Fahrenheit (2 degrees C) and ideally to less than 2.7 degrees Fahrenheit (1.5 degrees C) as compared with "pre-industrial levels." It should be noted that the UN does not define the time frame of the "pre-industrial" era or specify which global temperature from that era should be used as the baseline.

Unlike the Kyoto Protocol, the Paris Agreement does not bind parties to specific emissions targets. Instead, each party devises and pledges to meet a nonbinding nationally determined contribution (NDC). The UN (http://www4.unfccc.int/ndcregistry/Pages/Home.aspx) maintains a database of all the NDCs. For example, the United States'

NDC (http://www4.unfccc.int/ndcregistry/PublishedDocuments/United%20States%20of%20America%20First/U.S.A.%20First%20NDC%20Submission.pdf) is to reduce its greenhouse gas emissions by 26% to 28% by 2025 as compared with the 2005 level. Canada (http://www4.unfccc.int/ndcregistry/PublishedDocuments/Canada%20First/Canada%20First%20NDC-Revised%20submission%202017-05-11.pdf) pledges to reduce its greenhouse gas emissions by 30% by 2030 as compared with 2005. China's NDC is more complex. The nation (http://www4.unfccc.int/ndcregistry/PublishedDocuments/China%20First/China%27s%20First%20NDC%20Submission.pdf) commits to a variety of actions, including "to achieve the peaking of carbon dioxide emissions around 2030 and making best efforts to peak early." In addition, China pledges to lower its carbon dioxide emissions per unit of gross domestic product (the total market value of final goods and services that are produced within an economy in a given year), to generate more energy from nonfossil fuels, and to increase its forest volume.

It is important to understand that the NDCs are voluntary. Coral Davenport explains in "Nations Approve Landmark Climate Accord in Paris" (NYTimes.com, December 12, 2015) that the parties are legally required to "publicly monitor, verify and report what they are doing." Davenport notes that the requirements "are designed to create a 'name-and-shame' system of global peer pressure." In other words, a country failing to make progress toward its NDC could not hide that fact and would face international criticism for its shortcomings.

According to the UN (http://unfccc.int/paris_agreement/items/9444.php), the Paris Agreement entered into force in November 2016 and had been ratified by 174 parties as of January 2018. The ratifying parties included the EU and key nations such as Australia, Canada, China, India, and Japan. One major holdout was Russia. The article "Russia Says Still Likely to Back Paris Climate Deal Despite U.S. Withdrawal" (Reuters.com, June 2, 2017) explains that "Russian officials have said they need more time to assess [the agreement's] potential impact on their economy."

President Obama officially accepted the Paris Agreement on behalf of the United States during a visit to China in August 2016. He did not, however, submit the agreement to the Senate for ratification. This proved very controversial and initiated debate over the constitutional validity of the president's action. Nevertheless, the UN considers the United States to be a ratifying party to the Paris Agreement.

In June 2017 President Donald Trump (1946–) announced his intention to withdraw the United States from the agreement. During a speech (June 1, 2017, https://www.whitehouse.gov/the-press-office/2017/06/01/statement-president-trump-paris-climate-accord), he stated,

"The Paris Climate Accord is simply the latest example of Washington entering into an agreement that disadvantages the United States to the exclusive benefit of other countries, leaving American workers ... and taxpayers to absorb the cost in terms of lost jobs, lower wages, shuttered factories, and vastly diminished economic production."

Officially withdrawing from the Paris Agreement is a lengthy process. The agreement (like the UNFCCC) forbids any party from withdrawing until the agreement has been in force for at least three years. Then, there is a one-year waiting period before the withdrawal becomes final. The Paris Agreement went into force in November 4, 2016. Even if Trump did pursue a formal withdrawal, it would not become effective until November 4, 2020. This is one day after the scheduled presidential election for that year. Alternatively, Trump could pull the United States out of the UNFCCC. That would also withdraw the United States from the Paris Agreement and could be accomplished within one year. However, UNFCCC withdrawal would likely require Senate approval because that body originally ratified the UNFCCC. As of January 2018, it was unclear how the Trump administration would proceed given the political complexities of the situation. Some analysts speculated that Trump will not pursue any formal withdrawal, but simply ignore the United States' voluntary commitment under the Paris Agreement.

THE UNITED STATES GOES ITS OWN WAY

The United States has been very reluctant to be bound by international agreements such as the Kyoto Protocol and the Paris Agreement. Instead, it has focused on domestic policies and legislation that address global warming and climate change. These activities actually began before the Kyoto Protocol was adopted in 1997.

In 1989 President George H. W. Bush established the US Global Change Research Program (USGCRP), which was authorized by Congress in the Global Change Research Act of 1990. President Clinton took office in January 1993. That same year the United States released, in accordance with the UNFCCC, *The Climate Change Action Plan*, which called for measures to reduce emissions for all greenhouse gases to 1990 levels by 2000. However, the US economy grew at a more robust rate than anticipated, which led to increased emissions. Furthermore, Congress did not provide full funding for the actions contained in the plan.

The Clinton administration implemented some policies that did not require congressional approval. These included tax incentives and investments that focused on improving energy efficiency and renewable energy technologies, coordinating federal efforts to develop renewable fuels technology, and requiring all federal government agencies to reduce greenhouse gas emissions

below 1990 levels by 2010. Clinton also established the US Climate Change Research Initiative to study areas of uncertainty about global climate change science and identify priorities for public investments.

President George W. Bush took office in January 2001. He established a new cabinet-level management structure to oversee government investments in climate change science and technology. Both the US Climate Change Research Initiative and the USGCRP were placed under the oversight (supervision) of the interagency US Climate Change Science Program (beginning in 2009 it was renamed the US Global Change Research Program).

Although numerous bills regarding global warming were introduced in Congress during the Bush administration, they failed to move forward because of a lack of consensus among legislators about how to deal with the issue. The exclusion of developing countries, such as China and India, from the Kyoto Protocol's emissions limits was a major sticking point for many US politicians, who feared that the United States would be put at an economic disadvantage if it had to meet specific emissions limits. The United States' refusal to ratify the Kyoto Protocol or develop a similar control plan at the national level elicited strong criticism from foreign and domestic sources.

Obama and Trump

As is noted in Chapter 1, the November 2008 election of President Obama was hailed by many environmentalists as the beginning of a green revolution in the United States. Obama publicly expressed support for the Kyoto Protocol; he did not, however, try to achieve ratification of it by the Senate. He advocated for mandatory limits on US emissions of global warming gases and suggested that the federal government charge a permit fee to facilities that emit certain carbon levels. He proposed a cap-and-trade system that would include a nationwide cap (upper limit) on carbon emissions from industries. Facilities that reduced their emissions below the cap would receive credits (or allowances) that they could sell to facilities emitting carbon levels above the cap. As is described in Chapter 5, the cap-and-trade approach has been used successfully in the United States to curtail emissions of chemicals, such as sulfur dioxide, that cause acid rain. Nevertheless, the United States' carbon dioxide emissions dwarf those of sulfur dioxide, meaning that many facilities would be subject to a carbon cap-and-trade system. Although mandatory limits would spur research and development into alternative fuels and emissions controls, they would also raise energy and production costs for industry. These expenses would likely be passed onto consumers, making a carbon cap-and-trade scheme a politically risky endeavor.

In June 2009 the US House of Representatives passed by a thin margin (219–212) the American Clean Energy and Security Act. This legislation included a carbon cap-and-trade program that was projected to reduce emissions of greenhouse gases by 17% by 2020 compared with 2005 emissions. However, the bill was not considered by the Senate and thus did not become law. During the November 2010 midterm elections Republicans gained control of the House of Representatives and made large gains in the Senate. This was viewed politically as a public rebuke of Obama's policies. Neela Banerjee reports in "EPA Delays Rule on Industrial Emissions" (LATimes.com, May 17, 2011) that following the midterm elections the Obama administration chose to "postpone controversial environmental regulations and steer a more business-friendly course."

Following his reelection in 2012, Obama adopted a much stronger stance on global warming and climate change. By that point the US economy was strengthening, and the administration was emboldened to take action on greenhouse gas emissions. In June 2013 Obama released *The President's Climate Action Plan* (http://www.whitehouse.gov/sites/default/files/image/president27sclimateactionplan.pdf), which laid out a series of executive actions that were designed to reduce US carbon emissions and prepare the nation for the expected impacts of climate change. The executive branch of the US government includes the president and all the agencies that report to him. Thus, Obama opted not to pursue climate change action through the legislative branch, which is made up by the Senate and the House of Representatives.

In 2015 Obama acted through the EPA to impose carbon emissions limits on power plants and transportation vehicles. As shown in Table 3.4, these two sources account for the majority of the carbon dioxide emissions from fossil fuel combustion. For example, in 2015 coal-based electricity generation emitted 1,350.5 MMT of CO_2 equivalents, while petroleum-based transportation vehicles emitted 1,697.6 MMT of CO_2 equivalents. Together, they accounted for 60% of the total carbon dioxide emissions attributed to fossil fuel combustion.

TABLE 3.4

Carbon dioxide emissions from fossil fuel combustion by fuel type and economic sector, selected years 1990–2015

Fuel/sector	1990	2005	2011	2012	2013	2014	2015
Coal	**1,718.4**	**2,112.3**	**1,813.9**	**1,592.8**	**1,653.8**	**1,652.6**	**1,423.3**
Residential	3.0	0.8	NO	NO	NO	NO	NO
Commercial	12.0	9.3	5.8	4.1	3.9	3.8	2.9
Industrial	155.3	115.3	82.0	74.1	75.7	75.6	65.9
Transportation	NE	NE	NE	NE	NE	NE	NE
Electricity generation	1,547.6	1,983.8	1,722.7	1,511.2	1,571.3	1,569.1	1,350.5
US territories	0.6	3.0	3.4	3.4	2.8	4.0	4.0
Natural gas	**1,000.3**	**1,166.7**	**1,291.5**	**1,352.6**	**1,391.2**	**1,422.0**	**1,463.6**
Residential	238.0	262.2	254.7	224.8	266.2	277.9	252.8
Commercial	142.1	162.9	170.5	156.9	179.1	189.3	175.4
Industrial	408.9	388.5	417.3	434.8	451.9	468.4	467.5
Transportation	36.0	33.1	38.9	41.3	47.0	40.3	38.8
Electricity generation	175.3	318.8	408.8	492.2	444.0	443.2	526.1
US territories	NO	1.3	1.4	2.6	3.0	3.0	3.0
Petroleum[a]	**2,021.2**	**2,467.6**	**2,121.3**	**2,078.8**	**2,111.1**	**2,127.3**	**2,162.5**
Residential	97.4	94.9	70.9	57.7	63.4	67.5	66.8
Commercial	63.3	51.3	44.1	35.7	38.0	35.6	67.9
Industrial	278.3	324.2	275.7	274.1	284.6	262.1	272.2
Transportation	1,457.7	1,854.0	1,668.8	1,655.4	1,666.0	1,702.5	1,697.6
Electricity generation	97.5	97.9	25.8	18.3	22.4	25.3	23.7
US territories	26.9	45.4	36.0	37.5	36.6	34.3	34.3
Geothermal[b]	**0.4**	**0.4**	**0.4**	**0.4**	**0.4**	**0.4**	**0.4**
Total	**4,740.3**	**5,746.9**	**5,227.1**	**5,024.6**	**5,156.5**	**5,202.3**	**5,049.8**

+Does not exceed 0.05 MMT CO_2 Eq.
NE (Not estimated)
NO (Not occurring)
[a]In 2016, FHWA changed its methods for estimating the share of gasoline used in on-road and non-road applications, which created a time-series inconsistency between 2015 and previous years in this Inventory. The method changes resulted in a decrease in the estimated motor gasoline consumption for the transportation sector and a subsequent increase in the commercial and industrial sectors of this Inventory for 2015.
[b]Although not technically a fossil fuel, geothermal energy-related CO_2 emissions are included for reporting purposes.
Note: Totals may not sum due to independent rounding.
MMT CO_2 Eq. = million metric tons of carbon dioxide equivalent. CO_2 = carbon dioxide; FHWA = Federal Highway Administration.

SOURCE: "Table 3-5. CO_2 Emissions from Fossil Fuel Combustion by Fuel Type and Sector (MMT CO_2 Eq.)," in *Inventory of US Greenhouse Gas Emissions and Sinks, 1990–2015*, US Environmental Protection Agency, April 2017, https://www.epa.gov-/sites/production/files/2017–02/documents/2017_complete_report.pdf (accessed November 8, 2017)

CARBON EMISSIONS LIMITS FOR POWER PLANTS. Previously, in June 2013 Obama released "Presidential Memorandum—Power Sector Carbon Pollution Standards" (https://obamawhitehouse.archives.gov/the-press-office/2013/06/25/presidential-memorandum-power-sector-carbon-pollution-standards), which directed the EPA to propose carbon pollution standards for fossil fuel–fired power plants. Republicans expressed intense disapproval over this proposal and decried the standards as energy taxes in disguise. (Under the US Constitution, only Congress has the power to levy taxes.) Republicans also accused the Obama administration of waging a war on coal because the proposed standards would mostly affect coal-burning power plants.

In "12 States Sue the EPA over Proposed Power Plant Regulations" (LATimes.com, August 4, 2014), Banerjee notes that in 2014 a dozen states (Alabama, Indiana, Kansas, Kentucky, Louisiana, Nebraska, Ohio, Oklahoma, South Carolina, South Dakota, West Virginia, and Wyoming) sued the EPA in a failed effort to stop implementation of the proposed rule. Many of these states have large coal industries and view carbon emissions standards as economically harmful to those industries and the people they employ.

In August 2015 the EPA finalized the standards for the Clean Power Plan. The agency explains in the fact sheet "Components of the Clean Power Plan: Setting State Goals to Cut Carbon Pollution" (August 3, 2015 https://19january2017snapshot.epa.gov/sites/production/files/2015-08/documents/fs-cpp-state-goals.pdf) that it established interim and final goals for power plants to meet, but that states can develop and implement their own customized plans to ensure their compliance. The plan gives states various options for meeting their emissions goals, including emissions trading. It was originally expected that the states would submit their plans between 2016 and 2018 and the compliance period would begin in 2020.

The EPA's issuance of the final rule was staunchly criticized by the coal industry and the governors of numerous states. More than two dozen states, mostly represented by Republican governors, filed lawsuits against the EPA over the Clean Power Plan. Dozens of industry groups also joined in the litigation. In February 2016 the US Supreme Court granted a stay. Implementation of the new rule was put on hold pending the outcome of the legal battle. During the 2016 presidential campaign Trump championed the coal industry and decried the Clean Power Plan as part of the Obama administration's "war on coal." Two months after entering office President Trump signed an executive order that called for the EPA to review the Clean Power Plan.

In October 2017 the EPA formally proposed repealing the Clean Power Plan in "Repeal of Carbon Pollution Emission Guidelines for Existing Stationary Sources: Electric Utility Generating Units" (*Federal Register*, vol. 82, no. 198). As of January 2018, the proposal had not been finalized. It did, however, trigger a flurry of lawsuits from environmental groups and other parties opposed to the repeal.

CARBON EMISSIONS LIMITS FOR VEHICLES. Figure 3.13 shows the total carbon dioxide emissions for various transportation sources between 1995 and 2014. Cars and light-duty trucks accounted for the vast majority of the emissions. However, manufacturers have achieved significant reductions over time in the tons of carbon dioxide emitted annually by newer models. For example, on average, a model year 2016 car or light-duty truck emitted far less tons of carbon dioxide than comparable vehicles manufactured in earlier years. (See Figure 3.14.) These changes have been driven in large part by ever-stricter emissions standards for new vehicles.

FIGURE 3.13

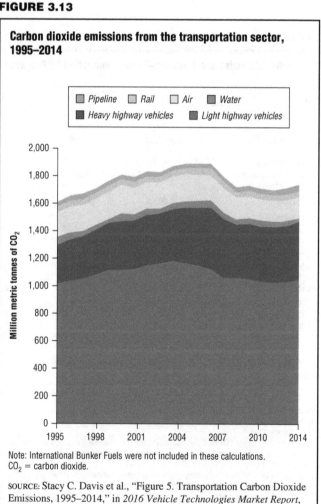

Carbon dioxide emissions from the transportation sector, 1995–2014

Note: International Bunker Fuels were not included in these calculations. CO_2 = carbon dioxide.

SOURCE: Stacy C. Davis et al., "Figure 5. Transportation Carbon Dioxide Emissions, 1995–2014," in *2016 Vehicle Technologies Market Report*, Oak Ridge National Laboratory, May 25, 2017, http://cta.ornl.gov/vtmarketreport/pdf/2016_vtmarketreport_full_doc.pdf (accessed November 9, 2017)

FIGURE 3.14

Average annual carbon dioxide emissions for cars and light-duty trucks, model years 1975–2016

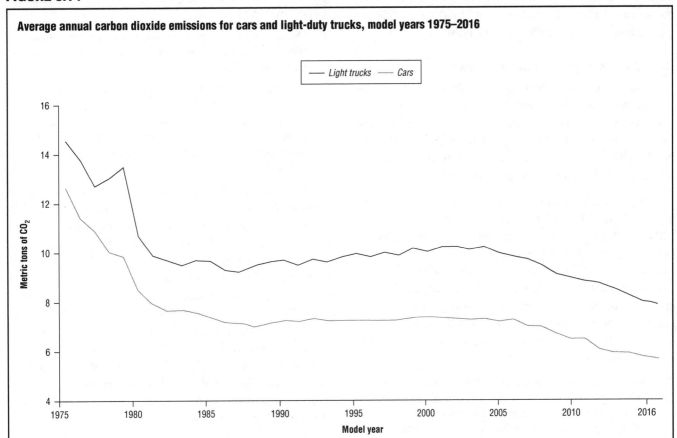

Note: Light trucks include pickups, vans, and 4-wheel drive sport utility vehicles. Carbon footprint is calculated using results from Argonne National Laboratory's GREET model. CO_2 = carbon dioxide.

SOURCE: Stacy C. Davis et al., "Figure 7. Average Carbon Footprint for Cars and Light Trucks Sold, MY 1975–2016," in *Vehicle Technologies Market Report*, Oak Ridge National Laboratory, May 25, 2017, http://cta.ornl.gov/vtmarketreport/pdf/2016_vtmarketreport_full_doc.pdf (accessed November 9, 2017)

As is described in Chapter 2, in 2010 and 2012 the EPA and the National Highway Transportation Safety Administration (NHTSA) established fuel economy and carbon dioxide standards for cars and light-duty trucks for model years 2012 to 2025. The EPA notes in "Carbon Pollution from Transportation" (July 17, 2017, https://www.epa.gov/air-pollution-transportation/carbon-pollution-transportation) that the standards were designed to cut 6.6 billion tons (6 billion t) of greenhouse gas emissions over the lifetime of the covered vehicles.

Chapter 2 also describes the midterm evaluation that was initiated in 2016 to assess the appropriateness of the carbon dioxide emissions standards scheduled to go into effect during the early 2020s. In January 2017, during the last days of the Obama administration, the EPA announced that the standards would remain in place. Under the incoming Trump administration, however, the EPA took a far different stance and reopened the midterm evaluation. As of January 2018, this process was still ongoing. As shown in Table 2.6 in Chapter 2, the standards for model years 2021 through 2025 were being reviewed, and it was widely expected that these standards would be loosened.

In 2011 the EPA and the NHTSA established fuel economy and carbon dioxide standards for medium- and heavy-duty vehicles, such as large pickup trucks, vans, buses, motor homes, and combination tractors (semi-trucks that typically pull trailers loaded with freight) for model years 2014 to 2018. In the fact sheet *EPA and NHTSA Adopt First-Ever Program to Reduce Greenhouse Gas Emissions and Improve Fuel Efficiency of Medium- and Heavy-Duty Vehicles* (August 2011, https://nepis.epa.gov/Exe/ZyPDF.cgi/P100BOT1.PDF?Dockey=P100BOT1.PDF), the EPA notes that the standards are expected to reduce greenhouse gas emissions by approximately 297.6 million tons (270 million t) over the lifetime of the covered vehicles.

In October 2016 the EPA and the NHTSA finalized an extension of the medium- and heavy-duty vehicle standards beyond the model year 2018. According to the EPA, in "Greenhouse Gas Emissions and Fuel Efficiency Standards for Medium- and Heavy-Duty Engines and

Vehicles—Phase 2" (*Federal Register*, vol. 81, no. 206), the so-called Phase 2 standards would reduce greenhouse gas emissions by 1.1 billion tons (1 billion t).

Recent US Reports on Climate Science

Since 2000 the USGCRP (http://www.globalchange.gov/browse/reports) has published dozens of reports related to climate science, including three complete national climate assessments (NCAs): NCA1 (2000), NCA2 (2009), and NCA3 (2014). As of January 2018, work on NCA4 was ongoing and was expected to be completed in late 2018.

In the NCA3 report, *Climate Change Impacts in the United States: The Third National Climate Assessment* (2014, http://s3.amazonaws.com/nca2014/low/NCA3 _Climate_Change_Impacts_in_the_United%20States_Low Res.pdf), the USGCRP compiles and explains information from numerous publications from various US government agencies. It examines existing and expected climate change impacts on the United States by economic sector and geographical region. Overall, it lists 12 key findings:

1. Global climate is changing and this is apparent across the United States in a wide range of observations. The global warming of the past 50 years is primarily due to human activities, predominantly the burning of fossil fuels.

2. Some extreme weather and climate events have increased in recent decades, and new and stronger evidence confirms that some of these increases are related to human activities.

3. Human-induced climate change is projected to continue, and it will accelerate significantly if global emissions of heat-trapping gases continue to increase.

4. Impacts related to climate change are already evident in many sectors and are expected to become increasingly disruptive across the nation throughout this century and beyond.

5. Climate change threatens human health and well-being in many ways, including through more extreme weather events and wildfire, decreased air quality, and diseases transmitted by insects, food, and water.

6. Infrastructure is being damaged by sea level rise, heavy downpours, and extreme heat; damages are projected to increase with continued climate change.

7. Water quality and water supply reliability are jeopardized by climate change in a variety of ways that affect ecosystems and livelihoods.

8. Climate disruptions to agriculture have been increasing and are projected to become more severe over this century.

9. Climate change poses particular threats to Indigenous Peoples' health, well-being, and ways of life.

10. Ecosystems and the benefits they provide to society are being affected by climate change. The capacity of ecosystems to buffer the impacts of extreme events like fires, floods, and severe storms is being overwhelmed.

11. Ocean waters are becoming warmer and more acidic, broadly affecting ocean circulation, chemistry, ecosystems, and marine life.

12. Planning for adaptation (to address and prepare for impacts) and mitigation (to reduce future climate change, for example by cutting emissions) is becoming more widespread, but current implementation efforts are insufficient to avoid increasingly negative social, environmental, and economic consequences.

Climate Science Special Report: Fourth National Climate Assessment, Volume 1 was released in November 2017. At nearly 500 pages long, the document includes input from dozens of scientists from government agencies and academia. They reiterate the 12 key findings from the NCA3 and summarize new observations and research related to climate change. In the executive summary, D. J. Wuebbles et al. note that the report "serves as the climate science foundation of the NCA4 and is generally intended for those who have a technical background in climate science." Overall, the researchers conclude that the global annual average surface air temperature increased by approximately 1.8 degrees Fahrenheit (1 degree C) between 1895 and 2016.

In Chapter 6 of the report "Temperature Changes in the United States," R. S. Vose et al. note that the annual average temperature of the contiguous United States increased by 1.23 degrees Fahrenheit (0.68 degrees C) between the early portion of the last century (1901–60) and recent decades (1986–2016). (See Table 3.5.) Every

TABLE 3.5

Annual average temperature changes by region

[Changes are the difference between the average for recent decades (1986–2016) and the average for the first half of the 20th century (1901–1960 for the contiguous United States, 1925–1960 for Alaska, Hawaii, and the Caribbean)]

NCA region	Change in annual average temperature	Change in annual average maximum temperature	Change in annual average minimum temperature
Contiguous US	1.23°F	1.06°F	1.41°F
Northeast	1.43°F	1.16°F	1.70°F
Southeast	0.46°F	0.16°F	0.76°F
Midwest	1.26°F	0.77°F	1.75°F
Great Plains north	1.69°F	1.66°F	1.72°F
Great Plains south	0.76°F	0.56°F	0.96°F
Southwest	1.61°F	1.61°F	1.61°F
Northwest	1.54°F	1.52°F	1.56°F
Alaska	1.67°F	1.43°F	1.91°F
Hawaii	1.26°F	1.01°F	1.49°F
Caribbean	1.35°F	1.08°F	1.60°F

NCA = National Climate Assessment.

SOURCE: D. J. Wuebbles et al., eds., "Table 6.1. Observed Changes in Annual Average Temperature (°F) for Each National Climate Assessment Region," in *Climate Science Special Report: Fourth National Climate Assessment, Volume 1*, US Global Change Research Program, 2017, https://science2017 .globalchange.gov/ (accessed November 9, 2017)

region of the United States experienced some level of net warming through 2016. This effect was most acute in Alaska and western areas. In Chapter 13, "Ocean Acidification and Other Ocean Changes," L. Jewett and A. Romanou assess the effects of global warming on the world's oceans, including the seas along the US coastline. Table 3.6 shows both historical trends and projected trends in sea surface temperatures. The projections are based on scenarios called representative concentration pathways (RCPs), which were developed by the IPCC. Each scenario represents a set of assumptions related to the atmospheric changes expected from greenhouse gas emissions. RCP4.5 and RCP8.5 represent relatively low and high emissions growth, respectively. As shown in Table 3.6, the global sea surface temperature increased by approximately 1.8 degrees Fahrenheit (1 degree C) between 1950 and 2016. The rates of increase for US coastal waters were greater than the global average rate around Alaska and the southwestern and northeastern coastlines. Model projections indicate continued high rates of growth to 2080 for all regions.

In June 2015 the EPA published *Climate Change in the United States: Benefits of Global Action* (https://www.epa.gov/sites/production/files/2015-06/documents/cirareport.pdf). The agency states, "The goal of this work is to estimate to what degree climate change impacts and damages to multiple U.S. sectors (e.g., human health, infrastructure, and water resources) may be avoided or reduced in a future with significant global action to reduce GHG emissions, compared to a future in which current emissions continue to grow." Table 3.7 provides an overview of the results with a listing of the expected benefits of mitigation in 2050 and 2100 to the nation's health and well-being and to various major resources and economic sectors. Overall, hundreds of billions of dollars in benefits are projected to occur.

Local and State Governments Take Action

During the first decade of the 21st century growing concern about climate change and the federal government's lack of involvement in the Kyoto Protocol spurred some local and state governments to establish their own campaigns against greenhouse gases. In 2007 the Sierra Club launched the Cool Counties Initiative for county governments that were committed to reducing their contributions to global warming. Some state and local governments adopted specific emissions targets.

Dozens of states joined with other states (and some Canadian provinces) in regional initiatives to reduce greenhouse gas emissions. These collaborations include the Western Climate Initiative (2017, http://www.wci-inc.org/) and the Regional Greenhouse Gas Initiative (2017, http://www.rggi.org/). This initiative is particularly notable because it is "the first market-based regulatory program in the United States to reduce greenhouse gas emissions." The collaborating states are Connecticut, Delaware, Maine, Maryland, Massachusetts, New Hampshire, New York,

TABLE 3.6

Sea surface temperature trends, 1900 to 2016 and 1950 to 2016 and projected for 2080

Region	Latitude and longitude	Historical trend (°C/100 years)		Projected trend 2080 (relative to 1976–2005 climate) (°C)	
		1900–2016	1950–2016	RCP4.5	RCP8.5
Global		0.70 ± 0.08	1.00 ± 0.11	1.3 ± 0.6	2.7 ± 0.7
Alaska	50°–66°N, 150°–170°W	0.82 ± 0.26	1.22 ± 0.59	2.5 ± 0.6	3.7 ± 1.0
Northwest (NW)	40°–50°N, 120°–132°W	0.64 ± 0.30	0.68 ± 0.70	1.7 ± 0.4	2.8 ± 0.6
Southwest (SW)	30°–40°N, 116°–126°W	0.73 ± 0.33	1.02 ± 0.79		
Hawaii (HI)	18°–24°N, 152°–162°W	0.58 ± 0.19	0.46 ± 0.39	1.6 ± 0.4	2.8 ± 0.6
Northeast (NE)	36°–46°N, 64°–76°W	0.63 ± 0.31	1.10 ± 0.71	2.0 ± 0.3	3.2 ± 0.6
Southeast (SE)	24°–34°N, 64°–80°W	0.40 ± 0.18	0.13 ± 0.34	1.6 ± 0.3	2.7 ± 0.4
Gulf of Mexico (GOM)	20°–30°N, 80°–96°W	0.52 ± 0.14	0.37 ± 0.27	1.6 ± 0.3	2.8 ± 0.3
Caribbean	10°–20°N, 66°–86°W	0.76 ± 0.15	0.77 ± 0.32	1.5 ± 0.4	2.6 ± 0.3

°C = degrees Celsius. RCP = representative concentration pathway.

SOURCE: D. J. Wuebbles et al., eds., "Table 13.1. Historical Sea Surface Temperature Trends (°C per Century) and Projected Trends by 2080 (°C) for Eight US Coastal Regions and Globally," in *Climate Science Special Report: Fourth National Climate Assessment, Volume 1*, US Global Change Research Program, 2017, https://science2017.globalchange.gov/ (accessed November 9, 2017)

TABLE 3.7

National benefits expected in 2050 and 2100 from limiting global temperature rise to approximately 3.6 degrees Fahrenheit (2 degrees Celsius) above preindustrial levels

	In the year 2050, global GHG mitigation is projected to result in...	In the year 2100, global GHG mitigation is projected to result in...
Health		
Air quality	An estimated 13,000 fewer deaths from poor air quality, valued at $160 billion.[a]	An estimated 57,000 fewer deaths from poor air quality, valued at $930 billion.[a]
Extreme temperature	An estimated 1,700 fewer deaths from extreme heat and cold in 49 major US cities, valued at $21 billion.	An estimated 12,000 fewer deaths from extreme heat and cold in 49 major US cities, valued at $200 billion.
Labor	An estimated avoided loss of 360 million labor hours, valued at $18 billion.	An estimated avoided loss of 1.2 billion labor hours, valued at $110 billion.
Water quality	An estimated $507–$700 million in avoided damages from poor water quality.[b]	An estimated $2.6–$3.0 billion in avoided damages from poor water quality.[b]
Infrastructure		
Bridges	An estimated 160–960 fewer bridges made structurally vulnerable, valued at $0.12–$1.5 billion.[b]	An estimated 720–2,200 fewer bridges made structurally vulnerable, valued at $1.1–$1.6 billion.[b]
Roads	An estimated $0.56–$2.3 billion in avoided adaptation costs.[b]	An estimated $4.2–$7.4 billion in avoided adaptation costs.[b]
Urban drainage	An estimated $56 million to $2.9 billion in avoided adaptation costs from the 50-year, 24-hour storm in 50 US cities.[b]	An estimated $50 million to $6.4 billion in avoided adaptation costs from the 50-year, 24-hour storm in 50 US cities.[b]
Coastal property	An estimated $0.14 billion in avoided damages and adaptation costs from sea level rise and storm surge.	An estimated $3.1 billion in avoided damages and adaptation costs from sea level rise and storm surge.
Electricity		
Demand and supply	An estimated 1.1%–4.0% reduction in energy demand and $10–$34 billion in savings in power system costs.[c]	Not estimated.
Water resources		
Inland flooding	An estimated change in flooding damages ranging from $260 million in damages to $230 million in avoided damages.[b]	An estimated change in flooding damages ranging from $32 million in damages to $2.5 billion in avoided damages.[b]
Drought	An estimated 29%–45% fewer severe and extreme droughts, with corresponding avoided damages to the agriculture sector of approximately $1.2–$1.4 billion.[b]	An estimated 40%–59% fewer severe and extreme droughts, with corresponding avoided damages to the agriculture sector of $2.6–$3.1 billion.[b]
Water supply and demand	An estimated $3.9–$54 billion in avoided damages due to water shortages.[b]	An estimated $11–$180 billion in avoided damages due to water shortages.[b]
Agriculture & forestry		
Agriculture	An estimated $1.5–$3.8 billion in avoided damages.	An estimated $6.6–$11 billion in avoided damages.
Forestry	Estimated damages of $9.5–$9.6 billion.	An estimated $520 million to $1.5 billion in avoided damages.
Ecosystems		
Coral reefs	An estimated avoided loss of 53% of coral in Hawaii, 3.7% in Florida, and 2.8% in Puerto Rico. These avoided losses are valued at $1.4 billion.	An estimated avoided loss of 35% of coral in Hawaii, 1.2% in Florida, and 1.7% in Puerto Rico. These avoided losses are valued at $1.2 billion.
Shellfish	An estimated avoided loss of 11% of the US oyster supply, 12% of the US scallop supply, and 4.6% of the US clam supply, with corresponding consumer benefits of $85 million.	An estimated avoided loss of 34% of the US oyster supply, 37% of the US scallop supply, and 29% of the US clam supply, with corresponding consumer benefits of $380 million.
Freshwater fish	An estimated change in recreational fishing ranging from $13 million in avoided damages to $3.8 million in damages.[b]	An estimated $95–$280 million in avoided damages associated with recreational fishing.[b]
Wildfire	An estimated 2.1–2.2 million fewer acres burned and corresponding avoided wildfire response costs of $160–$390 million.[†]	An estimated 6.0–7.9 million fewer acres burned and corresponding avoided wildfire response costs of $940 million to $1.4 billion.[†]
Carbon storage	An estimated 26–78 million fewer metric tons of carbon stored, and corresponding costs of $7.5–$23 billion.[b]	An estimated 1–26 million fewer metric tons of carbon stored, and corresponding costs of $880 million to $12 billion.[b]

[a]These results do not reflect additional benefits to air quality and human health that would stem from the co-control of traditional air pollutants along with GHG emissions.
[b]For sectors sensitive to changes in precipitation, the estimated range of results is generated using projections from two climate models showing different patterns of future precipitation in the contiguous US The IGSM-CAM model projects a relatively "wetter" future for most of the contiguous US compared to the "drier" MIROC model.
[c]Estimated range of benefits from the reduction in demand and system costs resulting from lower temperatures associated with GHG mitigation. The electricity section in this report presents an analysis that includes the costs to the electric sector of reducing GHG emissions.
Notes: GHG = greenhouse gas.

SOURCE: "National Highlights," in *Climate Change in the United States: Benefits of Global Action*, US Environmental Protection Agency, Office of Atmospheric Programs, June 2015, https://www.epa.gov/sites/production/files/2015-06/documents/cirareport.pdf (accessed November 9, 2017)

Rhode Island, and Vermont. They have agreed to a regional cap on emissions (in total tons) that declines each year. The states use an auction trading program through which power plants with lower emissions sell emissions credits to power plants with higher emissions.

According to the Center for Climate and Energy Solutions (2017, http://www.c2es.org/what_s_being_done/targets), 20 states and the District of Columbia have established specific carbon emissions target goals. Climate action plans have sometimes been stymied by legal challenges. In 2014 a federal court overturned portions of Minnesota's Next Generation Energy Act of 2007. According to David Shaffer, in "Judge Strikes down Minnesota's Anti-coal Energy Law" (StarTribune.com, April 18, 2014), the judge ruled that the law—which put restrictions on energy from coal-fired power plants—violates the commerce clause of the US Constitution.

However, some state and local governments have persisted in their efforts to limit carbon emissions within their jurisdictions. In "Malloy 'Recommits' State to Climate Change Battle" (Courant.com, April 22, 2015), Brian Dowling indicates that during the early 1990s Connecticut became the first state "to pass legislation requiring actions to control carbon emissions." This was followed by adoption of a climate change action plan in 2005 and passage of the Global Warming Solutions Act of 2008. The law commits the state to reducing its greenhouse gas emissions by 2020 to 10% below 1990 levels and by 2050 to 80% of 2001 levels.

CALIFORNIA LEADS WITH LEGISLATION. California has been the most aggressive of the states in implementing legislation related to global warming and climate change. In 2005 it set targets for greenhouse gas emissions under an executive order issued by Governor Arnold Schwarzenegger (1947–). He also created a Climate Action Team under the direction of the California Environmental Protection Agency to coordinate the state's climate policy.

In August 2006 the California legislature passed AB 32, the Global Warming Solutions Act, which adopted Schwarzenegger's plans into law. It calls for the state to reduce its greenhouse gas emissions to 1990 levels by 2020. This represents an approximate 25% reduction, compared with what emissions would be without the act. The act also includes a cap-and-trade program and a market-based trading program in which industries emitting greenhouse gases can buy or sell credits among themselves to meet the limits. The state's carbon market began trading in 2012 and quickly grew to be the second largest in the world, behind the EU's Emissions Trading System. Lynn Doan reports in "California Adopts Regulation to Link Carbon Markets with Quebec" (Bloomberg.com, April 19, 2013) that in April 2013 the state modified its cap-and-trade program to align it with Quebec, a Canadian province with an aggressive policy toward reducing greenhouse gas emissions.

Opponents to AB 32 worry about its economic consequences, fearing that it will drive businesses from California and raise consumer prices, particularly for gasoline. Advocates counter that California companies will create profitable technological innovations for the world marketplace that will ultimately offset and even surpass the short-term costs of tighter emissions limits.

California has also targeted carbon emissions from transportation vehicles. The state's Low Carbon Fuel Standard (https://www.arb.ca.gov/fuels/lcfs/lcfs.htm) was implemented in April 2009 through a new regulation that targets providers, refiners, importers, and blenders of transportation fuels. It is designed to reduce greenhouse gas emissions from transportation fuels and encourage development and investment in alternative fuels other than gasoline.

MITIGATING CARBON BUILDUP IN THE ATMOSPHERE

To mitigate means to relieve or reduce in harshness. Limiting greenhouse gas emissions is one way to mitigate carbon buildup in the atmosphere and the main method that is focused on in legislation and government policy, such as through cap-and-trade programs or other emissions controls.

Carbon Sequestration

Besides emissions controls, scientists are increasingly exploring techniques for long-term storage of carbon to keep it out of the atmosphere. This is known as carbon sequestration. Carbon storage media are known as repositories or sinks.

NATURAL SINKS: OCEANS, VEGETATION, AND SOILS. The earth's oceans, vegetation (particularly forests), and soils act naturally to mitigate the effect of carbon buildup by absorbing and storing carbon. The oceans are, by far, the largest reservoir of carbon in the earth's carbon cycle. Some scientists believe the oceans can absorb between 1 billion and 2 billion tons (907 million and 1.8 billion t) of carbon dioxide per year. Living vegetation, especially trees, also naturally absorbs and neutralizes carbon dioxide. Deforestation (the clearing of forests) reduces natural carbon sequestration. The burning of the Amazon rain forest and other forests has a twofold effect: the immediate release of large amounts of carbon dioxide into the atmosphere from the fires and the loss of trees to absorb the carbon dioxide in the atmosphere. Natural disasters, such as hurricanes, can also destroy large swaths of trees. Soil can also be a carbon sink due to the presence of tiny carbon-storing microbes. Disturbing the soil, for example, through plowing, releases the carbon.

PURPOSEFUL CARBON CAPTURE. Purposeful carbon capture is carbon sequestration facilitated by humans. Afforestation (establishing new forest) is one method. However, massive amounts of forested land are required to offset anthropogenic emissions.

Geological sequestration is the injection of carbon dioxide into sealed formations or reservoirs deep beneath the earth's surface. These include already tapped oil and natural gas reservoirs, saline formations (formations of porous rock that is saturated with saltwater), unmineable deep coal seams, and basalt formations (formations of solidified lava). According to the Department of Energy's National Energy Technology Laboratory, the use of tapped oil reservoirs could be particularly beneficial because the injection of carbon dioxide would help push hard-to-pump oil out of the reservoir. This process is known as CO_2-enhanced oil recovery and is already being used by the petroleum industry. The laboratory believes that widespread use of CO_2-enhanced oil recovery could significantly boost US oil production while sequestering away a potent greenhouse gas.

The Department of Energy is engaged in public-private partnerships to further research and development of carbon sequestration in the commercial power industry. The National Carbon Capture Center (https://www.national carboncapturecenter.com/) was launched in May 2009 to develop and test technologies that can be used to capture carbon dioxide emissions from coal-based power plants.

GLOBAL WARMING SKEPTICS

Although there is widespread agreement among scientists that the earth's temperature has warmed in recent years, there is lingering debate over the causes of this warming. Some scientists believe major climate events should be viewed in terms of thousands of years, not just a century. A record of only the past century may indicate, but not prove, that a major change has occurred. Is it caused by anthropogenic greenhouse gases or is it natural variability?

Critics of global warming contend that there are several reasons for the change in climate, including:

- Climate has been known to change dramatically within a relatively short period without any human influence.

- Temperature readings already showed increased temperatures before carbon dioxide levels rose significantly (before 1940).

- Natural variations in climate may exceed any human-caused climate change.

- Some of the increase in temperatures can be attributed to sunspot activity.

- Although clouds are crucial to climate predictions, so little is known about them that computer models cannot produce accurate predictions.

There are a handful of scientists notably known for their criticism of the IPCC and its conclusions about anthropogenic causes of global warming. They believe modeling results exaggerate the role of carbon dioxide emissions on climate and attack what they see as

environmental hysteria on a subject about which much is still unknown by the scientific community.

PUBLIC OPINION ABOUT GLOBAL WARMING

Polling conducted by Gallup, Inc., indicates that a majority of Americans recognize that many scientists believe global warming is taking place. In 2017 more than seven out of 10 (71%) poll respondents expressed their agreement with the statement "Most scientists believe that global warming is occurring." (See Table 3.8.) However, 22% of the respondents said they are "unsure," and 5% agreed with the statement "Most scientists believe that global warming is not occurring." The remaining 2% of respondents had no opinion on the matter. Thus, there is far from universal acceptance in the United States that most scientists believe that global warming is taking place.

Americans have doubts about the science underpinning the purported cause of global warming. As shown in Table 3.9, a 2017 Gallup poll found that 68% of Americans believe global warming is due to "the effects of pollution from human activities," whereas 29% blame global warming on "natural changes in the environment." Previous Gallup polls have found sharp differences of opinion on this topic based on party affiliation. In *Conservative Republicans Alone on Global Warming's Timing*

TABLE 3.8

Public opinion on the belief in global warming by scientists, selected years 1997–2017

JUST YOUR IMPRESSION, WHICH ONE OF THE FOLLOWING STATEMENTS DO YOU THINK IS MOST ACCURATE—MOST SCIENTISTS BELIEVE THAT GLOBAL WARMING IS OCCURRING, MOST SCIENTISTS BELIEVE THAT GLOBAL WARMING IS NOT OCCURRING OR MOST SCIENTISTS ARE UNSURE ABOUT WHETHER GLOBAL WARMING IS OCCURRING OR NOT?

	Is occurring	Is not occurring	Unsure	No opinion
	%	%	%	%
2017 Mar 1–5	71	5	22	2
2016 Mar 2–6	65	7	25	3
2015 Mar 5–8	62	8	27	3
2014 Mar 6–9	60	8	29	3
2013 Mar 7–10	62	6	28	4
2012 Mar 8–11	58	7	32	3
2011 Mar 3–6	55	8	33	4
2010 Mar 4–7	52	10	36	2
2008 Mar 6–9	65	7	26	3
2006 Mar 13–16	65	3	29	3
2001 Mar 5–7	61	4	30	5
1997 Nov 21–23	48	7	39	6

SOURCE: "Just your impression, which one of the following statements do you think is most accurate—most scientists believe that global warming is occurring, most scientists believe that global warming is NOT occurring or most scientists are unsure about whether global warming is occurring or not?" in *In Depth: Topics A to Z: Environment*, Gallup, Inc., 2017, http://news.gallup.com/poll/1615/environment.aspx (accessed November 7, 2017). Copyright © 2017. Republished with permission of Gallup, Inc.; permission conveyed through Copyright Clearance Center, Inc.

TABLE 3.9

Public opinion about the causes of Earth's increasing temperatures, selected years 2003–17

AND FROM WHAT YOU HAVE HEARD OR READ, DO YOU BELIEVE INCREASES IN THE EARTH'S TEMPERATURE OVER THE LAST CENTURY ARE DUE MORE TO—THE EFFECTS OF POLLUTION FROM HUMAN ACTIVITIES (OR) NATURAL CHANGES IN THE ENVIRONMENT THAT ARE NOT DUE TO HUMAN ACTIVITIES?

	Human activites	Natural causes	No opinion
	%	%	%
2017 Mar 1–5	68	29	3
2016 Mar 2–6	65	31	4
2015 Mar 5–8	55	41	4
2014 Mar 6–9	57	40	3
2013 Mar 7–10	57	39	4
2012 Mar 8–11	53	41	6
2011 Mar 3–6	52	43	5
2010 Mar 4–7	50	46	5
2008 Mar 6–9	58	38	5
2007 Mar 11–14	61	35	5
2006 Mar 13–16	58	36	6
2003 Mar 3–5	61	33	6

SOURCE: "And from what you have heard or read, do you believe increases in the Earth's temperature over the last century are due more to—the effects of pollution from human activities (or) natural changes in the environment that are not due to human activities?" in *In Depth: Topics A to Z: Environment*, Gallup, Inc., 2017, http://news.gallup.com/poll/1615/environment.aspx (accessed November 7, 2017). Copyright © 2017. Republished with permission of Gallup, Inc.; permission conveyed through Copyright Clearance Center, Inc.

(April 22, 2015, http://news.gallup.com/poll/182807/conservative-republicans-alone-global-warming-timing.aspx), Andrew Dugan notes that in 2015, 81% of liberal Democrats agreed that global warming is due to pollution from human activities, compared with only 27% of conservative Republicans. There is obviously deep disbelief among Republicans that humans are the cause of global warming. These beliefs help explain why President Trump and other like-minded policy makers refuse to take aggressive action against emissions linked by many scientists to global warming.

CHAPTER 4
A HOLE IN THE SKY: OZONE DEPLETION

THE EARTH'S PROTECTIVE OZONE LAYER

Ozone is a gas naturally present in the earth's atmosphere. Unlike ordinary oxygen, a diatomic molecule that contains two oxygen atoms (O_2), ozone, a triatomic molecule, contains three oxygen atoms (O_3). A molecule of ordinary oxygen can be converted to ozone by ultraviolet (UV) radiation, electrical discharge (such as from lightning), or complex chemical reactions. These processes split apart the two oxygen atoms, which are then free to bind with other loose oxygen atoms to form ozone.

Ozone exists in the earth's atmosphere at two levels: the troposphere and the stratosphere. (See Figure 4.1.) Tropospheric (ground-level) ozone accounts for only a small portion of the earth's total ozone, but it is a potent air pollutant with serious health consequences. Ground-level ozone is the primary component in smog and is formed via complex chemical reactions involving emissions of industrial chemicals and through fossil fuel combustion. Tropospheric ozone formation is intensified during hot weather, when more radiation reaches the ground. Smog retards crop and tree growth, impairs health, and limits visibility.

Approximately 90% of the earth's ozone lies in the stratosphere at altitudes greater than about 9.3 miles (15 km). (See Figure 4.1.) Ozone molecules at this level protect life on the earth by absorbing UV radiation from the sun and preventing it from reaching the ground. The so-called ozone layer is actually a scattering of molecules constantly undergoing change from oxygen to ozone and back. Although most of the ozone changes back to oxygen, a small amount of ozone persists. As long as this natural process stays in balance, the overall ozone layer remains thick enough to protect the earth from harmful UV radiation from the sun. The amount of ozone in the stratosphere varies greatly, depending on location, altitude, and temperature.

EVIDENCE OF OZONE DEPLETION

Many scientists believe the introduction of certain chemicals into the stratosphere alters the natural ozone balance by depleting ozone molecules. Chlorine and bromine atoms are particularly destructive. They bind to oxygen atoms that are loose and prevent them from reforming either oxygen or ozone. Chlorine and bromine are found in the sea salt from ocean spray. Chlorine is also present in the form of hydrochloric acid, which is emitted with volcanic gases. These are natural sources of ozone-depleting chemicals.

During the mid-1970s scientists began speculating that the ozone layer was rapidly being destroyed by reactions involving industrial chemicals that contained chlorine and bromine. Two chemists, F. Sherwood Rowland (1927–2012) and Mario J. Molina (1943–), discovered that chlorofluorocarbons (CFCs) could break down in the stratosphere, releasing chlorine atoms that could destroy thousands of ozone molecules. This discovery led to a ban on CFCs as a propellant in aerosols in the United States and in other countries.

In 1985 Joseph C. Farman, Brian G. Gardiner, and Jonathan D. Shanklin reported in "Large Losses of Total Ozone in Antarctica Reveal Seasonal ClO_x/NO_x Interaction" (*Nature*, vol. 315, no. 6016, May 16, 1985) about alarmingly low concentrations of stratospheric ozone above Halley Bay in Antarctica (the South Pole). Measurements indicated ozone levels were about 30% lower during the springs of 1980 to 1984, compared with the springs of 1957 to 1973. (The Antarctic spring coincides with the fall season in North America.)

Scientists report ozone concentrations in Dobson units. The unit is named after Gordon M. B. Dobson (1889–1975), a British scientist who invented an instrument for measuring ozone concentrations from the ground. One Dobson unit (DU) corresponds to a layer of atmospheric ozone that would be 0.001 of a millimeter

FIGURE 4.1

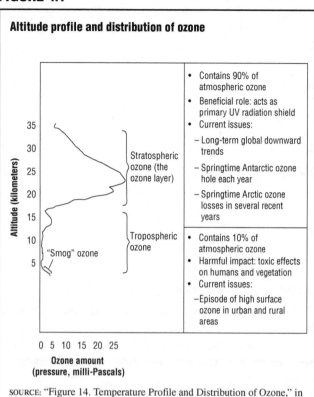

Altitude profile and distribution of ozone

- Contains 90% of atmospheric ozone
- Beneficial role: acts as primary UV radiation shield
- Current issues:
  – Long-term global downward trends
  – Springtime Antarctic ozone hole each year
  – Springtime Arctic ozone losses in several recent years

Stratospheric ozone (the ozone layer)

Tropospheric ozone

- Contains 10% of atmospheric ozone
- Harmful impact: toxic effects on humans and vegetation
- Current issues:
  –Episode of high surface ozone in urban and rural areas

SOURCE: "Figure 14. Temperature Profile and Distribution of Ozone," in *Science: Ozone Basics*, US Department of Commerce, National Oceanic and Atmospheric Administration, March 20, 2008, http://www.ozonelayer.noaa.gov/science/basics.htm (accessed November 17, 2017)

TABLE 4.1

Average yearly ozone hole area and minimum ozone level for the Southern Hemisphere for September through October, 1979–2017

Year	Mean ozone hole area (millions of square kilometers)	Minimum yearly average ozone level (Dobson units)
1979	0.1	225
1980	1.4	203
1981	0.6	209.5
1982	4.8	185
1983	7.9	172.9
1984	10.1	163.6
1985	14.2	146.5
1986	11.3	157.8
1987	19.3	123
1988	10	171
1989	18.7	127
1990	19.2	124.2
1991	18.8	119
1992	22.3	114.3
1993	24.2	112.6
1994	23.6	92.3
1996	22.8	108.8
1997	22.1	108.8
1998	25.9	98.8
1999	23.3	102.9
2000	24.8	98.7
2001	25	100.9
2002	12	157.4
2003	25.8	108.7
2004	19.5	123.5
2005	24.4	113.8
2006	26.6	98.4
2007	22	116.2
2008	25.2	114
2009	22	107.9
2010	19.4	128.5
2011	24.7	106.5
2012	17.8	139.3
2013	21	132.7
2014	20.9	128.6
2015	25.6	117.2
2016	20.7	123.2
2017	17.4	141.8

SOURCE: "Annual Records," in *NASA Ozone Watch*, National Aeronautics and Space Administration, Goddard Institute for Space Studies, October 16, 2017, https://ozonewatch.gsfc.nasa.gov/statistics/annual_data.html (accessed November 9, 2017)

thick if it was compressed into a layer at standard temperature and pressure at the earth's surface. Atmospheric ozone is considered "thin" if its concentration falls below 220 DU. A thin spot in the ozone layer is commonly called an ozone hole.

The extreme cold and unique climate conditions over the poles are thought to make the ozone layers there particularly susceptible to thinning. Where cloud and ice particles are present, reactions that hasten ozone destruction also occur on the surface of ice particles. Since 1982 an ozone hole has appeared each year over Antarctica beginning in August and lasting until November. The hole formation is linked to polar clouds that form during the dark Antarctic winter (May through September). These clouds provide reaction surfaces for chlorine-containing compounds to release their chlorine. As sunlight returns in August or September, the released chlorine begins destroying ozone molecules.

The Antarctic ozone hole increased in size throughout the 1980s. By the early 1990s it was consistently larger than the area of Antarctica. Throughout most of the first decade of the 21st century the hole was larger in size than the continent of North America. In 2002 the size of the hole dropped dramatically because of unusually warm weather at the South Pole. The 2017 hole measured 6.7 million square miles (17.4 million square km) in size.

(See Table 4.1.) This corresponded with a minimum ozone concentration of 141.8 DU. The largest ozone hole on record was 10.3 million square miles (26.6 million square km) in 2006. The minimum ozone concentration at that time was 98.4 DU.

Scientists also monitor stratospheric ozone levels over the Arctic (the North Pole). Historically, Arctic winters have been warmer than those in Antarctica. This helps protect the northern pole from ozone depletion. During the winter months (December to March) of 2011 the Arctic experienced an unusually low ozone level. In "NASA Pinpoints Causes of 2011 Arctic Ozone Hole" (March 11, 2013, https://www.nasa.gov/topics/earth/features/2011-ozone-hole.html), the National Aeronautics and Space Administration (NASA) notes that scientists believe a combination of very cold weather, high chlorine pollution, and unusual wind conditions combined to lower stratospheric ozone approximately 20% below its normal seasonal average. Ozone concentrations did not, however, drop below 220 DU, which is the threshold of an ozone hole. Yearly Arctic ozone maps compiled by NASA (https://ozonewatch.gsfc.nasa.gov/monthly/climatology_03_NH.html) indicate that the unusually low ozone levels of 2011 were not seen between 2012 and 2017.

The World Meteorological Organization (WMO) explains in *Scientific Assessment of Ozone Depletion: 2002* (2002, https://www.esrl.noaa.gov/csd/assessments/ozone/2002/) that the average total ozone column on a global basis was approximately 3% lower between 1997 and 2001 when compared with pre-1980 average values. The most dramatic changes were recorded in the polar regions and midlatitudes (between the tropics and the poles). Most of the global population lives in the midlatitudes of the Northern and Southern Hemispheres. For example, the US mainland lies approximately in the range of 30 degrees to 50 degrees north latitude.

CONSEQUENCES OF OZONE DEPLETION

The sun emits radiation at a variety of wavelengths. The ozone layer acts as a protective shield against UV radiation (radiation with wavelengths of approximately 10 to 400 nanometers; a nanometer is one billionth of a meter). As the ozone layer diminishes in the upper atmosphere, the earth receives more UV radiation.

Scientists are particularly worried about the increased exposure to radiation in the ultraviolet-B (UVB) spectrum (wavelengths of approximately 290 to 320 nanometers). This wavelength can be damaging to human health because it is linked with adverse effects to deoxyribonucleic acid, skin, eyes, and the immune system. In addition, excessive exposure to UV radiation can negatively affect terrestrial and aquatic ecosystems and damage synthetic materials.

In "Health and Environmental Effects of Ozone Layer Depletion" (December 28, 2016, https://www.epa.gov/ozone-layer-protection/health-and-environmental-effects-ozone-layer-depletion), the US Environmental Protection Agency (EPA) reports that the amount of UVB radiation reaching the surface in Antarctica can double during the time of its annual ozone hole.

UV radiation alters photosynthesis, plant yield, and growth in plant species. Phytoplankton (one-celled organisms found in the ocean) are the backbone of the marine food web. According to the EPA, excessive exposure to UVB radiation reduces the productivity and survival rate for these organisms. Diminishing phytoplankton supplies would likely harm many fish species that depend on them for food. Studies performed during the mid-1990s blamed the rise in UV radiation caused by the thinning of the ozone layer for a decline in the number of frogs and other amphibians.

Increased UV radiation also affects synthetic materials. Plastics are especially vulnerable, tending to weaken, become brittle and discolored, and break.

OZONE-DEPLETING CHEMICALS

Most ozone destruction in the atmosphere is believed to be anthropogenic (caused by humans). In 1998 the WMO estimated in *Scientific Assessment of Ozone Depletion: 1998* (March 1999, https://www.esrl.noaa.gov/csd/assessments/ozone/1998/ExecSum98.pdf) that only 18% of the sources contributing to ozone depletion during the 1990s were natural. The remaining 82% of sources contributing to ozone depletion were industrial chemicals. The blame was largely placed on the chemicals that were developed by modern society for use as refrigerants, air-conditioning fluids, solvents, cleaning agents, and foam-blowing agents. These chemicals can persist in the atmosphere for years. Thus, there is a significant lag between the time that emissions decline at the earth's surface and the time at which ozone levels in the stratosphere recover.

Table 4.2 lists the chemicals of particular concern to scientists. Each chemical is assigned a value called an ozone depletion potential (ODP) based on its harmfulness to the ozone layer. CFC-11 and CFC-13 are arbitrarily assigned an ODP of 1. The ODPs for other chemicals are

TABLE 4.2

Lifetime, ozone depletion potential, and global warming potential of various chemicals

	Lifetime, in years	Ozone depletion potential	Global warming potential*
Class I			
CFC-11	45	1	4,750
CFC-12	100	0.82–1	10,900
CFC-13	640	1	14,420
CFC-113	85	0.8–0.85	6,130
CFC-114	190	0.58–1	10,000
CFC-115	1,020	0.5–0.6	7,370
Halon 1211	16	3–7.9	1,890
Halon 1301	65	10–15.9	7,140
Halon 2402	20	6–13	1,640
Carbon tetrachloride	26	0.82–1.1	1,400
Methyl bromide	0.8	0.66–0.7	5
Methyl chloroform	5	0.1–0.16	146
Class II			
HCFC-21	1.7	0.04	151
HCFC-22	11.9	0.04–0.055	1,810
HCFC-123	1.3	0.01–0.02	77
HCFC-124	5.9	0.022	609
HCFC-141b	9.2	0.11–0.12	725
HCFC-142b	17.2	0.06–0.065	2,310
HCFC-225ca	1.9	0.02–0.025	122
HCFC-225cb	5.9	0.03–0.033	595

*Global warming potential over a 100-year time horizon.
CFC = Chlorofluorocarbon; HCFC = Hydrochlorofluorocarbon.

SOURCE: Adapted from "Class I ODS" and "Class II ODS," in *Ozone Layer Protection: Ozone-Depleting Substances*, US Environmental Protection Agency, December 28, 2016, https://www.epa.gov/ozone-layer-protection/ozone-depleting-substances (accessed November 9, 2017)

determined by comparing their relative harmfulness with that of CFC-11 and CFC-13. In general, Class I chemicals are those with an ODP value greater than or equal to 0.1, and Class II chemicals have ODP values less than 0.1.

Class I Chemicals

Although a number of chemicals can destroy stratospheric ozone, CFCs are the main offenders because they are so prevalent. When CFCs were invented in 1928, they were welcomed as chemical wonders. Discovered by the chemist Thomas Midgley Jr. (1889–1944), they proved to be nontoxic, nonflammable, noncorrosive, stable, and inexpensive. Their artificial cooling provided refrigeration for food and brought comfort to warm climates. The CFC compound was originally marketed under the trademark Freon.

Over time, new formulations and applications were discovered. CFCs could be used not only as coolants in air conditioners and refrigerators but also as propellants in aerosol sprays, in certain plastics such as polystyrene, in insulation, in fire extinguishers, and as cleaning agents. Production grew dramatically as new uses were discovered—primarily as a solvent to clean circuit boards and computer chips.

CFCs are extremely stable; it is this stability that allows them to float intact through the troposphere and into the ozone layer. CFCs do not degrade in the lower atmosphere but, after entering the stratosphere, the sun's intense UV radiation eventually breaks them down into chlorine, fluorine, and carbon. Many scientists believe it is the chlorine that damages the ozone layer.

Although CFCs are primarily blamed for ozone loss, other gases are also at fault. One of these gases is halon, which contains bromine. Halons have much higher ODP values than do CFCs. (See Table 4.2.) The bromine atoms in halons destroy ozone, but they are chemically more powerful than chlorine atoms. This means that the impact to ozone of a particular mass of halon is more destructive than a similar mass of CFC. Halons are relatively long lived in the atmosphere, lingering for up to 65 years before being broken down. Halon is used primarily for fighting fires. Civilian and military firefighting training accounts for much of the halon emissions.

Other Class I ozone destroyers include carbon tetrachloride, methyl bromide, and methyl chloroform. These chemicals are commonly used as solvents and cleaning agents.

Class II Chemicals

The most common Class II ozone-depleting chemicals are hydrochlorofluorocarbons (HCFCs). HCFCs contain hydrogen. This makes them more susceptible to atmospheric breakdown than CFCs. As shown in Table 4.2, most HCFCs have a lifetime of less than six years. HCFCs have much lower ODP values than CFCs, halons, and industrial ozone depleters. HCFCs are considered good short-term replacements for CFCs. Although HCFCs are less destruc-

tive to ozone than the chemicals they are replacing, scientists believe that HCFC use must also be phased out to allow the ozone layer to fully recover.

A LANDMARK IN INTERNATIONAL DIPLOMACY: THE MONTREAL PROTOCOL

Ozone depletion was a global problem that necessitated international cooperation, but countries mistrusted one another's motives. As with the issues of climate change and pollution, developing countries resented being asked to sacrifice their economic development for a problem they believed the industrialized countries had created. To complicate matters, gaps in scientific proof led to disagreements over the extent and urgency of the ozone depletion situation.

In 1985, 20 countries signed an agreement in Vienna, Austria, known as the Convention for the Protection of the Ozone Layer (or the Vienna Convention). It called for data gathering, cooperation, and a political commitment to take action at a later date. In a 1987 negotiators' meeting in Montreal, Canada, the participants finalized a landmark in international environmental diplomacy: the Montreal Protocol on Substances That Deplete the Ozone Layer. It is generally referred to as the Montreal Protocol. The protocol was signed by 29 countries, including the United States, Australia, Canada, Japan, Mexico, all of Western Europe, and a handful of other countries.

The protocol called for industrial countries to cut CFC emissions in half by 1998 and to reduce halon emissions to 1986 levels by 1992. Developing countries were granted deferrals to compensate for their low levels of production. More importantly, the protocol also called for further amending as new data became available.

Throughout the 1990s and the first decade of the 21st century new scientific information revealed that ozone depletion was occurring faster than expected. This news spurred calls to revise the treaty. Four amendments to the Montreal Protocol were adopted during this period. They are known as the London Amendment (effective 1992), the Copenhagen Amendment (effective 1994), the Montreal Amendment (effective 1999), and the Beijing Amendment (effective 2002).

The United Nations Environment Programme (UNEP; http://ozone.unep.org/en/treaties-and-decisions) indicates that as of January 2018, 197 countries (including the United States) had ratified (formally approved into law) the original Montreal Protocol and its first four amendments. The final phaseout schedule for ozone-depleting substances (ODS) is shown in Table 4.3. In 2016 a fifth amendment was added to the Montreal Protocol to address the climate change impact of chemicals that became popular ODS substitutes. This amendment is discussed in detail later in the chapter.

TABLE 4.3

Phase-out schedule under the Montreal Protocol for ozone-depleting substances

Ozone-depleting substance	Developed countries must phase out by:	Developing countries must phase out by:
Halons	1994	2010
Carbon tetrachloride	1996	2010
Chlorofluorocarbons (CFCs)	1996	2010
Hydrobromofluorocarbons (HBFCs)	1996	1996
Methyl chloroform	1996	2015
Bromochloromethane	2002	2002
Methyl bromide	2005	2015
Hydrochlorofluorocarbons (HCFCs)	2030	2040

SOURCE: Created by Kim Masters Evans for Gale, © 2017

TABLE 4.4

US actions to meet the phase-out schedule under the Montreal Protocol for Class II ozone-depleting substances

Year to be implemented	Implementation of HCFC phase-out through clean air act regulations	Year to be implemented	Percent reduction in HCFC consumption and production from baseline
2003	No production or import of HCFC-141b	2004	35.0%
2010	No production or import of HCFC-142b and HCFC-22, except for use in equipment manufactured before January 1, 2010	2010	75.0%
2015	No production or import of any other HCFCs, except as refrigerants in equipment manufactured before January 1, 2020	2015	90.0%
2020	No production or import of HCFC-142b and HCFC-22	2020	99.5%
2030	No production or import of any HCFCs	2030	100.0%

HCFC = hydrochlorofluorocarbon.

SOURCE: "US Action to Meet the Montreal Protocol Phaseout Schedule," in *Phaseout of Class II Ozone-Depleting Substances*, US Environmental Protection Agency, December 5, 2016, https://www.epa.gov/ods-phaseout/phaseout-class-ii-ozone-depleting-substances (accessed November 10, 2017)

EPA Regulatory Programs

The EPA is responsible for ensuring that the United States meets its obligations under the Montreal Protocol. In "Ozone Protection under Title VI of the Clean Air Act" (June 5, 2017, https://www.epa.gov/ozone-layer-protection/ozone-protection-under-title-vi-clean-air-act), the agency provides information about rules governing the use, import, management, and destruction of ODS. For example, technicians that service stationary refrigeration and air-conditioning systems must be certified and follow specific practices for handling, labeling, and disposing of ODS. Similar requirements apply to other types of equipment, including air-conditioning systems for motor vehicles and halon-based fire suppression systems.

Funding for Developing Countries

The Montreal Protocol includes special provisions for so-called Article 5 countries (developing countries). These are countries that annually produce and consume less than 0.66 of a pound (0.3 kg) per capita of ODS. The London Amendment established the Multilateral Fund for the Implementation of the Montreal Protocol. Industrial countries agreed to set up the fund to reimburse developing countries that complied with the protocol for "all agreed incremental costs," meaning all additional costs above any they would have expected to incur had they developed their infrastructure in the absence of the protocol.

The Multilateral Fund is a financial resource for developing countries that are party to the agreement. The UNEP explains in "OzonAction: About Montreal Protocol" (2018, http://web.unep.org/ozonaction/who-we-are/about-montreal-protocol) that "the Multilateral Fund has supported over 8,100 projects including industrial conversion, technical assistance, training and capacity building worth over US$3.3 billion." In *2017 Consolidated Project Completion Report* (July 3–7, 2017, http://www.multilateralfund.org/79/English/1/7915.docx), the UNEP briefly describes some of the funded projects in various countries in 2017. For example, a project in Mozambique was devoted to eliminating the use of methyl bromide for soil fumigation.

Phasing Out HCFCs

In 2007 the parties to the Montreal Protocol agreed to certain changes to their commitments to phase out HCFCs. According to the UNEP, in "2007 Montreal Adjustment on Production and Consumption of HCFCs" (November 30, 2007, http://ozone.unep.org/Meeting_Documents/mop/19mop/Adjustments_on_HCFCs.pdf), the changes do not affect the final phaseout deadlines shown in Table 4.3, but the intermediate deadlines. For example, developed countries had committed to achieve a 65% reduction in HCFCs by 2010. Instead, these countries agreed to achieve a 75% reduction by 2010. They agreed to a 90% reduction by 2015 and must achieve a 99.5% reduction by 2020. Table 4.4 shows an EPA listing of US milestones for the HCFC phaseout schedule.

Article 5 countries agreed to the following new intermediate HCFC deadlines:

- 2013—a freeze on consumption based on the average of their 2009 and 2010 production and consumption figures
- 2015—10% reduction
- 2020—35% reduction
- 2025—67.5% reduction

Technically, developing countries must achieve a 100% reduction by 2030. However, they are allowed to devote a small amount of HCFCs to servicing refrigeration and air-conditioning equipment until 2040.

PROGRESS AND PROBLEMS

The Montreal Protocol has been hailed as historic—the most ambitious attempt ever to combat environmental degradation on a global scale. It ushered in a new era of environmental diplomacy. Some historians view the signing of the accord as a defining moment, the point at which the definition of international security was expanded to include environmental issues as well as military matters. In addition, an important precedent was established: that science and policy makers had a new relationship. Many observers thought that the decision to take precautionary action in the absence of complete proof of a link between CFCs and ozone depletion was an act of foresight that would now be possible with other issues.

Progress reports published by the UNEP highlight the success of the Montreal Protocol in terms of party (country) compliance and reduced ODS atmospheric levels. Researchers, however, have raised troubling questions about some types of ODS and how they are being controlled by the parties. In addition, black market trade of banned ODS is a vexing and growing problem. (ODS black market trade is discussed later in the chapter.)

Progress

In August 2012 the UNEP released a progress report on the 25th anniversary of the Montreal Protocol—*OzonAction: Protecting Our Atmosphere for Generations to Come: 25 Years of the Montreal Protocol* (http://www.igsd.org/wp-content/uploads/2014/10/OzonActionSpecial Issue2012_Englishcopy.pdf). OzonAction is a UNEP program that helps developing countries meet their obligations under the international agreement. The UNEP notes that as of 2012, 197 countries had ratified the Montreal Protocol, making it "the world's most widely ratified treaty." The developing countries reportedly met the 2010 deadline to phase out CFCs, halons, and carbon tetrachloride. The UNEP predicts that continued implementation of the Montreal Protocol by all parties will result in a return by "midcentury" to pre-1980 levels of stratospheric ozone.

Table 4.5 shows the progress achieved by the United States at meeting its Montreal Protocol commitments for Class I ODS. Production of all of the chemicals was phased out by the required deadlines. As of January 2018, the United States was still in the process of phasing out its HCFC production and importation in accordance with the schedule shown in Table 4.4.

Monitoring Data and Modeling Results

Article 6 of the Montreal Protocol requires that the ratifying countries base their decision-making on scientific information assessed and presented by an international panel of ozone experts. This panel includes the WMO, the UNEP, the European Commission, the National Oceanic and Atmospheric Administration (NOAA), and

TABLE 4.5

US progress at phasing out Class I ozone-depleting substances under the Montreal Protocol

Chemical group	Production phaseout dates	Deadline met
Halons	January 1, 1994	✓
Chlorofluorocarbons (CFCs)	January 1, 1996	✓
Carbon tetrachloride	January 1, 1996	✓
Hydrobromofluorocarbons (HBFCs)	January 1, 1996	✓
Methyl chloroform	January 1, 1996	✓
Chlorobromomethane	August 18, 2003	✓
Methyl bromide	January 1, 2005	✓

SOURCE: "US Production of First-Generation Ozone-Depleting Substances Phased out on Schedule," in *Achievements in Stratospheric Ozone Protection: Progress Report*, US Environmental Protection Agency, April 2007, https://www.epa.gov/sites/production/files/2015-07/documents/achievements_in_stratospheric_ozone_protection.pdf (accessed November 10, 2017)

NASA. As of January 2018, the most recent comprehensive UNEP assessment was published in December 2014—*Scientific Assessment of Ozone Depletion: 2014* (https://www.esrl.noaa.gov/csd/assessments/ozone/2014/chapters/2014OzoneAssessment.pdf). This is the 10th scientific assessment of the world's ozone condition and is based on analysis of data collected from satellites, aircraft, balloons, and ground-based instruments and the results of laboratory investigations and computer modeling. The UNEP indicates that as of 2014, most of the ODS controlled under the Montreal Protocol were decreasing "largely as projected." Levels of HCFCs and halon-1301 were still increasing. The UNEP notes that carbon tetrachloride was more abundant in the atmosphere than expected due to "unknown or unreported sources." The organization projects that full compliance with the Montreal Protocol will allow the ozone layer to recover "over most of the globe." Recovery is expected before "midcentury" over the middle latitudes and the Arctic region, and "somewhat later" over Antarctica.

In "Quantifying the Ozone and Ultraviolet Benefits Already Achieved by the Montreal Protocol" (*Nature Communications*, vol. 6, May 26, 2015), Martyn P. Chipperfield et al. report on modeling results that predict how the ozone layer would have been affected if the Montreal Protocol had not been implemented. The researchers conclude that the Antarctic ozone hole would have increased in size by 40% by 2013. Ozone layer losses over the middle latitudes of the Northern Hemisphere would have more than doubled. Chipperfield et al. note that these changes would have resulted in higher rates of skin cancer due to greater atmospheric penetration of UV rays from the sun. They predict that the ozone layer will gradually improve and that the Antarctic ozone hole will disappear sometime around 2050.

NOAA operates the Earth System Research Laboratory (ESRL), which is headquartered in Boulder, Colorado. The

ESRL collects data from its observatories around the world and does research related to global trends in air quality. Historical data on atmospheric concentrations of ODS have been collected at five ESRL observatories:

- Point Barrow, Alaska
- Niwot Ridge, Colorado
- Mauna Loa, Hawaii
- Cape Matatula, American Samoa
- South Pole, Antarctica

ESRL graphs dating back to the 1970s indicate that atmospheric concentrations of CFC-11 peaked during the early 1990s and then began declining. (See Figure 4.2.) CFC-12 concentrations peaked during the first decade of the 21st century and then slowly began decreasing. Concentrations of other ODS have also declined since 1990.

Other monitoring data, however, show troubling trends. Johannes C. Laube et al. report in "Newly Detected Ozone-Depleting Substances in the Atmosphere" (*Nature Geoscience*, vol. 7, no. 4, 2014) measurements for four ODS—CFC-112, CFC-112a, CFC-113a, and HCFC-133a—in the atmosphere. The researchers state, "The reported emissions are clearly contrary to the intentions behind the Montreal Protocol, and raise questions about the sources of these gases." According to Laube et al., emissions of CFC-113a, in particular, have risen sharply since the 1980s.

The Environmental Investigation Agency is a London-based nonprofit organization that focuses on environmental crimes. In November 2014 the agency provided a briefing to international representatives at the 26th Meeting of the Montreal Protocol in Paris. In *New Trends in ODS Smuggling* (https://eia-international.org/wp-content/uploads/EIA-New-Trends-in-ODS-Smuggling-lo-res.pdf), the agency suggests that the rising CFC-113a emissions detected by Laube et al. could be related to feedstock use. CFCs and HCFCs are used as raw materials to manufacture other types of chemicals. In other words, the ODS are converted into non-ODS chemicals. This ODS usage is not restricted by the Montreal Protocol, because it has long been assumed that the emissions associated with feedstock conversion are minimal.

In 2017 there was further troubling news about CFC-113a. Karina E. Adcock et al. report in *Continued Increase of CFC-113a (CCl₃CF₃) Mixing Ratios in the Global Atmosphere: Emissions, Occurrence and Potential Sources* (November 10, 2017, https://www.atmos-chem-phys-discuss.net/acp-2017-978/acp-2017-978.pdf) on new data that were collected through February 2017 and state, "CFC-113a is the only known CFC for which abundances are still substantially increasing in the atmosphere." The researchers further note, "The sources of CFC-113a are still unclear, but we present evidence that indicates large

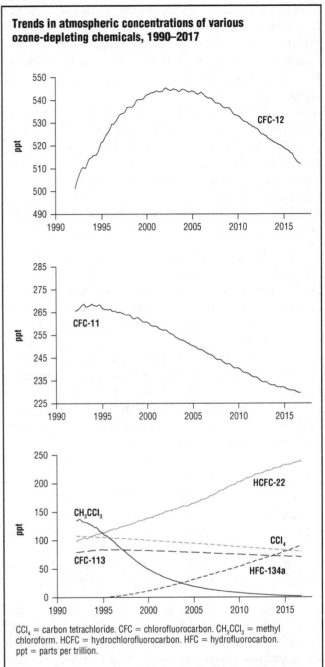

FIGURE 4.2

Trends in atmospheric concentrations of various ozone-depleting chemicals, 1990–2017

CCl₄ = carbon tetrachloride. CFC = chlorofluorocarbon. CH₃CCl₃ = methyl chloroform. HCFC = hydrochlorofluorocarbon. HFC = hydrofluorocarbon. ppt = parts per trillion.

SOURCE: "Trends of the CFCs, HCFCs, Halons, Chlorinated Solvents, and Effective Equivalent Chlorine (EECl) from the GMD Halocarbon Flask and in Situ Network," in *Halocarbons and Other Atmospheric Trace Gases*, US Department of Commerce, National Oceanic and Atmospheric Administration, Earth System Research Laboratory, 2017, https://www.esrl.noaa.gov/gmd/hats/graphs/totalCl_NOAA-HATS.pdf (accessed November 10, 2017)

emissions in East Asia, most likely due to its use as a chemical involved in the production of hydrofluorocarbons."

The Environmental Investigation Agency has a similar concern about carbon tetrachloride (CCl₄), another feedstock. As shown in Figure 4.2, atmospheric concentrations of this chemical have declined since the 1990s. The decrease, however, has not been as pronounced as expected. According to NASA, in "Ozone-Depleting Compound Persists, NASA Research Shows" (August 20, 2014, https://www.nasa.gov/press/2014/august/ozone-depleting-compound-persists-nasa-research-shows/#.Vjnh wberSUn), "For almost a decade, scientists have debated why the observed levels of CCl_4 in the atmosphere have declined slower than expectations, which are based on what is known about how the compound is destroyed by solar radiation and other natural processes." In *New Trends in ODS Smuggling*, the Environmental Investigation Agency expresses deep concern about these levels, noting, "They are an indication that either significant quantities of [carbon tetrachloride] are being emitted during their use as feedstocks or that significant non-feedstock production and use is occurring despite the Montreal Protocol ban."

Ryan Hossaini et al. report in "The Increasing Threat to Stratospheric Ozone from Dichloromethane" (June 27, 2017, https://www.nature.com/articles/ncomms15962.epdf) on another troubling chemical: dichloromethane, which is also called methylene chloride. It is a chlorine-containing chemical commonly used in paint strippers and industrial solvents and is not controlled under the Montreal Protocol. Data reveal rising atmospheric concentrations of the chemical since the early years of the first decade of the 21st century. The researchers warn, "If these increases continue into the future, the return of Antarctic ozone to pre-1980 levels could be substantially delayed."

Illegal Trade Problems

The black market trading of ODS became a significant challenge after implementation of the Montreal Protocol. As shown in Table 4.3, developing countries were not required to phase out many ODS, particularly CFCs, until 2010 and after. Thus, production continued in these countries well into the first decade of the 21st century.

According to Joydeep Gupta, in "India Largest Source of Smuggled CFCs: UN Official" (Hindustan Times.com, April 26, 2008), a UNEP regional coordinator in Southeast Asia reported in 2008 that India was the largest source of black market ODS. In 2006 the UNEP began Project Skyhole Patching, a collaboration with customs officers throughout the Asia Pacific region to stem the illegal trade in ODS and hazardous waste. The article "Customs Seize over 108 Tonnes of Refrigerant" (ACR-News.com, December 2, 2010) indicates that Project Skyhole Patching I, which ran through 2009, resulted in the seizure of more than 771.6 tons (700 t) of ODS. Project Skyhole Patching II was conducted in 2010 and reaped more than 119 tons (108 t) of ODS.

In *New Trends in ODS Smuggling*, the Environmental Investigation Agency describes major ODS smuggling cases between 2010 and 2014 involving China, India, the Philippines, Russia, and Spain. In many of the cases the product seized was believed to be of Chinese origin and

had been mislabeled in an attempt to deceive customs inspectors. For example, in 2010 Russian authorities discovered 43 tons (39 t) of CFCs that had been mislabeled as "recycled." The Environmental Investigation Agency indicates that the shipment actually contained "virgin" CFCs of Chinese origin. The agency states it "is concerned that CFCs were still available for export from China, given that production was phased out in 2007. Whether the source was stockpiled material or unlicensed production is unknown."

The Environmental Investigation Agency notes in "Update on the Illegal Trade in Ozone-Depleting Substances" (July 2016, https://eia-international.org/report/update-illegal-trade-ozone-depleting-substances) that it is also concerned about HCFCs. As shown in Table 4.3, they are to be phased out by 2030 by developed countries and by 2040 by developing countries. The agency explains, "Global demand for refrigerants has risen significantly in recent years, with peak hydrochlorofluorocarbon (HCFC) consumption approximately three times greater than CFC peak production. The scale of illegal HCFC trade could potentially be larger than that previously seen with CFCs."

THE US BLACK MARKET. In 1996 the ban on CFCs was implemented in the developed countries, including the United States. The CFC called Freon was widely used in automobile air conditioners before that time. After the ban went into effect, there were still millions of American cars that used Freon as a refrigerant. Although alternative refrigerants were available, they were more expensive than Freon. The result was a black market for the product. This market expanded in the United States during the first decade of the 21st century with the boom in the illegal production of methamphetamine at so-called meth labs. Freon is commonly used in meth labs as part of the production process.

Several US government agencies—the EPA, the US Customs and Border Protection, the US Departments of Commerce and Justice, and the Internal Revenue Service (IRS)—began intensive antismuggling efforts. The IRS became involved because of the Revenue Reconciliation Act of 1989, which imposes an excise tax on most US manufacturers, producers, and importers of ODS. In "Enforcement Actions under Title VI of the Clean Air Act" (November 20, 2017, https://www.epa.gov/ozone-layer-protection/enforcement-actions-under-title-vi-clean-air-act), the EPA documents major compliance and enforcement actions related to ODS under Title VI of the Clean Air Act. Most of the cases involved alleged rules violations by companies, such as releasing ODS because of failure to repair faulty refrigeration systems. As of November 2017, the most recent completed case involving smuggling occurred in 2013, when a supplier and distributor of air-conditioning and heating products pleaded guilty to receiving and selling HCFC-22 that had been smuggled into the United States. The company was sentenced to three years of probation and fined $100,000.

SUBSTITUTES AND NEW TECHNOLOGIES

As pressure increased to discontinue the use of CFCs and halons, substitute chemicals and technologies began being developed. The EPA's Significant New Alternative Policy (SNAP) program evaluates these alternatives under the Clean Air Act and determines their acceptability for use. As of June 2017, the SNAP program (https://www.epa.gov/snap/overview-snap) listed dozens of approved substitute chemicals and technologies for use in various applications, including refrigeration and air-conditioning, foam blowing, and fire suppression and protection.

A class of compounds called hydrofluorocarbons (HFCs) became one of the most popular substitutes for ODS. HFCs do not contain chlorine, which is a potent ozone destroyer. HFCs are also relatively short lived in the atmosphere—most survive intact for less than 12 years. As a result, they have ODP values of zero. Although HFCs do not deplete the earth's protective ozone layer, they are believed to be potent greenhouse gases that contribute to global warming and climate change. (See Table 4.6.) A different class of chemicals called hydrocarbons are slowly gaining favor as substitutes for ODS and HFCs in some applications. In 2011

TABLE 4.6

Uses for common ozone-depleting substances and their alternatives

Substance	Uses
Chlorofluorocarbons (CFCs)	Refrigerants, cleaning solvents, aerosol propellants, and blowing agents for plastic foam manufacture.
Halons	Fire extinguishers/fire suppression systems, explosion protection.
Carbon tetrachloride (CCl$_4$)	Production of CFCs (feedstock), solvent/diluents, fire extinguishers.
Methyl chloroform (CHCl$_3$)	Industrial solvent for cleaning, inks, correction fluid.
Methyl bromide (CH$_3$Br)	Fumigant used to control soil-borne pests and diseases in crops prior to planting and in commodities such as stored grains. Fumigants are substances that give off fumes; they are often used as disinfectants or to kill pests.
Hydrochlorofluorocarbons (HCFCs)	Transitional CFC replacements used as refrigerants, solvents, blowing agents for plastic foam manufacture, and fire extinguishers. HCFCs deplete stratospheric ozone, but to a much lesser extent than CFCs; however, they are greenhouse gases.
Hydrofluorocarbons (HFCs)	CFC replacements used as refrigerants, aerosol propellants, solvents, and fire extinguishers. HFCs do not deplete stratospheric ozone, but they are greenhouse gases.

Note: This is a limited list and does not represent all of the alternatives approved by EPA's Significant New Alternatives Policy (SNAP) program.

SOURCE: Adapted from "Common Ozone-Depleting Substances and Some Alternatives," in *Achievements in Stratospheric Ozone Protection: Progress Report*, US Environmental Protection Agency, April 2007, https://www.epa.gov/sites/production/files/2015-07/documents/achievements_in_stratospheric_ozone_protection.pdf (accessed November 10, 2017)

the EPA approved the use of three hydrocarbon alternatives: propane, isobutane, and R-441A (a hydrocarbon blend) as refrigerants. Leon Walker indicates in "EPA Approves Three Alternative Refrigerants to Replace HFCs" (EnvironmentalLeader.com, December 15, 2011) that hydrocarbons are "substances with zero ozone depletion potential, and also [have] a low global warming potential."

THE CLIMATE CHANGE CONNECTION

As is described in Chapter 3, the earth's climate has been warming in recent decades and is expected to continue to do so. This warming is widely blamed on a buildup in the atmosphere of anthropogenic emissions of greenhouse gases, such as carbon dioxide. Many ODS are also considered to be greenhouse gases. Table 4.2 shows the global warming potential (GWP) of some common ODS compared with a GWP value of 1 for carbon dioxide. Most of the ODS have GWP values that are several hundreds to several thousand times that of carbon dioxide.

Scientists note that the phaseout of ODS under the Montreal Protocol provides a dual benefit by reducing damage to the earth's ozone layer and decreasing greenhouse gas emissions. These positive effects are expected to continue as the full phaseout of HCFCs unfolds through 2040. As a result, attention has turned to the impact of HFCs on global warming and climate change. Since the 1990s the use of HFCs has increased dramatically. Table 3.1 in Chapter 3 lists emissions of HFCs for various years between 1990 and 2015. NOAA reports that atmospheric levels of some HFCs also surged during this period. (See Figure 4.2 and Figure 4.3.)

Under the administration of President Barack Obama (1961–), the EPA touted the "climate-friendly" attributes of hydrocarbon substitutes for HFCs. Concurrently, the agency prohibited the use of many HFCs that had formerly been accepted. For example, in July 2015 the EPA (https://www.epa.gov/sites/production/files/2016-12/documents/snap_regulatory_factsheet_july20_2015.pdf) issued a final rule (later revised in December 2016) that banned the use of dozens of HFCs across multiple applications and industry sectors. The bans have a phaseout schedule with compliance dates ranging from 2016 to 2026.

The Kigali Amendment to the Montreal Protocol

In October 2016 a meeting of the parties to the Montreal Protocol was held in Kigali, Rwanda. The delegates hashed out a new amendment that specifically targets HFCs. In "The Kigali Amendment to the Montreal Protocol: Another Global Commitment to Stop Climate Change" (December 8, 2016, https://www.unenvironment.org/news-and-stories/news/kigali-amendment-montreal-protocol-another-global-commitment-stop-climate), the United Nations explains that "HFCs are man-made chemicals that are primarily used in air conditioning, refrigeration and

FIGURE 4.3

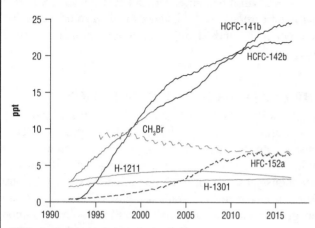

Trends in atmospheric concentrations of various ozone-depleting chemicals, 1990–2017

CH_3Br = methyl bromide (or bromomethane).
H-1211 = Halon 1211.
H-1301 = Halon 1301.
HCFC = hydrochlorofluorocarbon.
ppt = parts per trillion.

SOURCE: "Trends of the CFCs, HCFCs, Halons, Chlorinated Solvents, and Effective Equivalent Chlorine (EECl) from the GMD Halocarbon Flask and in Situ Network," in *Halocarbons and Other Atmospheric Trace Gases*, US Department of Commerce, National Oceanic and Atmospheric Administration, Earth System Research Laboratory, 2017, https://www.esrl.noaa.gov/gmd/hats/graphs/totalCl_NOAA-HATS.pdf (accessed November 10, 2017)

foam insulation, and are powerful greenhouse gases that can be thousands of times more potent than carbon dioxide in contributing to climate change."

The Kigali Amendment (http://ozone.unep.org/en/handbook-montreal-protocol-substances-deplete-ozone-layer/41453) includes a schedule for countries to freeze or reduce their production and consumption of HFCs. The delegates from the United States and the European Union agreed to reduce their production and consumption beginning in 2019. The delegates of many other countries agreed to freeze their usage of HFCs by various dates during the 2020s. The amendment was scheduled to go into effect after at least 20 countries ratified it. This milestone was reached in November 2017. As such, the Kigali Amendment is slated to go into effect in 2019.

According to the UNEP (http://ozone.unep.org/en/treaties-and-decisions), as of January 2018, 24 countries had ratified the Kigali Amendment. The United States was not among them. Ratification of a treaty by the United States requires the consent of the US Senate. As Chapter 3 explains, President Donald Trump (1946–) is staunchly opposed to US participation in international agreements that are devoted to combating climate change. Thus, it is uncertain if he will submit the Kigali Amendment to the Senate for its consideration. Approval by the Senate is also highly uncertain given the politicized nature of the climate change debate.

CHAPTER 5

ACID RAIN

WHAT IS ACID RAIN?

Acid rain is the common name for acidic deposits that fall to the earth from the atmosphere. The term was coined in 1872 by the Scottish chemist Robert Angus Smith (1817–1884) to describe the acidic precipitation in Manchester, England. In the 21st century scientists study both wet and dry acidic deposits. Although there are natural sources of acid in the atmosphere, acid rain is primarily caused by emissions from electric utilities that burn fossil fuels, especially coal. The main culprits are sulfur dioxide (SO_2) and nitrogen oxides (NO_x). As is noted in Chapter 2, the chemical formula NO_x is used to collectively refer to nitrogen oxide, nitrogen dioxide, and other nitrogen oxides. Sulfur dioxide and NO_x are converted to sulfuric acid and nitric acid, respectively, in the atmosphere and can be carried by the winds for many miles from where the original emissions took place. (See Figure 5.1.)

Volatile organic compounds also contribute to acid rain. These are carbon-containing chemicals that easily become vapors or gases. Sources of volatile organic compounds include paint thinners, degreasers, and other solvents and burning fuels such as coal, gasoline, natural gas, and wood. It should be noted that acid rain is an environmental problem in developed countries in North America and Europe and is becoming increasingly troublesome in developing countries that are undergoing heavy industrialization, such as China and India.

Wet deposition occurs when acid falls in precipitation (rain, snow, or ice). Dry deposition is caused by tiny particles (or particulates) in combustion emissions. They may stay dry as they fall or pollute cloud water and precipitation. Moist deposition occurs when the acid is trapped in cloud or fog droplets. This is most common at high altitudes and in coastal areas. Whatever its form, acid rain can create dangerously high levels of acidic impurities in plants, soil, and water.

Measuring Acid Rain

The acidity of any solution is measured on a potential hydrogen (pH) scale numbered from 0 to 14, with a pH value of 7 considered neutral. (See Figure 5.2.) Values higher than 7 are considered more alkaline or basic (the pH of baking soda is 8); values lower than 7 are considered acidic (the pH of lemon juice is 2). The pH scale is a logarithmic measure. This means that every pH change of one is a 10-fold change in acid content. Therefore, a decrease from pH 7 to pH 6 is a 10-fold increase in acidity; a drop from pH 7 to pH 5 is a 100-fold increase in acidity; and a drop from pH 7 to pH 4 is a 1,000-fold increase.

Pure, distilled water has a neutral pH of 7. Normal rainfall has a pH value of about 5 to 6. It is slightly acidic because it accumulates naturally occurring sulfur oxides and nitrogen oxides as it passes through the atmosphere. Acid rain has a pH of less than 5.

SOURCES OF SULFATE AND NITRATE IN THE ATMOSPHERE

Natural Sources

Natural sources of sulfate in the atmosphere include ocean spray, volcanic emissions, and readily oxidized hydrogen sulfide, which is released from the decomposition of organic matter found in the earth. Natural sources of nitrogen or nitrates include nitrogen oxides produced by microorganisms in soils, by lightning during thunderstorms, and by forest fires.

Sources Caused by Human Activity

According to the US Environmental Protection Agency (EPA), in "What Is Acid Rain?" (March 1, 2017, https://www.epa.gov/acidrain/what-acid-rain), the primary anthropogenic (human-related) contributors to acid rain are sulfur dioxide and nitrogen oxides, resulting from the burning of fossil fuels, such as coal, oil, and natural gas.

FIGURE 5.1

Origins of acid rain

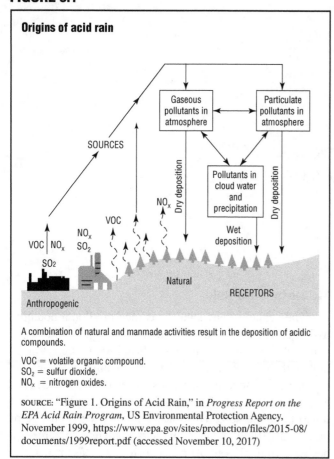

A combination of natural and manmade activities result in the deposition of acidic compounds.

VOC = volatile organic compound.
SO₂ = sulfur dioxide.
NOₓ = nitrogen oxides.

SOURCE: "Figure 1. Origins of Acid Rain," in *Progress Report on the EPA Acid Rain Program*, US Environmental Protection Agency, November 1999, https://www.epa.gov/sites/production/files/2015-08/documents/1999report.pdf (accessed November 10, 2017)

FIGURE 5.2

The potential hydrogen scale

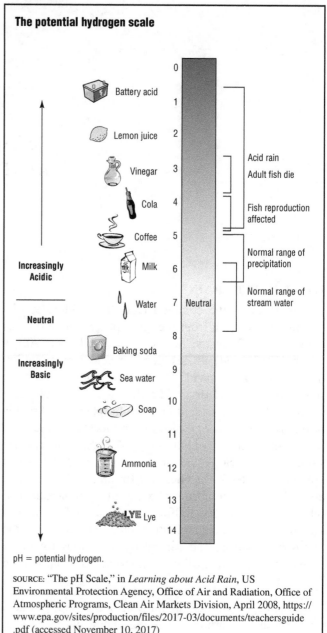

pH = potential hydrogen.

SOURCE: "The pH Scale," in *Learning about Acid Rain*, US Environmental Protection Agency, Office of Air and Radiation, Office of Atmospheric Programs, Clean Air Markets Division, April 2008, https://www.epa.gov/sites/production/files/2017-03/documents/teachersguide.pdf (accessed November 10, 2017)

As is described in Chapter 2, stationary fuel combustion (as in fossil-fueled electric utilities) accounted for 73% of sulfur dioxide emissions in 2016. Industrial and other processes contributed another 20%. The three largest sources of nitrogen oxides emissions in 2016 were highway vehicles (34%), stationary fuel combustion (26%), and off-highway vehicles (23%).

NATURAL FACTORS THAT AFFECT ACID RAIN DEPOSITION

Major natural factors that contribute to the impact of acid rain on an area include air movement, climate, topography, and geology. Transport systems—primarily the movement of air—distribute acid emissions in definite patterns around the planet. The movement of air masses transports emitted pollutants many miles, during which the pollutants are transformed into sulfuric and nitric acid by mixing with clouds of water vapor.

In drier climates, such as those of the western United States, windblown alkaline dust moves more freely through the air and tends to neutralize atmospheric acidity. The effects of acid rain can be greatly reduced by the presence of basic (also called alkali) substances. Sodium, potassium, and calcium are examples of basic chemicals. When a basic and an acid chemical come into contact, they react chemically and neutralize each other. By contrast, in more humid climates where there is less dust, such as along the Eastern Seaboard, precipitation is more acidic.

Areas that are most sensitive to acid rain contain hard, crystalline bedrock and thin surface soils. When no alkaline-buffering particles are in the soil, runoff from rainfall directly affects surface waters, such as mountain streams. By contrast, a thick soil covering or soil with a high buffering capacity, such as flat land, neutralizes acid rain better. Lakes tend to be most susceptible to acid rain because of low alkaline content in lake beds. A lake's depth, its watershed (the area draining into the lake), and the amount of time the water has been in the lake are also factors.

EFFECTS OF ACID RAIN ON THE ENVIRONMENT

In nature the combination of rain and oxides is part of a natural balance that nourishes plants and aquatic life. However, when the balance is upset by acid rain, the effects on the environment can be harmful and destructive. (See Table 5.1.)

Aquatic Systems

Although pH levels vary considerably from one body of water to another, a typical pH range for the lakes, rivers, and streams in the United States is 6 to 8. Low pH levels kill fish, their eggs, and fish food organisms. The degree of damage depends on several factors, one of which is the buffering capacity of the watershed soil—the higher the alkalinity, the more slowly the lakes and streams acidify. The exposure of fish to acidified freshwater lakes and streams has been intensely studied since the 1970s. Scientists distinguish between sudden shocks and chronic (long-term) exposure to low pH levels.

Sudden, short-term shifts in pH levels result from snowmelts, which release acidic materials that accumulated during the winter, or from sudden rainstorms that can wash residual acid into lakes and streams. The resulting acid shock can be devastating to fish and their ecosystems. Figure 5.3 shows the pH tolerance of various aquatic creatures. The shaded boxes indicate safe pH levels for each species. Frogs, for instance, have a high tolerance for acidity and can survive in water with a pH level as low as 4. Clams and snails are much more sensitive and must have pH levels above 5.5 to survive.

Because many species of fish hatch in the spring, even mild increases in acidity can harm or kill the new life. Temporary increases in acidity also affect insects and other invertebrates, such as snails and crayfish, on which the fish feed. Gradual decreases of pH levels over time affect fish reproduction and spawning. In addition, excessive acid levels in female fish cause low amounts of calcium, thereby preventing the production of eggs. Even if eggs are produced, their development is often abnormal. Increased acidity can also cause the release of aluminum and manganese particles that are stored in a lake or river bottom. High concentrations of these metals are toxic to fish.

Soil and Vegetation

Acid rain is believed to harm vegetation by changing soil chemistry. Soils exposed to acid rain can gradually lose valuable nutrients, such as calcium and magnesium, and become too concentrated with dissolved inorganic aluminum, which is toxic to vegetation. Long-term changes in soil chemistry may have already affected sensitive soils, particularly in forests. Nutrient-poor trees are more vulnerable to climatic extremes, pest invasion, and the effects of other air pollutants, such as ozone, a toxic gas.

The effect of acid rain on trees is influenced by many factors. Some trees adapt to environmental stress better than others; the type of tree, its height, and its leaf structure (deciduous or evergreen) influence how well it will adapt to acid rain. Scientists believe acid rain directly harms trees by leaching calcium from their foliage and indirectly harms them by lowering their tolerance to other stresses.

Birds

Increased freshwater acidity harms some species of migratory birds. Experts believe the dramatic decline of the North American black duck population since the

TABLE 5.1

Effects of acid rain on human health and selected ecosystems and anticipated recovery benefits

Human health and ecosystem	Effects	Recovery benefits
Human health	In the atmosphere, sulfur dioxide and nitrogen oxides become sulfate and nitrate aerosols, which increase morbidity and mortality from lung disorders, such as asthma and bronchitis, and impacts to the cardiovascular system.	Decrease emergency room visits, hospital admissions, and deaths.
Surface waters	Acidic surface waters decrease the survivability of animal life in lakes and streams and in the more severe instances eliminate some or all types of fish and other organisms.	Reduce the acidic levels of surface waters and restore animal life to the more severely damaged lakes and streams.
Forests	Acid deposition contributes to forest degradation by impairing trees' growth and increasing their susceptibility to winter injury, insect infestation, and drought. It also causes leaching and depletion of natural nutrients in forest soil.	Reduce stress on trees, thereby reducing the effects of winter injury, insect infestation, and drought, and reduce the leaching of soil nutrients, thereby improving overall forest health.
Materials	Acid deposition contributes to the corrosion and deterioration of buildings, cultural objects, and cars, which decreases their value and increases costs of correcting and repairing damage.	Reduce the damage to buildings, cultural objects, and cars, and reduce the costs of correcting and repairing future damage.
Visibility	In the atmosphere, sulfur dioxide and nitrogen oxides form sulfate and nitrate particles, which impair visibility and affect the enjoyment of national parks and other scenic views.	Extend the distance and increase the clarity at which scenery can be viewed, thus reducing limited and hazy scenes and increasing the enjoyment of national parks and other vistas.

SOURCE: "Appendix I. Effect of Acid Rain on Human Health and Selected Ecosystems and Anticipated Recovery Benefits," in *Acid Rain: Emissions Trends and Effects in the Eastern United States*, US General Accounting Office, March 2000, http://www.gao.gov/archive/2000/rc00047.pdf (accessed November 10, 2017)

FIGURE 5.3

Tolerance of various aquatic species to low potential hydrogen levels

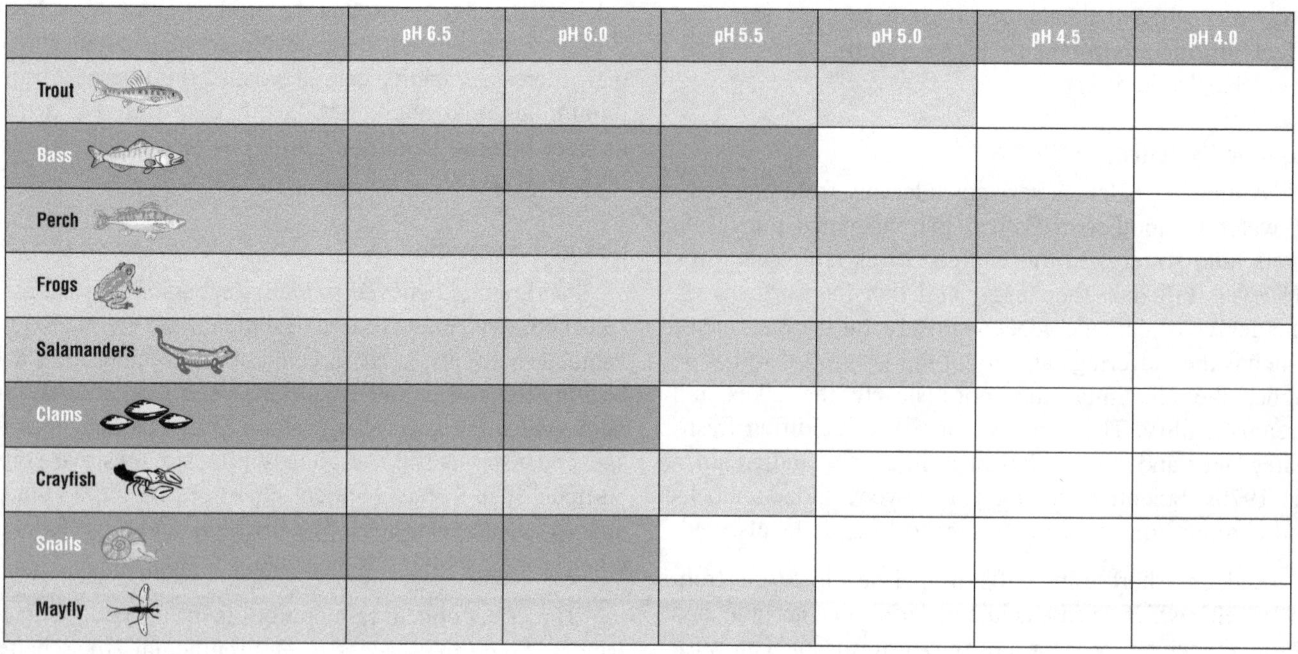

	pH 6.5	pH 6.0	pH 5.5	pH 5.0	pH 4.5	pH 4.0
Trout	■	■	■	■		
Bass	■	■	■			
Perch	■	■	■	■	■	
Frogs	■	■	■	■	■	■
Salamanders	■	■	■	■	■	■
Clams	■	■	■			
Crayfish	■	■	■	■		
Snails	■	■	■			
Mayfly	■	■	■	■	■	■

pH = potential hydrogen.

SOURCE: "pH Tolerance Chart on Aquatic Life," in *Learning about Acid Rain*, US Environmental Protection Agency, Office of Air and Radiation, Office of Atmospheric Programs, Clean Air Markets Division, April 2008, https://www3.epa.gov/acidrain/education/teachersguide.pdf (accessed November 17, 2017)

1950s is because of decreased food supplies in acidified wetlands. Acid rain leaches calcium out of the soil and robs snails of the calcium they need to form shells. Because some species of songbirds get most of their calcium from the shells of snails, the birds are also perishing. The eggs they lay are defective—thin and fragile. The chicks either do not hatch or have bone malformations and die.

Materials

Acid rain can also be harmful to materials, such as building stones, marble statues, metals, and paints. Historical monuments and buildings composed of these materials in the eastern United States have been affected by acid rain. For example, in "Acid Rain's Slow Dissolve" (April 10, 2015, https://www.nps.gov/nama/blogs/acid-rains-slow-dissolve.htm), Megan Nortrup of the US National Park Service describes the damage done to monuments in the District of Columbia, such as the Jefferson Memorial (which is made of marble) and the Ulysses S. Grant Memorial (which is made of bronze). In both cases acid rain has caused accelerated deterioration of these monuments.

Human Health

Acid rain has several direct and indirect effects on humans. Particulates are extremely small pollutant particles that can threaten human health. Particulates related to acid rain include fine particles of sulfur oxides and nitrates. These particles can travel long distances and, when inhaled, penetrate deep into the lungs. Acid rain and the pollutants that cause it can lead to the development of bronchitis and asthma in children. Acid rain is also believed to be responsible for increasing health risks for those with asthma, chronic bronchitis, and emphysema; pregnant women; and those with histories of heart disease.

THE POLITICS OF ACID RAIN

Scientific research on acid rain was sporadic and largely focused on local problems until the late 1960s, when Scandinavian scientists began more systematic studies. Acid precipitation in North America was not identified until 1972, when scientists found that precipitation was acidic in eastern North America, especially in eastern and northeastern Canada. In 1975 the First International Symposium on Acid Precipitation and the Forest Ecosystem convened in Columbus, Ohio, to define the acid rain problem. Scientists used the meeting to propose a precipitation-monitoring network in the United States that would cooperate with the European and Scandinavian networks and set up protocols for collecting and testing precipitation.

In 1977 the Council on Environmental Quality was asked to develop a national acid rain research program. Several scientists drafted a report that eventually became the basis for the National Acid Precipitation Assessment Program. This initiative eventually translated into legislative action with the Energy Security Act of 1980. Title VII (Acid Precipitation Act of 1980) of the act produced a formal proposal that created the program and authorized federally financed support.

The first international treaty that aimed to limit air pollution was the United Nations Economic Commission for Europe (UNECE) Convention on Long-Range Transboundary Air Pollution, which went into effect in 1983. It was ratified (formally approved into law) by 38 of the 54 UNECE members, which included not only European countries but also Canada and the United States. The treaty targeted sulfur emissions, requiring that countries reduce emissions 30% from 1980 levels—the so-called Thirty Percent Club.

The early acid rain debate centered almost exclusively on the eastern United States and Canada. The controversy was often defined as a problem of property rights. The highly valued production of electricity in coal-fired utilities in the Ohio River valley caused acid rain to fall on land in the northeastern United States and eastern Canada. An important part of the acid rain controversy during the 1980s was the adversarial relationship between US and Canadian government officials over emissions controls of sulfur dioxide and nitrogen dioxide. More of these pollutants crossed the border into Canada than the reverse. Canadian officials very quickly came to a consensus over the need for more stringent controls, whereas this consensus was lacking among US officials.

Throughout the 1980s the major lawsuits involving acid rain all came from eastern states, and the states that passed their own acid rain legislation were those in the eastern part of the United States.

Legislative attempts to restrict emissions of pollutants were often defeated after strong lobbying by the coal industry and utility companies. These industries advocated further research on pollution control technology rather than placing restrictions on utility company emissions.

ACID RAIN CONTROL MEASURES

Congress created the Acid Rain Program (ARP) under Title IV (Acid Deposition Control) of the Clean Air Act Amendments of 1990. The goal of the program is to reduce annual emissions of sulfur dioxide and nitrogen oxide from electric power plants nationwide. The program set a permanent cap on the total amount of sulfur dioxide that could be emitted by these power plants. According to the EPA, in *2015 Program Progress—Cross-State Air Pollution Rule and Acid Rain Program*

(August 2017, https://www3.epa.gov/airmarkets/prog ress/reports/pdfs/2015_full_report.pdf), this cap was set for 2010 at 8.95 million tons (8.1 million t), which is approximately half the amount of sulfur dioxide emitted by these plants in 1980. The program also established nitrogen oxide emissions limitations for certain coal-fired electric utility plants.

As is described in Chapter 2, in 2005 the EPA issued the Clean Air Interstate Rule to address problems with cross-border contaminants, such as particulate matter, ground-level ozone, and acid rain. The rule established permanent caps on emissions of sulfur dioxide and NO_x in more than two dozen eastern states. The Clean Air Interstate Rule underwent numerous legal challenges but remained in effect as its proposed replacement—the Cross-State Air Pollution Rule (CSAPR)—was also challenged in court. In April 2014 the US Supreme Court ruled in *Environmental Protection Agency v. EME Homer City Generation* (No. 12-1182) that the EPA could implement the CSAPR. The first phase of the rule went into effect in January 2015, and the second phase began in January 2017.

Table 2.4 in Chapter 2 lists the states that are affected by the CSAPR. Many of them must meet annual limits on emissions of sulfur dioxide and NO_x. In addition, most states must reduce their NO_x emissions during the "ozone season," the warm summer months when ground-level ozone concentrations are at their highest. Nitrogen oxides are an ozone precursor, meaning that their presence leads to the formation of ozone. The EPA defines the ozone season as May 1 to September 30.

The EPA notes in *2015 Program Progress—Cross-State Air Pollution Rule and Acid Rain Program* that the two rules (the CSAPR and the ARP) covered the following electricity generating units (EGUs) in 2015:

- ARP sulfur dioxide program—3,520 EGUs

- ARP nitrogen oxides program—795 EGUs

- CSAPR sulfur dioxide program—2,820 EGUs; most (79%) of them were also covered by the ARP

- CSAPR nitrogen oxides annual program—2,820 EGUs; most (79%) of them were also covered by the ARP

- CSAPR nitrogen oxides ozone season program—3,228 EGUs; most (79%) of them were also covered by the ARP

It should be noted that there is significant overlap between the ARP and the CSAPR, with many units covered by both programs. Table 5.2 provides a breakdown by fuel type of the affected units in the programs. The vast majority of the units rely on coal or natural gas as their fuel type.

Both the ARP and the CSAPR were designed as cap-and-trade systems that feature overall caps on emissions for an entire industry (or group of industries). Affected utilities or industrial sources have some flexibility in choosing how to achieve emissions reductions. For example, they can switch to low-sulfur coal, install pollution control devices called scrubbers, or shut down older, less-efficient plants. In "Clean Air Markets—Allowance Markets" (March 2, 2017, https://www.epa.gov/airmarkets/clean-air-markets-allowance-markets), the EPA explains that it allocates allowances to the utilities or industrial sources in the programs. Each allowance allows a source to emit 1 ton (0.9 t) of emissions during a specified compliance period. Sources that reduce their emissions below the required caps can sell their extra allowances to other sources, trade them, or "bank" them to use in future years. Table 5.3 shows the allowance reconciliation summary for 2015 for the ARP sulfur dioxide program. In total, nearly 36 million allowances were held that year, and around 2.2 million were deducted to achieve acid rain compliance. This left 33.7 million banked allowances.

As shown in Table 5.4, emissions of sulfur dioxide from all covered units under the ARP and the CSAPR dropped from 11.2 million tons (10.2 million t) in 2000 to 2.2 million tons (2 million t) in 2015, an 80% decrease. The units easily achieved the original goal of the ARP to reduce emissions to less than 8.95 million tons (8.1 million t) by 2010. The EPA indicates in *2015 Program Progress—Cross-State Air Pollution Rule and Acid Rain Program* that the 2015 emissions were below the target goal of 3.5 million tons (3.2 million t).

Table 5.5 provides a summary of trends for annual NO_x emissions. They declined 73%, from 5.1 million tons (4.6 million t) in 2000 to 1.4 million tons (1.3 million t) in 2015. According to the EPA, the 2015 emissions were below the target goal of 1.3 million tons (1.2 million t).

The EPA notes that NO_x emissions covered by the seasonal programs declined 70% between 2000 and 2015. The amount emitted in 2015 was 450,000 tons (408,233 t), which was below the target goal of 628,392 tons (570,068 t).

ARE US ECOSYSTEMS RECOVERING?

As shown in Figure 2.8 and Figure 2.4 in Chapter 2, atmospheric levels of sulfur dioxide and nitrogen dioxide averaged nationwide between 1990 and 2016 were below

TABLE 5.2

Number of electricity-generating units affected by the Acid Rain Program and the Cross-State Air Pollution Rule, 2015

Fuel	ARP NO_x	ARP SO_2	CSAPR SO_2 and annual NO_x	CSAPR ozone season NO_x
Coal	760	855	710	706
Gas	31	2,494	1,779	2,135
Oil	0	134	287	339
Other	4	28	37	40
Unclassified	0	9	7	8
Total units	**795**	**3,520**	**2,820**	**3,228**

Notes: "Unclassified" units have not submitted a fuel type in their monitoring plan and did not report emissions.
"Other" fuel refers to units that burn waste, wood, petroleum coke, tire-derived fuel, etc.
ARP = Acid Rain Program.
CSAPR = Cross-state Air Pollution Rule.
NO_x = nitrous oxides.
SO_2 = sulfur dioxide.

SOURCE: "Figure 2. Affected Units in CSAPR and ARP Programs, 2015," in *2015 Program Progress: Cross-State Air Pollution Rule and Acid Rain Program*, US Environmental Protection Agency, 2017, https://www3.epa.gov/airmarkets/progress/reports/pdfs/2015_-full_report.pdf (accessed November 8, 2017)

TABLE 5.3

Acid Rain Program SO_2 allowances, 2015

Total allowances held (1995–2015 vintage)	35,892,022	Held by affected facility accounts	23,510,854
		Held by other accounts (general and non-affected facility accounts)	12,381,168
Allowances deducted for acid rain compliance	2,190,248		
Penalty allowance deductions	0		
Banked allowances	33,701,774	Held by affected facility accounts	21,320,606
		Held by other accounts (general and non-affected facility accounts)	12,381,168

ARP SO_2 program compliance results

Reported emissions (tons)	2,189,307
Compliance issues, rounding, and report resubmission adjustments (tons)	941
Emissions not covered by allowances (tons)	0
Total allowances deducted for emissions	**2,190,248**

Notes: Each allowance allows a source to emit 1 ton (0.9t) of emissions during a specific compliance period.
Compliance emissions data may vary from other report sections as a result of variation in rounding conventions, changes due to resubmissions by sources, or allowance compliance issues at certain units.
Reconciliation and compliance data are current as of January 2017 and subsequent adjustments of penalties are not reflected.
SO_2 = sulfur dioxide.

SOURCE: "Figure 1. ARP SO_2 Program Allowance Reconciliation Summary, 2015," in *2015 Program Progress: Cross-State Air Pollution Rule and Acid Rain Program*, US Environmental Protection Agency, 2017, https://www3.epa.gov/airmarkets/progress/reports/pdfs/2015_full_report.pdf (accessed November 8, 2017)

TABLE 5.4

Trends in sulfur dioxide emissions from electricity-generating units affected by the Acid Rain Program and the Cross-State Air Pollution Rule, selected years 2000–15

Primary fuel	SO₂ emissions (thousand tons)				SO₂ rate (lb/mmBtu)				Heat input (billion mmBtu)			
	2000	2005	2010	2015	2000	2005	2010	2015	2000	2005	2010	2015
Coal	10,708	9,835	5,051	2,182	1.04	0.95	0.53	0.30	20.67	20.77	19.04	14.39
Gas	110	96	20	8	0.06	0.04	0.01	0.00	3.93	5.53	7.07	9.75
Oil	383	288	28	11	0.76	0.71	0.19	0.12	1.01	0.81	0.29	0.17
Other	1	4	22	12	0.22	0.27	0.57	0.17	0.01	0.03	0.08	0.14
Total	**11,201**	**10,223**	**5,120**	**2,213**	**0.88**	**0.75**	**0.39**	**0.18**	**25.61**	**27.13**	**26.48**	**24.45**

Notes:
The data shown here reflect totals for those facilities required to comply with each program in each respective year. This means that CSAPR-only SO₂ program facilities are not included in the SO₂ emissions data prior to 2015.
Fuel type represents primary fuel type; units might combust more than one fuel.
Totals may not reflect the sum of individual rows due to rounding.
The emission rate reflects the emissions (pounds) per unit of heat input (mmBtu) for each fuel category. The total SO₂ emission rate in each column of the table is not cumulative and does not equal the arithmetic mean of the four fuel-specific rates. The total for each year indicates the average rate across all units in the program because each facility influences the annual emission rate in proportion to its heat input, and heat input is unevenly distributed across the fuel categories.
Unless otherwise noted, EPA data are current as of January 2017, and may differ from past or future reports as a result of resubmissions by sources and ongoing data quality assurance activities.
lb = pounds.
mmBtu = million British thermal units.
SO₂ = sulfur dioxide.

SOURCE: "Figure 4. CSAPR and ARP SO₂2 Emissions Trends," in *2015 Program Progress: Cross-State Air Pollution Rule and Acid Rain Program*, US Environmental Protection Agency, 2017, https://www3.epa.gov/airmarkets/progress/reports/pdfs/2015_full_report.pdf (accessed November 8, 2017)

TABLE 5.5

Trends in nitrogen oxides emissions from electricity-generating units affected by the Acid Rain Program and the Cross-State Air Pollution Rule, selected years 2000–15

Primary fuel	NOₓ emissions (thousand tons)				NOₓ rate (lb/mmBtu)				Heat input (billion mmBtu)			
	2000	2005	2010	2015	2000	2005	2010	2015	2000	2005	2010	2015
Coal	4,587	3,356	1,896	1,208	0.44	0.32	0.20	0.17	20.67	20.77	19.04	14.39
Gas	357	170	143	146	0.18	0.06	0.04	0.03	3.93	5.53	7.07	9.75
Oil	159	101	19	11	0.32	0.25	0.13	0.13	1.01	0.81	0.29	0.17
Other	2	6	5	7	0.25	0.42	0.13	0.10	0.01	0.03	0.08	0.14
Total	**5,104**	**3,633**	**2,063**	**1,373**	**0.40**	**0.27**	**0.16**	**0.11**	**25.61**	**27.13**	**26.48**	**24.45**

Notes:
The data shown here reflect totals for those facilities required to comply with each program in each respective year. This means that CSAPR-only annual NOₓ program facilities are not included in the NOₓ emissions data prior to 2015.
Fuel type represents primary fuel type; units might combust more than one fuel.
Totals may not reflect the sum of individual rows due to rounding.
The emission rate reflects the emissions (pounds) per unit of heat input (mmBtu) for each fuel category. The total NOₓ emission rate in each column of the table is not cumulative and does not equal the arithmetic mean of the four fuel-specific rates. The total for each year indicates the average rate across all units in the program because each facility influences the annual emission rate in proportion to its heat input, and heat input is unevenly distributed across the fuel categories.
Unless otherwise noted, EPA data are current as of January 2017, and may differ from past or future reports as a result of resubmissions by sources and ongoing data quality assurance activities.
lb = pounds.
mmBtu = million British thermal units.
NOₓ = nitrogen oxides.

SOURCE: "Figure 4. CSAPR and ARP Annual NOₓ Emissions Trends," in *2015 Program Progress: Cross-State Air Pollution Rule and Acid Rain Program*, US Environmental Protection Agency, 2017, https://www3.epa.gov/airmarkets/progress/reports/pdfs/2015_full_report.pdf (accessed November 8, 2017)

the national standards for these pollutants. These trends are also evident on a regional basis. (See Table 5.6.) When comparing the annual average for 2013–15 with the annual average for 1989–91, the mid-Atlantic region, in particular, experienced dramatic decreases in its ambient concentrations of sulfate (down 70%), sulfur dioxide (down 85%), and nitrate (down 52%). The EPA also tracks regional trends in wet and dry deposition of sulfur and nitrogen. (See Table 5.7). All regions had deposition declines between 1989–91 and 2013–15.

Monitoring data clearly indicate decreased emissions, atmospheric concentrations, and deposition related to sulfur dioxide and nitrogen oxide. These improvements have resulted in the recovery of many sensitive aquatic and terrestrial ecosystems. Recovery, however, has been slow in some areas. The EPA reports that ecosystems harmed by acid rain deposition can take a long time to fully recover even after harmful emissions cease. The most chronic aquatic problems can take years to be resolved. Forest health is even slower to improve

TABLE 5.6

Regional trends in air quality, 1989–91 compared with 2013–15

Measurement	Region	Annual average, 1989–1991	Annual average, 2013–2015	Percent change	Number of sites	Statistical significance
Ambient	Mid-Atlantic	6.3	1.9	−70	12	*
particulate	Midwest	5.8	2.0	−66	9	*
sulfate	Northeast	3.4	1.1	−68	4	
concentration (μg/m³)	Southeast	5.5	1.7	−69	8	*
Ambient	Mid-Atlantic	13.0	2.0	−85	12	*
sulfur dioxide	Midwest	11.0	1.0	−83	9	*
concentration	Northeast	5.2	0.7	−87	4	
(μg/m³)	Southeast	5.1	0.7	−86	8	*
Ambient total	Mid-Atlantic	3.3	1.6	−52	12	*
nitrate	Midwest	4.6	2.5	−46	9	*
concentration	Northeast	1.7	0.8	−53	4	
(μg/m³)	Southeast	2.2	1.1	−50	8	*

μg/m³ = micrograms per cubic meter.

*Statistical significance was determined at the 95 percent confidence level (p <0.05) using student's t-test. Changes that are not statistically significant may be unduly influenced by measurements at only a few locations or large variability in measurements.

Notes: Averages are the arithmetic mean of all sites in a region that were present and met the completeness criteria in both averaging periods. Thus, average concentrations for 1989 to 1991 may differ from past reports.

SOURCE: "Figure 2. Regional Changes in Air Quality," in *2015 Program Progress: Cross-State Air Pollution Rule and Acid Rain Program*, US Environmental Protection Agency, 2017, https://www3.epa.gov/airmarkets/progress/reports/pdfs/2015_full_report.pdf (accessed November 8, 2017)

TABLE 5.7

Regional trends in deposition of nitrogen and sulfur, 1989–91 compared with 2013–15

Measurement	Region	Annual average, 1989–1991	Annual average, 2013–2015	Percent change	Number of sites	Statistical significance
Dry inorganic	Mid-Atlantic	2.5	0.9	−64	12	*
nitrogen deposition	Midwest	2.4	1.2	−50	9	*
(kg–N/ha)	Northeast	1.3	0.4	−69	4	
	Southeast	1.7	0.7	−59	8	*
Dry sulfur deposition	Mid-Atlantic	7.0	1.2	−83	12	*
(kg–S/ha)	Midwest	6.6	1.4	−79	9	*
	Northeast	2.6	0.4	−85	4	
	Southeast	3.1	0.6	−81	8	*
Total inorganic	Mid-Atlantic	8.8	3.8	−57	12	*
nitrogen deposition	Midwest	8.6	4.8	−44	9	*
(kg–N/ha)	Northeast	6.6	2.9	−56	4	
	Southeast	6.4	3.1	−52	8	*
Total sulfur deposition	Mid-Atlantic	16.0	4.0	−75	12	*
(kg–S/ha)	Midwest	15.0	5.0	−67	9	*
	Northeast	9.5	2.5	−74	4	
	Southeast	10.4	3.3	−68	8	*
Wet nitrogen	Mid-Atlantic	6.2	3.9	−37	11	*
deposition from	Midwest	5.8	5.3	−9	27	*
inorganic nitrogen	Northeast	5.7	4.0	−30	16	*
(kg–N/ha)	Southeast	4.3	3.5	−19	22	*
Wet sulfur	Mid-Atlantic	9.2	2.7	−71	11	*
deposition from	Midwest	7.1	2.9	−59	27	*
sulfate (kg–S/ha)	Northeast	7.5	2.4	−68	16	*
	Southeast	5.9	2.4	−59	22	*

kg-N/ha = kilograms of nitrogen per hectare.
kg-S/ha = kilograms of sulfur per hectare.

*Statistical significance was determined at the 95 percent confidence level (p <0.05) using student's t-test. Changes that are not statistically significant may be unduly influenced by measurements at only a few locations or large variability in measurements.

Notes: Averages are the arithmetic mean of all sites in a region that were present and met the completeness criteria in both averaging periods. Thus, average concentrations for 1989 to 1991 may differ from past reports. Total deposition is estimated from raw measurement data, not rounded, and may not equal the sum of dry and wet deposition.

SOURCE: "Figure 3. Regional Trends in Deposition," in *2015 Program Progress: Cross-State Air Pollution Rule and Acid Rain Program*, US Environmental Protection Agency, 2017, https://www3.epa.gov/airmarkets/progress/reports/pdfs/2015_full_report.pdf (accessed November 8, 2017)

following decreases in emissions, taking decades to recover. Finally, soil nutrient reserves (such as calcium) can take centuries to replenish.

Table 5.8 summarizes environmental trends between 1990 and 2015 for monitoring sites at water bodies in the Adirondack Mountains, New England, the Catskills and northern Appalachian plateau, and the central Appalachians. Overall, the vast majority of sites (80% to 100%) in the first three areas showed improving sulfate trends. However, only 27% of sampled water bodies in the central Appalachians showed improvement. The results were also mixed for three other environmental indicators: nitrates, acid neutralizing capacity, and base cations, which are ions of important minerals, such as calcium and magnesium.

The EPA calculates the total amount of sulfur and nitrogen deposits that water bodies can receive while remaining ecologically healthy. These thresholds are called "critical loads." Table 5.9 shows a regional analysis of the number of sites at which lakes and streams exceeded their calculated critical loads. Overall, 13% of the sites exceeded their critical loads in 2013–15. This was an improvement compared with 2000–02, when 34% of the sites had exceedances. Although much progress

TABLE 5.8

Regional trends in water chemistry, 1990–2015

Region	Water bodies covered	% of sites with improving sulfate trend	% of sites with improving nitrate trend	% of sites with improving ANC trend	% of sites with improving base cations trend
Adirondack Mountains	44 lakes in NY*	100%	57%	91%	89%
New England	26 lakes in ME and VT	100%	25%	67%	60%
Catskills/N. Appalachian Plateau	9 streams in NY and PA	80%	40%	58%	90%
Central Appalachians	66 streams in VA	27%	74%	11%	23%

ANC = acid neutralizing capacity.
Ca = calcium.
K = potassium.
Mg = magnesium.
Na = sodium.
µeq/L = microequivalents per liter.
*Trends are based on a new subsite of 38 lakes in NY where 26 of the lakes have ANC less than 25 µeq/L.
Notes: Trends are determined by multivariate Mann-Kendall tests. Trends are significant at the 95 percent confidence interval (p <0.05). Sum of base cations calculated as (Ca+Mg+K+Na).

SOURCE: "Figure 2. Regional Trends in Sulfate, Nitrate, ANC, and Base Cations at Long-term Monitoring Sites, 1990–2015," in *2015 Program Progress: Cross-State Air Pollution Rule and Acid Rain Program*, US Environmental Protection Agency, 2017, https://www3.epa.gov/airmarkets/progress/reports/pdfs/2015_full_report.pdf (accessed November 8, 2017)

TABLE 5.9

Water bodies with exceedances of critical loads for nitrogen and sulfur, 2000–02 compared with 2013–15

Region	Number of water bodies modeled	Water bodies in exceedance of critical load				Percent reduction
		2000–2002		2013–2015		
		Number of sites	Percent of sites	Number of sites	Percent of sites	
New England (CT, MA, ME, NH, RI, VT)	2,027	461	23%	185	9%	60%
Adirondacks (NY)	315	144	46%	58	18%	60%
Northern Mid-Atlantic (NY, NJ, PA)	1,166	279	24%	95	8%	66%
Southern Mid-Atlantic (MD, VA, WV)	1,597	856	54%	356	22%	58%
Southern Appalachian Mountains (AL, GA, NC, SC, TN)	896	286	32%	115	13%	60%
Total units	**6,001**	**2,026**	**34%**	**809**	**13%**	**60%**

Notes: Surface water samples from the represented lakes and streams were compiled from surface WATER monitoring programs, such as National Surface Water Survey (NSWS), Environmental Monitoring and Assessment Program (EMAP), Wadeable Stream Assessment (WSA), National Lake Assessment (NLA), Temporally Integrated Monitoring of Ecosystems (TIME), Long-term Monitoring (LTM), and other water quality monitoring programs. Steady state exceedances calculated in units of meq/m²/yr.
meq/m²/yr = microequivalents per square meter per year.

SOURCE: "Figure 2. Critical Load Exceedances by Region, 2000–2002 Versus 2013–2015," in *2015 Program Progress: Cross-State Air Pollution Rule and Acid Rain Program*, US Environmental Protection Agency, 2017, https://www3.epa.gov/airmarkets/progress/reports/pdfs/2015_full_report.pdf (accessed November 8, 2017)

was achieved, the EPA believes that further acid rain control measures could be justified. In *2015 Program Progress—Cross-State Air Pollution Rule and Acid Rain Program*, the agency states that "sulfur and nitrogen deposition loadings in 2015 still exceed levels required for recovery of some lakes and streams, indicating that additional emission reductions would be necessary for some acid-sensitive aquatic ecosystems along the Appalachian Mountains to recover and be protected from acid deposition."

CHAPTER 6
NONHAZARDOUS WASTE

All waste materials that are not specifically deemed hazardous under federal law are considered nonhazardous wastes. The vast majority of waste produced in the United States is not inherently hazardous. It includes paper, wood, plastics, glass, metals, and chemicals, as well as other materials that are generated by industrial, commercial, agricultural, and residential sources. Although these wastes are not defined as hazardous, improper management of them poses significant risks to the environment and human health. Therefore, the handling, transport, and disposal of nonhazardous wastes is regulated by the government, largely at the state and local levels.

LAWS REGARDING WASTE

In 1965 the US government passed the Solid Waste Disposal Act, the first of many solid waste management laws. It was amended several times, most notably in 1976 with the Resource Conservation and Recovery Act (RCRA), which is administered by the US Environmental Protection Agency (EPA). The law applies to solid waste. In *RCRA Orientation Manual 2014* (October 2014, https://www.epa.gov/sites/production/files/2015-07/documents/rom.pdf), the EPA notes that the RCRA definition of solid waste includes garbage and other materials ordinarily considered "solid," as well as sludges, semisolids, liquids, and even containers of gases.

The agency explains in "EPA History: Resource Conservation and Recovery Act" (October 18, 2016, https://www.epa.gov/history/epa-history-resource-conservation-and-recovery-act) that the RCRA's primary goal is "protecting human health and the environment from the potential hazards of waste disposal." The RCRA is also concerned with reducing the amount of solid waste that is generated, ensuring that solid wastes are managed properly, and conserving natural resources and energy.

The RCRA consists of 10 subtitles. (See Table 6.1.) Subtitle C concerns the management of hazardous waste, which makes up only a small portion of all the solid waste that is generated. Hazardous wastes are discussed in detail in Chapter 8. Subtitle D concerns the management of nonhazardous wastes. As noted earlier, nonhazardous wastes can come from many different sources, including residential, commercial, and industrial sources; agriculture; construction and demolition; and medical practices. Certain batteries and lightbulbs disposed by businesses fall under hazardous waste regulations. Thus, the extent to which a particular waste is deemed nonhazardous depends on both its physical and chemical nature and the source from which it comes.

The RCRA assigns to the states responsibility for permitting and monitoring landfills for municipal solid waste (MSW; or common garbage) and other nonhazardous wastes. Regulations established under Subtitle D describe minimum federal standards for the design, location, and operation of solid waste landfills to protect the environment. The states can develop their own permitting programs, so long as they include the federal landfill criteria. The EPA has the authority to review and approve the state programs.

State and local governments are mainly responsible for passing laws concerning nonhazardous waste, although the federal government will supply money and guidance to local governments so they can better manage their garbage systems.

It is difficult to calculate exactly how much nonhazardous waste is generated in the United States and what becomes of it. Under the RCRA the federal government collects data primarily on hazardous waste. In addition, the EPA estimates the production of MSW each year using surveys, studies, population data, and other information. MSW, however, makes up only a small portion of all nonhazardous waste that is generated. The vast majority of nonhazardous waste is not tracked or

TABLE 6.1

Outline of the Resource Conservation and Recovery Act

Subtitle	Provisions
A	General provisions
B	Office of Solid Waste; authorities of the administrator and Interagency Coordinating Committee
C	Hazardous waste management
D	State or regional solid waste plans
E	Duties of the Secretary of Commerce in resource and recovery
F	Federal responsibilities
G	Miscellaneous provisions
H	Research, development, demonstration, and information
I	Regulation of underground storage tanks
J	Standards for the tracking and management of medical waste

SOURCE: "Figure 1-2. Outline of the Act," in *RCRA Orientation Manual 2014: Resource Conservation and Recovery Act*, US Environmental Protection Agency, Solid Waste and Emergency Response, October 2014, https://www.epa.gov/sites/production/files/2015-07/documents/rom.pdf (accessed November 10, 2017)

estimated by the federal government but falls under varying state and local regulatory schemes.

NONHAZARDOUS INDUSTRIAL WASTES: SOURCES AND REGULATION

Nonhazardous industrial wastes come from a variety of sources. For example, the Texas Commission on Environmental Quality (the state's environmental agency) explains in "Nonhazardous Industrial Waste Storage, Treatment or Disposal: Am I Regulated?" (November 27, 2017, http://www.tceq.texas.gov/permitting/waste_permits/ihw_permits/NHW_Am_I_Regulated.html) that "industrial waste is waste resulting from or incidental to operations of industry, manufacturing, mining, or agriculture. For example, wastes from power generation plants, manufacturing facilities, and laboratories serving an industry are considered industrial waste while wastes from schools, hospitals, dry cleaners, most service stations, and laboratories serving the public are not considered industrial waste."

Nonhazardous industrial wastes are believed to be the largest single type of waste produced in the United States. Many big manufacturing plants have sites on their own property where they dispose of waste or treat it so it will not become dangerous. Still others ship it to private disposal sites for dumping or for treatment. Smaller manufacturers might use private waste disposal companies or even the city garbage company. State and local governments have regulatory responsibility for the management of most nonhazardous wastes.

AGRICULTURAL WASTES

Agricultural wastes are made up primarily of livestock manure, urine, and bedding material. The management of livestock waste, particularly on large agricultural facilities, is an issue of concern because of the potential environmental impacts. The US Government Accountability

Office notes in *Concentrated Animal Feeding Operations: EPA Needs More Information and a Clearly Defined Strategy to Protect Air and Water Quality from Pollutants of Concern* (September 2008, https://www.gao.gov/new.items/d08944.pdf) that large farms raising thousands of animals can produce "over 2,800 tons to more than 1.6 million tons a year. To further put this in perspective, the amount of manure produced by large farms that raise animals can exceed the amount of waste produced by some large U.S. cities."

Manure is of particular concern because it is produced in huge amounts at agricultural facilities that confine large numbers of livestock in relatively small spaces. Although manure can be beneficially applied to the ground, care must be taken so that it does not adversely affect local water bodies. The runoff of nutrients from manure collection and storage facilities poses a threat to the water quality of lakes, rivers, and streams. For this reason agricultural operations that confine large numbers of animals and use manure management methods that could allow the waste to come into contact with water are regulated by the state and federal governments under water laws and regulations. (Water issues are discussed in detail in Chapter 9.)

CONSTRUCTION AND DEMOLITION DEBRIS

Construction and demolition (C&D) debris is a nonhazardous waste stream that is generated from the construction, renovation, and demolition of buildings, roads, and bridges. Table 6.2 lists typical examples of C&D wastes. Most C&D debris is managed through disposal at specially designated landfills.

Table 6.3 shows EPA estimates of the C&D wastes generated in the United States in 2012, 2013, and 2014. Overall, 534.1 million tons (484.5 million t) of materials

TABLE 6.2

Typical components of construction and demolition debris

Material components	Content examples
Wood	Forming and framing lumber, stumps/trees, engineered wood
Drywall	Sheetrock (wallboard)
Metals	Pipes, rebar, flashing, wiring, framing
Plastics	Vinyl siding, doors, windows, flooring, pipes, packaging
Roofing	Asphalt, wood, slate, and tile shingles, roofing felt
Masonry	Cinder blocks, brick, masonry cement
Glass	Windows, mirrors, lights
Miscellaneous	Carpeting, fixtures, insulation, ceramic tile
Cardboard	From newly installed items such as appliances and tile
Concrete	Foundations, driveways, sidewalks, floors, road surfaces (all concrete containing portland cement)
Asphalt pavement	Sidewalks and road structures made with asphalt binder

SOURCE: "Table 1-1. Typical Components of C&D Materials," in *Estimating 2003 Building-Related Construction and Demolition Materials Amounts*, US Environmental Protection Agency, March 2009, https://www.epa.gov/sites/production/files/2017-09/documents/estimating2003buildingrelatedcanddmaterialsamounts.pdf (accessed November 10, 2017)

TABLE 6.3

Construction and demolition debris generation by material and activity, 2012–14

[In thousand tons]

	Waste during construction			Demolition debris			Total C&D debris		
	2012	**2013**	**2014**	**2012**	**2013**	**2014**	**2012**	**2013**	**2014**
Concrete	19,017	19,939	21,664	345,376	349,603	353,633	364,394	369,542	375,297
Wood products	2,506	2,691	2,922	35,158	35,481	35,757	37,664	38,172	38,680
Drywall & plasters	2,881	2,896	3,319	9,636	9,935	10,271	12,517	12,832	13,590
Steel	0	0	0	4,229	4,282	4,349	4,229	4,282	4,349
Brick & clay tile	265	212	211	11,914	11,844	11,829	12,179	12,057	12,041
Asphalt shingles	1,023	832	828	11,783	11,567	12,713	12,806	12,400	13,542
Asphalt concrete	0	0	0	72,020	76,868	76,565	72,020	76,868	76,565
Total	**25,693**	**26,571**	**28,947**	**490,118**	**499,583**	**505,121**	**515,812**	**526,155**	**534,068**

C&D = construction and demolition.

SOURCE: "Table 6. C&D Debris Generation by Material and Activity (Thousand Tons)," in *Construction and Demolition Debris Generation in the United States, 2014*, US Environmental Protection Agency, Office of Resource Conservation and Recovery, December 2016, https://www.epa.gov/sites/production/files/2016-12/documents/construction_and_demolition_debris_generation_2014_11302016_508.pdf (accessed November 10, 2017)

FIGURE 6.1

Breakdown of construction and demolition debris composition by material, 2014

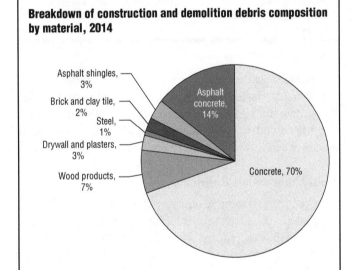

Asphalt shingles, 3%
Brick and clay tile, 2%
Steel, 1%
Drywall and plasters, 3%
Wood products, 7%
Asphalt concrete, 14%
Concrete, 70%

SOURCE: "Figure 7. C&D Debris Generation Composition by Material," in *Construction and Demolition Debris Generation in the United States, 2014*, US Environmental Protection Agency, Office of Resource Conservation and Recovery, December 2016, https://www.epa.gov/sites/production/files/2016-12/documents/construction_and_demolition_debris_generation_2014_11302016_508.pdf (accessed November 10, 2017)

TABLE 6.4

Construction and demolition debris composition by material and source, 2014

	Total generation in 2014 (thousand tons)	% of total generation in 2014
Concrete from buildings	84,763	15.9%
Concrete from roads and bridges	157,384	29.5%
Concrete from other structures	133,150	24.9%
Lumber from buildings	26,572	5.0%
Railroad ties	1,376	0.3%
Wood panel products	8,663	1.6%
Plywood and veneer	2,067	0.4%
Drywall and plasters	13,590	2.5%
Steel	4,349	0.8%
Brick	11,344	2.1%
Clay tile	696	0.1%
Asphalt shingles	13,542	2.5%
Asphalt concrete	76,565	14.3%
Total	**534,068**	**100%**

SOURCE: "Table 7. C&D Debris Generation Composition by Material and Source," in *Construction and Demolition Debris Generation in the United States, 2014*, US Environmental Protection Agency, Office of Resource Conservation and Recovery, December 2016, https://www.epa.gov/sites/production/files/2016-12/documents/construction_and_demolition_debris_generation_2014_11302016_508.pdf (accessed November 10, 2017)

were generated in 2014. The vast majority of the waste was demolition debris (505.1 million tons [458.2 million t]). The remainder was waste generated during construction activities. Figure 6.1 gives an overview of C&D composition by material category for 2014. Concrete was, by far, the most common material type, accounting for 70% of the total. A more detailed breakdown is provided in Table 6.4, which also includes information about debris sources. In 2014 most concrete waste came from roads and bridges (29.5%). The remainder came from buildings and other structures. Chapter 7 discusses the recovery and reuse of C&D materials for useful purposes.

MEDICAL WASTE

Medical waste attracted widespread attention during the mid-1980s, when used needles and similar items washed up onto beaches in the Northeast. Congress responded with the Medical Waste Tracking Act of 1988. This temporary act called on the states to use better tracking and disposal methods for medical waste. The act, which expired in 1991, defined medical waste as "any solid waste that is generated in the diagnosis, treatment, or immunization of human beings or animals, in research pertaining thereto, or in the production or testing of biologicals." Examples include bloody bandages, tissue samples, and used scalpels and needles. Medical waste is generated at facilities such as health care facilities, medical research facilities, veterinary clinics, and medical laboratories.

Medical waste is primarily regulated by state agencies. For example, the California Department of Public Health (https://www.cdph.ca.gov/Programs/CEH/DRSEM/Pages/EMB/MedicalWaste/MedicalWaste.aspx#) regulates medical waste in that state under the Medical Waste Management Act.

There are different regulatory categories of medical wastes, including infectious, hazardous, radioactive, and general wastes. According to the EPA, in "Medical Waste" (November 7, 2017, https://www.epa.gov/rcra/medical-waste), prior to 1997 more than 90% of infectious medical waste was incinerated. The federal government regulates emissions from medical waste incinerators. Tighter restrictions introduced in 1997 have prompted the use of alternative measures for the treatment and disposal of some medical wastes. Such measures include thermal treatment (e.g., microwaving), steam sterilization, electropyrolysis (destruction at very high temperatures), and chemical disinfection.

SPECIAL WASTES

When the RCRA regulations were promulgated in 1987, the EPA included a list of six wastes that were deemed "special wastes" and exempted them from classification as hazardous wastes until further studies could be conducted. According to the EPA, in "Special Wastes" (March 23, 2017, https://www.epa.gov/hw/special-wastes), many studies on the toxicity of these wastes have been conducted, and the following are considered to be special wastes under federal law:

- Cement kiln dust, which is the fine-grained, highly alkaline dust removed by air pollution control devices during the production of cement

- Wastes generated during the exploration, development, and production of crude oil, natural gas, and geothermal energy

- Certain wastes produced from the mining of uranium ore

- Wastes produced from the burning of fossil fuels (coal, oil, and natural gas) and including all ash and slag (metal waste) and any particulates removed from flue gases

- 20 waste streams from mineral processing that are generated during physical and chemical processes, such as smelting or acid treatment, and that result in wastes that are no longer considered earthen. (See Table 6.5.)

- Most wastes generated from the extraction and beneficiation (treating ore to make it more beneficial for smelting) of hard rock (metal ores and phosphate rock)

TABLE 6.5

Mineral processing wastes considered "Special Wastes" under the Resource Conservation and Recovery Act

- Slag from primary copper processing
- Slag from primary lead processing
- Red and brown muds from bauxite refining
- Phosphogypsum from phosphoric acid production
- Slag from elemental phosphorous production
- Gasifier ash from coal gasification
- Process wastewater from coal gasification
- Calcium sulfate wastewater treatment plant sludge from primary copper processing
- Slag tailings from primary copper processing
- Flurogypsum from hydrofluoric acid production
- Process wastewater from hydrofluoric acid production
- Air pollution control dust/sludge from iron blast furnaces
- Iron blast furnace slag
- Treated residue from roasting/leaching of chrome ore
- Process wastewater from primary magnesium processing by the anhydrous process
- Process wastewater from phosphoric acid production
- Basic oxygen furnace and open hearth furnace air pollution control dust/sludge from carbon steel production
- Basic oxygen furnace and open hearth furnace slag from carbon steel production
- Chloride process waste solids from titanium tetrachloride production
- Slag from primary zinc processing

SOURCE: "Mineral Processing Wastes Covered by the Mining Waste Exclusion," in *Special Wastes*, US Environmental Protection Agency, March 23, 2017, https://www.epa.gov/hw/special-wastes (accessed November 13, 2017)

These waste streams are also known as high-volume, low-toxicity wastes. Although some components, particularly cement kiln dust, can be reused within the processes involved or sold for commercial purposes, most special wastes are disposed in land-based disposal units.

Coal Combustion Residuals

Coal combustion residuals (CCRs) or coal ash is a designated special waste that results from the combustion of coal at power plants. Table 6.6 lists the types of by-products that make up CCRs. In December 2008 more than 5 million cubic yards (3.8 million cubic m) of impounded coal ash spilled into water bodies and wetlands surrounding a power plant in Harriman, Tennessee, after an embankment failed. More than 300 acres (121 ha) were affected.

The spill prompted the EPA to propose in June 2010 the regulation of CCRs under either RCRA Subtitle C (as hazardous waste) or RCRA Subtitle D (as nonhazardous waste). Linda Luther, James E. McCarthy, and James D. Werner of the Congressional Research Service explain in *Analysis of Recent Proposals to Amend the Resource Conservation and Recovery Act (RCRA) to Create a Coal Combustion Residuals Permit Program* (March 19, 2013, https://digital.library.unt.edu/ark:/67531/metadc815918/m2/1/high_res_d/R43003_2013Mar19.pdf) that the EPA proposals triggered a political battle in Congress over the roles that the EPA and the states should play in regulating CCRs.

In December 2014 the EPA finalized a rule regulating CCRs under RCRA Subtitle D. The regulations went

TABLE 6.6

Coal combustion residuals

Fly ash	A very fine, powdery material composed mostly of silica made from the burning of finely ground coal in a boiler.
Bottom ash	A coarse, angular ash particle that is too large to be carried up into the smoke stacks so it forms in the bottom of the coal furnace.
Boiler slag	Molten bottom ash from slag tap and cyclone type furnaces that turns into pellets that have a smooth glassy appearance after it is cooled with water.
Flue gas desulfurization material (FGD)	A material leftover from the process of reducing sulfur dioxide emissions from a coal-fired boiler that can be a wet sludge consisting of calcium sulfite or calcium sulfate or a dry powered material that is a mixture of sulfites and sulfates.

SOURCE: "What Is Coal Ash?" in *Frequent Questions about the Coal Ash Disposal Rule*, US Environmental Protection Agency, February 9, 2017, https://www.epa.gov/coalash/frequent-questions-about-coal-ash-disposal-rule#1 (accessed November 13, 2017)

into effect in 2015 and include specific requirements for existing and new CCR landfills and surface impoundments. The EPA explains in "Permit Programs for Coal Combustion Residual Disposal Units" (January 4, 2018, https://www.epa.gov/coalash/permit-programs-coal-combustion-residual-disposal-units) that the Water Infrastructure Improvements for the Nation Act of 2016 amended the RCRA to allow states to develop their own CCR permit programs. A state's permit program rules can be more protective of the environment than the federal rules, but not less protective. In the press release "EPA to Reconsider Certain Coal Ash Rule Provisions" (September 14, 2017, https://www.epa.gov/newsreleases/epa-reconsider-certain-coal-ash-rule-provisions), the EPA indicates that, as of September 2017, it was reconsidering "substantive provisions" of its CCR rules after being petitioned to do so by two power companies. As of January 2018, no changes to the rules had been officially proposed.

MUNICIPAL SOLID WASTE

MSW is common garbage or trash. As such, it is nonhazardous. It includes items such as food scraps, paper, containers and packaging, appliances, and yard trimmings. They may come from residential, commercial, industrial, and institutional (e.g., schools, libraries, hospitals, and prisons) sources. MSW is generally collected and managed by local municipal agencies.

Since 1995 the EPA (https://www.epa.gov/smm/advancing-sustainable-materials-management-facts-and-figures-report) has published a report nearly every year on the generation and disposal of MSW in the United States. As of January 2018, the most recent reports were *Advancing Sustainable Materials Management: 2014 Tables and Figures* (December 2016, https://www.epa.gov/sites/production/files/2016-11/documents/2014_smm_tablesfigures_508.pdf) and *Advancing Sustainable Materials Management: 2014 Fact Sheet* (November 2016, https://www.epa.gov/sites/production/files/2016-11/documents/2014_smmfactsheet_508.pdf), which include data through 2014.

Determining the amount and types of MSW generated in the United States is difficult because people are not required to track or report how much MSW they produce or what it contains. The EPA uses information supplied by trade groups and industrial sources, combined with estimated product life spans and population and sales data, to estimate how much and what types of MSW are generated.

In 2014, 258.5 million tons (234.5 million t) of MSW were generated in the United States. (See Figure 6.2.) The tons of MSW generated annually increased dramatically between 1960 and 2000. Most of this increase occurred during the 1960s, 1970s, and 1980s. Between 1990 and 2000 MSW generation increased 17%, from 208.3 million tons (189 million t) to 243.5 million tons (220.9 million t). Generation then leveled off; it increased only 6% between 2000 and 2014.

The EPA indicates that in 1960 each American generated on average 2.68 pounds (1.22 kg) of MSW per day. (See Figure 6.2.) This value steadily increased until 1990, when it reached 4.57 pounds (2.07 kg) per day. The rate leveled off during the 1990s and then began to decline after 2000. In 2014 the per capita generation was 4.44 pounds (2.01 kg) per day.

MSW Composition

Since 1960 paper and paperboard (boxboard and containerboard) have consistently been the largest single component of MSW generated. (See Table 6.7 and Table 6.8.) The amount of paper waste grew dramatically through 2000 before leveling off and then declining through 2013. Paper and paperboard waste generation was up slightly in 2014 at 68.6 million tons (62.2 million t). The amounts of other materials, particularly plastics, in the total MSW stream have grown over time, with the exception of glass, which decreased after 1980 and leveled off after 2010.

Figure 6.3 shows EPA estimates of the breakdown by material of MSW produced in 2014. Paper made up the largest single component by weight, composing 26.6% of the waste stream. Food (14.9%), yard trimmings (13.3%), and plastics (12.9%) each also accounted for more than 10% of the total. (Note that these values may be slightly different from those shown in Table 6.8 due to rounding.)

FIGURE 6.2

Trends in total and per capita municipal solid waste generation, 1960–2014

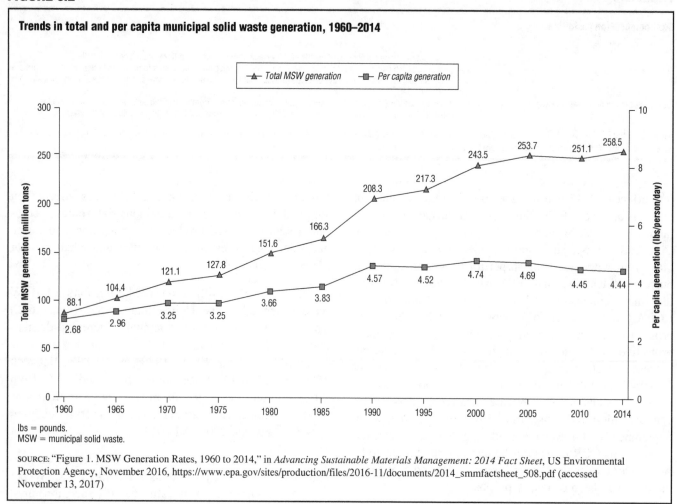

lbs = pounds.
MSW = municipal solid waste.

SOURCE: "Figure 1. MSW Generation Rates, 1960 to 2014," in *Advancing Sustainable Materials Management: 2014 Fact Sheet*, US Environmental Protection Agency, November 2016, https://www.epa.gov/sites/production/files/2016-11/documents/2014_smmfactsheet_508.pdf (accessed November 13, 2017)

Another way in which the EPA characterizes MSW is by product category. The categories include durable goods (consumer items with a life expectancy in excess of three years), nondurable goods (consumer items with a life expectancy of less than three years), containers and packaging, and other wastes. In this system, a particular type of material can be classified under multiple categories. For example, steel is found in durable goods (e.g., in appliances) and in containers and packaging (e.g., in steel drums). As shown in Table 6.9 and Table 6.10, containers and packaging have consistently made up the largest portion of the total MSW stream since 1960. In 2014 they amounted to 76.7 million tons (69.6 million t), or 29.7% of the total stream.

CONSUMER ELECTRONICS. Consumer electronics include televisions, computers, compact disc and digital video disc players, digital and video cameras, radios, telephones and cellular phones, printers, scanners, and other miscellaneous equipment. Historically, the EPA has lumped such products under the category "other miscellaneous durable goods."

In *Advancing Sustainable Materials Management: 2014 Tables and Figures*, the EPA notes that beginning in 2000 consumer electronics were categorized separately. That year an estimated 1.9 million tons (1.7 million t) entered the MSW stream. In 2014 this value climbed to 3.4 million tons (3 million t), representing 1.3% of the total 258.5 million tons (234.5 million t) of MSW generated. Although this percentage is small, it is expected to increase quickly during the 21st century as more electronic products reach the end of their useful lives.

Disposal of electronic goods in MSW poses environmental risks because of the presence of metals and other hazardous contaminants in the products. As a result, some states forbid electronic waste from MSW, as described in Chapter 7.

MSW Management

The EPA divides MWS management methods into three broad categories.

- Combustion with energy recovery—this is the burning of waste to produce energy. As shown in Figure 6.4, 12.8% of the nation's MSW in 2014 was combusted with energy recovery.

TABLE 6.7

Materials generated in the municipal waste stream, selected years 1960–2014

Materials	1960	1970	1980	1990	2000	2005	2010	2012	2013	2014
					Thousands of tons					
Paper and paperboard	29,990	44,310	55,160	72,730	87,740	84,840	71,310	68,620	68,560	68,610
Glass	6,720	12,740	15,130	13,100	12,770	12,540	11,520	11,590	11,540	11,480
Metals										
Ferrous	10,300	12,360	12,620	12,640	14,150	15,210	16,920	16,940	17,720	17,690
Aluminum	340	800	1,730	2,810	3,190	3,330	3,510	3,510	3,500	3,530
Other nonferrous	180	670	1,160	1,100	1,600	1,860	2,020	1,980	2,010	2,040
Total metals	**10,820**	**13,830**	**15,510**	**16,550**	**18,940**	**20,400**	**22,450**	**22,430**	**23,230**	**23,260**
Plastics	390	2,900	6,830	17,130	25,550	29,380	31,400	31,920	32,620	33,250
Rubber and leather	1,840	2,970	4,200	5,790	6,670	7,290	7,750	8,100	8,350	8,210
Textiles	1,760	2,040	2,530	5,810	9,480	11,510	13,220	14,500	15,320	16,220
Wood	3,030	3,720	7,010	12,210	13,570	14,790	15,710	15,820	15,770	16,120
Other*	70	770	2,520	3,190	4,000	4,290	4,710	4,570	4,440	4,440
Total materials in products	**54,620**	**83,280**	**108,890**	**146,510**	**178,720**	**185,040**	**178,070**	**177,550**	**179,830**	**181,590**
Other wastes										
Food	12,200	12,800	13,000	23,860	30,700	32,930	35,740	36,430	37,060	38,400
Yard trimmings	20,000	23,200	27,500	35,000	30,530	32,070	33,400	33,960	34,200	34,500
Miscellaneous inorganic wastes	1,300	1,780	2,250	2,900	3,500	3,690	3,840	3,900	3,930	3,970
Total other wastes	**33,500**	**37,780**	**42,750**	**61,760**	**64,730**	**68,690**	**72,980**	**74,290**	**75,190**	**76,870**
Total MSW generated-weight	**88,120**	**121,060**	**151,640**	**208,270**	**243,450**	**253,730**	**251,050**	**251,840**	**255,020**	**258,460**

Note: Generation before materials recycling, composting, combustion with energy recovery, or landfilling. Does not include construction & demolition debris, industrial process wastes, or certain other wastes. Details may not add to totals due to rounding.
*Includes electrolytes in batteries and fluff pulp, feces, and urine in disposable diapers.
MSW = municipal solid waste.

SOURCE: Adapted from "Table 1. Materials Generated in the Municipal Waste Stream, 1960 to 2014," in *Advancing Sustainable Materials Management: 2014 Tables and Figures*, US Environmental Protection Agency, December 2016, https://www.epa.gov/sites/production/files/2016-11/documents/2014_smm_tablesfigures_508.pdf (accessed November 13, 2017)

TABLE 6.8

Breakdown of materials generated in the municipal waste stream, by type, selected years 1960–2014

Materials	1960	1970	1980	1990	2000	2005	2010	2012	2013	2014
					Percent of total generation					
Paper and paperboard	34.0%	36.6%	36.4%	34.9%	36.0%	33.4%	28.4%	27.2%	26.9%	26.5%
Glass	7.6%	10.5%	10.0%	6.3%	5.2%	4.9%	4.6%	4.6%	4.5%	4.4%
Metals										
Ferrous	11.7%	10.2%	8.3%	6.1%	5.8%	6.0%	6.7%	6.7%	6.9%	6.8%
Aluminum	0.4%	0.7%	1.1%	1.3%	1.3%	1.3%	1.4%	1.4%	1.4%	1.4%
Other nonferrous	0.2%	0.6%	0.8%	0.5%	0.7%	0.7%	0.8%	0.8%	0.8%	0.8%
Total metals	**12.3%**	**11.4%**	**10.2%**	**7.9%**	**7.8%**	**8.0%**	**8.9%**	**8.9%**	**9.1%**	**9.0%**
Plastics	0.4%	2.4%	4.5%	8.2%	10.5%	11.6%	12.5%	12.7%	12.8%	12.9%
Rubber and leather	2.1%	2.5%	2.8%	2.8%	2.7%	2.9%	3.1%	3.2%	3.3%	3.2%
Textiles	2.0%	1.7%	1.7%	2.8%	3.9%	4.5%	5.3%	5.8%	6.0%	6.3%
Wood	3.4%	3.1%	4.6%	5.9%	5.6%	5.8%	6.3%	6.3%	6.2%	6.2%
Other*	0.1%	0.6%	1.7%	1.5%	1.6%	1.7%	1.9%	1.8%	1.7%	1.7%
Total materials in products	**62.0%**	**68.8%**	**71.8%**	**70.3%**	**73.4%**	**72.9%**	**70.9%**	**70.5%**	**70.5%**	**70.3%**
Other wastes										
Food	13.8%	10.6%	8.6%	11.5%	12.6%	13.0%	14.2%	14.5%	14.5%	14.9%
Yard trimmings	22.7%	19.2%	18.1%	16.8%	12.5%	12.6%	13.3%	13.5%	13.4%	13.3%
Miscellaneous inorganic wastes	1.5%	1.5%	1.5%	1.4%	1.4%	1.5%	1.5%	1.5%	1.5%	1.5%
Total other wastes	**38.0%**	**31.2%**	**28.2%**	**29.7%**	**26.6%**	**27.1%**	**29.1%**	**29.5%**	**29.5%**	**29.7%**
Total MSW generated-%	**100.0%**	**100.0%**	**100.0%**	**100.0%**	**100.0%**	**100.0%**	**100.0%**	**100.0%**	**100.0%**	**100.0%**

Note: Generation before materials recycling, composting, combustion with energy recovery, or landfilling. Does not include construction & demolition debris, industrial process wastes, or certain other wastes. Details may not add to totals due to rounding.
*Includes electrolytes in batteries and fluff pulp, feces, and urine in disposable diapers.
MSW = municipal solid waste.

SOURCE: Adapted from "Table 1. Materials Generated in the Municipal Waste Stream, 1960 to 2014," in *Advancing Sustainable Materials Management: 2014 Tables and Figures*, US Environmental Protection Agency, December 2016, https://www.epa.gov/sites/production/files/2016-11/documents/2014_smm_tablesfigures_508.pdf (accessed November 13, 2017)

- Recovery through recycling or composting—recycling is the reuse of a material in another product or application. Composting is a method of decomposing yard trimmings and other biodegradable wastes for reuse as fertilizer or mulch. Recycling and composting are discussed at length in Chapter 7. As shown in Figure 6.4, more than one-third (34.6%) of the MSW stream was recycled or composted in 2014.

- Landfilling—MSW components that are not combusted with energy recovery or recovered through recycling or composting are landfilled. They are piled on or below the ground, primarily at facilities called landfills. In 2014 land disposal was the most common method of managing MSW in the United States. More than half (52.6%) of the MSW generated was discarded via land disposal. (See Figure 6.4.) Note that the EPA includes within this category MSW that was combusted (reduced to ash) without energy recovery.

In 1960 paper and paperboard were the largest single component of landfilled MSW, making up 30.2% of the total. (See Table 6.11 and Table 6.12.) Over time, paper's contribution has declined, while other materials—particularly plastics and food—have become more predominant. Figure 6.5 provides a breakdown by material of the 136 million tons (123.4 million t) of MSW that was landfilled in 2014. Food (21.6%) made up the largest portion, followed by plastics (18.5%) and paper and paperboard (14.3%).

As shown in Table 6.13, the EPA estimates that in 1960 each person in the United States discarded to landfills or otherwise disposed of 2.5 pounds (1.1 kg) of MSW per day. This represented 93% of the total 2.7 pounds (1.2 kg) of MSW per day that were generated. Over the decades, other types of waste management became more prominent. In 2014 each person generated 4.4 pounds (2 kg) of MSW per day. Only 2.3 pounds

FIGURE 6.3

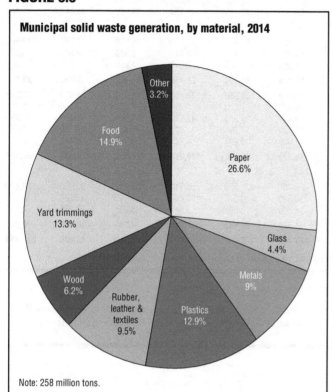

Municipal solid waste generation, by material, 2014

Note: 258 million tons.

SOURCE: "Figure 5. Total MSW Generation (by Material), 2014," in *Advancing Sustainable Materials Management: 2014 Fact Sheet*, US Environmental Protection Agency, November 2016, https://www.epa.gov/sites/production/files/2016-11/documents/2014_smmfactsheet_508.pdf (accessed November 13, 2017)

TABLE 6.9

Products generated in the municipal waste stream, by product category, selected years 1960–2014

Products	Thousands of tons									
	1960	1970	1980	1990	2000	2005	2010	2012	2013	2014
Durable goods	9,920	14,660	21,800	29,810	38,870	45,060	49,350	50,890	52,520	52,650
Nondurable goods	17,330	25,060	34,420	52,170	64,010	63,650	53,250	51,430	51,540	52,270
Containers and packaging	27,370	43,560	52,670	64,530	75,840	76,330	75,470	75,230	75,770	76,670
Total product* wastes	**54,620**	**83,280**	**108,890**	**146,510**	**178,720**	**185,040**	**178,070**	**177,550**	**179,830**	**181,590**
Other wastes										
Food	12,200	12,800	13,000	23,860	30,700	32,930	35,740	36,430	37,060	38,400
Yard trimmings	20,000	23,200	27,500	35,000	30,530	32,070	33,400	33,960	34,200	34,500
Miscellaneous inorganic wastes	1,300	1,780	2,250	2,900	3,500	3,690	3,840	3,900	3,930	3,970
Total other wastes	**33,500**	**37,780**	**42,750**	**61,760**	**64,730**	**68,690**	**72,980**	**74,290**	**75,190**	**76,870**
Total MSW generated-weight	**88,120**	**121,060**	**151,640**	**208,270**	**243,450**	**253,730**	**251,050**	**251,840**	**255,020**	**258,460**

Note: Generation before materials recycling, composting, combustion with energy recovery, or landfilling. Does not include construction & demolition debris, industrial process wastes, or certain other wastes. Details may not add to totals due to rounding.
*Other than food products.
MSW = municipal solid waste.

SOURCE: Adapted from "Table 10. Products Generated in the Municipal Waste Stream, 1960 to 2014," in *Advancing Sustainable Materials Management: 2014 Tables and Figures*, US Environmental Protection Agency, December 2016, https://www.epa.gov/sites/production/files/2016-11/documents/2014_smm_tablesfigures_508.pdf (accessed November 13, 2017)

TABLE 6.10

Breakdown of products generated in the municipal waste stream, by product category, selected years 1960–2014

Products	Percent of total generation									
	1960	1970	1980	1990	2000	2005	2010	2012	2013	2014
Durable goods	11.3%	12.1%	14.4%	14.3%	16.0%	17.8%	19.7%	20.2%	20.6%	20.4%
Nondurable goods	19.7%	20.7%	22.7%	25.0%	26.3%	25.1%	21.2%	20.4%	20.2%	20.2%
Containers and packaging	31.1%	36.0%	34.7%	31.0%	31.2%	30.1%	30.1%	29.9%	29.7%	29.7%
Total product* wastes	**62.0%**	**68.8%**	**71.8%**	**70.3%**	**73.4%**	**72.9%**	**70.9%**	**70.5%**	**70.5%**	**70.3%**
Other wastes										
Food	13.8%	10.6%	8.6%	11.5%	12.6%	13.0%	14.2%	14.5%	14.5%	14.9%
Yard trimmings	22.7%	19.2%	18.1%	16.8%	12.5%	12.6%	13.3%	13.5%	13.4%	13.3%
Miscellaneous inorganic wastes	1.5%	1.5%	1.5%	1.4%	1.4%	1.5%	1.5%	1.5%	1.5%	1.5%
Total other wastes	**38.0%**	**31.2%**	**28.2%**	**29.7%**	**26.6%**	**27.1%**	**29.1%**	**29.5%**	**29.5%**	**29.7%**
Total MSW generated -%	**100.0%**	**100.0%**	**100.0%**	**100.0%**	**100.0%**	**100.0%**	**100.0%**	**100.0%**	**100.0%**	**100.0%**

Note: Generation before materials recycling, composting, combustion with energy recovery, or landfilling. Does not include construction & demolition debris, industrial process wastes, or certain other wastes. Details may not add to totals due to rounding.
*Other than food products.
MSW = municipal solid waste.

SOURCE: Adapted from "Table 10. Products Generated in the Municipal Waste Stream, 1960 to 2014," in *Advancing Sustainable Materials Management: 2014 Tables and Figures*, US Environmental Protection Agency, December 2016, https://www.epa.gov/sites/production/files/2016-11/documents/2014_smm_tablesfigures_508.pdf (accessed November 13, 2017)

FIGURE 6.4

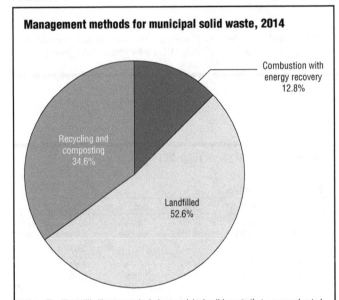

Management methods for municipal solid waste, 2014

Combustion with energy recovery 12.8%

Recycling and composting 34.6%

Landfilled 52.6%

Note: The "Landfilled" category includes municipal solid waste that was combusted without energy recovery.

SOURCE: "Figure 4. Management of MSW in the United States, 2014," in *Advancing Sustainable Materials Management: 2014 Fact Sheet*, US Environmental Protection Agency, November 2016, https://www.epa.gov/sites/production/files/2016-11/documents/2014_smmfactsheet_508.pdf (accessed November 13, 2017)

(1 kg), or 52%, of this total was discarded to landfills or other disposal. The remainder was recovered for recycling, composting, or combustion with energy recovery.

Municipal Landfills

Municipal (or sanitary) landfills are areas where MSW waste is placed into and onto the land. Although some landfilled wastes will decompose, many of the wastes in MSW are not biodegradable. Landfills provide a centralized location in which these wastes can be contained.

HOW BIODEGRADABLE MATTER DECOMPOSES IN LANDFILLS. Biodegradable waste comes from materials that were once alive, such as paper and wood products, food scraps, and clothing made of natural fibers. These materials decompose in the following way: first, aerobic (oxygen-using) bacteria use the material as food and begin the decomposition process. Note that in compacted, layered, and covered landfills the availability of oxygen may be low. The principal by-products of the aerobic stage are water, carbon dioxide, nitrates, and heat.

After the available oxygen is used, anaerobic bacteria (those that do not use oxygen) continue the decomposition. They generally produce carbon dioxide and organic acids. This stage can last many months. During a final anaerobic stage of decomposition lasting several years or decades, methane gas is formed along with carbon dioxide. The duration of this stage and the amount of decomposition depend on landfill conditions, including temperature, soil permeability, and water levels.

Landfills and the Environment

METHANE. Methane, a flammable gas, is produced when biodegradable matter decomposes in the absence of oxygen. If not properly vented or controlled, it can cause explosions and underground fires that smolder for years. Methane is also deadly to breathe. The RCRA requires landfill operators to monitor methane gas.

Methane gas can be recovered through pipes that are inserted into landfills, and the gas can be used to generate energy. The EPA indicates in "Project and Landfill Data by State" (https://www.epa.gov/lmop/project-and-land

TABLE 6.11

Materials in the municipal waste stream that were landfilled, selected years 1960–2014

Materials	Thousands of tons									
	1960	1970	1980	1990	2000	2005	2010	2012	2013	2014
Paper and paperboard	24,910	37,390	42,560	43,570	40,450	35,080	22,000	19,490	20,170	19,470
Glass	6,620	12,520	14,080	8,660	8,100	8,290	7,030	6,900	6,940	7,040
Metals										
Ferrous	10,250	12,150	12,000	8,720	7,860	8,550	9,310	9,330	9,810	9,830
Aluminum	340	790	1,390	1,500	1,940	2,230	2,390	2,330	2,340	2,360
Other nonferrous	180	350	600	310	490	530	520	530	590	630
Total metals	**10,770**	**13,290**	**13,990**	**10,530**	**10,290**	**11,310**	**12,220**	**12,190**	**12,740**	**12,820**
Plastics	390	2,900	6,670	13,780	19,950	23,270	24,370	24,140	24,720	25,100
Rubber and leather	1,510	2,710	4,000	4,590	3,880	4,130	4,400	4,250	4,150	4,150
Textiles	1,710	1,970	2,320	4,270	6,280	7,570	8,900	9,420	9,910	10,460
Wood	3,030	3,710	6,860	10,000	9,910	10,690	11,120	10,860	10,800	11,010
Other*	70	470	1,990	2,100	2,480	2,570	2,800	2,670	2,560	2,580
Total materials in products	**49,010**	**74,960**	**92,470**	**97,500**	**101,340**	**102,910**	**92,840**	**89,920**	**91,990**	**92,630**
Other wastes										
Food	12,200	12,750	12,740	19,800	24,200	26,370	28,620	27,860	28,250	29,310
Yard trimmings	20,000	23,110	26,950	25,560	11,900	9,990	11,690	11,540	10,910	10,790
Miscellaneous inorganic wastes	1,300	1,770	2,200	2,410	2,820	3,020	3,160	3,130	3,150	3,190
Total other wastes	**33,500**	**37,630**	**41,890**	**47,770**	**38,920**	**39,380**	**43,470**	**42,530**	**42,310**	**43,290**
Total MSW landfilled-weight	**82,510**	**112,590**	**134,360**	**145,270**	**140,260**	**142,290**	**136,310**	**132,450**	**134,300**	**135,920**

Note: Landfilling after recycling, composting, and combustion with energy recovery. Does not include construction & demolition debris, industrial process wastes, or certain other wastes. Details may not add to totals due to rounding.
*Includes electrolytes in batteries and fluff pulp, feces, and urine in disposable diapers.
MSW = municipal solid waste.

SOURCE: Adapted from "Table 4. Materials Landfilled in the Municipal Waste Stream, 1960 to 2014," in *Advancing Sustainable Materials Management: 2014 Tables and Figures*, US Environmental Protection Agency, December 2016, https://www.epa.gov/sites/production/files/2016-11/documents/2014_smm_tablesfigures_508.pdf (accessed November 13, 2017)

TABLE 6.12

Breakdown of materials in the municipal waste stream that were landfilled by type, selected years 1960–2014

Materials	Percent of total landfilled									
	1960	1970	1980	1990	2000	2005	2010	2012	2013	2014
Paper and paperboard	30.2%	33.2%	31.7%	30.0%	28.8%	24.7%	16.1%	14.7%	15.0%	14.3%
Glass	8.0%	11.1%	10.5%	6.0%	5.8%	5.8%	5.1%	5.2%	5.2%	5.2%
Metals										
Ferrous	12.4%	10.8%	8.9%	6.0%	5.6%	6.0%	6.8%	7.0%	7.3%	7.2%
Aluminum	0.4%	0.7%	1.0%	1.0%	1.4%	1.6%	1.8%	1.8%	1.7%	1.7%
Other nonferrous	0.2%	0.3%	0.4%	0.2%	0.3%	0.3%	0.4%	0.4%	0.5%	0.5%
Total metals	**13.0%**	**11.8%**	**10.3%**	**7.2%**	**7.3%**	**7.9%**	**9.0%**	**9.2%**	**9.5%**	**9.4%**
Plastics	0.5%	2.6%	5.0%	9.5%	14.2%	16.4%	17.9%	18.2%	18.4%	18.5%
Rubber and leather	1.8%	2.4%	3.0%	3.2%	2.8%	2.9%	3.2%	3.2%	3.1%	3.1%
Textiles	2.1%	1.7%	1.7%	2.9%	4.5%	5.3%	6.5%	7.1%	7.4%	7.7%
Wood	3.7%	3.3%	5.1%	6.9%	7.1%	7.5%	8.2%	8.2%	8.0%	8.1%
Other*	0.1%	0.4%	1.5%	1.4%	1.8%	1.8%	2.1%	2.0%	1.9%	1.9%
Total materials in products	**59.4%**	**66.6%**	**68.8%**	**67.1%**	**72.3%**	**72.3%**	**68.1%**	**67.9%**	**68.5%**	**68.2%**
Other wastes										
Food	14.8%	11.3%	9.5%	13.6%	17.3%	18.5%	21.0%	21.0%	21.0%	21.6%
Yard trimmings	24.2%	20.5%	20.1%	17.6%	8.5%	7.0%	8.6%	8.7%	8.1%	7.9%
Miscellaneous inorganic wastes	1.6%	1.6%	1.6%	1.7%	1.9%	2.2%	2.3%	2.4%	2.4%	2.3%
Total other wastes	**40.6%**	**33.4%**	**31.2%**	**32.9%**	**27.7%**	**27.7%**	**31.9%**	**32.1%**	**31.5%**	**31.8%**
Total MSW landfilled-%	**100.0%**	**100.0%**	**100.0%**	**100.0%**	**100.0%**	**100.0%**	**100.0%**	**100.0%**	**100.0%**	**100.0%**

Note: Landfilling after recycling, composting, and combustion with energy recovery. Does not include construction & demolition debris, industrial process wastes, or certain other wastes. Details may not add to totals due to rounding.
*Includes electrolytes in batteries and fluff pulp, feces, and urine in disposable diapers.
MSW = municipal solid waste.

SOURCE: Adapted from "Table 4. Materials Landfilled in the Municipal Waste Stream, 1960 to 2014," in *Advancing Sustainable Materials Management: 2014 Tables and Figures*, US Environmental Protection Agency, December 2016, https://www.epa.gov/sites/production/files/2016-11/documents/2014_smm_tablesfigures_508.pdf (accessed November 13, 2017)

fill-data-state) that, as of November 2017, there were 637 operational landfill gas-to-energy projects in the United States. The states with the most projects were California (76), Michigan (42), and Pennsylvania (39). The EPA's Landfill Methane Outreach Program estimates that approximately 400 other landfill sites presented attractive opportunities for project development.

According to the EPA (https://www.epa.gov/lmop/basic-information-about-landfill-gas), about 75% of the landfill gas-to-energy projects in the United States as of January 2018 were devoted to generating electricity. The remaining projects used the gas for other purposes (e.g., to fuel equipment such as heaters, boilers, and dryers).

Landfill Design Standards

The RCRA standards require landfill operators to do several things to lessen the chance of polluting the underlying groundwater. Groundwater can become contaminated when liquid chemicals or contaminated rainfall runoff seep down through the ground underneath the landfill. This liquid is called leachate.

The RCRA requirements are as follows:

- Landfill operators must monitor the groundwater for pollutants. This is usually accomplished with a groundwater monitoring well system.

- Landfills must have plastic liners underneath their waste, as well as a leachate collection system. (See Figure 6.6.)

- Debris must be covered daily with soil to prevent odors and stop refuse from being blown away.

- Methane gas must be monitored, which is usually accomplished with an explosive-gas monitoring well.

- Landfill owners are responsible for cleanup of any contamination.

Landfills are not open dumps but managed facilities in which wastes are controlled. MSW is often compacted before it is placed in a landfill and covered with soil.

FIGURE 6.5

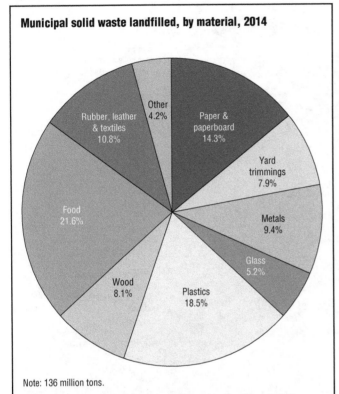

Municipal solid waste landfilled, by material, 2014

Note: 136 million tons.

SOURCE: "Figure 8. Total MSW Landfilled (by Material), 2014," in *Advancing Sustainable Materials Management: 2014 Fact Sheet*, US Environmental Protection Agency, November 2016, https://www.epa.gov/sites/production/files/2016-11/documents/2014_smmfactsheet_508.pdf (accessed November 13, 2017)

TABLE 6.13

Generation, recovery, and discard amounts for municipal solid waste, selected years 1960–2014

[In pounds per day]

Activity	1960	1970	1980	1990	2000	2005	2010	2012	2013	2014
Generation	2.7	3.3	3.7	4.6	4.7	4.7	4.4	4.4	4.4	4.4
Recycling	0.2	0.2	0.4	0.6	1.0	1.1	1.1	1.1	1.1	1.1
Composting[a]	neg.	neg.	neg.	0.1	0.3	0.4	0.4	0.4	0.4	0.4
Combustion with energy recovery[b]	0.0	neg.	0.1	0.7	0.7	0.6	0.5	0.6	0.6	0.6
Landfilling and other disposal[c]	2.5	3.1	3.2	3.2	2.7	2.6	2.4	2.3	2.3	2.3
Population (in millions)	180.0	204.0	227.3	249.9	281.4	296.4	309.1	313.9	316.1	318.9

[a]Composting of yard trimmings, food and other MSW organic material. Does not include backyard composting.
[b]Includes combustion of MSW in mass burn or refuse-derived fuel form, and combustion with energy recovery of source separated materials in MSW (e.g., wood pallets, tire-derived fuel).
[c]Landfilling after recycling, composting and combustion with energy recovery. Includes combustion without energy recovery. Details might not add to totals due to rounding.
MSW = municipal solid waste.
neg. = Negligible = less than 5,000 tons or 0.05 percent.

SOURCE: "Table 4. Generation, Recycling, Composting, Combustion with Energy Recovery and Landfilling of MSW, 1960 to 2014 (in Pounds per Person per Day)," in *Advancing Sustainable Materials Management: 2014 Fact Sheet*, US Environmental Protection Agency, November 2016, https://www.epa.gov/sites/production/files/2016-11/documents/2014_smmfactsheet_508.pdf (accessed November 13, 2017)

FIGURE 6.6

Example of a properly closed landfill

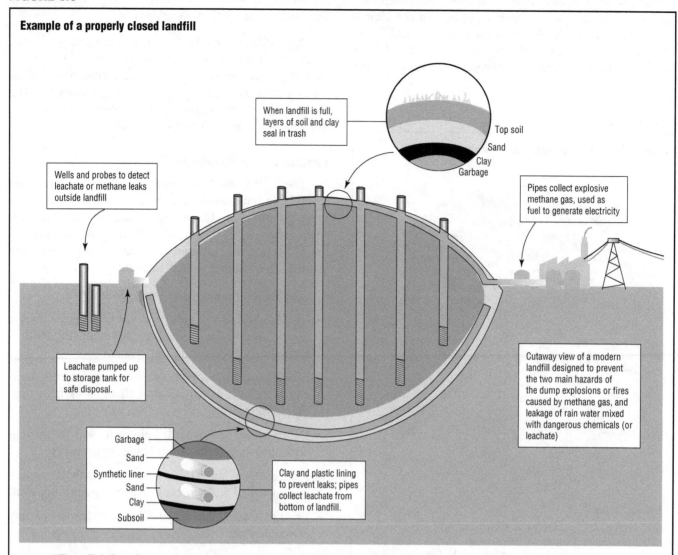

When landfill is full, layers of soil and clay seal in trash

Top soil
Sand
Clay
Garbage

Wells and probes to detect leachate or methane leaks outside landfill

Pipes collect explosive methane gas, used as fuel to generate electricity

Leachate pumped up to storage tank for safe disposal.

Cutaway view of a modern landfill designed to prevent the two main hazards of the dump explosions or fires caused by methane gas, and leakage of rain water mixed with dangerous chemicals (or leachate)

Garbage
Sand
Synthetic liner
Sand
Clay
Subsoil

Clay and plastic lining to prevent leaks; pipes collect leachate from bottom of landfill.

SOURCE: "Figure II-4. Cross-Section of a Municipal Solid Waste Landfill," in *RCRA Orientation Manual 2014: Resource Conservation and Recovery Act*, US Environmental Protection Agency, Solid Waste and Emergency Response, October 2014, https://www.epa.gov/sites/production/files/2015-07/documents/rom.pdf (accessed November 13, 2017)

Modern landfills have liner systems and other safeguards to prevent groundwater contamination. When they are full, landfills are usually capped with a clay liner to prevent contamination. (See Figure 6.6.)

Interstate Imports and Exports of Garbage

The lack of landfill space has encouraged some municipalities to send their garbage to other states. Although shipments do occur across the Mexican and Canadian borders, the vast majority of US MSW is managed within the United States.

Several states have tried to ban the importing of garbage into their respective state. In 1992 the US Supreme Court ruled in *Chemical Waste Management v. Hunt* (504 US 334) that the constitutional right to conduct commerce across state borders protects such shipments. Experts point out that newer, state-of-the-art landfills

with multiple liners and sophisticated pollution control equipment must accept waste from a wide region to be financially viable.

Trends in Landfill Development

Before using landfills, cities used open dumps—areas in which garbage and trash were simply discarded into huge piles. Open dumps, however, produced unpleasant odors and attracted animals. During the early 1970s the number of operating landfills in the United States was estimated at about 20,000. In 1979, as part of the RCRA, the EPA designated conditions under which solid waste disposal facilities and practices would not pose adverse effects to human health and the environment. As a result of the implementation of these criteria, open dumps had to be closed or upgraded to meet the criteria for landfills.

Additionally, many more landfills closed during the early 1990s because they could not conform to the new standards that took effect in 1993 under the 1992 RCRA amendment. Other landfills closed as they became full. According to the EPA, in *Advancing Sustainable Materials Management: 2014 Tables and Figures*, there were 1,956 MSW landfills operating in the United States in 2014.

Landfilling is expected to continue to be the single most predominant MSW management method. In the coming decades it will be economically prohibitive to develop and maintain small-scale, local landfills. There will likely be fewer, larger, and more regional operations. More MSW is expected to move away from its point of generation, resulting in increased import and export rates.

Landfill protection methods will likely become stronger in the future with more options for leachate and gas recovery. To make landfills more acceptable to neighborhoods, operators will likely establish larger buffer zones, use more green space, and show more sensitivity to land-use compatibility and landscaping.

Waste-to-Energy Processes

Combustion with energy recovery has become a popular disposal choice for nonhazardous wastes. In the past waste was burned in incinerators primarily to reduce its volume. During the 1980s technology was developed that allowed waste to be burned for energy recovery. The use of waste as a fuel is commonly called combustion; however, the terms *combustion* and *incineration* are often used interchangeably. The EPA refers to waste combustion as a waste-to-energy (WTE) process.

In a traditional WTE facility, waste is burned in a furnace, heating a boiler that changes water into steam; the rapid flow of steam is directed over the blades of a turbine, forcing it to rotate and produce electricity. Ash collects at the bottom of the furnace, where it is later removed and taken to a landfill for disposal. The combustion process also produces gaseous emissions that must be "scrubbed" using pollution control devices or technologies.

According to the EPA, in *Advancing Sustainable Materials Management: 2014 Tables and Figures*, WTE facilities operating in the United States combusted 33.1 million tons (30.1 million t) of MSW in 2014. As shown in Figure 6.7, the largest components were food (21.6%); rubber, leather, and textiles (17.4%); and plastics (15%). Table 6.14 provides a historical breakdown of the MWS combusted with energy recovery during selected years between 1970 and 2014. In 1970 paper and paperboard made up one-third (33.3%) of the waste that was disposed of in this manner. Over the decades, paper recycling has become much more common, reducing the proportion of paper and paperboard in the total MSW stream that is combusted for energy recovery.

FIGURE 6.7

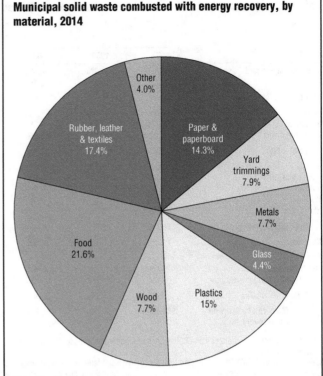

Municipal solid waste combusted with energy recovery, by material, 2014

Note: 33 million tons.

SOURCE: "Figure 7. Total MSW Combusted with Energy Recovery (by Material), 2014," in *Advancing Sustainable Materials Management: 2014 Fact Sheet*, US Environmental Protection Agency, November 2016, https://www.epa.gov/sites/production/files/2016-11/documents/2014_smmfactsheet_508.pdf (accessed November 13, 2017)

Overall, combustion with energy recovery was the disposal method for 12.8% of the total MSW generated in 2014. (See Figure 6.4.) This is a significant change since 1960, when, according to the EPA, zero MSW was combusted for energy recovery. (See Table 6.15.) The US Department of Energy reports in *Monthly Energy Review: January 2018* (January 26, 2018, https://www.eia.gov/totalenergy/data/monthly/pdf/mer.pdf) that 0.503 quadrillion British thermal units of waste-derived energy were consumed in the United States in 2016. This was about 0.5% of the nation's total energy consumption of 97.410 quadrillion British thermal units.

The Energy Recovery Council is a trade organization that represents companies, local governments, and organizations that recover energy and materials from waste. In *Energy Recovery Council 2016 Directory of Waste-to-Energy Facilities* (May 2016, http://energyrecoverycouncil.org/wp-content/uploads/2016/05/ERC-2016-directory.pdf), the council notes that 77 WTE facilities were operating across the country in 2016. The states with the highest numbers were Florida (11), New York (10), and Minnesota (8). The council explains that WTE facilities practice material recovery by removing recyclable items from the waste stream before

TABLE 6.14

Materials in the municipal solid waste stream that were combusted with energy recovery, selected years 1970–2014

Materials	Percent of total combusted								
	1970	1980	1990	2000	2005	2010	2012	2013	2014
Paper and paperboard	33.3%	31.2%	30.0%	28.8%	24.6%	16.2%	14.7%	15.0%	14.3%
Glass	13.3%	10.9%	6.1%	5.3%	5.2%	4.6%	4.6%	4.4%	4.4%
Metals									
Ferrous	13.3%	9.0%	5.7%	4.8%	5.2%	6.2%	6.2%	6.2%	6.1%
Aluminum	0.0%	1.1%	1.0%	1.2%	1.3%	1.5%	1.4%	1.4%	1.4%
Other nonferrous	0.0%	0.7%	0.2%	0.1%	0.1%	0.2%	0.2%	0.2%	0.2%
Total metals	**13.3%**	**10.8%**	**6.9%**	**6.1%**	**6.6%**	**7.9%**	**7.8%**	**7.8%**	**7.7%**
Plastics	Neg.	5.1%	10.0%	12.2%	13.7%	15.5%	15.4%	14.8%	15.0%
Rubber and leather	2.2%	2.5%	2.8%	5.9%	6.7%	6.5%	7.2%	8.2%	7.9%
Textiles	2.2%	1.8%	2.9%	5.6%	6.7%	7.7%	8.6%	9.1%	9.5%
Wood	2.2%	5.4%	7.0%	6.8%	7.2%	7.9%	7.8%	7.5%	7.7%
Other*	Neg.	1.1%	1.4%	1.6%	1.6%	1.8%	1.8%	1.7%	1.7%
Total materials in products	**66.6%**	**68.8%**	**67.1%**	**72.3%**	**72.3%**	**68.1%**	**67.9%**	**68.5%**	**68.1%**
Other wastes	**11.1%**	**9.4%**	**13.6%**	**17.3%**	**18.5%**	**21.0%**	**21.0%**	**21.0%**	**21.6%**
Food									
Yard trimmings	20.0%	20.0%	17.6%	8.5%	7.0%	8.6%	8.7%	8.1%	7.9%
Miscellaneous inorganic wastes	2.3%	1.8%	1.7%	1.9%	2.1%	2.3%	2.4%	2.4%	2.4%
Total other wastes	**33.4%**	**31.2%**	**32.9%**	**27.7%**	**27.7%**	**31.9%**	**32.1%**	**31.5%**	**31.9%**
Total MSW combusted with energy recovery-%	**100.0%**	**100.0%**	**100.0%**	**100.0%**	**100.0%**	**100.0%**	**100.0%**	**100.0%**	**100.0%**

*Includes electrolytes in batteries and fluff pulp, feces, and urine in disposable diapers.
MSW = municipal solid waste.
Note: Products and materials combusted with energy recovery estimated at percentage total MSW after recycling and composting. In 2014, 19.6 percent of MSW after recycling and composting was combusted with energy recovery except for major appliances, tires, and lead-acid batteries. No combustion with energy recovery in 1960. Does not include construction & demolition debris, industrial process wastes, or certain other wastes. Details may not add to totals due to rounding.

SOURCE: Adapted from "Table 3. Materials Combusted with Energy Recovery in the Municipal Waste Stream, 1960 to 2014," in *Advancing Sustainable Materials Management: 2014 Tables and Figures*, US Environmental Protection Agency, December 2016, https://www.epa.gov/sites/production/files/2016-11/documents/2014_smm_tablesfigures_508.pdf (accessed November 13, 2017)

TABLE 6.15

Breakdown of municipal solid waste stream generation and disposition, selected years 1960–2014

	Percent of total generation									
	1960	1970	1980	1990	2000	2005	2010	2012	2013	2014
Generation	100.0%	100.0%	100.0%	100.0%	100.0%	100.0%	100.0%	100.0%	100.0%	100.0%
Recycling	6.4%	6.6%	9.6%	14.0%	21.8%	23.3%	26.0%	26.0%	25.5%	25.7%
Composting[a]	Neg.	Neg.	Neg.	2.0%	6.7%	8.1%	8.0%	8.5%	8.8%	8.9%
Combustion with energy recovery[b]	0.0%	0.3%	1.8%	14.2%	13.9%	12.5%	11.7%	12.9%	13.0%	12.8%
Landfilling and other disposal[c]	93.6%	93.1%	88.6%	69.8%	57.6%	56.1%	54.3%	52.6%	52.7%	52.6%

[a]Composting of yard trimmings, food and other MSW organic material. Does not include backyard composting.
[b]Includes combustion with energy recovery of MSW in mass burn or refuse-derived fuel form, and combustion with energy recovery of source separated materials in MSW (e.g., wood pallets and tire-derived fuel). 2014 includes 29,540 MSW, 520 wood, and 3,080 tires (1,000 tons).
[c]Landfilling after recycling and composting minus combustion with energy recovery. Includes combustion without energy recovery. Details may not add to totals due to rounding.
MSW = municipal solid waste.
Neg. = negligible.

SOURCE: Adapted from "Table 35. Generation, Recycling, Composting, Combustion with Energy Recovery, and Landfilling of Municipal Solid Waste, 1960 to 2014," in *Advancing Sustainable Materials Management: 2014 Tables and Figures*, US Environmental Protection Agency, December 2016, https://www.epa.gov/sites/production/files/2016-11/documents/2014_smm_tablesfigures_508.pdf (accessed November 13, 2017)

incineration and by recovering nuggets of recyclable metals from the ash after incineration.

MSW INCINERATION EMISSIONS. Incineration of MSW fell into disfavor during the 1980s because of concerns about air emissions from the combustion process. These emissions can include mercury and other heavy metals and acid gases (such as hydrochloric acid) from the burning of paints, lightbulbs, electronics, and so on. Chlorine-containing chemicals within MSW are of particular concern, because their combustion can produce dioxins and furans, two groups of complex organic and toxic compounds. WTE facilities are required to use air pollution control equipment to reduce the emissions of toxic chemicals.

ALTERNATIVE WASTE-TO-ENERGY PROCESSES. Incineration/combustion via furnace heat is, by far, the most predominant WTE process used on MSW. There are alternatives that are slowly gaining favor for some applications. One example is plasma gasification. (Plasma is a hot ionized gas very unlike other gases.) According to the Westinghouse Electric Corporation, in "Waste to Energy" (2018, http://westinghouse.com/story-waste-to-energy/), plasma torches can generate "super-high" heat at a temperature of 5,432 degrees Fahrenheit (3,000 degrees C) or more. This extreme heat breaks down many solid materials into their component elements (such as carbon and hydrogen). The elements then recombine to form a synthetic (human-made) gas that can be used as a fuel. The company notes that, as of 2018, its plasma gasification technology was in use at "several facilities around the world" that produce electricity from waste streams, including MSW.

Another WTE option for MSW is pyrolysis. In "What Is Pyrolysis?" (April 14, 2017, https://www.ars.usda.gov/northeast-area/wyndmoor-pa/eastern-regional-research-center/docs/biomass-pyrolysis-research-1/what-is-pyrolysis/), the US Department of Agriculture explains that pyrolysis is the heating of an organic material in the absence of oxygen. This process causes the organic compounds in the material to "thermally decompose into combustible gases and charcoal." Pyrolysis is well suited for the carbon-rich materials in MSW, such as plastics and biodegradables (e.g., food waste and yard trimmings).

Anaerobic digestion is also an emerging waste-conversion process for MSW. The American Biogas Council notes in "What Is Anaerobic Digestion?" (2018, https://www.americanbiogascouncil.org/biogas_what.asp) that "anaerobic digestion is a series of biological processes in which microorganisms break down biodegradable material in the absence of oxygen. One of the end products is biogas, which is combusted to generate electricity and heat, or can be processed into renewable natural gas and transportation fuels." The council notes that anaerobic digestion can be used on organic waste streams, such as food waste, that are biodegradable.

THE FEDERAL ROLE IN MSW MANAGEMENT

The federal government plays a key role in waste management. Its legislation has established landfill standards under the RCRA and incinerator and landfill emissions standards under the Clean Air Act.

Some waste management laws have been controversial, resulting in legal challenges. Consequently, the federal government has also had an effect on waste management programs through federal court rulings. In a series of rulings, including US Supreme Court decisions such as *Chemical Waste Management v. Hunt*, federal courts have held that shipments of waste are protected under the interstate commerce clause of the US Constitution. As a result, state and local governments may not prohibit landfills from accepting waste from other states, nor may they impose fees on waste disposal that discriminate on the basis of origin.

Flow-Control Laws

Flow-control laws require private waste collectors to dispose of their waste in specific landfills. State and local governments institute these laws to guarantee that any new landfill they build will be used. This way, when they sell bonds to get the money to build a new landfill, the bond purchasers will not worry that they will not be repaid. In 1994 the US Supreme Court held in *C & A Carbone Inc. v. Clarkstown* (511 US 383) that flow-control laws violate the interstate commerce clause. However, since that time the courts have carved out various exceptions for specific circumstances. For example, in 2007 in *United Haulers Association, Inc., v. Oneida-Herkimer Solid Waste Management Authority* (550 US 330), the US Supreme Court upheld a local flow-control ordinance in New York. Local governments have strongly pushed for the restoration of full flow-control authority. They have appealed to Congress, which has the authority to regulate interstate commerce, to restore the use of flow control. As of January 2018, bills proposed to grant full flow control to local governments had failed to pass.

CHAPTER 7
NONHAZARDOUS MATERIALS RECOVERY: RECYCLING AND COMPOSTING

Materials recovery is considered one of the most promising ways to reduce the amount of nonhazardous waste requiring disposal. The terms *recovery* and *recycling* are often used interchangeably. Both mean that a waste material is reused rather than put in a landfill or incinerated. In general, reuse as a fuel does not fall under the definition of recovery.

Recycling involves the sorting, collecting, and processing of wastes such as paper, glass, plastic, and metals, which are then refashioned or incorporated into new marketable products. Composting is a recovery method in which organic waste materials, such as yard trimmings and food waste, are isolated and allowed to decompose. The resulting soil-like substance can be used as a soil amendment (e.g., to adjust its ability to retain moisture), fertilizer, or mulch (a layer of material spread on the surface of the soil around a plant).

Waste recovery offers many advantages. It conserves energy otherwise used to incinerate the waste; reduces the amount of landfill space needed for the disposal of waste; reduces possible environmental pollution because of waste disposal; generates jobs and small-scale enterprises; reduces dependence on foreign imports of raw materials; and replaces some chemical fertilizers with composting material, which further lessens possible environmental pollution. However, recovery sometimes requires more energy and water consumption than waste disposal. It depends on how far the materials must be transported and what is necessary to process them before they can be reused. Demand for some recyclable materials is weak, making them economically unfeasible to recycle in a market-driven society.

Many Americans view waste recovery primarily as a way to help the environment. For example, if paper is recycled, fewer trees have to be cut down to make paper. State and local governments see recycling and composting as a way to save money on waste disposal costs and prolong the life of landfill space. Thus, waste recovery has both environmental and economic components.

INDUSTRIAL WASTE RECOVERY

As is noted in Chapter 6, industrial waste is believed to be the largest nonhazardous waste stream generated in the United States. It is produced by various sources, including factories, mines, power plants, and water and sewage treatment plants.

Some industrial wastes can be recycled either within a facility or between facilities and/or companies. The use of wastes from one facility as raw materials at another facility is called by-product synergy. Examples include the recycling of industrial wastewaters, such as process rinse waters, cooling water, and scrubber water. Reuse often requires sophisticated treatment technologies to cleanse wastewaters of impurities. These technologies produce wastes, typically sludges, that contain the concentrated impurities stripped from the wastewaters. Nontoxic, industrial wastewater sludges can themselves be reused, for example, in agricultural applications or construction materials.

By-product synergy is enhanced by materials exchange services that operate throughout the country. For example, the Materials Marketplace (http://materialsmarketplace .org/) facilitates by-product synergy in the United States and is sponsored by two private organizations: the US Business Council for Sustainable Development and Pathway21. As of January 2018, the Materials Marketplace noted that dozens of companies and local governments participated in its exchange.

The Industrial Resources Council (2018, http://www .industrialresourcescouncil.org/AboutUs/tabid/360/Default .aspx), an industry organization, reports that its member industries (power generation, metal casting, steel manufacturing, construction, rubber manufacturing, and pulp and paper manufacturing) produce more than 600 million

TABLE 7.1

Industrial materials that can be recycled

Coal combustion products
• Fly and bottom ash
• Boiler slag
• Flue gas desulfurization material

Can be recycled in
• Portland cement and concrete
• Flowable and structural fill
• Wallboard

Construction and demolition debris
• Concrete gypsum from drywall
• Metals
• Bricks
• Asphalt from roads and
  roofing shingles
• Wood from buildings

Can be recycled in
• Asphalt paving
• Concrete
• Re-milled lumber
• Wallboard

Foundry sand
• Spent sand used in metal casting

Can be recycled in
• Road embankments
• Flowable and structural fill
• Base and sub-base for road
  construction

SOURCE: "Industrial Materials," in *Industrial Materials Recycling: Managing Resources for Tomorrow*, US Environmental Protection Agency, Office of Solid Waste and Emergency Response, January 2007, https://nepis.epa.gov/Exe/ZyPURL.cgi?Dockey=60000E1A.txt (accessed November 13, 2017)

tons (544 million t) of materials annually. These industries are particularly interested in recycling the following products:

• Coal combustion residuals—ash, boiler slag (molten ash that crystallizes as it cools), and fine solid materials collected in flue gas treatment equipment can be reused in cement and concrete production or as a filler or solidifier. (See Table 7.1 for examples of reuses.)

• Construction and demolition (C&D) wastes—wastes resulting from the construction, renovation, and demolition of buildings, roads, and bridges. Typical C&D wastes include concrete, wood, asphalt, drywall, metals, bricks, glass, and cleared trees, stumps, and earth. Figure 7.1 shows building components and materials with a high recovery potential that are typically found in buildings. C&D debris from roads, bridges, and similar infrastructures is also reusable. (See Table 7.1 for examples of reuses.)

• Foundry sand—sand used in the manufacturing of metal parts produced in molds eventually becomes degraded and can be reused in engineering applications, such as embankments, or as a component of commercially available topsoil. (See Table 7.1 for examples of reuses.)

• Metal slags—mixtures of minerals and other impurities separated from metals during melting and cooled to form glassy granules that can be ground into a powder and reused, for example, in cement and concrete.

• Pulp and paper processing residuals—sludges containing wood fibers and minerals and other pulping liquors and residues can be used as soil amendments (e.g., fertilizers) or as cover materials at landfills.

• Scrap tires—because of their high petroleum content, scrap tires are widely combusted in waste-to-energy facilities. Scrap tires are also reused in civil engineering applications, such as roads and landfills, septic tank leach fields, and other construction projects. In addition, ground rubber from scrap tires is used to produce new rubber products and as a surface material at playgrounds and sports arenas, such as running tracks.

Organic by-products encompass a variety of carbon-containing materials from agricultural, commercial, industrial, municipal, and residential sources. (See Table 7.2.) Some wastes with high organic contents can be recycled into soil-enrichment products or mulch. One of the largest waste streams is biosolids, which are wastewater treatment sludges from municipal (sewage) plants or industrial facilities with organic-based processes, such as pulp and paper mills. Whatever their source, organic by-products usually require some type of treatment or processing before they can be reused.

STRIVING FOR "ZERO WASTE"

Some businesses strive to generate no waste that requires land disposal or incineration. This "zero waste" goal is espoused by various organizations. For example, Green Business Certification Inc. (GBCI; http://www.gbci.org/) operates a certification program to advance zero waste business practices. The TRUE Zero Waste certification system (http://true.gbci.org/) recognizes companies and other entities (such as universities) that divert 90% or more of their nonhazardous wastes from landfills, incineration, or other environmental disposal. Viable actions include recycling, reuse, recovery, and composting. GBCI (http://true.gbci.org/projects) indicates that, as of 2018, nearly 140 projects around the world had met its certification requirements. One example is a printing plant in Norcross, Georgia, operated by the *Atlanta Journal-Constitution* newspaper. According to GBCI (http://true.gbci.org/atlanta-journal-constitution-ajc-printing-plant), the newspaper's parent company, Cox Enterprises, established a goal of achieving "Zero Waste to Landfill by 2024."

MUNICIPAL SOLID WASTE RECOVERY

Municipal solid waste (MSW) is the everyday garbage produced by homes and businesses. As is described in Chapter 6, the US Environmental Protection Agency (EPA) conducts detailed estimates on the generation and recovery of this nonhazardous waste stream. The most recent estimates are provided in *Advancing Sustainable Materials Management: 2014 Tables and Figures* (December 2016, https://www.epa.gov/sites/production/files/2016-11/documents/2014_smm_tablesfigures_508.pdf), which includes data through 2014. The EPA reports that Americans recovered (recycled or composted)

FIGURE 7.1

Reuse of industrial materials in building construction

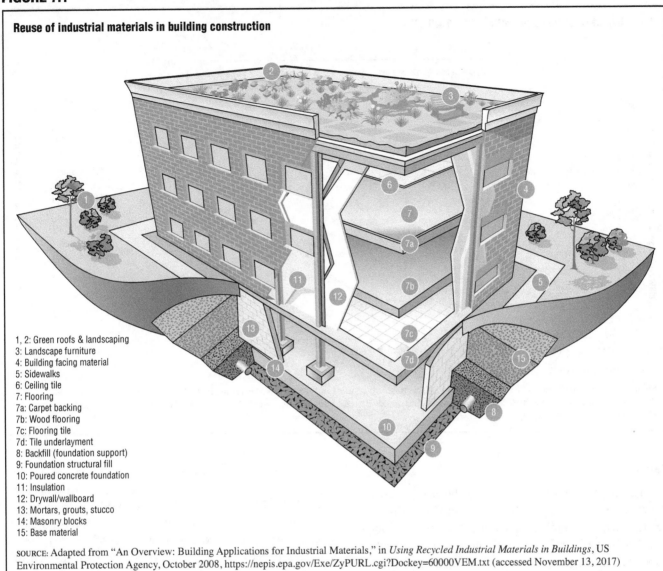

1, 2: Green roofs & landscaping
3: Landscape furniture
4: Building facing material
5: Sidewalks
6: Ceiling tile
7: Flooring
7a: Carpet backing
7b: Wood flooring
7c: Flooring tile
7d: Tile underlayment
8: Backfill (foundation support)
9: Foundation structural fill
10: Poured concrete foundation
11: Insulation
12: Drywall/wallboard
13: Mortars, grouts, stucco
14: Masonry blocks
15: Base material

SOURCE: Adapted from "An Overview: Building Applications for Industrial Materials," in *Using Recycled Industrial Materials in Buildings*, US Environmental Protection Agency, October 2008, https://nepis.epa.gov/Exe/ZyPURL.cgi?Dockey=60000VEM.txt (accessed November 13, 2017)

TABLE 7.2

Organic by-products

Animal manure and bedding
Biosolids
Food processing residuals (fruit and vegetable peelings, pulp, pits)
Food scraps
Hatchery wastes
Meat, seafood, poultry and dairy processing wastewater and solids
Mixed refuse (food scraps, paper etc.)
Pharmaceutical and brewery waste
Pulp and paper mill residues
Spent mushroom substrate
Textile residuals
Waste grain, silage
Wood ash
Yardwaste (leaves, grass clippings, woodchips)

SOURCE: Adapted from "Other Organic By-Products," in *Guide to Field Storage of Biosolids*, US Environmental Protection Agency, July 2000, https://www.epa.gov/sites/production/files/2015-05/documents/guide_to_field_storage_of_biosolids.pdf (accessed November 13, 2017)

89.4 million tons (81.1 million t) of MSW in 2014, accounting for 34.6% of the total MSW generated. (See Figure 7.2.) The recovery rate has more than doubled since 1990, when it stood at 16%. Figure 7.3 provides a breakdown by material for 2014. Paper and paperboard was the largest component, accounting for nearly half (49.7%) of the recovery total.

Figure 7.4 shows recovery rates as a percentage of generation for specific MSW components in 2014. Overall, lead-acid batteries had the highest recovery rate (98.9%), followed by corrugated boxes (89.5%) and steel cans (70.7%). Table 7.3 provides a more detailed breakdown of the entire MSW stream for 2014. Nonferrous metals other than aluminum had the highest recovery rate at 66.7%. Paper and paperboard (64.7%) and yard trimmings (61.1%) also had rates in excess of 50%.

FIGURE 7.2

Recycling rates for municipal solid waste, 1960–2014

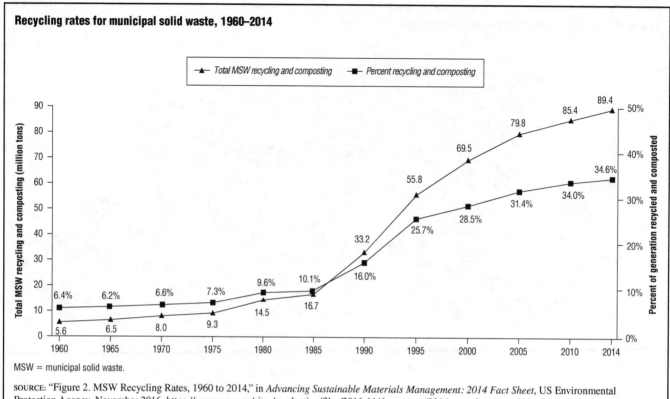

MSW = municipal solid waste.

SOURCE: "Figure 2. MSW Recycling Rates, 1960 to 2014," in *Advancing Sustainable Materials Management: 2014 Fact Sheet*, US Environmental Protection Agency, November 2016, https://www.epa.gov/sites/production/files/2016-11/documents/2014_smmfactsheet_508.pdf (accessed November 13, 2017)

Paper

The paper industry has been at the leading edge of the recycling revolution. Used paper-based products can be de-inked in chemical baths and reduced to a fibrous slurry that can be reformulated into new paper products. Paper can undergo this process several times before the fibers become too damaged for reuse. Paper products vary greatly in the type (hardwood versus softwood) and length of fibers that are used to make them. Recycled papers must typically be sorted into particular usage categories (e.g., newsprint or fine writing papers) before being reprocessed.

Table 7.4 shows EPA estimates of the percentage of paper (and paperboard) products recovered in selected years between 1960 and 2014. Overall, the recovery rate in 2014 was 64.7%. By contrast, only 16.9% of paper and paperboard was recovered in 1960.

Glass

Waste glass can be melted down and formed into new glass products over and over without losing its structural integrity. Virgin raw materials, such as sand, limestone, and soda ash, are added as needed to formulate new glass products. However, colored glass cannot be easily decolorized. This means that glass products must be sorted by color before reprocessing.

Table 7.4 shows EPA estimates of the percentage of glass products recovered in selected years between 1960 and 2014. Most glass that becomes MSW is from bottles and jars that were manufactured for food and drink products. The glass recovery rate in 1960 was 1.5%; it increased between 1970 and 2010 and then leveled off. In 2014 it was 26%.

Metals

Ferrous metals (iron and steel) are primarily used in durable goods such as appliances, furniture, and tires. Aluminum is used extensively in drink and food cans and packaging materials. Lead, zinc, and copper fall under the category "other nonferrous metals." They are found in batteries, appliances, and consumer electronics.

Metals recovery was virtually nonexistent in 1960, and it remained relatively flat until the 1980s, when it began increasing dramatically. (See Table 7.4.) Recovery leveled off during the first decade of the 21st century. Recovery rates differed greatly from metal to metal in 2014. Two-thirds (66.7%) of other nonferrous metals in the MSW stream were recovered, compared with only 33% of ferrous metals and 19.8% of aluminum.

Plastics

Plastic products are manufactured from chemical resins that are molded into various shapes. There are dozens

FIGURE 7.3

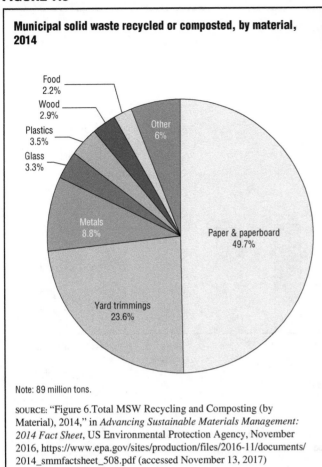

Municipal solid waste recycled or composted, by material, 2014

Food 2.2%
Wood 2.9%
Plastics 3.5%
Glass 3.3%
Metals 8.8%
Other 6%
Paper & paperboard 49.7%
Yard trimmings 23.6%

Note: 89 million tons.

SOURCE: "Figure 6. Total MSW Recycling and Composting (by Material), 2014," in *Advancing Sustainable Materials Management: 2014 Fact Sheet*, US Environmental Protection Agency, November 2016, https://www.epa.gov/sites/production/files/2016-11/documents/2014_smmfactsheet_508.pdf (accessed November 13, 2017)

of resins in common use, each with a different chemical formulation. Although waste plastic products can be melted down and reformulated into new products, they must first be sorted by resin type.

As shown in Table 6.7 and Table 6.8 in Chapter 6, in 1960 there were virtually no plastic products in MSW. In 2014 the MSW stream contained 33.3 million tons (30.2 million t) of plastic products. This massive increase in generation has been accompanied by low rates of recovery. Only 9.5% of all plastic products generated in MSW in 2014 were recovered. (See Table 7.4.)

Consumer Electronics

Computers and other electronic devices contain materials that are valuable for reuse, particularly metals, plastics, and glass. The most common metals in personal computers are aluminum, steel, and copper. Small amounts of precious metals, such as gold, palladium, platinum, and silver, are also found in computer circuit boards. Some of the metals used in personal computers (antimony, arsenic, cadmium, chromium, cobalt, lead, mercury, and selenium) are classified as hazardous by the Resource Conservation and Recovery Act and cannot be disposed of in MSW landfills. As a result, some states

mandate the recycling of computers and other consumer electronic products.

The primary source of plastics in electronic devices is computer casings. Plastic can be melted down to produce new materials or used as a fuel in certain industrial processes. Most of the glass content of computers is in monitors, both the older types containing cathode-ray tubes (CRTs) and the newer liquid crystal display (LCD) and light-emitting diode (LED) monitors. CRT glass contains lead, which is a hazardous material. Likewise, older LCD monitors contain mercury, another hazardous material; however, many newer models are mercury free. LED monitors contain neither mercury nor lead. LCD and LED monitors and television screens pose their own recycling challenges, however, mainly because they contain very thin layers of materials that are difficult to separate.

As is noted in Chapter 6, the EPA estimates that 3.4 million tons (3.1 million t) of consumer electronic products entered the MSW stream in 2014. This included selected products, such as televisions, compact disc and digital video disc players, video cameras, stereo systems, telephones, and computer equipment. Figure 7.4 shows that 41.7% of consumer electronic products were recovered for recycling in 2014.

The EPA's Sustainable Materials Management Electronics Challenge program (2018, https://www.epa.gov/smm-electronics) is a partnership between the agency and consumer companies that manufacture and/or sell electronic goods and companies that provide mobile services, such as cell phone service. Participants in the program offer the public opportunities to drop off or mail in unwanted electronic products. These products are typically reused, refurbished, or have their valuable components (e.g., gold, lead, or copper) recovered. This reduces the amount of electronic waste requiring disposal, thereby decreasing the risk of heavy metals and other toxic chemicals within the products leaching into the environment.

The electronics challenge program encourages manufacturers to use reverse supply chain methods to reduce MSW generation. A supply chain is the series of activities and feedstocks that go into manufacturing a final product. In "The Reverse Supply Chain" (HBR.org, February 2002), V. Daniel R. Guide Jr. and Luk N. Van Wassenhove define the reverse supply chain as "the series of activities required to retrieve a used product from a customer and either dispose of it or reuse it." High consumer demand for electronic products makes them particularly attractive candidates for reverse supply chain methods that result in reusable products. For example, cell phone and computer manufacturers acquire used products and refurbish them for resale. Guide and Wassenhove note that these companies "target customers who cannot afford the new products but who would jump at the chance to buy used versions at lower prices."

FIGURE 7.4

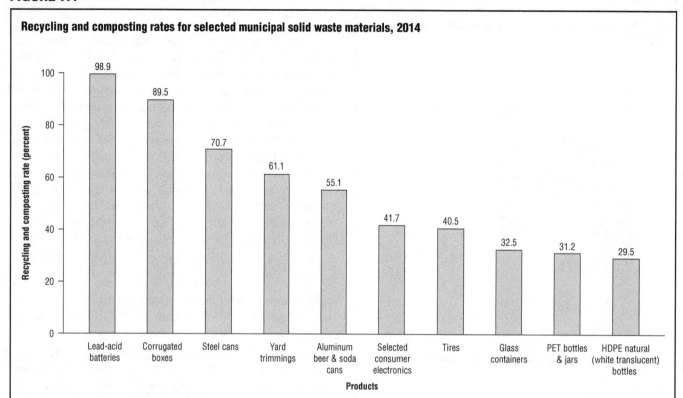

Recycling and composting rates for selected municipal solid waste materials, 2014

Note: Does not include combustion with energy recovery.
PET = polyethylene terephthalate. HDPE = high density polyethylene.

SOURCE: "Figure 3. Recycling and Composting Rates of Selected Products, 2014," in *Advancing Sustainable Materials Management: 2014 Fact Sheet*, US Environmental Protection Agency, November 2016, https://www.epa.gov/sites/production/files/2016-11/documents/2014_smmfactsheet_508.pdf (accessed November 13, 2017)

Yard Trimmings and Food Waste

Yard trimmings and food waste can be recovered through composting. The materials biodegrade into a soil-like product that can be used as a soil amendment or mulch. Compostable wastes in MSW include grass and garden cuttings, leaves, and kitchen refuse, such as potato peelings, coffee grounds, and eggshells. Compost created on a large scale is often used in landscaping, land reclamation, and landfill cover and to provide high-nutrient soil for farms and nurseries. As shown in Table 6.7 in Chapter 6, in 2014 the MSW stream contained 34.5 million tons (31.3 million t) of yard trimmings and 38.4 million tons (34.8 million t) of food waste. In 1960 recovery of these waste materials was negligible. (See Table 7.4.) The recovery rates grew during later decades and by 2014 had reached 61.1% for yard trimmings and 5.1% for food waste.

The EPA states in *Advancing Sustainable Materials Management: 2014 Tables and Figures* that in 2014 residential food collection and composting programs served 2.8 million households in the United States. These community-based operations offer curbside pickup of compostable wastes and/or drop-off facilities for public convenience.

Yard trimmings and food waste are also recovered through backyard composting; however, the EPA does not provide estimates of the amounts involved. The agency does offer tips for people who engage in backyard composting. For example, Table 7.5 lists organic materials that the EPA believes are well suited for backyard composting. Table 7.6 lists organic materials that the EPA, for various reasons, does not recommend for backyard composting. Some organic materials are deemed unsuitable for backyard composting because they cause odors, attract pests, pose a threat to human health, or are otherwise harmful to the environment. Community-based composting operations may accept materials (such as dairy products and meat scraps) that are not typically recommended for backyard composting.

MSW Recycling Programs

The successful recycling of any product within MSW depends on the success of three key components in the recycling process:

- Collection and sorting of the products to be recycled

- Processing and manufacturing technologies to convert waste materials into new products

- Consumer demand for recycled products and those containing recycled materials

TABLE 7.3

Generation and disposition of municipal solid waste, 2014

[In millions of tons and percent of generation of each material]

Material	Weight generated	Weight recycled	Weight composted	Weight combusted with energy recovery	Weight landfilled	Recycling as percent of generation	Composting as percent of generation	Combustion as percent of generation	Landfilling as percent of generation
Paper and paperboard	68.61	44.40		4.74	19.47	64.7%		6.9%	28.4%
Glass	11.48	2.99		1.45	7.04	26.0%		12.6%	61.3%
Metals									
Steel	17.69	5.84		2.02	9.83	33.0%		11.4%	55.6%
Aluminum	3.53	0.70		0.47	2.36	19.8%		13.3%	66.9%
Other nonferrous metals[a]	2.04	1.36		0.05	0.63	66.7%		2.5%	30.9%
Total metals	**23.26**	**7.90**		**2.54**	**12.82**	**34.0%**		**10.9%**	**55.1%**
Plastics	33.25	3.17		4.98	25.10	9.5%		15.0%	75.5%
Rubber and leather	8.21	1.44		2.62	4.15	17.5%		31.9%	50.5%
Textiles	16.22	2.62		3.14	10.46	16.2%		19.4%	64.5%
Wood	16.12	2.57		2.54	11.01	15.9%		15.8%	68.3%
Other materials	4.44	1.29		0.57	2.58	29.1%		12.8%	58.1%
Total materials in products	**181.59**	**66.38**		**22.58**	**92.63**	**36.6%**		**12.4%**	**51.0%**
Other wastes									
Food, other[b]	38.40		1.94	7.15	29.31		5.1%	18.6%	76.3%
Yard trimmings	34.50		21.08	2.63	10.79		61.1%	7.6%	31.3%
Miscellaneous inorganic wastes	3.97			0.78	3.19			19.6%	80.4%
Total other wastes	**76.87**		**23.02**	**10.56**	**43.29**		**29.9%**	**13.7%**	**56.3%**
Total municipal solid waste	**258.46**	**66.38**	**23.02**	**33.14**	**135.92**	**25.7%**	**8.9%**	**12.8%**	**52.6%**

[a]Includes lead from lead-acid batteries.
[b]Includes collection of other MSW organics for composting.
MSW = municipal solid waste.
Note: Includes waste from residential, commercial and institutional sources.
Details might not add to totals due to rounding.

SOURCE: "Table 1. Generation, Recycling, Composting, Combustion with Energy Recovery and Landfilling of Materials in MSW, 2014," in *Advancing Sustainable Materials Management: 2014 Fact Sheet*, US Environmental Protection Agency, November 2016, https://www.epa.gov/sites/production/files/2016-11/documents/2014_smmfactsheet_508.pdf (accessed November 13, 2017)

Lack of any one of these components seriously jeopardizes recovery efforts for a particular material within the MSW stream. The following discussion is based on information provided by the EPA in *Advancing Sustainable Materials Management: 2014 Tables and Figures*.

COLLECTION METHODS. Curbside programs are those in which recyclable items are collected from bins placed outside residences. Some municipalities offer reward programs to encourage curbside recycling. These programs typically provide residents with points based on the number of pounds of materials they place in their recycling bins for curbside pickup. The points can be redeemed for items such as gift certificates to restaurants or stores.

Drop-off centers for recyclable materials are operated by various entities, including cities, grocery stores, charitable organizations, and apartment complexes. Typically, they accept a broader range of materials than curbside collection programs.

Two systems provide a cash incentive to encourage recycling. These are buy-back centers and deposit programs. Buy-back centers are typically businesses that pay cash for recovered materials, such as scrap metal, aluminum cans, or paper. Deposit programs charge consumers a deposit or fee on beverage containers at the time of purchase, typically ranging from 5 cents to 10 cents per container. The deposit can be redeemed if the container is returned empty for reuse. The EPA reports that in 2014 there were 10 states operating deposit-type programs for bottles: California, Connecticut, Hawaii, Iowa, Maine, Massachusetts, Michigan, New York, Oregon, and Vermont. Deposit amounts vary by state.

Materials recovery facilities (MRFs) sort collected recyclables, process them, and ship them to companies that can use them to produce new or reformulated products. For example, an MRF may sort and crush various types of glass recovered from curbside programs and then ship the processed glass to a bottle factory, where it can be used to produce new bottles. The EPA notes that in 2014 there were 797 MRFs operating in the United States, which processed more than 140,000 tons (127,006 t) of materials per day.

Commercial establishments recycle large quantities of MSW. Commonly recycled materials in the business sector are old corrugated containers and office papers, which are typically picked up by paper dealers. Likewise, many businesses collect used office paper, which they turn over to paper dealers.

TABLE 7.4

Materials recycled and composted in municipal solid waste, selected years 1960–2014

Materials	Percent of generation of each material									
	1960	1970	1980	1990	2000	2005	2010	2012	2013	2014
Paper and paperboard	16.9%	15.3%	21.3%	27.8%	42.8%	49.5%	62.5%	64.6%	63.3%	64.7%
Glass	1.5%	1.3%	5.0%	20.1%	22.6%	20.7%	27.2%	27.7%	27.3%	26.0%
Metals										
Ferrous	0.5%	1.2%	2.9%	17.6%	33.1%	33.0%	34.3%	33.0%	33.1%	33.0%
Aluminum	Neg.	1.3%	17.9%	35.9%	27.0%	20.7%	19.4%	20.2%	20.0%	19.8%
Other nonferrous	Neg.	47.8%	46.6%	66.4%	66.3%	68.8%	71.3%	70.2%	68.2%	66.7%
Total metals	**0.5%**	**3.5%**	**7.9%**	**24.0%**	**34.8%**	**34.3%**	**35.3%**	**34.3%**	**34.2%**	**34.0%**
Plastics	Neg.	Neg.	0.3%	2.2%	5.8%	6.1%	8.0%	8.7%	9.2%	9.5%
Rubber and leather	17.9%	8.4%	3.1%	6.4%	12.3%	14.4%	18.6%	18.5%	17.8%	17.5%
Textiles	2.8%	2.9%	6.3%	11.4%	13.9%	15.9%	15.5%	15.8%	15.5%	16.2%
Wood	Neg.	Neg.	Neg.	1.1%	10.1%	12.4%	14.5%	15.2%	15.7%	15.9%
Other[a]	Neg.	39.0%	19.8%	21.3%	24.5%	28.2%	29.1%	28.7%	29.3%	29.1%
Total materials in products	**10.3%**	**9.6%**	**13.3%**	**19.8%**	**29.7%**	**32.0%**	**36.6%**	**36.9%**	**36.2%**	**36.6%**
Other wastes	Neg.	Neg.	Neg.	Neg.	2.2%	2.1%	2.7%	4.8%	5.0%	5.1%
Food, other[b]										
Yard trimmings	Neg.	Neg.	Neg.	12.0%	51.7%	61.9%	57.5%	57.7%	60.2%	61.1%
Miscellaneous inorganic wastes	Neg.	Neg.	Neg.	Neg.	Neg.	Neg.	Neg.	Neg.	Neg.	Neg.
Total other wastes	**Neg.**	**Neg.**	**Neg.**	**6.8%**	**25.4%**	**29.9%**	**27.6%**	**28.7%**	**29.8%**	**29.9%**
Total MSW recycled and composted-%	**6.4%**	**6.6%**	**9.6%**	**16.0%**	**28.5%**	**31.4%**	**34.0%**	**34.5%**	**34.3%**	**34.6%**

[a]Collection of electrolytes in batteries; probably not recycled.
[b]Includes paper and mixed MSW for composting.
Neg = Less than 5,000 tons or 0.05 percent.
MSW = municipal solid waste.
Note: Recycling and composting of postconsumer wastes; does not include converting/fabrication scrap. Details may not add to totals due to rounding.

SOURCE: Adapted from "Table 2. Materials Recycled and Composted in Municipal Solid Waste, 1960 to 2014," in *Advancing Sustainable Materials Management: 2014 Tables and Figures*, US Environmental Protection Agency, December 2016, https://www.epa.gov/sites/production/files/2016-11/documents/2014_smm_tablesfigures_508.pdf (accessed November 13, 2017)

TABLE 7.5

Waste materials that the US Environmental Protection Agency recommends for backyard composting

- Fruits and vegetables
- Eggshells
- Coffee grounds and filters
- Tea bags
- Nut shells
- Shredded newspaper
- Cardboard
- Paper
- Yard trimmings
- Grass clippings
- Houseplants
- Hay and straw
- Leaves
- Sawdust
- Wood chips
- Cotton and wool rags
- Dryer and vacuum cleaner lint
- Hair and fur
- Fireplace ashes

SOURCE: "What to Compost," in *Composting at Home*, US Environmental Protection Agency, March 20, 2017, https://www.epa.gov/recycle/composting-home (accessed November 14, 2017)

TABLE 7.6

Waste materials that the US Environmental Protection Agency does not recommend for backyard composting

Material	Why it is not appropriate for composting
Black walnut tree leaves or twigs	Releases substances that might be harmful to plants
Coal or charcoal ash	Might contain substances harmful to plants
Dairy products (e.g., butter, milk, sour cream, yogurt) and eggs*	Create odor problems and attract pests such as rodents and flies
Diseased or insect-ridden plants	Diseases or insects might survive and be transferred back to other plants
Fats, grease, lard, or oils*	Create odor problems and attract pests such as rodents and flies
Meat or fish bones and scraps*	Create odor problems and attract pests such as rodents and flies
Pet wastes (e.g., dog or cat feces, soiled cat litter)*	Might contain parasites, bacteria, germs, pathogens, and viruses harmful to humans
Yard trimmings treated with chemical pesticides	Might kill beneficial composting organisms

*Check with your local composting or recycling coordinator to see if these organics are accepted by your community curbside or drop-off composting program.

SOURCE: "What Not to Compost and Why," in *Composting at Home*, US Environmental Protection Agency, March 20, 2017, https://www.epa.gov/recycle/composting-home (accessed November 14, 2017)

The Role of Government in MSW Recycling

The oldest recycling law in the United States is the Oregon Recycling Opportunity Act, which was passed in 1983 and went into effect in 1986. The act established curbside residential recycling opportunities in large cities and set up drop-off depots in small towns and rural areas. Since that time, many US cities and states have set recycling/recovery goals for their municipal waste. In addition, some jurisdictions provide financial assistance, incentive money, or tax credits or exemptions for recycling businesses (such as companies that manufacture or process recycled products).

For recycling programs to work, there must be markets for recycled products. A growing number of states require that many consumer goods sold must be made from recycled products. For example, newspaper publishers may have to use a minimum proportion of recycled paper. All states have some kind of "buy recycled" program that requires their government agencies to purchase recycled products when possible.

The federal government helps create a market for recycled goods as well. The Resource Conservation and Recovery Act requires federal procuring agencies to purchase recycled-content products that are designated by the EPA in its overall Comprehensive Procurement Guidelines (https://www.epa.gov/smm/comprehensive-procurement-guideline-cpg-program). EPA guidance regarding the purchase of recycled-content products is also included in the Recovered Materials Advisory Notices, which are published periodically and include recommended recycled-content ranges for Comprehensive Procurement Guidelines products that are commercially available.

THE HISTORY AND CURRENT STRENGTH OF MSW RECYCLING

As with any business, recycling is subject to the cyclical highs and lows of supply and demand. During the early years of recycling, there was not enough demand for all the plastic, paper, and other materials that were recovered. It was difficult for private recycling companies to make a profit. Instead of earning money from recycling, the programs cost them money. Some cities even started dumping their recycled materials into landfills because they could not sell them. Eventually, markets grew for some recycled materials, particularly in the paper sector. Market growth has been helped by the widespread public support that recycling receives.

Table 7.4 and Figure 7.5 show that the recovery of materials in MSW grew dramatically during the 1990s compared with previous decades. After 2000, however, the proportion of recovered MSW grew much more

FIGURE 7.5

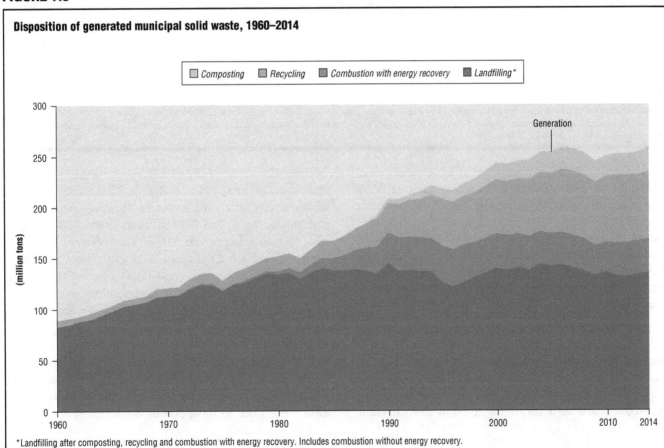

Disposition of generated municipal solid waste, 1960–2014

*Landfilling after composting, recycling and combustion with energy recovery. Includes combustion without energy recovery.

SOURCE: "Figure 12. Recycling, Composting, Combustion with Energy Recovery and Landfilling of Materials in MSW, 1960 to 2014," in *Advancing Sustainable Materials Management: 2014 Tables and Figures*, US Environmental Protection Agency, December 2016, https://www.epa.gov/sites/production/files/2016-11/documents/2014_smm_tablesfigures_508.pdf (accessed November 13, 2017)

TABLE 7.7

Examples of source reduction practices

Source reduction practice	MSW product categories			
	Durable goods	Nondurable goods	Containers & packaging	Organics (wood, yard waste, food, etc.)
Product or packaging redesign				
Materials reduction	• Downgauge metals in appliances	• Paperless purchase orders • Concentrated products	• Container lightweighting • Right size packaging • Eliminate unnecessary layers of packaging • Refillable/reusable containers, including use of flexible pouches for refills for rigid containers	• Xeriscaping • Just in time ordering/ inventory control • Adjust menus to reduce frequently uneaten or wasted items
Materials substitution	• Use of composites in appliances and electronic circuitry		• Replace rigid or heavy packaging with lighter or more compact options, e.g., cereal in bags, coffee in brick packs • Use life cycle data to choose material with lower lifecycle impact	
Lengthen life	• High mileage tires • Electronic components reduce moving parts	• Regular servicing • Consider purchasing warranties to make repair more affordable • Extend warranties	• Design for secondary use • Design for upgrades (e.g., add computer memory or processing capacity, battery upgrades) • Reusable packaging	• Clearer label information on food expiration date • Avoid spoilage by changing: — Packaging — Storage and transportation — Supply chain management
Consumer practices				
	• Purchase long lived products • Regular servicing • Repair • Buying less stuff	• Repair • Duplex printing • Sharing • Reduce unwanted mail • Purchasing concentrated products • Buying less stuff	• Purchasing products in bulk (less packaging) • Reusable bags and containers • Buying less stuff	• Food donation • Avoid spoilage by monitoring and tracking food and purchases and use • Reduce over-purchasing • Proper food storage and preparation • Repurposing (e.g., older bread can be made into croutons) • Backyard composting • Vermi-composting • Grasscycling

MSW = municipal solid waste.

SOURCE: Adapted from "Table 30. Selected Examples of Source Reduction Practices," in *Advancing Sustainable Materials Management: 2014 Tables and Figures*, US Environmental Protection Agency, December 2016, https://www.epa.gov/sites/production/files/2016-11/documents/2014_smm_tablesfigures_508.pdf (accessed November 13, 2017)

slowly. Some analysts believe recycling rates for MSW have reached a plateau and cannot easily be increased because of the supply-and-demand imbalance in recycled-content markets. They prefer to focus on source reduction (reducing the amount of municipal waste produced originally). Table 7.7 lists examples of source reduction practices for product and packaging companies and for consumers.

One method for reducing MSW generation is a principle called extended producer responsibility. Extended producer responsibility regulations require manufacturers and producers to take some responsibility for the final disposition of their products. This provides an incentive for products and their packaging to be more recoverable

and contain less toxic materials. Extended producer responsibility is a cornerstone of recycling requirements in Canada, Japan, and the European Union and is beginning to play a larger role in the United States. The Electronics TakeBack Coalition (2018, http://www.electronicstakeback.com/promote-good-laws/state-legislation), a national coalition of nonprofit organizations, notes that as of January 2018, 25 states had passed legislation mandating some form of electronic waste recycling. For example, the New York State Department of Environmental Conservation (2018, http://www.dec.ny.gov/chemical/65583.html) indicates that New York "requires manufacturers to provide free and convenient recycling of electronic waste to most consumers in the state."

CHAPTER 8
HAZARDOUS AND RADIOACTIVE WASTE

The most toxic and dangerous waste materials produced in the United States are those classified by the government as hazardous or radioactive.

WHAT IS HAZARDOUS WASTE?

Hazardous waste is dangerous solid waste. The federal government's definition of solid waste includes materials one would ordinarily consider solid, as well as sludges, semisolids, liquids, and even containers of gases. The vast majority of hazardous waste is generated by industrial sources. Small amounts come from commercial and residential sources.

Officially, hazardous waste is defined by the federal government as a waste that is either listed as such in regulations issued by the US Environmental Protection Agency (EPA) or that exhibits one or more of the following characteristics: corrosivity, ignitability, reactivity, or toxicity. (See Figure 8.1.) As of January 2018, the EPA had a list of more than 1,500 hazardous wastes. The list is published in the Code of Federal Regulations (CFR; January 30, 2018, https://www.ecfr.gov/cgi-bin/ECFR?page=browse) under Title 40, Section 261.31–33.

Because of its dangerous characteristics, hazardous waste requires special care when being stored, transported, or discarded. Most hazardous wastes are regulated under Subtitle C of the Resource Conservation and Recovery Act (RCRA). The EPA has the primary responsibility for permitting facilities that treat, store, and dispose of hazardous waste. The states can adopt more stringent regulations if they wish.

Contamination of the air, water, and soil with hazardous waste can frequently lead to serious health problems. Exposure to some hazardous wastes is believed to cause cancer, degenerative diseases, intellectual disabilities, birth defects, and chromosomal changes. Although most scientists agree that exposure to high doses of hazardous waste is dangerous, there is less agreement on the danger of exposure to low doses.

INDUSTRIAL HAZARDOUS WASTE

Every two years since 1991 the EPA, in partnership with the states, has conducted an inventory of the nation's industrial hazardous waste. As of January 2018, the most recent data available were from 2015 (https://rcrainfo.epa.gov/rcrainfoweb/action/modules/br/summary/view).

As shown in Table 8.1, 33.6 million tons (30.5 million t) of RCRA hazardous waste were generated in 2015. Texas was, by far, the leading generator among the states, accounting for 16.3 million tons (14.8 million t), or 48% of the total. It was followed by Louisiana (5 million tons [4.5 million t]) and Mississippi (1.9 million tons [1.8 million t]). These Gulf Coast states are home to many large facilities that are engaged in chemical production and petroleum refining.

According to the EPA (https://rcrainfo.epa.gov/rcrainfoweb/action/modules/br/naics/view), the 10 industries that generated the most hazardous waste in 2015 were:

- Basic chemical manufacturing—19.7 million tons (17.9 million t)

- Petroleum and coal products manufacturing—4.8 million tons (4.4 million t)

- Waste treatment and disposal—3.2 million tons (2.9 million t)

- Iron and steel mills and ferroalloy manufacturing—1.3 million tons (1.2 million t)

- Nonferrous metal (except aluminum) production and processing—914,990 tons (830,065 t)

- Semiconductor and other electronic component manufacturing—429,611 tons (389,737 t)

FIGURE 8.1

Types of hazardous waste

- Corrosive—A corrosive material can wear away (corrode) or destroy a substance. For example, most acids are corrosives that can eat through metal, burn skin on contact, and give off vapors that burn the eyes.

- Ignitable—An ignitable material can burst into flames easily. It poses a fire hazard; can irritate the skin, eyes, and lungs; and may give off harmful vapors. Gasoline, paint, and furniture polish are ignitable.

- Reactive—A reactive material can explode or create poisonous gas when combined with other chemicals. For example, chlorine bleach and ammonia are reactive and create a poisonous gas when they come into contact with each other.

- Toxic—Toxic materials or substances can poison people and other life. Toxic substances can cause illness and even death if swallowed or absorbed through the skin. Pesticides, weed killers, and many household cleaners are toxic.

SOURCE: "Fast Flash I: Hazardous Substances and Hazardous Waste," in *HAZ-ED: Classroom Activities for Understanding Hazardous Waste*, US Environmental Protection Agency, April 1996, https://nepis.epa .gov/Exe/ZyNET.exe/10001XBX.TXT?ZyActionD=ZyDocument& Client=EPA&Index=1995+Thru+1999&Docs=&Query=&Time=&End Time=&SearchMethod=1&TocRestrict=n&Toc=&TocEntry=&QField= &QFieldYear=&QFieldMonth=&QFieldDay=&IntQFieldOp=0&ExtQ FieldOp=0&XmlQuery=&File=D%3A%5Czyfiles%5CIndex%20Data %5C95thru99%5CTxt%5C00000000%5C10001XBX.txt&User= ANONYMOUS&Password=anonymous&SortMethod=h%7C-& MaximumDocuments=1&FuzzyDegree=0&ImageQuality=r75g8/ r75g8/x150y150g16/i425&Display=hpfr&DefSeekPage=x&Search Back=ZyActionL&Back=ZyActionS&BackDesc=Results%20page &MaximumPages=1&ZyEntry=1&SeekPage=x&ZyPURL (accessed November 14, 2017)

- Pharmaceutical and medicine manufacturing—268,951 tons (243,988 t)

- Pesticide, fertilizer, and other agricultural chemical manufacturing—262,367 tons (238,015 t)

- Coating, engraving, heat treating, and allied activities—246,546 tons (223,663 t)

- Resin, synthetic rubber, and artificial synthetic fibers and filaments—234,920 tons (213,116 t)

METHODS OF MANAGING HAZARDOUS WASTE

Before the 1970s most industrial hazardous waste was dumped in landfills, stored on-site, burned, or discharged into surface waters with little or no treatment.

TABLE 8.1

Resource Conservation and Recovery Act hazardous waste generated, by state, 2015

Location	Number of generators	Hazardous waste generated (tons)
National	26,794	33,646,785
Alabama	432	709,666
Alaska	45	3,965
American Samoa	0	0
Arizona	320	38,696
Arkansas	109	338,703
California	3,395	309,123
Colorado	209	40,440
Connecticut	458	35,939
Delaware	101	12,577
District of Columbia	74	1,078
Florida	520	90,847
Georgia	821	172,752
Guam	19	140
Hawaii	100	484,603
Idaho	72	7,049
Illinois	1,083	601,542
Indiana	822	930,379
Iowa	209	56,946
Kansas	257	1,280,076
Kentucky	326	135,106
Louisiana	508	5,010,182
Maine	138	2,606
Maryland	342	125,807
Massachusetts	813	39,108
Michigan	535	407,754
Minnesota	362	120,862
Mississippi	147	1,946,349
Missouri	482	291,067
Montana	72	6,773
Navajo Nation	1	45
Nebraska	104	26,839
Nevada	141	13,141
New Hampshire	232	3,714
New Jersey	948	333,804
New Mexico	89	5,631
New York	3,636	281,259
North Carolina	611	81,153
North Dakota	35	265,051
Northern Marianas	1	2
Ohio	1,324	1,711,110
Oklahoma	242	105,306
Oregon	252	52,830
Pennsylvania	1,422	293,947
Puerto Rico	97	20,312
Rhode Island	184	7,252
South Carolina	519	154,595
South Dakota	43	1,917
Tennessee	290	47,756
Texas	1,686	16,288,728
Trust territories	1	0
Utah	167	33,927
Vermont	62	288,019
Virgin Islands	5	299
Virginia	567	62,418
Washington	512	135,461
West Virginia	259	52,168
Wisconsin	559	172,716
Wyoming	34	7,250

SOURCE: Adapted from "Biennial Report Summary," in *2015 Biennial Report Summary Results for National*, US Environmental Protection Agency, 2017, https://rcrainfo.epa.gov/rcrainfoweb/action/modules/br/ summary/view (accessed November 14, 2017)

Since the Pollution Prevention Act of 1990, industrial waste management follows a hierarchy introduced by the EPA that advocates source reduction first, followed by recycling or reuse, and then treatment. (See Figure 8.2.)

FIGURE 8.2

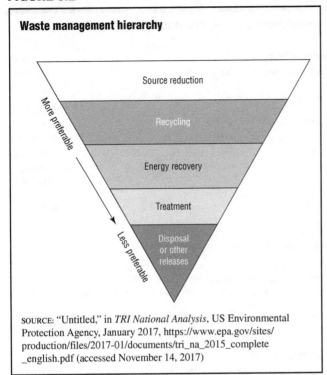

Waste management hierarchy

Source reduction

Recycling

Energy recovery

Treatment

Disposal or other releases

More preferable

Less preferable

SOURCE: "Untitled," in *TRI National Analysis*, US Environmental Protection Agency, January 2017, https://www.epa.gov/sites/production/files/2017-01/documents/tri_na_2015_complete_english.pdf (accessed November 14, 2017)

FIGURE 8.3

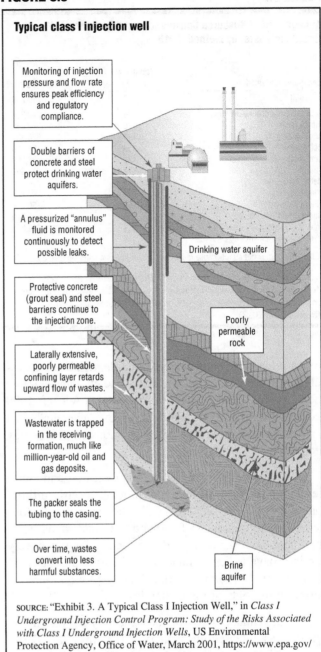

Typical class I injection well

Monitoring of injection pressure and flow rate ensures peak efficiency and regulatory compliance.

Double barriers of concrete and steel protect drinking water aquifers.

A pressurized "annulus" fluid is monitored continuously to detect possible leaks.

Protective concrete (grout seal) and steel barriers continue to the injection zone.

Laterally extensive, poorly permeable confining layer retards upward flow of wastes.

Wastewater is trapped in the receiving formation, much like million-year-old oil and gas deposits.

The packer seals the tubing to the casing.

Over time, wastes convert into less harmful substances.

Drinking water aquifer

Poorly permeable rock

Brine aquifer

SOURCE: "Exhibit 3. A Typical Class I Injection Well," in *Class I Underground Injection Control Program: Study of the Risks Associated with Class I Underground Injection Wells*, US Environmental Protection Agency, Office of Water, March 2001, https://www.epa.gov/sites/production/files/2015-07/documents/study_uic-class1_study_risks_class1.pdf (accessed November 14, 2017)

Source reduction is an activity that prevents the generation of waste initially, such as a change in operating practices or raw materials. The second choice is recycling, followed by energy recovery. If none of these methods is feasible, then treatment before disposal is recommended.

A variety of chemical, biological, and thermal processes can be applied to neutralize or destroy toxic compounds in hazardous waste. For example, microorganisms and chemicals can remove hazardous hydrocarbons from contaminated water. State and federal regulations require the pretreatment of most hazardous wastes before they are discarded in landfills. These treated materials can only be placed in specially designed land disposal facilities. Besides land disposal, hazardous wastes may be injected under high pressure into underground wells that are thousands of feet deep. (See Figure 8.3.) Hazardous waste can also be burned in incinerators. As waste is burned, however, hot gases are released into the atmosphere, carrying toxic materials not consumed by the flames. In 1999 the federal government imposed a ban on new hazardous waste incinerators.

Table 8.2 lists the management methods that were used in 2015 to handle 33.1 million tons (30.1 million t) of RCRA hazardous wastes. The vast majority of it—23.8 million tons (21.6 million t), or 72% of the total—was managed through deep well or underground injection. Note that the total amount of hazardous waste managed in 2015 was less than the total amount generated; the remaining waste was managed during subsequent years.

FEDERAL REGULATION OF HAZARDOUS WASTES

The Toxics Release Inventory

The Toxics Release Inventory (TRI; https://www.epa.gov/toxics-release-inventory-tri-program) was established under the Emergency Planning and Community Right-to-Know Act of 1986. Under the program certain industrial facilities that use specific toxic chemicals must report annually on their waste management activities and toxic chemical releases. These releases are to air, land, or water. According to the EPA, in "Learn about the Toxics Release Inventory" (May 15, 2017, https://www.epa.gov/

TABLE 8.2

Management of Resource Conservation and Recovery Act hazardous waste, by method, 2015

Management method	Number of facilities	Managed (tons)
Total	**1,332**	**33,130,299**
Deepwell/underground injection	40	23,780,226
Energy recovery	70	1,562,283
Fuel blending	116	676,381
Incineration	159	1,126,330
Land treatment/application	21	32,208
Landfill	77	1,263,309
Metals recovery	125	746,362
Other recovery	84	209,706
Other treatment	186	350,947
Sludge trtmnt/stab/encap	84	632,710
Solvents recovery	421	241,803
Wastewater treatment	428	2,508,033

Note: Column may not sum because facilities can have multiple handling methods.

SOURCE: "Management Method," in *2015 Biennial Report: Management Methods*, US Environmental Protection Agency, 2017, https://rcrainfo.epa.gov/rcrainfoweb/action/modules/br/management/view (accessed November 14, 2017)

TABLE 8.3

Toxics Release Inventory Program, 2015

Number of TRI facilities	**21,849**
Production-related waste managed	**27.24 billion lb**
Recycled	11.91 billion lb
Energy recovery	3.10 billion lb
Treated	8.83 billion lb
Disposed of or otherwise released	3.41 billion lb
Total disposal or other releases	**3.36 billion lb**
On-site	**2.89 billion lb**
Air	0.69 billion lb
Water	0.19 billion lb
Land	2.01 billion lb
Off-site	**0.46 billion lb**

lb = pounds.
TRI = Toxics Release Inventory.
Note: Numbers do not sum exactly due to rounding.

SOURCE: "Quick Facts for 2015," in *TRI National Analysis*, US Environmental Protection Agency, January 2017, https://www.epa.gov/sites/production/files/2017-01/documents/tri_na_2015_complete_english.pdf (accessed November 14, 2017)

toxics-release-inventory-tri-program/learn-about-toxics-release-inventory), more than 650 toxic chemicals are on the TRI list. The Pollution Prevention Act of 1990 requires the EPA to collect data on toxic chemicals that have been recycled, treated, or combusted for energy recovery.

Manufacturing facilities, federal facilities, and facilities involved in metal and coal mining, electric utilities that burn coal or oil, chemical wholesale distributors, petroleum terminals, RCRA Subtitle C hazardous water treatment and disposal facilities, and solvent recovery services have to report under the TRI program, but only if they have 10 or more full-time employees and use certain thresholds of toxic chemicals.

As of January 2018, the most recently published TRI report was released in January 2017. In *2015 Toxics Release Inventory National Analysis* (https://www.epa.gov/sites/production/files/2017-01/documents/tri_na_2015_complete_english.pdf), the EPA summarizes data for 2015. As shown in Table 8.3, 27.2 billion pounds (12.4 billion kg) of TRI chemicals were waste managed in 2015 by 21,849 TRI facilities. The breakdown by management method is shown in Figure 8.4. Overall, 44% of the waste was recycled, 32% was treated, 13% was released to the environment or otherwise disposed, and 11% was used for energy recovery. The EPA reports that 3.4 billion pounds (1.5 billion kg) of TRI chemicals were released in 2015. (See Table 8.3.) The vast majority of the releases (2.9 billion pounds [1.3 billion kg]) were on-site releases. The remaining 460 million pounds (208.7 million kg) were off-site releases. Figure 8.5 shows the distribution of releases to the environment in 2015. More than half (60%) of the disposed waste went

FIGURE 8.4

Management of Toxics Release Inventory production-related wastes, by method, 2015

[27.24 billion pounds]

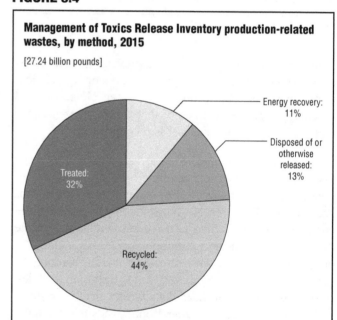

Energy recovery: 11%
Disposed of or otherwise released: 13%
Treated: 32%
Recycled: 44%

SOURCE: "Production-Related Waste Managed, 2015," in *TRI National Analysis*, US Environmental Protection Agency, January 2017, https://www.epa.gov/sites/production/files/2017-01/documents/tri_na_2015_complete_english.pdf (accessed November 14, 2017)

to on-site land disposal. Another 21% was released to the air on-site. Much smaller percentages went to on-site surface water discharges (6%) and off-site disposal or other releases to the environment (14%).

A breakdown of disposed and released wastes by industry in 2015 is provided in Figure 8.6. The metal mining industry was responsible for more than one-third (37%) of the releases, followed by chemicals production (15%) and electric utilities (13%). Figure 8.7 shows

FIGURE 8.5

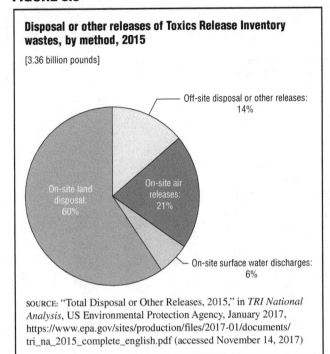

Disposal or other releases of Toxics Release Inventory wastes, by method, 2015

[3.36 billion pounds]

SOURCE: "Total Disposal or Other Releases, 2015," in *TRI National Analysis*, US Environmental Protection Agency, January 2017, https://www.epa.gov/sites/production/files/2017-01/documents/tri_na_2015_complete_english.pdf (accessed November 14, 2017)

FIGURE 8.6

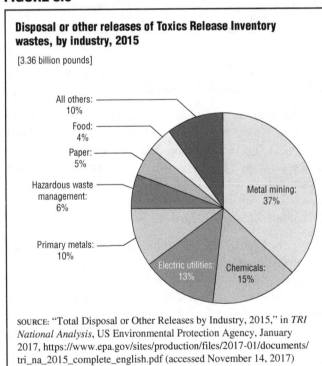

Disposal or other releases of Toxics Release Inventory wastes, by industry, 2015

[3.36 billion pounds]

SOURCE: "Total Disposal or Other Releases by Industry, 2015," in *TRI National Analysis*, US Environmental Protection Agency, January 2017, https://www.epa.gov/sites/production/files/2017-01/documents/tri_na_2015_complete_english.pdf (accessed November 14, 2017)

a breakdown by chemical. Only eight chemicals accounted for most of the releases, with zinc (19%) and lead (17%) taking the top-two spots.

As shown in Figure 8.8, the amount of TRI releases varied from year to year between 2005 and 2015, but has generally declined over time. The number of facilities with TRI releases also decreased during this period.

FIGURE 8.7

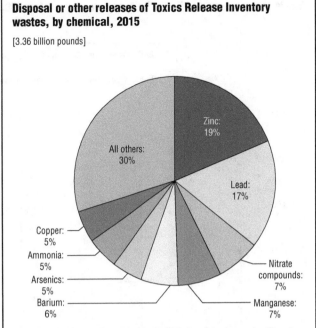

Disposal or other releases of Toxics Release Inventory wastes, by chemical, 2015

[3.36 billion pounds]

Note: In this graph, metals are combined with their metal compounds, although metals and compounds of the same metal are usually listed separately on the TRI list (e.g. lead is listed separately from lead compounds).

SOURCE: "Total Disposal or Other Releases by Chemical, 2015," in *TRI National Analysis*, US Environmental Protection Agency, January 2017, https://www.epa.gov/sites/production/files/2017-01/documents/tri_na_2015_complete_english.pdf (accessed November 14, 2017)

The Resource Conservation and Recovery Act

The RCRA, which was first enacted by Congress in 1976 and expanded by amendments in 1980, 1984, 1992, and 1996, was designed to manage the disposal, incineration, treatment, and storage of waste in landfills, surface impoundments, waste piles, tanks, and container storage areas. It regulates the production and disposal of hazardous waste and provides guidelines and mandates to improve waste disposal practices. The EPA also has the authority under the RCRA to require businesses with hazardous waste operations to take corrective action to clean up the waste they have released into the environment.

The RCRA imposes design and maintenance standards for waste disposal facilities, such as the installation of liners to prevent waste from leaking into groundwater. Land disposal facilities in operation after November 1980 are regulated under the act and are required to meet RCRA standards or close. Owners of facilities that ceased operation before November 1980 are required to clean up any hazardous waste threats their facilities still pose. Abandoned sites and those that owners cannot afford to clean up under the RCRA are usually referred to the national Superfund program.

FIGURE 8.8

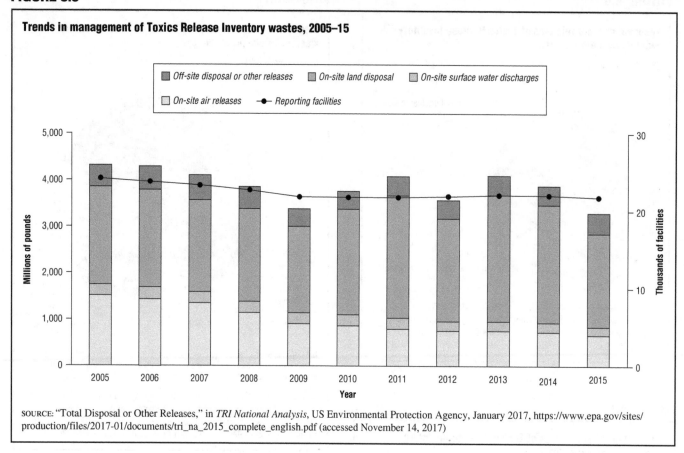

Trends in management of Toxics Release Inventory wastes, 2005–15

Legend:
- Off-site disposal or other releases
- On-site land disposal
- On-site surface water discharges
- On-site air releases
- Reporting facilities

SOURCE: "Total Disposal or Other Releases," in *TRI National Analysis*, US Environmental Protection Agency, January 2017, https://www.epa.gov/sites/production/files/2017-01/documents/tri_na_2015_complete_english.pdf (accessed November 14, 2017)

The Comprehensive Environmental Response, Compensation, and Liability Act and the Superfund

The Comprehensive Environmental Response, Compensation, and Liability Act (CERCLA) of 1980 established the Superfund program to pay for cleaning up highly contaminated hazardous waste sites that had been abandoned or where a sole responsible party could not be identified. Originally a $1.6 billion, five-year program, the Superfund was focused initially on cleaning up leaking dumps that jeopardized groundwater.

During the original mandate of the Superfund, only six sites were cleaned up. When the program expired in 1985, many observers viewed it as a billion-dollar fiasco rampant with scandal and mismanagement. Nonetheless, the negative publicity surrounding the program increased public awareness of the magnitude of the cleanup job in the United States. Consequently, in 1986 and later in 1990 the Superfund was reauthorized.

THE NATIONAL PRIORITIES LIST. CERCLA requires the government to maintain a list of hazardous waste sites that pose the highest potential threat to human health and the environment. This list is known as the National Priorities List (NPL) and includes hazardous waste sites in the country that are being cleaned up under the Superfund program. The NPL constitutes Appendix B to the National Oil and Hazardous Substances Pollution Contingency Plan, 40 CFR Part 300, which the EPA promulgated pursuant to Section 105 of CERCLA.

The NPL is constantly changing as new sites are officially added (finalized) and other sites are deleted (removed). Table 8.4 shows NPL site actions and milestones achieved by fiscal year (FY; October through September) between 1983 and 2017. These data were reported in April 2017, so only data for seven months are included for FY 2017.

According to the EPA (https://www.epa.gov/superfund/npl-site-totals-status-and-milestone), as of January 30, 2018, there were 1,344 sites on the NPL. Another 55 sites had been proposed for listing. Overall, 1,195 sites had been declared as "construction completed." The EPA determines construction completed when all physical construction of cleanup actions are completed, all immediate threats have been addressed, and all long-term threats are under control. This does not mean that a site has met its cleanup goals. It simply means that the engineering/construction phase of site cleanup is completed. The EPA had deleted 396 sites from the NPL as of January 30, 2018. According to the agency, in "National Oil and Hazardous Substances Pollution Contingency" (*Federal Register*, vol. 61, no. 21, January 31, 1996), sites are deleted when the agency determines that "no further Fund-financed CERCLA response action is appropriate."

TABLE 8.4

National Priorities List site actions and milestones, fiscal years 1983–2017

	Proposed NPL sites	NPL sites	Deleted NPL sites	NPL sites with construction completions	NPL sites with partial deletions	Partial deletion actions
2017*	4	7	2	7	3	4
2016	16	15	2	11	0	1
2015	13	8	6	13	1	2
2014	16	21	14	8	3	4
2013	9	9	7	14	1	2
2012	18	24	11	22	0	2
2011	35	25	7	22	2	3
2010	8	20	7	18	3	5
2009	23	20	8	20	3	3
2008	17	18	9	30	3	3
2007	17	12	7	24	2	3
2006	10	10	7	40	1	3
2005	12	18	18	40	5	5
2004	26	11	16	40	3	7
2003	14	20	9	40	6	7
2002	9	19	17	42	5	7
2001	45	29	30	47	3	4
2000	40	39	19	87	5	5
1999	37	43	23	85	3	3
1998	34	17	20	87	7	7
1997	20	18	32	88	6	6
1996	27	13	34	64	0	0
1995	9	31	25	68	0	0
1994	36	43	13	61	0	0
1993	52	33	12	68	0	0
1992	30	0	2	88	0	0
1991	23	7	9	12	0	0
1990	25	300	1	8	0	0
1989	64	101	10	10	0	0
1988	246	0	5	12	0	0
1987	71	99	0	3	0	0
1986	45	170	8	8	0	0
1985	317	3	0	3	0	0
1984	0	132	0	0	0	0
1983	552	406	5	5	0	0

NPL = National Priorities List.
*As of April 2017.
Notes: A fiscal year is October 1 through September 30.
The policy to allow partial deletions at sites was implemented in fiscal year 1996.
The total number of NPL Sites with Partial Deletions represents the number of sites that have had partial site deletions. Some sites have had multiple partial deletions.
The total number of Partial Deletion Actions represents the number of partial deletion actions that have occurred at all of the sites and may include multiple partial deletions at a single site.

SOURCE: "Number of NPL Site Actions and Milestones by Fiscal Year," in *Superfund*, US Environmental Protection Agency, April 5, 2017, https://www.epa.gov/superfund/number-npl-site-actions-and-milestones-fiscal-year (accessed November 15, 2017)

Beginning in FY 1996 the EPA started designating "partial deletions" to indicate that portions of NPL sites had reached the deletion criteria. As of January 30, 2018, the agency indicated that 65 sites had achieved partial deletions.

FUNDING FOR SUPERFUND. Funding for the Superfund program has historically come from three major sources: responsible parties, a so-called Superfund tax, and monies appropriated from the federal government's general fund. In addition, there is interest earned on the fund balance.

The EPA is authorized to compel parties responsible for creating hazardous pollution (such as waste generators, waste haulers, site owners, or site operators) to clean up the sites. In "Superfund Remedial Annual Accomplishments: Fiscal Year 2016 Superfund Remedial Program Accomplishments Report" (January 4, 2018, https://www.epa.gov/superfund/superfund-remedial-annual-accomplishments), the EPA notes that it received Superfund program commitments of approximately $1 billion from private responsible parties for FY 2016. The EPA obtains the money through fines, penalties, and cost recoveries (money recovered through legal settlements with the responsible parties). If responsible parties cannot be found, or if a settlement cannot be reached, public monies finance the cleanup. After completing a cleanup, the EPA can take action against the responsible parties to recover costs. The agency indicates that in FY 2016 responsible parties agreed to reimburse the agency for $55.3 million in past costs related to cleanup work at Superfund sites.

The Superfund tax was set up as part of the original Superfund legislation of 1980. It was financed by dedicated taxes collected from companies in the chemical and crude oil industries and a special income tax on corporate profits. This system was extremely unpopular with many corporations, which argued that environmentally responsible companies should not have to pay for the mistakes of others. The tax was eliminated in 1995. By the end of FY 2003 the Superfund tax monies had been exhausted. As of January 2018, several bills had been introduced in Congress to reinstate the tax, but none had been passed. Reinstating the tax is a controversial issue. Advocates argue that it is unfair for all US taxpayers to have to pay to clean up hazardous waste sites. Opponents counter that it is unfair to tax corporations that are complying with environmental rules for the sins of polluting companies.

The third primary source of money for the Superfund program is money appropriated from the federal government's general fund. This means that all US taxpayers assume some of the financial burden to clean up hazardous waste sites. After the depletion of the Superfund tax fund in FY 2003, general appropriation funds became the only government source of money for the program. The US Government Accountability Office (GAO) reports in *Superfund: EPA's Costs to Remediate Existing and Future Sites Will Likely Exceed Current Funding Levels* (June 22, 2010, https://www.gao.gov/new.items/d10857t .pdf) that appropriations averaged about $1.2 billion per year between FYs 1981 and 2009. Annual funding has fallen slightly since that time. As shown in Table 1.6 in Chapter 1, $1 billion per year was allocated to the Superfund program in FYs 2016 and 2017. President Donald Trump (1946–) requested only $745.7 million for the program in his proposed budget for FY 2018. As of January 2018, Congress had not passed a final appropriations bill to fund the EPA for FY 2018; thus, it was uncertain how much money would be allocated to the Superfund program for that year.

THE FEDERAL AGENCY HAZARDOUS WASTE COMPLIANCE DOCKET. CERCLA requires the EPA to maintain a list of federal lands or facilities (e.g., military bases) that are contaminated or potentially contaminated with hazardous waste. The Federal Agency Hazardous Waste Compliance Docket (the Docket) is regularly reported in the *Federal Register*. As of January 2018, the most recent Docket, "Thirty-Second Update of the Federal Agency Hazardous Waste Compliance Docket" (*Federal Register*, vol. 82, no. 235), was published in December 2017 and included 2,349 federal sites. The GAO has previously complained that the number should be larger. For example, in *Hazardous Waste Cleanup: Numbers of Contaminated Federal Sites, Estimated Costs, and EPA's Oversight Role* (September 11, 2015, http://www.gao.gov/assets/680/672464.pdf), the GAO indicates that federal agencies were aware of many more contaminated or potentially contaminated sites, but had not yet officially inventoried them.

The GAO notes that the federal government owns more than 700 million acres (280 million ha) of land.

Much of it is located in the western United States and is managed by the Bureau of Land Management (BLM), an agency within the US Department of the Interior. According to the GAO, the BLM knows of 4,722 sites on its land with "confirmed or likely contamination." In addition, the BLM has identified more than 30,000 abandoned mines on its land that have not yet been assessed for contamination. (See Figure 8.9.) The GAO further states that the BLM "estimated that there may be approximately 100,000 abandoned mines that had not yet been inventoried in California, Nevada, and Utah." A full inventory of abandoned mine sites by the BLM is expected to take "decades." In addition, the US Forest Service estimates that its lands hold between 27,000 and 39,000 abandoned mines and that approximately 20% of these mines "may pose some level of risk to human health or the environment."

The GAO indicates that officials with the Department of the Interior and the US Department of Agriculture "believed that abandoned mines should not be listed on EPA's Docket because the agencies did not cause the contamination and, therefore, the sites should not be considered federal sites." The EPA, however, disagrees with this opinion. The GAO recommends that the federal agencies work together to ensure that contaminated or potentially contaminated sites on federal lands are identified and assessed.

Abandoned mine sites have received heightened public attention since August 2015, when a spill of contaminated water occurred at the defunct Gold King mine in Colorado. That mine is located on private land along the headwaters of the upper Animas River. In "Upper Animas Mining District" (July 6, 2016, https://www.epa .gov/region8/upper-animas-mining-district), the EPA notes that it previously investigated the upper Animas River to assess the possibility of listing the watershed on the NPL. The agency states that a 2008 investigation "indicated that the area would qualify [for listing], although after receiving additional community input, EPA again postponed efforts to include the area on the NPL." As a result, state and local agencies in Colorado were responsible for the cleanup of the watershed. Nevertheless, the EPA indicates that its Superfund Remedial Program "contributed resources" to assist in these efforts.

SUPERFUND FINANCIAL RESPONSIBILITY REGULATIONS. The EPA explains in "Superfund Financial Responsibility" (December 1, 2017, https://www.epa.gov/super fund/superfund-financial-responsibility) that CERCLA Section 108(b) "gives EPA the authority to require that classes of facilities establish and maintain evidence of financial responsibility to cover the costs associated with releases or threatened releases of hazardous substances from their facilities." This authority has existed since 1980; however, the agency has been slow to exercise it.

FIGURE 8.9

Locations of abandoned mine sites on western land managed by the US Department of the Interior's Bureau of Land Management

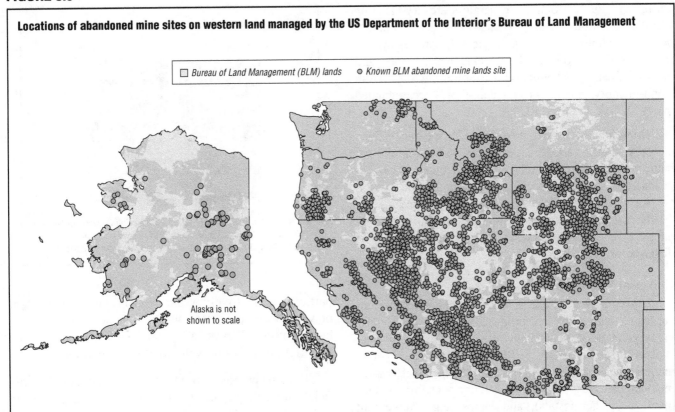

☐ *Bureau of Land Management (BLM) lands*   ⊙ *Known BLM abandoned mine lands site*

Alaska is not
shown to scale

SOURCE: "Figure 1. Known BLM Abandoned Mine Sites in the Western United States," in *Hazardous Waste: Agencies Should Take Steps to Improve Information on USDA's and Interior's Potentially Contaminated Sites*, US Government Accountability Office, January 2015, https://www.gao.gov/assets/670/667959.pdf (accessed November 15, 2017)

In 2008 a coalition of environmental groups led by the Sierra Club sued the EPA for failing to establish financial responsibility rules under CERCLA. The agency responded in 2009 and 2010 by choosing several industries for which it intended to develop such rules. Chief among them was the rock mining industry, which mines materials such as copper, gold, iron, lead, silver, and zinc. Additional targeted industries included chemical manufacturing, petroleum and coal products manufacturing, and electric power generation, transmission, and distribution. All these industries opposed development of the new rules, arguing that they were already strictly regulated.

At the time, the EPA was under President Barack Obama (1961–), a Democrat who generally favored tighter environmental restrictions. Nevertheless, the agency delayed issuing financial responsibility rules. In 2014 environmental groups sued the federal government again. As part of the settlement, the EPA proposed in "Financial Responsibility Requirements under CERCLA § 108(b) for Classes of Facilities in the Hardrock Mining Industry" (*Federal Register*, vol. 82, no. 7, January 11, 2017) a financial responsibility regulation for certain rock mining facilities. This proposal was published during the last days of the Obama administration. His successor, President Trump, a Republican, had campaigned

with a promise to reduce the regulatory burden on US businesses. In December 2017 the EPA announced in "Final Action: Financial Responsibility Requirements under CERCLA Section 108(b) for Classes of Facilities in the Hardrock Mining Industry" (https://www.epa.gov/superfund/final-action-financial-responsibility-requirements-under-cercla-section-108b-classes) that it would not issue the rock mining rule. In the press release "EPA Determines Risks from Hardrock Mining Industry Minimal and No Need for Additional Federal Requirements" (December 1, 2017, https://www.epa.gov/newsreleases/epa-determines-risks-hardrock-mining-industry-minimal-and-no-need-additional-federal), Scott Pruitt (1968–), the agency's head, expressed the EPA's confidence in "modern industry practices" and existing federal and state rules. Pruitt noted, "Additional financial assurance requirements are unnecessary and would impose an undue burden on this important sector of the American economy and rural America, where most of these mining jobs are based." Environmental groups were dismayed by the decision and threatened to sue in federal court.

HAZARDOUS WASTE FROM SMALL BUSINESSES AND HOUSEHOLDS

A small percentage of hazardous waste comes from thousands of small-quantity generators—businesses that produce less than 2,200 pounds (1,000 kg) of hazardous waste per month. Common generators are dry-cleaning facilities, furniture-making plants, construction companies, and photo processors. Typical hazardous wastes include spent solvents, leftover chemicals, paints, and unused cleaning chemicals. Hazardous wastes from small-quantity generators and households are regulated under Subtitle D of the RCRA.

Household hazardous waste includes solvents, paints, cleaners, stains, varnishes, pesticides, motor oil, and car batteries. Because of the relatively low amount of hazardous substances in individual products, household hazardous waste is not regulated as a hazardous waste. Since the 1980s many communities have held special collection days for household hazardous waste to ensure that it is disposed of properly.

Universal Wastes

Universal wastes are a federally defined subset of hazardous wastes that are produced in small amounts by many generators. According to the EPA, in "Universal Wastes" (September 21, 2017, https://www.epa.gov/hw/universal-waste), the federal list of universal wastes includes batteries, pesticides, mercury-containing equipment (e.g., thermostats), and lamps (e.g., fluorescent bulbs). Although these wastes sometimes wind up in the municipal waste stream, they contain worrisome components, such as heavy metals, that pose an environmental hazard. Thus, the EPA regulates them separately from other hazardous wastes with simpler streamlined requirements that are designed to encourage generators to recycle or dispose of the wastes properly. The EPA's universal waste regulations are published in 40 CFR 273 and apply only to businesses, not to residential generators. The states are allowed to adopt the federal universal waste regulations or add to them, as they see fit.

RADIOACTIVE WASTE

Radioactive waste results from the mining, processing, and use of radioactive materials for commercial, military, medical, and research purposes. In *2017–2018 Information Digest* (August 2017, https://www.nrc.gov/docs/ML1722/ML17228A057.pdf), the US Nuclear Regulatory Commission (NRC) defines radioactivity as "the property possessed by some elements (such as uranium) of spontaneously emitting energy in the form of radiation as a result of the decay (or disintegration) of an unstable atom." As the decay or disintegration takes place, the nucleus of an unstable atom emits nuclear radiation in the form of alpha particles, beta particles, neutrons, or gamma rays. They are examples of ionizing radiation because they can displace or remove electrons from other materials with which they come into contact. Thus, high doses of ionizing radiation can damage skin or tissue. As shown in Figure 8.10, alpha and beta

FIGURE 8.10

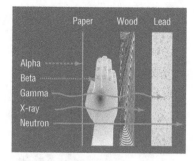

Radiation types and their penetrating capacities

SOURCE: "Untitled," in *2017–2018 Information Digest*, US Nuclear Regulatory Commission, August 2017, https://www.nrc.gov/docs/ML1722/ML17228A057.pdf (accessed November 15, 2017)

particles are relatively weak; neutrons and gamma rays, however, can pass through (and hence damage) the human body. X-rays, a nonnuclear ionizing form of radiation, can also pass through the human body.

Humans purposely produce nuclear radiation by artificially breaking apart atomic nuclei. Such a process is called nuclear fission. The fission of uranium 235 (U-235) releases several neutrons that can penetrate other U-235 nuclei. In this way the fission of a single U-235 atom can begin a cascading chain of nuclear reactions. If this series of reactions is regulated to occur slowly, as it is in nuclear power plants, the energy emitted can be captured for a variety of uses, such as generating electricity. If this series of reactions is allowed to occur all at once, as in a nuclear bomb, the energy emitted is explosive. (Plutonium-239 can also be used to generate a chain reaction similar to that of U-235.)

In general, the US Department of Energy (DOE) is responsible for managing radioactive waste that is associated with the nation's military and defense operations. The NRC has primary responsibility for managing radioactive wastes that are produced by other sources. Some state agencies have also been authorized to regulate aspects of radioactive waste management within their jurisdictions. The EPA regulates the release of radioactive materials to the environment.

Nuclear Power Plants

The primary commercial source of radioactive waste is associated with electricity generation at nuclear power plants. These plants rely on controlled slow fission reactions with nuclear fuel pellets to produce heat to create steam. Figure 8.11 shows the locations of the nation's 99 operational nuclear power plants as of 2017. Nuclear power plant construction was robust through the 1970s and then ceased. The drop-off is attributed to a variety of

FIGURE 8.11

Locations of commercial operating nuclear power reactors, 2017

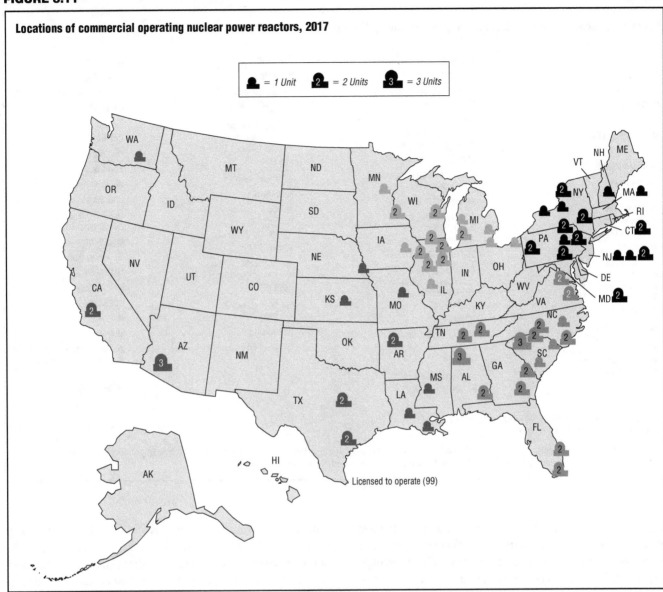

factors including construction and regulatory difficulties, availability of cheap supplies of natural gas, and public opposition to nuclear power. Opposition grew dramatically following an emergency at the Three Mile Island nuclear power plant near Harrisburg, Pennsylvania. On March 28, 1979, equipment failures, design problems, and operator errors led to a partial meltdown in the nuclear core of one of the reactors. A meltdown occurs when cooling of the nuclear fuel rods is inadequate and the fuel overheats and melts, releasing radioactivity to the atmosphere.

Although no one was directly injured or killed by the accident, it did expose a substantial population of nearby residents to radioactive gases. The NRC indicates in the fact sheet "Three Mile Island Accident" (February 2013, https://www.nrc.gov/reading-rm/doc-collections/fact-sheets/3mile-isle.pdf) that approximately 2 million people in the area were exposed to an average dose of 1 millirem. This is

roughly one-sixth the amount of radiation that is associated with a full set of chest x-rays.

Public fears about nuclear power were rekindled in 1986, when an explosion occurred at a nuclear power plant near the town of Chernobyl in the Soviet Union (now Ukraine). During the early morning hours of April 26, 1986, operators decided to test one of the reactors to see what would happen if the station lost electrical power. A combination of design flaws and operator errors during the test resulted in a massive power surge that overheated and ruptured some of the fuel rods. The resulting explosions destroyed the nuclear reactor core and ripped the roof off the reactor building, sending radioactive debris and smoke into the atmosphere.

Dozens of people, mostly plant workers, died during the explosions or soon thereafter from acute radiation poisoning. Hundreds, possibly thousands, more people

FIGURE 8.11

Locations of commercial operating nuclear power reactors, 2017 [CONTINUED]

Region I

CONNECTICUT
- Millstone 2 and 3

MARYLAND
- Calvert Cliffs 1 and 2

MASSACHUSETTS
- Pilgrim

NEW HAMPSHIRE
- Seabrook

NEW JERSEY
- Hope Creek
- Oyster Creek
- Salem 1 and 2

NEW YORK
- Fitz Patrick
- Ginna
- Indian Point 2 and 3
- Nine Mile Point 1 and 2

PENNSYLVANIA
- Beaver Valley 1 and 2
- Limerick 1 and 2
- Peach Bottom 2 and 3
- Susquehanna 1 and 2
- Three Mile Island 1

Region II

ALABAMA
- Browns Ferry 1, 2, and 3
- Farley 1 and 2

FLORIDA
- St. Lucie 1 and 2
- Turkey Point 3 and 4

GEORGIA
- Edwin I. Hatch 1 and 2
- Vogtle 1 and 2

NORTH CAROLINA
- Brunswick 1 and 2
- McGuire 1 and 2
- Harris 1

SOUTH CAROLINA
- Catawba 1 and 2
- Oconee 1, 2, and 3
- Robinson 2
- Summer

TENNESSEE
- Sequoyah 1 and 2
- Watts Bar 1 and 2

VIRGINIA
- North Anna 1 and 2
- Surry 1 and 2

Region III

ILLINOIS
- Braidwood 1 and 2
- Byron 1 and 2
- Clinton
- Dresden 2 and 3
- LaSalle 1 and 2
- Quad Cities 1 and 2

IOWA
- Duane Arnold

MICHIGAN
- Cook 1 and 2
- Fermi 2
- Palisades

MINNESOTA
- Monticelol
- Prairie Island 1 and 2

OHIO
- Davis-Besse
- Perry

WISCONSIN
- Point Beach 1 and 2

Region IV

ARKANSAS
- Arkansas Nuclear 1 and 2

ARIZONA
- Palo Verde 1, 2, and 3

CALIFORNIA
- Diablo Canyon 1 and 2

KANSAS
- Wolf Creek 1

LOUISIANA
- River Bend 1
- Waterford 3

MISSISSIPPI
- Grand Gulf

MISSOURI
- Callaway

NEBRASKA
- Cooper

TEXAS
- Comanche Peak 1 and 2
- South Texas Project 1 and 2

WASHINGTON
- Columbia

Note: NRC-abbreviated reactor names listed. Dated are as of May 2017.
NRC = US Nuclear Regulatory Commission.

SOURCE: "Figure 11. US Operating Commercial Nuclear Power Reactors," in *2017–2018 Information Digest*, US Nuclear Regulatory Commission, August 2017, https://www.nrc.gov/docs/ML1722/ML17228A057.pdf (accessed November 15, 2017)

died later as a result of exposure to radiation that was released by the accident. More than 100,000 people were evacuated from the surrounding area. The Chernobyl disaster left a long-lasting negative public perception about nuclear power.

During the latter part of the first decade of the 21st century, however, high fuel prices and concerns about the contribution of fossil fuels to global warming prompted new interest in nuclear power in the United States. In response, President Obama made nuclear power a key element of his energy policy. In *Blueprint for a Secure Energy Future* (March 30, 2011, https://obamawhitehouse.archives.gov/sites/default/files/blueprint_secure_energy_future.pdf), the White House notes that in 2010 it issued a conditional loan guarantee for two new nuclear power units at the existing Plant Vogtle site near Augusta, Georgia. They were the first new nuclear power units ordered since the late 1970s.

The burgeoning support for nuclear power in the United States suffered a setback in March 2011, when an earthquake and tsunami seriously damaged Japan's Fukushima Daiichi nuclear power plant, one of the largest nuclear power plant facilities in the world. Loss of sufficient cooling water allowed fuel rod temperatures in several of the reactors to rise to dangerous levels. Subsequent explosions caused further structural damage. Some radioactive gases were released into the atmosphere, and tens of thousands of people in the region surrounding the plant had to be evacuated.

The long-term public health consequences of the disaster, such as higher cancer rates, remain to be seen. In February 2013 the World Health Organization (WHO) released its predictions in *Health Risk Assessment from the Nuclear Accident after the 2011 Great East Japan Earthquake and Tsunami, Based on a Preliminary Dose Estimation* (http://www.who.int/ionizing_radiation/pub_meet/fukushima_risk_assessment_2013/en/). Overall, the WHO notes, "This health risk assessment concludes that no discernible increase in health risks from the Fukushima event is expected outside Japan. With respect to Japan, this assessment estimates that the lifetime risk for some cancers may be somewhat elevated above baseline rates in certain age and sex groups that were in the areas most affected." The WHO cautions, however, that its estimates are based on preliminary data and that scientific knowledge is limited on the effects of low-level radiation on human health.

Following the Fukushima incident, the NRC ordered a task force to examine the causes of the accident and recommend ways in which the US nuclear power industry should respond to prevent a similar occurrence. In July 2011 the task force released *Recommendations for Enhancing Reactor Safety in the 21st Century: The Near Term Task Force Review of Insights from the Fukushima Dai-Ichi Accident* (https://www.nrc.gov/docs/ML1118/ML111861807.pdf). Overall, the task force states, "In light of the low likelihood of an event beyond the design basis of a U.S. nuclear power plant and the current mitigation capabilities at those facilities, the Task Force concludes that continued operation and continued licensing activities do not pose an imminent risk to the public health and safety." The task force, however, does provide specific recommendations to improve the NRC's regulatory framework and its oversight of plant safety performance;

strengthen protection methods against earthquakes and floods at nuclear power plants; enhance mitigation capabilities at the plants, such as through design changes and improved on-site emergency response procedures; and strengthen plant emergency preparedness measures, particularly in regards to total loss of electrical power. Figure 8.12 depicts some of the required safety enhancements that resulted from the task force's recommendations.

In February 2012 the NRC approved the license for the two new nuclear reactors at Plant Vogtle. A month later it approved a license for two new nuclear reactors at the Virgil C. Summer power plant in Jenkinsville, South Carolina. Both projects were subsequently plagued by construction delays and massive cost overruns as the lead contractor, the Westinghouse Electric Company, struggled to complete them. In March 2017 Westinghouse declared

FIGURE 8.12

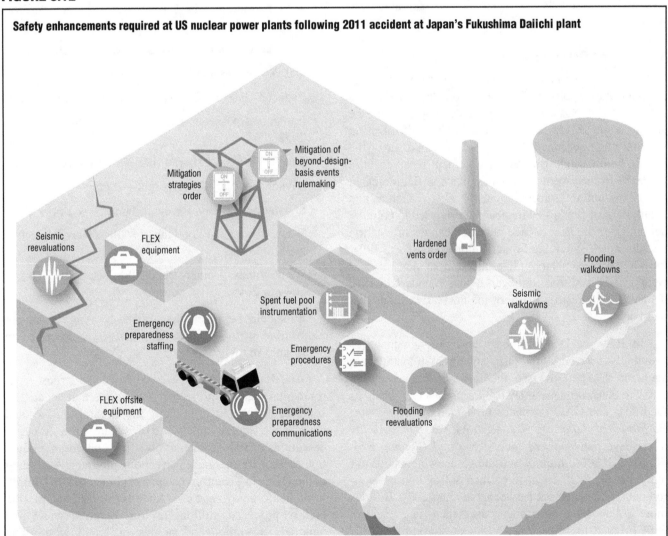

Safety enhancements required at US nuclear power plants following 2011 accident at Japan's Fukushima Daiichi plant

Note: FLEX refers to the industry's term for mitigation strategy equipment.

SOURCE: "Figure 13. NRC Post-Fukushima Safety Enhancements," in *2017–2018 Information Digest*, US Nuclear Regulatory Commission, August 2017, https://www.nrc.gov/docs/ML1722/ML17228A057.pdf (accessed November 15, 2017)

bankruptcy due to its financial woes. Months later, construction at the Summer plant ceased after the utility companies that had commissioned it decided to abandon the project. As of January 2018, the Plant Vogtle project was still under construction, but its future remained uncertain.

In "Combined License Applications for New Reactors" (http://www.nrc.gov/reactors/new-reactors/col.html), the NRC indicates that, as of September 2017, five other commercial nuclear reactor projects had active licenses. Three of them are expansion projects that would add additional units at existing nuclear power plants in Michigan (Fermi unit 3), Texas (South Texas units 3 and 4), and Virginia (North Anna unit 3). The other two projects would be new nuclear power plants in Florida (Levy units 1 and 2) and South Carolina (William States Lee III units 1 and 2). All the projects had been under consideration for many years. Media reports suggest that the nuclear projects are unlikely to proceed because of Westinghouse's bankruptcy and stiff competition from relatively inexpensive and domestically produced oil and natural gas to produce power.

Military and Defense Sources

The US government maintained an active program for nuclear weapons development from the early 1940s through the 1980s. It began with development of the atomic bomb during World War II (1939–1945). During the first three decades following the development of the atomic bomb, nuclear waste management received little attention from government policy makers. Beginning in the 1970s public concern about the environmental and health risks of stockpiled nuclear materials led to political action. Over the next decade nuclear weapons production was curtailed. When the Soviet Union collapsed in 1991, the DOE ceased nearly all production of new nuclear weapons. In addition, it began a major undertaking to dismantle and destroy many of the nuclear weapons that had been created.

In 1989 the DOE formed a new program that was eventually directed by the Office of Environmental Management (EM) to oversee the massive and expensive effort to clean up more than 100 former nuclear weapons facilities. The GAO estimates in *Nuclear Waste: Better Performance Reporting Needed to Assess DOE's Ability to Achieve the Goals of the Accelerated Cleanup Program* (July 2005, http://www.gao.gov/new.items/d05764.pdf) that the DOE spent more than $60 billion on environmental management between 1989 and 2001. Billions more dollars have been spent since then. In *Budget in Brief* (May 2017, https://energy.gov/sites/prod/files/2017/05/f34/FY2018BudgetinBrief_0.pdf), the DOE indicates that the funding levels for environmental management for FYs 2016 and 2017 were $6.2 billion and $6.3 billion, respectively. The agency's request for FY 2018 was $6.5

billion. The DOE notes that as of May 2017, the EM had completed cleanup at 91 sites. Most of the remaining 16 sites are massive projects that are expected to take decades to complete. The following projected completion dates are taken from the EM's FY 2018 budget request (May 2017, https://energy.gov/sites/prod/files/2017/06/f35/EMFY2018BudgetVolume5_0.pdf):

- Brookhaven National Laboratory, New York—2020
- Energy Technology Engineering Center, California—Undetermined
- Hanford Site, Washington—2070 to 2075
- Idaho National Engineering and Environmental Laboratory, Idaho—2042 to 2050
- Lawrence Livermore National Laboratory, California—2022
- Los Alamos National Laboratory, New Mexico—2036
- Moab: Uranium Mill Tailings Remedial Action Project, Utah—2034
- Nevada National Security Site, Nevada—2030
- Oak Ridge Reservation, Tennessee—2047
- Paducah Gaseous Diffusion Plant, Kentucky—2047
- Portsmouth Gaseous Diffusion Plant, Ohio—2044 to 2052
- Sandia National Laboratories, New Mexico—2028
- Savannah River Site, Georgia—2065
- Separations Process Research Unit, New York—2020
- Waste Isolation Pilot Plant (WIPP), New Mexico—2035 to 2042
- West Valley Demonstration Project, New York—2040 to 2045

It should be noted that WIPP is a repository for radioactive wastes from other sites. It is described in detail later in this chapter.

The Hanford Site is believed to be the largest environmental cleanup project in the world. It is located in southeastern Washington along the Columbia River and covers 586 square miles (1,518 square km). It began operations in 1944 as the nation's first plutonium production facility for the nuclear weapons program. According to the DOE, in "Hanford Cleanup" (June 26, 2017, http://www.hanford.gov/page.cfm/AboutHanfordCleanup), the facility produced millions of tons of solid waste and hundreds of billions of gallons of liquid waste. The agency notes, "These liquid wastes were disposed of by pouring them onto the ground or into trenches or holding ponds. Unintentional spills of liquids also took place." The site closed during the late 1980s, leaving behind tons of disintegrating nuclear fuel rods and contaminated sludge, soil, and groundwater.

The cleanup at Hanford (which began during the 1980s) has proved to be difficult and very expensive. In December 2012 the GAO issued a scathing report about the project's problems. In *Hanford Waste Treatment Plant: DOE Needs to Take Action to Resolve Technical and Management Challenges* (https://www.gao.gov/assets/660/650931.pdf), the GAO notes that the DOE is constructing a waste treatment plant (WTP) to handle millions of gallons of liquid waste. However, as of 2012 the WTP budget had tripled since 2000 to $13.4 billion, and the projected completion date slipped by nearly a decade to 2019. The GAO again addressed the WTP in May 2015 in *Hanford Waste Treatment: DOE Needs to Evaluate Alternatives to Recently Proposed Projects and Address Technical and Management Challenges* (https://www.gao.gov/assets/680/670080.pdf). The GAO states, "Significant technical and management challenges continue to affect the WTP and hinder its completion." The DOE has proposed two treatment facilities to treat some waste while it continues to struggle with completing the WTP. The new projects are expected to cost "at least $1 billion and take 6 to 8 years to construct." In yet another review published in May 2017, the GAO notes in *Nuclear Waste: Opportunities Exist to Reduce Risks and Costs by Evaluating Different Waste Treatment Approaches at Hanford* (https://www.gao.gov/assets/690/684468.pdf) that the WTP continued to face many technological hurdles and cost escalation problems. At that time, the WTP was expected to begin operations by the end of 2036.

Classes of Radioactive Waste

Federal and state agencies classify radioactive wastes based on their radioactivity, sources, and methods of management. These classifications differ from agency to agency, and there is sometimes overlap between classes. Major classes defined by the federal government are as follows:

- Uranium mill tailings—remnants from uranium mining, which was extensively practiced in the western United States in the decades following World War II. By the 1980s the United States imported most of the uranium it needed for nuclear power and weapons production. As a result, the vast majority of domestic uranium mines and processing facilities ceased operating. The DOE is responsible for cleaning up abandoned mill-tailing sites that were associated primarily with nuclear weapons production. The NRC oversees the cleanup operations to ensure that they meet environmental standards set by the EPA. In "Backgrounder on Uranium Mill Tailings" (October 2016, https://www.nrc.gov/reading-rm/doc-collections/fact-sheets/mill-tailings.html), the NRC indicates that as of 2016, 20 sites were undergoing cleanup operations.

- High-level radioactive waste (HLW)—the NRC explains in "High-Level Waste" (August 3, 2017, https://www.nrc.gov/waste/high-level-waste.html) that HLW is "a byproduct of the reactions that occur inside nuclear reactors." It can take hundreds of thousands of years before the waste is harmless to humans. According to the GAO, in *Nuclear Waste: Benefits and Costs Should Be Better Understood before DOE Commits to a Separate Repository for Defense Waste* (January 2017, https://www.gao.gov/assets/690/682385.pdf), HLW in the United States includes waste produced by defense-related activities through the 1980s and spent nuclear fuel (SNF) from commercial power plants. The GAO estimates that the defense-related activities produced about 15,400 tons (14,000 t) of HLW. As of 2017, commercial reactors had produced nearly 88,200 tons (80,000 t) of SNF. The latter amount is expected to grow to around 154,300 tons (140,000 t) "over the next several decades." As of 2017, no permanent long-term storage facility existed for HLW; therefore, it was stored on-site at the locations where it was generated or transported to other approved sites for temporary storage. Figure 8.13 is a map showing the nation's SNF storage facilities. In addition, the GAO indicates that HLW (mostly from defense sources) was also being stored at Fort St. Vrain in Colorado, the Hanford Site, the Idaho National Laboratory, the Savannah River Site, and the West Valley Demonstration Project.

- Low-level radioactive waste (LLW)—LLW includes items such as protective clothing, tools, equipment, rags, mops, and animal carcasses used in radiation research. Until the 1960s the United States dumped LLW into the ocean. Thereafter, various storage sites were developed around the country. As of 2017, four commercial LLW sites were operating in South Carolina, Texas, Utah, and Washington. In "Low-Level Waste Disposal Statistics" (December 6, 2017, https://www.nrc.gov/waste/llw-disposal/licensing/statistics.html), the NRC reports that in 2016 LLW disposal totaled 1.6 million cubic feet (46,700 cubic m). The wastes are enclosed in canisters buried underground, as shown in Figure 8.14.

- Transuranic (TRU) waste—waste that consists of chemical elements with an atomic number greater than that of uranium (92) and therefore are beyond (trans-) uranium. With the exception of plutonium, which is found in extremely small amounts in nature, all the TRU elements are artificially produced (made by humans). TRU waste remains radioactive for up to tens of thousands of years. Until 1999 all the wastes were in temporary storage at various DOE facilities around the country. In 1999 the DOE began moving the wastes to WIPP.

FIGURE 8.13

Spent nuclear fuel storage installations, 2017

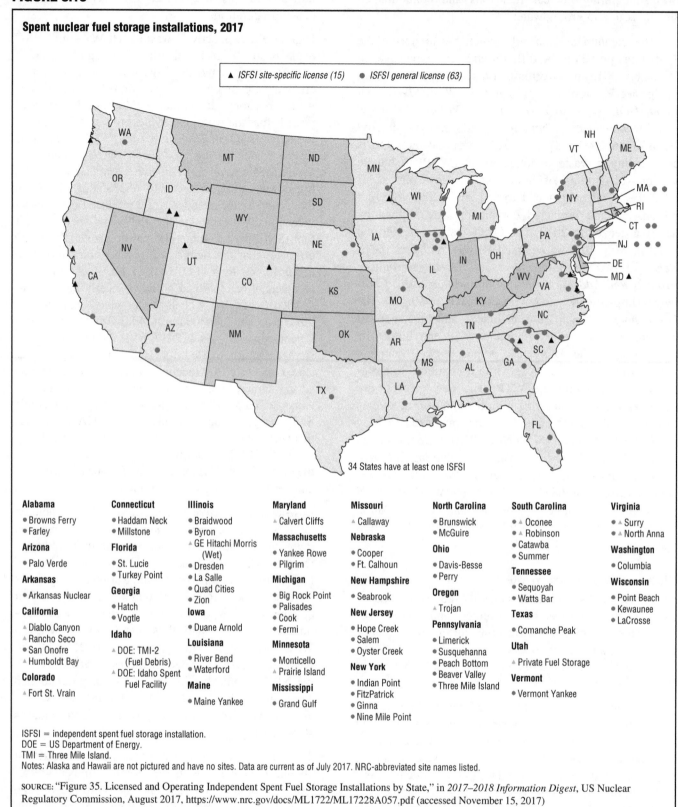

▲ ISFSI site-specific license (15)   ● ISFSI general license (63)

34 States have at least one ISFSI

Alabama
- ● Browns Ferry
- ● Farley

Arizona
- ● Palo Verde

Arkansas
- ▲ Arkansas Nuclear

California
- ▲ Diablo Canyon
- ▲ Rancho Seco
- ▲ San Onofre
- ▲ Humboldt Bay

Colorado
- ▲ Fort St. Vrain

Connecticut
- ● Haddam Neck
- ● Millstone

Florida
- ● St. Lucie
- ● Turkey Point

Georgia
- ● Hatch
- ● Vogtle

Idaho
- ▲ DOE: TMI-2 (Fuel Debris)
- ▲ DOE: Idaho Spent Fuel Facility

Illinois
- ● Braidwood
- ● Byron
- ▲ GE Hitachi Morris (Wet)
- ● Dresden
- ● La Salle
- ● Quad Cities
- ● Zion

Iowa
- ● Duane Arnold

Louisiana
- ● River Bend
- ● Waterford

Maine
- ● Maine Yankee

Maryland
- ▲ Calvert Cliffs

Massachusetts
- ● Yankee Rowe
- ● Pilgrim

Michigan
- ● Big Rock Point
- ● Palisades
- ● Cook
- ● Fermi

Minnesota
- ● Monticello
- ▲ Prairie Island

Mississippi
- ● Grand Gulf

Missouri
- ▲ Callaway

Nebraska
- ● Cooper
- ● Ft. Calhoun

New Hampshire
- ● Seabrook

New Jersey
- ● Hope Creek
- ● Salem
- ● Oyster Creek

New York
- ● Indian Point
- ● FitzPatrick
- ● Ginna
- ● Nine Mile Point

North Carolina
- ● Brunswick
- ● McGuire

Ohio
- ● Davis-Besse
- ● Perry

Oregon
- ▲ Trojan

Pennsylvania
- ● Limerick
- ● Susquehanna
- ● Peach Bottom
- ● Beaver Valley
- ● Three Mile Island

South Carolina
- ● ▲ Oconee
- ● ▲ Robinson
- ● Catawba
- ● Summer

Tennessee
- ● Sequoyah
- ● Watts Bar

Texas
- ● Comanche Peak

Utah
- ▲ Private Fuel Storage

Vermont
- ● Vermont Yankee

Virginia
- ● ▲ Surry
- ● ▲ North Anna

Washington
- ● Columbia

Wisconsin
- ● Point Beach
- ● Kewaunee
- ● LaCrosse

ISFSI = independent spent fuel storage installation.
DOE = US Department of Energy.
TMI = Three Mile Island.
Notes: Alaska and Hawaii are not pictured and have no sites. Data are current as of July 2017. NRC-abbreviated site names listed.

SOURCE: "Figure 35. Licensed and Operating Independent Spent Fuel Storage Installations by State," in *2017–2018 Information Digest*, US Nuclear Regulatory Commission, August 2017, https://www.nrc.gov/docs/ML1722/ML17228A057.pdf (accessed November 15, 2017)

Geologic Repositories for Radioactive Waste

The United States has been working for decades to establish permanent storage facilities for HLW and TRU waste. These facilities are geological repositories; that is, storage facilities constructed deep underground in ancient geological formations that are relatively dry and not subject to earthquakes or other stresses. WIPP is an example of a geologic repository for radioactive waste.

FIGURE 8.14

Low-level waste disposal facility

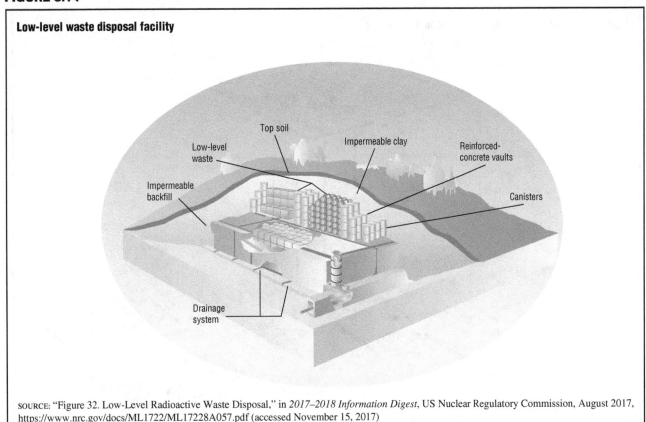

SOURCE: "Figure 32. Low-Level Radioactive Waste Disposal," in *2017–2018 Information Digest*, US Nuclear Regulatory Commission, August 2017, https://www.nrc.gov/docs/ML1722/ML17228A057.pdf (accessed November 15, 2017)

Engineers working on permanent storage facilities have designed barrier systems that combine multiple physical barriers with chemical controls to provide a high level of long-term containment for radioactive waste. Radioactive waste is chemically treated for long-term storage and placed into steel drums. The drums are then placed in a concrete container. Many of these drum-filled concrete containers, which are surrounded with a special chemically treated backfill material, are placed in a larger concrete container deep underground. The rock surrounding this large concrete container must have low groundwater flow. The multiple barriers, chemical conditions, and geologic conditions under which the wastes are stored ensure that the wastes dissolve slowly and pose little danger to the groundwater.

THE WASTE ISOLATION PILOT PLANT. WIPP became the world's first deep depository for nuclear waste when it received its first shipment in March 1999. The large facility is located in a desert region near Carlsbad, New Mexico. It was designed for permanent storage of the nation's TRU waste. WIPP is 2,150 feet (655 m) below the surface in the salt beds of the Salado Formation. The layout is depicted in Figure 8.15.

In February 2014 the facility suffered two serious incidents. On February 5, a salt haul truck caught fire in an underground area. (See Figure 8.16.) Nine days later

a radioactive release occurred in Room 7 of the underground waste disposal area. (See Figure 8.16.) The DOE indicates in *Waste Isolation Pilot Plant Recovery Plan, Revision 0* (September 30, 2014, http://www.wipp.energy .gov/Special/WIPP%20Recovery%20Plan.pdf) that 86 personnel in the mine at the time of the fire were safely evacuated. Seven of them were evaluated for smoke inhalation, and one of the victims received treatment for that condition. In regard to facility damage, the agency states, "The soot and smoke from the fire adversely affected key equipment and facilities of the WIPP repository, which has resulted in a widespread cleanup effort throughout the underground and identification of deficiencies in WIPP's emergency response, maintenance, and other operational procedures."

Details on the radioactive release at WIPP were reported by the DOE in April 2015 in *Accident Investigation Report: Phase 2: Radiological Release Event at the Waste Isolation Pilot Plant, February 14, 2014* (https:// www.energy.gov/sites/prod/files/2015/04/f21/WIPP%20 Rad%20Event%20Report%20Phase%202%2004.16.2015 .pdf). The agency concludes that the release occurred because of a chemical reaction between organic materials and nitrate salts inside a storage drum. The resulting pressure buildup popped open the lid of the drum and "propelled" TRU waste into the storage area. An airflow monitoring system sensed the release and set off an alarm.

FIGURE 8.15

Layout of the Waste Isolation Pilot Plant in New Mexico

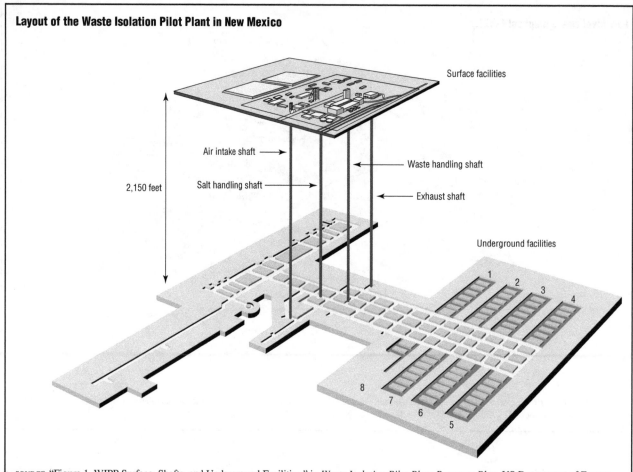

SOURCE: "Figure 1. WIPP Surface, Shafts, and Underground Facilities," in *Waste Isolation Pilot Plant Recovery Plan*, US Department of Energy, September 30, 2014, http://www.wipp.energy.gov/Special/WIPP%20Recovery%20Plan.pdf (accessed November 15, 2017)

The facility's ventilation system was activated to capture the contaminated air; however, "a small portion" leaked from the system and "exhausted directly to the atmosphere." The DOE's investigation revealed that the drum, which had come from the Los Alamos National Laboratory (LANL) in New Mexico, contained "incompatible materials." The DOE states, "If LANL had adequately developed and implemented repackaging and treatment procedures that incorporated suitable hazard controls and included a rigorous review and approval process, the release would have been preventable." In *Waste Isolation Pilot Plant Recovery Plan, Revision 0*, the DOE indicates that no employees were below ground when the release occurred.

WIPP ceased accepting new waste shipments following the February 2014 incidents and began implementing new safety measures outlined in the facility's recovery plan. The DOE indicates in "WIPP Update: April 10, 2017" (http://www.wipp.energy.gov/Special/WIPP%20Update%204_10_17.pdf) that the plant reopened in January 2017 and began receiving waste again in April 2017.

According to the DOE, in "Shipment & Disposal Information" (2018, http://www.wipp.energy.gov/shipments.htm),

through January 29, 2018, WIPP had received 12,040 shipments of TRU wastes totaling around 3.2 million cubic feet (92,000 cubic m). The total amount of TRU waste that can be deposited at WIPP is capped by the Waste Isolation Pilot Plant Land Withdrawal Act of 1992 at 6.2 million cubic feet (176,000 cubic m). It is estimated that WIPP will reach its full capacity during the 2020s or 2030s.

YUCCA MOUNTAIN. For decades the centerpiece of the federal government's geologic disposal plan for SNF and other HLW was the Yucca Mountain site in Nevada. The site is approximately 100 miles (160 km) northwest of Las Vegas, Nevada, on federal lands within the Nevada Test Site in Nye County. The mountain is located in a remote desert region.

The Nuclear Waste Policy Act of 1982 required the US secretary of energy to investigate the site and, if it was suitable, to recommend to the president that the site be established. In February 2002 President George W. Bush (1946–) received such a recommendation and approved it. Despite opposition from the Nevada governor Kenny Guinn (1936–2010), the project was subsequently approved by the US House of Representatives

FIGURE 8.16

Locations of two 2014 incidents at the Waste Isolation Pilot Plant

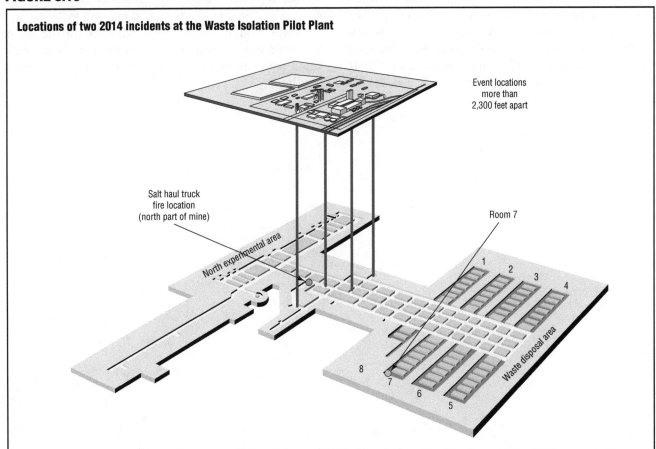

SOURCE: "Figure 4. Location of the Two Incidents at WIPP in February 2014," in *Waste Isolation Pilot Plant Recovery Plan*, US Department of Energy, September 30, 2014, http://www.wipp.energy.gov/Special/WIPP%20Recovery%20Plan.pdf (accessed November 15, 2017)

and the US Senate. In July 2002 President Bush signed the Yucca Mountain resolution into law.

In June 2008 the DOE submitted a license application for the facility to the NRC. Licensing documents are available from the NRC at https://www.nrc.gov/waste/hlw-disposal/yucca-lic-app.html.

Development of the Yucca Mountain repository was plagued by legal setbacks and political controversy. Nevada lawmakers, in particular, were vehemently opposed to it. President Obama also did not support the project and did not provide funding for it in his proposed federal budgets. In March 2010 the DOE filed a motion with the NRC to withdraw its license application. Some analysts complained the decision was driven solely by political motives. The GAO explained in *Commercial Spent Nuclear Fuel: Observations on the Key Attributes and Challenges of Storage and Disposal Options* (April 11, 2013, https://www.gao.gov/assets/660/653731.pdf) that lack of support from Nevada legislators and the Obama administration proved to be insurmountable challenges for the project. The GAO stated, "DOE officials did not cite technical or safety issues with the Yucca Mountain repository project when the project's

termination was announced but instead stated that other solutions could achieve broader support."

The DOE created a panel called the Blue Ribbon Commission on America's Nuclear Future to recommend steps for future action. In January 2012 the commission (https://cybercemetery.unt.edu/archive/brc/20120620220235/http://brc.gov/sites/default/files/documents/brc_finalreport_jan2012.pdf) issued its final report, noting, "This nation's failure to come to grips with the nuclear waste issue has already proved damaging and costly. It will be even more damaging and more costly the longer it continues." The commission recommended legislative and administration policy changes as the first steps toward finding a permanent solution to the nation's HLW disposal problem.

According to the GAO, in "Disposal of High-Level Nuclear Waste" (2018, https://www.gao.gov/key_issues/disposal_of_highlevel_nuclear_waste/issue_summary), in 2015 President Obama decided that the nation needed two permanent repositories: one for commercially produced SNF and one for defense-related HLW. However, Congress opposed this idea and included language in a 2016 defense appropriations bill that prohibited the use of the funds for a defense-only repository. President Obama remained opposed to the Yucca Mountain project through the end of his administration in January 2017. His successor, President Trump, has indicated his support for the project. The GAO notes that President Trump included $120 million in his proposed FY 2018 federal budget "for the resumption of the license review for the repository at Yucca Mountain and for interim storage of nuclear waste." It remained to be seen if Congress would approve appropriations for the Yucca Mountain project, which is expected to face fierce opposition from environmental groups and possibly Nevada legislators.

CHAPTER 9
WATER ISSUES

Water is precious for many reasons. It is an essential resource for sustaining human, animal, and vegetable life. Agriculture is absolutely dependent on water to produce food crops and livestock. Water is crucial to tourism, navigation, and industry. Enormous amounts are used to generate power, mine materials, and produce goods. Water is an ingredient, a medium, and a means of conveyance or cooling in most industrial processes. Water supplies a vital habitat for many of the earth's creatures, from the whale to the tadpole. There are entire ecosystems that are water based.

All these competing uses put an enormous strain on the earth's water supply. Overall, the amount of water on the earth remains constant, simply passing from one stage to another in a circular pattern known as the hydrologic cycle. (See Figure 9.1.) Water in the atmosphere condenses and falls to the earth as precipitation, such as rain, sleet, or snow. Precipitation seeps into the ground, saturating the soil and refilling underground aquifers; it is drawn from the soil by vegetation for growth and returned into the air by plant leaves through the process of transpiration; and some precipitation flows into surface waters such as rivers, streams, lakes, wetlands, and oceans. Moisture evaporates from surface water back into the atmosphere to repeat the cycle.

Humans have interrupted the hydrologic cycle to accommodate the many water demands of modern life. Flowing rivers and streams are dammed up. Groundwater and surface water are pumped from their sources to other places. Water is either consumed or discharged back to the environment, usually not in the same condition. Water quality is important to all users, as differing levels of quality are required for different uses. Although some industrial users can tolerate water containing high levels of contaminants, drinking water requirements are extremely strict.

WATER AVAILABILITY

Water covers nearly three-fourths of the planet; however, the vast majority of it is too salty to drink or nourish crops and too corrosive for many industrial processes. In general, saline water is defined as water that contains at least 1,000 milligrams of salt per liter of water. No cheap and effective method for desalinating large amounts of ocean water has been discovered. This makes freshwater an extremely valuable commodity. Although the overall water supply on the earth is enormous, freshwater is not often in the right place at the right time in the right amount to serve all the competing needs.

Overall Water Use in 2010

Every five years since 1950 the US Geological Survey (USGS) has collected comprehensive data on water use in the United States. As of January 2018, the most recent report available was published in 2014 and includes data through 2010.

Molly A. Maupin et al. of the USGS find in *Estimated Use of Water in the United States in 2010* (November 2014, https://pubs.usgs.gov/circ/1405/pdf/circ1405.pdf) that in 2010 an estimated 355 billion gallons of water per day (Bgal/d; 1.3 trillion L/d) were withdrawn from surface water and groundwater sources. Nearly half of the water—161 Bgal/d (609.5 billion L/d) or 45%—was withdrawn for generation of thermoelectric power. Maupin et al. note that nearly all (94%) of the water that was withdrawn for thermoelectric power generation in 2010 was used for once-through cooling purposes. In other words, the water was withdrawn, traveled through the facility, and discharged back to its source. This is considered a nonconsumptive use of water because little to none of the water is actually consumed. (Some very small amounts may be consumed by evaporation, leaks, or minor uses in facility equipment.)

FIGURE 9.1

The hydrologic cycle

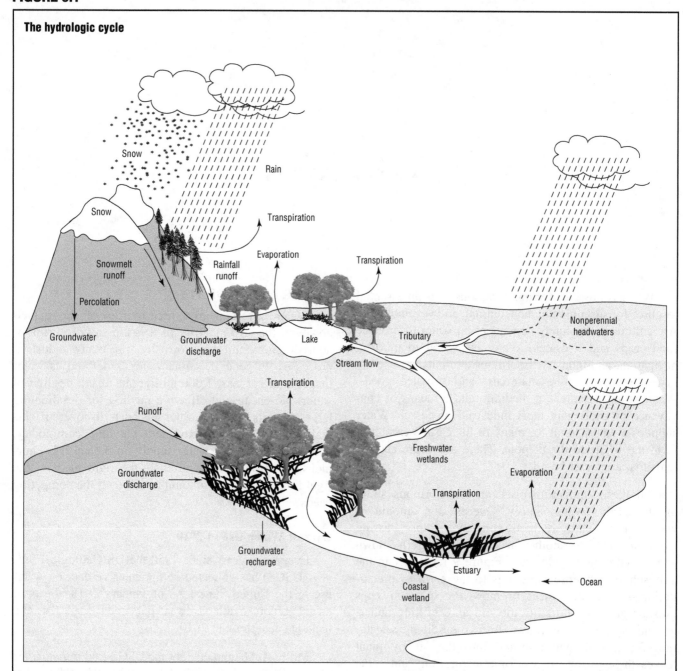

SOURCE: "The Water Cycle," in *National Water Quality Inventory: 1998 Report to Congress*, US Environmental Protection Agency, June 2000, https://www.epa.gov/sites/production/files/2015-09/documents/1998_national_water_quality_inventory_report_to_congress.pdf (accessed November 15, 2017)

Irrigation was the second-largest water withdrawal in 2010, accounting for 115 Bgal/d (435.3 billion L/d), or 32% of the total amount. Much of this water was consumed. It was absorbed by growing vegetation, ran off into surface waters, trickled down to groundwater, evaporated from the ground, or evaporated from vegetation (a process called transpiration). Thus, irrigation is a large consumptive use of freshwater.

Public water supply is another major consumptive use of freshwater. In 2010, 42 Bgal/d (159 billion L/d), or 12% of the total withdrawn, went to public water supply. This water was withdrawn from water sources by public and private water suppliers that provided water to at least 25 people or via a minimum of 15 connections. The water was potable (fit to drink) and used in homes, offices, and commercial and industrial facilities for a variety of purposes.

Maupin et al. report that the US population rose from 150.7 million in 1950 to 313 million in 2010, an increase of nearly 108%; in contrast, total water withdrawals went from 180 Bgal/d (681.4 billion L/d) in 1950 to 355 Bgal/d (1.6 trillion L/d) in 2010, an increase of 97%. In 1950 the per capita (per person) water withdrawal was 1,194 gallons per day (4,520 L/d). This value climbed steadily over the years, reaching a peak in 1975 of 1,940 gallons per day (7,344 L/d) per person. Per capita use has since declined and was 1,134 gallons per day (4,393 L/d) per person in 2010.

Groundwater

Groundwater is water that fills pores or cracks in subsurface rocks. When rain falls or snow melts on the earth's surface, water may run off into lower land areas or lakes and streams. Some is caught and diverted for human use. What is left absorbs into the soil, where it can be used by vegetation, seeps into deeper layers of soil and rock, or evaporates back into the atmosphere. (See Figure 9.2.)

An aquifer is an underground formation that contains enough water to yield significant amounts when a well is drilled into it. Aquifers vary from a few feet thick to tens or hundreds of feet thick. They can be located just below the earth's surface or thousands of feet beneath it, and one aquifer may be only a part of a large system of aquifers that feed into one another. They can cover a few acres of land or many thousands of square miles. Because runoff water can easily seep down to the water table (the boundary between saturated and unsaturated soils), aquifers are susceptible to contamination.

Modern technological developments allow massive quantities of water to be pumped out of the ground. When large amounts of water are removed from the ground, underground aquifers can become depleted much more quickly than they can naturally be replenished. Removal

of groundwater also disturbs the natural filtering process that occurs as water travels through rocks and sand.

CLEAN WATER ACT

On June 22, 1969, the Cuyahoga River in Cleveland, Ohio, burst into flames, the result of oil and debris that had accumulated on the river's surface. This episode thrust the problem of water pollution into the public consciousness. Many people became aware—and wary—of the nation's polluted waters, and in 1972 Congress passed the Federal Water Pollution Control Act, commonly known as the Clean Water Act (CWA).

The objective of the CWA was to "restore and maintain the chemical, physical, and biological integrity of the nation's waters." It called for ending the discharge of all pollutants into the navigable waters of the United States to achieve "wherever attainable, an interim goal of water quality which provides for the protection and propagation of fish, shellfish, and wildlife and provides for recreation in and on the water."

The CWA includes five titles as follows:

- Title I—Research and Related Programs
- Title II—Grants for the Construction of Treatment Works
- Title III—Standards and Enforcement
- Title IV—Permits and Licenses
- Title V—General Provisions

CWA Jurisdiction

Since its original passage, the scope of the water bodies subject to the CWA has been the subject of much litigation. The law gives the US Environmental Protection Agency (EPA) jurisdiction over "waters of the United States." This term has traditionally been interpreted to include navigable waters (waters that can be traversed by boat). The CWA's applicability to streams and small wetlands is a matter of extreme controversy.

The US Supreme Court has rendered three decisions on the definition of "waters of the United States": *United States v. Riverside Bayview Homes, Inc.* (474 US 121 [1985]), *Solid Waste Agency of Northern Cook County v. US Army Corps of Engineers* (531 US 159 [2001]), and *Rapanos v. United States* (547 US 715 [2006]). However, it is widely agreed that these decisions do not provide clearcut guidance. According to Jason Miller of the US Fish and Wildlife Service (FWS), in *Our Wetlands and Streams after Rapanos/Carabell ... Does the Clean Water Act Still Protect Them?* (July 2008, https://www.fws.gov/habitat conservation/rapanos_carabell/Post_Rapanos_pres_web.pdf), these decisions have been interpreted to mean that federal jurisdiction applies to wetlands that are adjacent to waters that are permanent, relatively permanent, standing, or

FIGURE 9.2

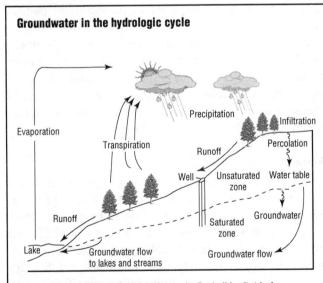

Groundwater in the hydrologic cycle

SOURCE: "Ground Water in the Hydrologic Cycle," in *Guide for Industrial Waste Management*, US Environmental Protection Agency, Office of Solid Waste and Emergency Response, June 1999, https://www.epa.gov/sites/production/files/2016-03/documents/industrial-waste-guide.pdf (accessed November 15, 2017)

flowing. In addition, it applies to wetlands that have a "significant nexus" to navigable waters.

In 2007 the EPA finalized a guidance document that informed its staff how to use these definitions to determine which waters are subject to federal jurisdiction. In 2011 the agency prepared *Draft Guidance on Identifying Waters Protected by the Clean Water Act* (https://www.epa.gov/cwa-404/guidance-identify-waters-protected-clean-water-act), which was a revised guidance document on the subject.

After a period of public comment and consideration, the EPA and the US Army Corps of Engineers (ACE) collaborated to draft a regulation to more clearly define the scope of the water bodies subject to the CWA. The ACE was involved because Section 404 of the law grants the ACE the authority to regulate developments that change waterways in certain ways, for example, dredging out bottom sediment from a river or dumping dirt into a swamp to fill it. In June 2015 the new regulation, called the Clean Water Rule (*Federal Register*, vol. 80, no. 124), was published. In "Clean Water Rule Protects Streams and Wetlands Critical to Public Health, Communities, and Economy" (May 27, 2015, https://www.nrcs.usda.gov/wps/portal/nrcs/detail/az/newsroom/releases/?cid=NRCSEPRD358025), the EPA notes that in addition to covering navigable waters, the rule also covers tributaries to them and their headwaters. Waters "next to" rivers and lakes and their tributaries are also included, as are small wetlands (such as prairie potholes), that "impact downstream waters." The Clean Water Rule went into effect in August 2015.

Critics decried the rule as a grievous overreach of power by the EPA and ACE and a massive infringement of private property rights. Dozens of states and private groups filed lawsuits against the agencies. In October 2015 the US Court of Appeals for the 6th Circuit granted a stay of the rule, making it unenforceable nationwide. The stay was still in effect when newly elected President Donald Trump (1946–) entered office in January 2017. The following month he issued an executive order instructing the EPA and ACE to review the Clean Water Rule to determine its cohesion with the following policy: "It is in the national interest to ensure that the Nation's navigable waters are kept free from pollution, while at the same time promoting economic growth, minimizing regulatory uncertainty, and showing due regard for the roles of the Congress and the States under the Constitution." As is explained in previous chapters, the president has focused on reducing the number and scope of federal regulations. In June 2017 the EPA and the ACE (https://www.epa.gov/wotus-rule) officially proposed rescinding the Clean Water Rule.

Meanwhile, the US Supreme Court had accepted a case related to Clean Water Rule litigation, specifically whether such lawsuits should be heard by district courts or by appeals courts. Miriam Seifter explains in "Argument Preview: Justices to Determine How Clean Water Act Litigation Flows" (October 5, 2017, http://www.scotusblog.com/2017/10/argument-preview-justices-determine-clean-water-act-litigation-flows/) that the case hinges on a section of the CWA that lists the types of EPA actions that are reviewable by the courts. As of January 2018, the Supreme Court had not reached a decision in the case, and the EPA and ACE had not finalized their repeal of the Clean Water Rule. The repeal is vehemently opposed by environmental groups, such as the Sierra Club, that want stricter federal regulation of the nation's water bodies.

Point Source Management

Point sources are those that disperse pollutants from a specific source or area, such as a sewage drain or an industrial discharge pipe. (See Figure 9.3.) Pollutants commonly discharged from point sources include bacteria (from wastewater treatment plants and sewer overflow), toxic chemicals, and heavy metals (from industrial plants). Point sources are regulated under the National Pollutant Discharge Elimination System (NPDES). Any facility using point sources to discharge to receiving waters must obtain an NPDES permit for them. States can operate their own NPDES-permitting program if they have been authorized to do so by the EPA. In "Specific State Program Status" (September 27, 2017, https://www.epa.gov/npdes/npdes-state-program-information), the EPA indicates that, as of 2017, most states had received that authorization.

NPDES permits include monitoring and reporting requirements and set specific limits on the amounts and types of pollutants that can be discharged to water bodies. The limits take into account any total maximum daily loads (TMDLs) that have been set for the water bodies. (A TMDL is the amount of a particular pollutant that can be safely released into a water body.) The EPA (https://www3.epa.gov/enviro/facts/pcs-icis/search.html) allows the public to access NPDES permit information, including any reported violations of the permit limits, via the Permit Compliance System and the Integrated Compliance Information System databases on the Envirofacts website.

Nonpoint Source Management

Nonpoint sources are those that are spread out over a large area and have no specific outlet or discharge point. (See Figure 9.3.) These include agricultural and urban runoff, runoff from mining and construction sites, and accidental or deliberate spills. Nonpoint sources are much more difficult to regulate than point sources but are increasingly blamed for contributing significantly to water pollution. Data presented later in this chapter show that sources such as agriculture and urban-related runoff and storm water are cited by the states as primary probable causes of water impairment.

FIGURE 9.3

Examples of point and nonpoint sources of pollution

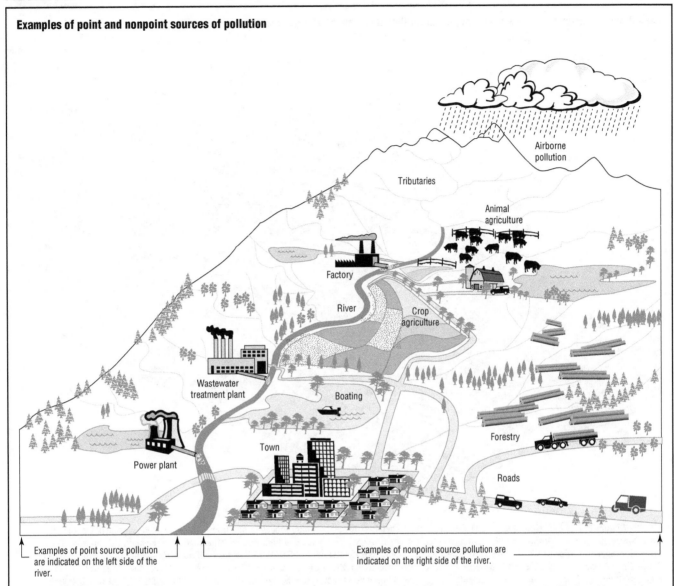

Examples of point source pollution are indicated on the left side of the river.

Examples of nonpoint source pollution are indicated on the right side of the river.

SOURCE: "Figure 3. Examples of Point and Nonpoint Sources of Pollution," in *Water Quality: Key EPA and State Decisions Limited by Inconsistent and Incomplete Data*, US General Accounting Office, March 2000, http://www.gao.gov/archive/2000/rc00054.pdf (accessed November 15, 2017)

Nonpoint source management at the federal level is not addressed directly in the CWA. Nevertheless, Title III, Section 319(b) of the law does require each state to establish a "management program for controlling pollution added from nonpoint sources to the navigable waters within the State and improving the quality of such waters." For example, California (January 2, 2018, https://www.water boards.ca.gov/water_issues/programs/nps/) operates an extensive Nonpoint Source Pollution Control Program.

In addition, nonpoint source management is achieved through nonregulatory measures, such as by encouraging voluntary practices by dischargers and by private water protection organizations that promote community actions. For example, the Iowa chapter of the Sierra Club recommends in "Protecting Iowa's Water Quality: Point and Non-point Sources of Pollution" (August 1, 2013,

https://www.sierraclub.org/sites/www.sierraclub.org/files/ sce/iowa-chapter/water/WaterQuality.pdf) that citizens, businesses, and local governments take measures to prevent or slow rainfall runoff from their properties, such as by using rain barrels or detention ponds. The organization notes, "These techniques hold water on the landscape longer and will serve to filter pollutants rather than allowing them to rush into water bodies."

Watershed Management

In "Healthy Watersheds Protection" (May 1, 2017, https://www.epa.gov/hwp/basic-information-and-answers-frequent-questions#what), the EPA defines a watershed as "the land area that drains to one stream, lake, or river." In other words, a watershed is determined geologically and hydrologically, rather than politically. Figure 9.4 shows a

FIGURE 9.4

Land drawing demonstrating watershed approach for the management of water resources

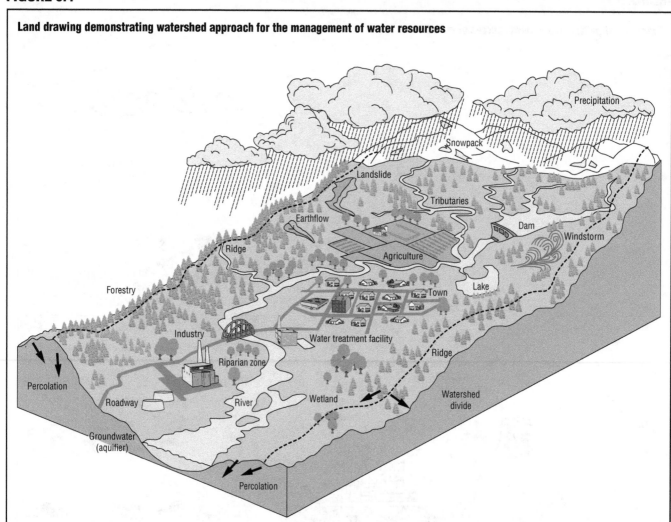

SOURCE: "Figure 1. The Area Hydrologically Defined by a Watershed Is Affected by Many Processes and Issues. A 'Watershed Approach' Coordinates Their Management," in *Protecting and Restoring America's Watersheds: Status, Trends and Initiatives in Watershed Management*, US Environmental Protection Agency, Office of Water, June 2001, https://nepis.epa.gov/Exe/ZyNET.exe/20004IC6.TXT?ZyActionD=ZyDocument&Client=EPA&Index= 2000+Thru+2005&Docs=&Query=&Time=&EndTime=&SearchMethod=1&TocRestrict=n&Toc=&TocEntry=&QField=&QFieldYear=&QFieldMonth= &QFieldDay=&IntQFieldOp=0&ExtQFieldOp=0&XmlQuery=&File=D%3A%5Czyfiles%5CIndex%20Data%5C00thru05%5CTxt%5C00000001% 5C20004IC6.txt&User=ANONYMOUS&Password=anonymous&SortMethod=h%7C-&MaximumDocuments=1&FuzzyDegree=0&ImageQuality= r75g8/r75g8/x150y150g16/i425&Display=hpfr&DefSeekPage=x&SearchBack=ZyActionL&Back=ZyActionS&BackDesc=Results%20page&Maximum Pages=1&ZyEntry=1&SeekPage=x&ZyPURL (accessed November 15, 2017)

watershed example and the many issues and processes that affect it. Obviously, a watershed can include both point sources and nonpoint sources that contribute to water impairment. Watersheds are delineated by the USGS and assigned unique 12-digit numbers that identify the region, subregion, basin, subbasin, watershed, and sub-watershed. (See Table 9.1.)

The EPA believes the nation's water quality problems cannot be solved by further regulating point-source discharges. Instead, the agency advocates a comprehensive approach that crosses jurisdictional boundaries and addresses all the air, water, land, social, and economic issues that affect a particular watershed. The EPA actively encourages the participation of private environmental and conservation groups in watershed protection.

The agency's Adopt Your Watershed program (https:// cfpub.epa.gov/surf/locate/index.cfm) provides a database that includes information about each of the nation's more than 2,600 watersheds. The database identifies thousands of local and regional groups that engage in activities to further watershed protection and improvement.

CWA-REQUIRED WATER QUALITY ASSESSMENTS

Two sections of CWA Title III require the states to assess the quality condition of their navigable waters and report the results to the EPA. Under Section 305(b) the states must report the extent to which their waters support the basic goals of the CWA and state water quality standards. Water quality standards are designed to protect designated uses (such as drinking water supply). Section 305(b) requires each state to submit data that indicate:

- The water quality of all navigable waters in the state

- The extent to which the waters provide for the protection and propagation of marine animals and allow recreation in and on the water

- The extent to which pollution has been eliminated or is under control

- The sources and causes of the pollution

The act stipulates that the states must submit this information to the EPA on a biennial basis (every two years).

Under Title III, Section 303(d) of the CWA, states are required to compile and submit a separate list of their waters that are considered to be impaired and requiring pollution controls.

Surface Water Quality Assessment Results

Since 2002 the EPA has electronically collected state water quality data on surface waters and compiled it into the "National Summary of State Information" (2018,

https://iaspub.epa.gov/tmdl_waters10/attains_nation_cy.control). As of 2018, most states had submitted data through 2014; thus, the following discussion of national water quality assumes 2014 as the reporting year.

In general, the states assess surface water quality in rivers and streams, lakes, ocean shoreline, and estuaries. Because of the tremendous resources required to assess all water bodies, only a small portion of each water body type is actually assessed for each reporting period.

Surface water bodies are rated on quality as follows:

- Good—meets applicable water quality standards and designated uses

- Threatened—qualifies for "good" rating, but is expected to degrade in the near future

- Impaired—fails to meet applicable water quality standards and designated uses

Table 9.2 provides a summary of the ratings for the different types of surface water bodies that were assessed by the states. It should be noted that the percentage of total waters assessed varied widely from only 1.1% of

TABLE 9.1

Watershed boundary definitions and examples

Definition	Example
A region, the largest drainage basin, contains the drainage area of a major river or the combined drainage areas of several rivers.	Mid-Atlantic (02)
Subregions divide regions and include the area drained by a river system.	Chesapeake Bay watershed (0207)
Basins divide or may be equivalent to subregions.	Potomac River watershed (020700)
Subbasins divide basins and represent part or all of a surface-drainage basin, a combination of drainage basins, or a distinct hydrologic feature.	Monocacy watershed (0207009)
Watersheds divide subbasins and usually range in size from 40,000 to 250,000 acres.	Monocacy River watershed (0207000905)
Subwatersheds divide or may be equivalent to watersheds and usually range in size from 10,000 to 40,000 acres.	Double Pipe Creek subwatershed (020700090502)

SOURCE: "Breaking down the Watershed," in *Handbook for Developing Watershed Plans to Restore and Protect Our Waters*, US Environmental Protection Agency, March 2008, https://www.epa.gov/sites/production/files/2015-09/documents/2008_04_18_nps_watershed_handbook_handbook-2.pdf (accessed November 15, 2017)

TABLE 9.2

Water bodies assessed for water quality, 2014

	Rivers and streams (miles)	Lakes, reservoirs, and ponds (acres)	Bays and estuaries (square miles)	Coastal shoreline (miles)	Ocean and near coastal (square miles)	Wetlands (acres)	Great Lakes shoreline (miles)	Great Lakes open water (square miles)
				Size of water				
Good waters	514,845	5,336,908	11,529	1,290	617	569,328	102	1
Threatened waters	4,495	30,309						
Impaired waters	582,031	12,950,960	44,619	3,325	6,218	665,494	4,355	39,230
Total assessed waters	**1,101,371**	**18,318,176**	**56,148**	**4,615**	**6,836**	**1,234,822**	**4,457**	**39,231**
Total waters	**3,533,205**	**41,666,049**	**87,791**	**58,618**	**54,120**	**107,700,000**	**5,202**	**196,343**
Percent of waters assessed	31.2	44.0	64.0	7.9	12.6	1.1	85.7	20.0

Note: Compilation of state-level data; while most data are from 2014, some data are from 2016, 2012, 2010, 2008, 2006, or 2004.

SOURCE: "Assessed Waters of United States," in *National Summary of State Information*, US Environmental Protection Agency, November 2017, https://ofmpub.epa.gov/waters10/attains_nation_cy.control (accessed November 15, 2017)

wetland acreage to 85.7% of the shoreline waters of the Great Lakes as measured in miles. Overall, the data indicate significant problems with impairment. For example, 582,031 river and stream miles (936,688 km) out of 1.1 million miles (1.8 million km) total or 53% were impaired. Likewise, 13 million lake, reservoir, and pond acres (excluding the Great Lakes; 5.3 ha) out of 18.3 million acres (7.4 million ha) total or 71% were impaired.

The EPA categorizes the many different (and sometimes overlapping) state-designated uses of water bodies into nine broad classes:

- Aesthetic value—water bodies valued for their aesthetic qualities, for example, beautiful scenery

- Agricultural—water bodies supporting the irrigation of agricultural land and the watering of livestock and wildlife

- Aquatic life harvesting—water bodies supporting the growth of harvestable aquatic life, such as fish and shellfish

- Exceptional recreational or ecological significance—water bodies supporting rare, threatened, or endangered species; serving as exceptional habitats; or being outstanding natural resource waters in some other way

- Fish, shellfish, and wildlife protection and propagation—water bodies supporting aquatic life and other wildlife that use them as part of their habitats; the spawning of salmon and other fish species; the migration of various species of aquatic organisms; and commercial and sport fishing

- Public water supply—water bodies serving as sources of public water supplies

- Industrial—water bodies supporting industrial operations

- Recreation—water bodies supporting recreational activities, such as boating and swimming

- Other—water bodies supporting other uses not specified, for example, navigational uses

In 2014 the designated use class with the highest level of impairment for each water body type was:

- Rivers and streams—Aquatic life harvesting (54.2% impaired). (See Table 9.3.)

- Lakes, reservoirs, and ponds—Aquatic life harvesting (73.4% impaired). (See Table 9.4.)

- Bays and estuaries—Public water supply (90% impaired). (See Table 9.5.)

- Coastal shoreline—Other uses (100% impaired). (See Table 9.6.)

- Ocean and near coastal—Aquatic life harvesting (91.2% impaired). (See Table 9.7.)

- Wetlands—Aquatic life harvesting (99.7% impaired). (See Table 9.8.)

- Great Lakes shoreline—Aquatic life harvesting (100% impaired). (See Table 9.9.)

- Great Lakes open water—Aquatic life harvesting (100% impaired). (See Table 9.10.)

Table 9.11 lists the general impairment causes reported by the states. Although dozens of factors were

TABLE 9.3

Percentage of rivers and streams supporting designated uses, 2014

Designated use group	Miles assessed	Percent good	Percent threatened	Percent impaired
Fish, shellfish, and wildlife protection and propagation	883,207	55.3	0.3	44.4
Recreation	444,746	56.4	0.8	42.9
Agricultural	374,761	95.6	0.0	4.4
Aquatic life harvesting	311,538	45.8	0.0	54.2
Public water supply	288,321	74.8	0.1	25.1
Industrial	192,126	98.2	0.0	1.8
Other	87,894	97.9	0.0	2.1
Aesthetic value	42,879	93.7	0.0	6.3
Exceptional recreational or ecological significance	5,213	82.3	0.0	17.7

Note: Compilation of state-level data; while most data are from 2014, some data are from 2016, 2012, 2010, 2008, 2006, or 2004. Waters assessed for more than one designated use are included in multiple designated use groups.

SOURCE: Adapted from "National Summary: Designated Use Support in Assessed Rivers and Streams," in *National Summary of State Information*, US Environmental Protection Agency, November 2017, https://ofmpub .epa.gov/waters10/attains_nation_cy.control (accessed November 15, 2017)

TABLE 9.4

Percentage of lakes, reservoirs, and ponds supporting designated uses, 2014

Designated use group	Acres assessed	Percent good	Percent threatened	Percent impaired
Aquatic life harvesting	10,870,229	26.6	0.0	73.4
Fish, shellfish, and wildlife protection and propagation	10,695,047	53.7	0.2	46.1
Recreation	8,750,341	74.6	0.3	25.0
Public water supply	6,939,810	77.4	0.0	22.6
Agricultural	5,484,831	97.2	0.0	2.8
Industrial	3,236,781	99.9	0.0	0.1
Other	2,477,695	87.2	0.0	12.8
Aesthetic value	1,215,548	62.6	0.0	37.4
Exceptional recreational or ecological significance	942	92.1	0.0	7.9

Note: Compilation of state-level data; while most data are from 2014, some data are from 2016, 2012, 2010, 2008, 2006, or 2004. Waters assessed for more than one designated use are included in multiple designated use groups.

SOURCE: Adapted from "National Summary: Designated Use Support in Assessed Lakes, Reservoirs, and Ponds," in *National Summary of State Information*, US Environmental Protection Agency, November 2017, https://ofmpub.epa.gov/waters10/attains_nation_cy.control (accessed November 15, 2017)

TABLE 9.5

Percentage of bays and estuaries supporting designated uses, 2014

Designated use group	Square miles assessed	Percent good	Percent threatened	Percent impaired
Aquatic life harvesting	46,066	21.7	0.0	78.3
Fish, shellfish, and wildlife protection and propagation	41,746	23.1	0.0	76.9
Recreation	15,962	78.1	0.0	21.9
Public water supply	7,583	10.0	0.0	90.0
Agricultural	3,732	96.6	0.0	3.4
Other	3,485	100.0	0.0	0.0
Industrial	3,166	100.0	0.0	0.0
Aesthetic value	72	71.1	0.0	28.9

Note: Compilation of state-level data; while most data are from 2014, some data are from 2016, 2012, 2010, 2008, 2006, or 2004. Waters assessed for more than one designated use are included in multiple designated use groups.

SOURCE: Adapted from "National Summary: Designated Use Support in Assessed Bays and Estuaries," in *National Summary of State Information*, US Environmental Protection Agency, November 2017, https://ofmpub .epa.gov/waters10/attains_nation_cy.control (accessed November 15, 2017)

TABLE 9.6

Percentage of coastal shoreline supporting designated uses, 2014

[Waters assessed for more than one designated use are included in multiple designated use groups below]

Designated use group	Miles assessed	Percent good	Percent threatened	Percent impaired
Aquatic life harvesting	3,401	24.2	0.0	75.8
Recreation	1,722	76.7	0.0	23.3
Fish, shellfish, and wildlife protection and propagation	840	22.7	0.0	77.3
Aesthetic value	235	100.0	0.0	0.0
Public water supply	118	91.4	0.0	8.6
Industrial	25	100.0	0.0	0.0
Other	4	0.0	0.0	100.0

Note: Compilation of state-level data; while most data are from 2014, some data are from 2016, 2012, 2010, 2008, 2006, or 2004.

SOURCE: Adapted from "National Summary: Designated Use Support in Assessed Coastal Shoreline," in *National Summary of State Information*, US Environmental Protection Agency, November 2017, https://ofmpub .epa.gov/waters10/attains_nation_cy.control (accessed November 15, 2017)

TABLE 9.7

Percentage of ocean and near coastal waters supporting designated uses, 2014

[Waters assessed for more than one designated use are included in multiple designated use groups below]

Designated use group	Square miles assessed	Percent good	Percent threatened	Percent impaired
Aquatic life harvesting	6,031	8.8	0.0	91.2
Recreation	1,493	86.1	0.0	13.9
Fish, shellfish, and wildlife protection and propagation	1,219	57.5	0.0	42.5
Other	376	46.7	0.0	53.3
Agricultural	201	100.0	0.0	0.0

Note: Compilation of state-level data; while most data are from 2014, some data are from 2016, 2012, 2010, 2008, 2006, or 2004.

SOURCE: Adapted from "National Summary: Designated Use Support in Assessed Ocean and Near Coastal," in *National Summary of State Information*, US Environmental Protection Agency, November 2017, https://ofmpub.epa.gov/waters10/attains_nation_cy.control (accessed November 15, 2017)

TABLE 9.8

Percentage of wetlands supporting designated uses, 2014

[Waters assessed for more than one designated use are included in multiple designated use groups below]

Designated use group	Acres assessed	Percent good	Percent threatened	Percent impaired
Fish, shellfish, and wildlife protection and propagation	1,231,502	52.1	0.0	47.9
Recreation	1,045,364	99.8	0.0	0.2
Public water supply	480,668	100.0	0.0	0.0
Aquatic life harvesting	121,322	0.3	0.0	99.7
Agricultural	55,401	35.0	0.0	65.0
Industrial	18,460	100.0	0.0	0.0
Other	985	100.0	0.0	0.0

Note: Compilation of state-level data; while most data are from 2014, some data are from 2016, 2012, 2010, 2008, 2006, or 2004.

SOURCE: Adapted from "National Summary: Designated Use Support in Assessed Wetlands," in *National Summary of State Information*, US Environmental Protection Agency, November 2017, https://ofmpub.epa .gov/waters10/attains_nation_cy.control (accessed November 15, 2017)

involved, the most highly reported causes across multiple water body types were mercury, nutrients, organic enrichment/oxygen depletion, pathogens, and polychlorinated biphenyls (PCBs). Table 9.12 identifies the probable sources of the impairment causes listed in Table 9.11. For many water bodies, the states could not determine specific sources, so they put the blame on "unknown" sources. The two leading impairment sources were agriculture and atmospheric deposition.

MERCURY. As shown in Table 9.11, mercury was the primary cause of impairment for several surface water body types in 2014, particularly lakes, reservoirs, and ponds. More than 8.3 million acres (3.4 million ha) of

lakes, reservoirs, and ponds were deemed impaired due to mercury. According to the EPA, in "Specific State Causes of Impairment That Make Up the National Mercury Cause of Impairment Group for Threatened and Impaired Lakes, Reservoirs, and Ponds" (2017, https://iaspub.epa.gov/ tmdl_waters10/attains_nation_cy.cause_detail?p_cause _group_name=MERCURY), this impairment factor was evidenced by widespread mercury detection in fish tissue. Mercury is said to bioaccumulate, meaning that it builds up in the tissues of the organisms that consume it. The chemical mostly reaches water bodies via atmospheric deposition. As is described in Chapter 2, mercury is present in fossil fuels, such as coal, and enters the atmosphere when the fuels are burned.

TABLE 9.9

Percentage of Great Lakes shoreline supporting designated uses, 2014

[Waters assessed for more than one designated use are included in multiple designated use groups below]

Designated use group	Miles assessed	Percent good	Percent threatened	Percent impaired
Aquatic life harvesting	4,333	0.0	0.0	100.0
Agricultural	3,131	100.0	0.0	0.0
Other	3,131	100.0	0.0	0.0
Industrial	3,131	100.0	0.0	0.0
Recreation	1,131	12.7	0.0	87.3
Fish, shellfish, and wildlife protection and propagation	953	7.0	0.0	93.0
Public water supply	916	35.4	0.0	64.6

Note: Compilation of state-level data; while most data are from 2014, some data are from 2016, 2012, 2010, 2008, 2006, or 2004.

SOURCE: Adapted from "National Summary: Designated Use Support in Assessed Great Lakes Shoreline," in *National Summary of State Information*, US Environmental Protection Agency, November 2017, https://ofmpub.epa.gov/waters10/attains_nation_cy.control (accessed November 15, 2017)

TABLE 9.10

Percentage of Great Lakes open water supporting designated uses, 2014

[Waters assessed for more than one designated use are included in multiple designated use groups below]

Designated use group	Square miles assessed	Percent good	Percent threatened	Percent impaired
Aquatic life harvesting	39,230	0.0	0.0	100.0
Agricultural	39,031	100.0	0.0	0.0
Industrial	39,031	100.0	0.0	0.0
Other	39,031	100.0	0.0	0.0
Fish, shellfish, and wildlife protection and propagation	200	100.0	0.0	0.0
Aesthetic value	196	0.1	0.0	99.9
Recreation	196	100.0	0.0	0.0
Public water supply	196	100.0	0.0	0.0

Note: Compilation of state-level data; while most data are from 2014, some data are from 2016, 2012, 2010, 2008, 2006, or 2004.

SOURCE: Adapted from "National Summary: Designated Use Support in Assessed Great Lakes Open Water," in *National Summary of State Information*, US Environmental Protection Agency, November 2017, https://ofmpub.epa.gov/waters10/attains_nation_cy.control (accessed November 15, 2017)

NUTRIENTS. Nutrients are substances that nourish vegetation; nitrogen and phosphorus and compounds that contain them (such as phosphate and nitrate) are prime examples. Excess levels of these nutrients can stimulate algal growth in water bodies, which can reduce oxygen concentrations to dangerous levels for aquatic creatures, such as fish and shellfish. In 2014 nutrients were one of the top causes of impairment for lakes, reservoirs, and ponds and for rivers and streams. (See Table 9.11.) Significant nitrogen and phosphorus sources include sewage/wastewater treatment plants, septic tanks, fertilizer, animal wastes, and certain industrial discharges. Nitrogen also makes its way into water bodies via atmospheric deposition.

ORGANIC ENRICHMENT/OXYGEN DEPLETION. Water bodies containing excessive nutrients and/or pathogens (disease-causing microorganisms, such as bacteria) can become overly rich in organic material, such as plant and algal growth. This process is called eutrophication and occurs through various mechanisms. High nutrient concentrations spur the growth of algal mats and aquatic plants. As they die off, they are degraded by aerobic (oxygen-gobbling) bacteria that thrive and multiply. Likewise, excessive algal mats on the water surface can block sunlight to underlying aquatic plants, causing them to die. The aerobic bacteria that flourish in this environment lower the dissolved oxygen content of the water, which is harmful to aquatic species, such as fish and invertebrate. As these creatures die, they perpetuate the cycle by further raising the organic content of the water. Aerobic bacteria also feast on fecal matter, which can enter water bodies via sewage and animal waste, such as from livestock.

As shown in Table 9.11, oxygen enrichment/oxygen depletion was the leading cause of impairment to wetlands in 2014 and negatively affected numerous other water body types.

PATHOGENS. Pathogens are disease-causing microorganisms. One of the most commonly measured pathogens in water bodies is *Escherichia coli* (*E. coli*), which is a type of fecal coliform. The latter is a group of bacteria with common characteristics that are found in the fecal matter of humans and animals. High pathogen levels are problematic for several reasons. First, they pose a threat to public health in water supplies that are used by humans for drinking water or recreational activities. Second, they can trigger organic enrichment/oxygen depletion problems. Pathogens make their way into water bodies via sewage and animal wastes, such as from livestock. In 2014 pathogens were among the leading causes of impairment to multiple types of water bodies, including lakes, reservoirs, ponds, rivers, and streams. (See Table 9.11.)

POLYCHLORINATED BIPHENYLS. Polychlorinated biphenyls (PCBs) are a group of synthetic organic chemicals that were widely used in the United States through the 1970s as lubricants and coolants for electrical equipment. After scientists became aware of their toxic nature, the chemicals fell into disfavor. The damage, however, was already done. PCBs are very long-lasting in the environment because they are not biodegradable. Also, like mercury, they bioaccumulate in the tissues of aquatic organisms. Eating contaminated fish and other aquatic creatures is one of the ways in which humans are exposed to PCBs. In "Polychlorinated Biphenyls" (April 8, 2013, http://www3.epa.gov/epawaste/hazard/tsd/pcbs/about.htm), the EPA explains that PCBs continue to enter the environment as old electrical equipment leaks or is landfilled or

TABLE 9.11

Causes of impairment in assessed water bodies, 2014

Cause of impairment group	Rivers and streams (miles)	Lakes, reservoirs, and ponds (acres)	Bays and estuaries (square miles)	Coastal shoreline (miles)	Ocean and near coastal (square miles)	Wetlands (acres)	Great Lakes shoreline (miles)	Great Lakes open water (square miles)
			Size of assessed waters with listed causes of impairment					
Algal growth	5,818	628,461	1,707	92	0	4,271		
Ammonia	12,005	212,104	28	22	1	171		
Biotoxins	6,450	66,142						
Cause unknown	44,768	21,930	1,838					
Cause unknown—fish kills	101	21						
Cause unknown—impaired biota	41,781	82,296	912	79		1,288		
Chlorine	585	50						
Dioxins	5,061	129,824	10,253		9	212	3,471	38,862
Fish consumption advisory	305	44,866	230					
Flow alteration(s)	41,084	185,227	1			2,086		
Habitat alterations	62,728	94,852	2		10	1,104	170	
Mercury	68,751	8,314,977	16,765	2,349	5,470	315,437	2,454	30,015
Metals (other than mercury)	93,032	1,231,409	8,124	11	110	94,630		0
Noxious aquatic plants	318	42,249	1,668					
Nuisance exotic species	1,219	600,501	656		35	1,142	380	
Nuisance native species	56	7,578						
Nutrients	117,917	3,920,336	18,275	131	8	67,849	380	196
Oil and grease	2,760	44,285	17	100	1			
Organic enrichment/ oxygen depletion	98,270	1,458,227	5,442	397	640	469,222	120	
Other cause	9,273	54,879	339					
Pathogens	178,755	502,367	5,947	798	374	72,385	521	
Pesticides	17,717	411,401	7,542	36	52	181	2,483	29,661
pH/acidity/caustic conditions	33,396	880,116	829	201	18	869		
Polychlorinated biphenyls (PCBs)	81,998	3,203,457	28,192	50	16	933	4,333	39,230
Radiation	1,101	48						
Salinity/total dissolved solids/chlorides/sulfates	37,626	867,572	38			82,164		
Sediment	138,871	502,200	400			1,237	290	0
Taste, color and odor	990	39,764	6					
Temperature	94,095	239,693	20	100	1	14,900		
Total toxics	10,230	243,538	336		29	13		
Toxic inorganics	4,830	5,770	3			28,053	5	
Toxic organics	4,649	24,783	6,017		14	44		
Trash	1,137	2,144	264			320		
Turbidity	47,618	1,473,536	15,321	490	36	5,551		

Note: Compilation of state-level data; while most data are from 2014, some data are from 2016, 2012, 2010, 2008, 2006, or 2004.

SOURCE: "National Causes of Impairment," in *National Summary of State Information*, US Environmental Protection Agency, November 2017, https://ofmpub.epa.gov/waters10/attains_nation_cy.control (accessed November 15, 2017)

incinerated. PCBs can enter water bodies via atmospheric deposition. As shown in Table 9.11, PCBs were a major impairment cause for several different water body types in 2014, including lakes (especially the Great Lakes), reservoirs, and ponds.

AGRICULTURE. In 2014 agricultural operations were singled out by the states as one of the top identifiable sources of impairment to assessed water bodies. (See Table 9.12.) This is primarily due to the harmful effects of nutrients, which are associated with fertilizers and livestock waste. The latter is also a source of pathogens. As is described in Chapter 6, manure production at large livestock facilities can be massive. Runoff from manure stockpiles or fields treated with the waste poses a threat to water quality.

The EPA explains in *NPDES Permit Writers' Manual for Concentrated Animal Feeding Operations* (February 2012, https://www.epa.gov/sites/production/files/2015-10/documents/cafo_permitmanual_entire.pdf) that it regulates concentrated animal feeding operations (CAFOs) that discharge to water bodies. CAFOs are a subset of animal feeding operations (AFOs), which the agency defines as facilities that stable, confine and feed, or maintain livestock for at least 45 days per year in noncrop-related areas. AFOs fall under federal CWA regulation when they are deemed CAFOs. This distinction is made on a case-by-case basis and depends on numerous factors, including the number of animals involved and how wastes are managed. As of 2012, the EPA estimates that there were approximately 20,000 CAFOs in the United States. CAFOs that discharge to water bodies must obtain NPDES permits.

ATMOSPHERIC DEPOSITION. Atmospheric deposition is explained in detail in Chapter 5, which concerns acid

TABLE 9.12

Probable sources of impairment to assessed water bodies, 2014

Probable source group	Size of assessed waters with probable sources of impairments							
	Rivers and streams (miles)	Lakes, reservoirs, and ponds (acres)	Bays and estuaries (square miles)	Coastal shoreline (miles)	Ocean and near coastal (square miles)	Wetlands (acres)	Great Lakes shoreline (miles)	Great Lakes open water (square miles)
Agriculture	133,164	1,111,390	3,423	58		203,199	620	4,373
Aquaculture	182	130	1					
Atmospheric deposition	84,798	4,612,679	13,852		1,485	199,741	3,283	39,230
Commercial harbor and port activities			0		0			
Construction	20,794	200,559	726	4	4			
Groundwater loadings/ withdrawals	172	2,944	0					
Habitat alterations (not directly related to hydromodification)	65,787	280,318	2,226			33	98	
Hydromodification	88,091	691,888	2,278	167	7	4,565	240	
Industrial	11,386	234,739	3,403	107	4	352	72	0
Land application/ waste sites			1					
Land application/ waste sites/tanks	8,526	27,199	63	44		680	11	
Legacy/historical pollutants	6,247	749,910	21,878	41			851	0
Military bases	21	204						
Municipal discharges/ sewage	55,758	640,413	5,854	415	6	21	304	
Natural/wildlife	49,433	1,095,805	3,575	1	1	288,418	1	
Other	9,067	839,429	3,839			372		
Recreation and tourism (non-boating)	1,725	174,518	7	0	67		1	
Recreational boating and marinas	132	24,616	257	140	15			
Resource extraction	33,187	519,509	120	8	10	32,112		
Silviculture (forestry)	40,822	170,181	0					
Spills/dumping	4,040	173,199	72	17	2	6	3	
Unknown	138,148	3,623,034	15,394	183	1,340	383,096	135	199
Unspecified nonpoint source	57,640	1,125,248	4,099	104	71	1,610	9	
Urban-related runoff/ stormwater	47,186	744,484	16,707	342	9	54	98	0

Note: Compilation of state-level data; while most data are from 2014, some data are from 2016, 2012, 2010, 2008, 2006, or 2004.

SOURCE: "National Probable Sources Contributing to Impairments," in *National Summary of State Information*, US Environmental Protection Agency, November 2017, https://ofmpub.epa.gov/waters10/attains_nation_cy.control (accessed November 15, 2017).

rain. Many chemicals that become airborne, such as the emissions from smokestacks, can fall back to the earth and impact water quality. These chemicals include organic compounds, such as PCBs, and metals, such as mercury. As shown in Table 9.12, atmospheric deposition was a leading source of impairment to water bodies in 2014. This was particularly true for lakes, reservoirs, and ponds in that atmospheric deposition was blamed by the states for impairing 4.6 million acres (1.9 million ha) of these water bodies. Obviously, the key to controlling atmospheric deposition lies in controlling the facilities that emit the offending chemicals. Chapter 2 and Chapter 5 describe the various regulatory programs that are designed to control air pollutants that contribute to the problem.

Pollution Controls

As noted earlier, Title III, Section 303(d) of the CWA requires the states to specifically identify any of their water bodies not meeting the water quality standards.

The states may then set a TMDL for each of the problematic water bodies. According to the EPA, in "Impaired Waters and TMDLs" (October 25, 2017, https://www.epa.gov/tmdl/developing-total-maximum-daily-loads-tmdl), a TMDL is the maximum amount of a particular pollutant that can be released into a water body without impairing its quality below that of the applicable water quality standard. TMDL calculations result in loading and reduction goals. For example, it might be determined that a river impaired by a pollutant needs to receive no more than 20 pounds (9.1 kg) per year of that pollutant from all dischargers in the future to improve and to meet the applicable water quality limit. In this case, 20 pounds per year is the loading goal. Assuming that the river currently receives 40 pounds (18.1 kg) per year of the pollutant means that discharges of the pollutant must be reduced by 50%. This is the reduction goal.

TMDL analyses provide numerical goals that are pollutant-specific and water body–specific. Achieving

The Environment

TABLE 9.13

Number of Total Maximum Daily Loads completed, by fiscal year, 1996–2018

[EPA fiscal year starts October 1 and ends September 30]

Fiscal year	Number of TMDLs	Number of causes of impairment addressed
1996	165	166
1997	394	418
1998	406	412
1999	331	374
2000	1,564	1,591
2001	2,584	2,620
2002	2,738	2,818
2003	3,001	3,273
2004	3,409	3,667
2005	4,269	4,586
2006	4,209	4,559
2007	4,323	4,653
2008	9,269	9,551
2009	4,403	4,627
2010	2,574	2,710
2011	2,849	3,132
2012	2,905	3,173
2013	15,536	15,626
2014	3,339	3,513
2015	968	1,092
2016	1,362	1,540
2017	3,348	4,471
2018	1	1
Total	**73,947**	**78,573**

TMDLs = Total Maximum Daily Loads.
Note: Data for fiscal year 2018 are for October 2018 only.

SOURCE: "National Cumulative Number of TMDLs," in *National Summary of State Information*, US Environmental Protection Agency, November 2017, https://ofmpub.epa.gov/waters10/attains_nation_cy.control (accessed November 15, 2017)

TABLE 9.14

Number of Total Maximum Daily Loads completed, by pollutant group, 1995–2017

[This chart includes TMDLs since October 1, 1995.]

Pollutant group	Number of TMDLs	Number of causes of impairment addressed
Mercury	21,624	21,654
Pathogens	14,144	14,459
Metals (other than mercury)	10,387	10,590
Nutrients	6,683	8,232
Sediment	4,031	4,689
Polychlorinated biphenyls (pcbs)	2,626	3,557
Temperature	2,454	2,464
Organic enrichment/ oxygen depletion	2,230	2,366
Ph/acidity/caustic conditions	2,033	2,092
Turbidity	1,817	2,081
Salinity/total dissolved solids/ chlorides/sulfates	1,762	1,821
Pesticides	1,395	1,558
Ammonia	1,148	1,259
Chlorine	341	347
Other cause	269	324
Toxic inorganics	219	223
Toxic organics	162	204
Cause unknown-impaired biota	128	132
Total toxics	**120**	**130**
Algal growth	104	112
Trash	92	92
Habitat alterations	83	84
Dioxins	27	28
Noxious aquatic plants	21	22
Radiation	21	24
Oil and grease	14	14
Cause unknown	7	7
Nuisance exotic species	3	6
Fish consumption advisory	2	2
Total	**73,947**	**78,573**

TMDLs = Total Maximum Daily Loads.
Note: Includes TMDLs completed since October 1, 1995.

SOURCE: "National Cumulative TMDLs by Pollutant," in *National Summary of State Information*, US Environmental Protection Agency, November 2017, https://ofmpub.epa.gov/waters10/attains_nation_cy.control (accessed November 15, 2017)

TMDL goals can be accomplished through various means. The options differ depending on whether the dischargers are point sources or nonpoint sources.

As of 2018, tens of thousands of TMDLs had been completed around the country. (See Table 9.13.) According to the EPA, in "National Summary of State Information," the states with the most TMDLs were North Carolina (13,523), Pennsylvania (7,157), New Hampshire (6,057), West Virginia (5,344), and Kansas (3,357). Table 9.14 breaks down the nation's TMDLs by pollutant group and lists the number of causes of impairment that are addressed. Mercury was, by far, the pollutant group that had triggered the most TMDLs as of 2017. It was followed by pathogens and metals other than mercury.

TMDLS FOR THE CHESAPEAKE BAY WATERSHED. The Chesapeake Bay is a massive estuary (an area where ocean and freshwater come together) located on the upper East Coast. (See Figure 9.5.) The estuary is fed by rivers and streams in multiple states and the District of Columbia; thus, the Chesapeake Bay watershed is enormous. Its water quality has long been a source of concern. During the late 1970s Congress ordered the EPA to conduct a comprehensive study of the watershed. Ben A. Franklin reports in "Chesapeake Bay Study Citing Pollution

Threats" (NYTimes.com, September 27, 1983) that the $27 million study took seven years to complete and revealed significant deterioration since the 1960s in the bay's water quality and ecological health. These problems were forecast to worsen as the area's population continued to grow.

Over the decades various federal-state programs have been implemented in an effort to improve the watershed but have failed to achieve desired goals. In early January 2009 a large group of plaintiffs sued the EPA alleging the agency had failed to meet its obligations under the CWA and federal-state agreements to restore and preserve the bay's water quality and ecological resources. The case, *Fowler v. EPA* (No. 1:09-CV-00005-CKK), reflects the name of one of the plaintiffs, the former Maryland state senator C. Bernard Fowler (1924–). Another major plaintiff was the Chesapeake Bay Foundation (http://www

FIGURE 9.5

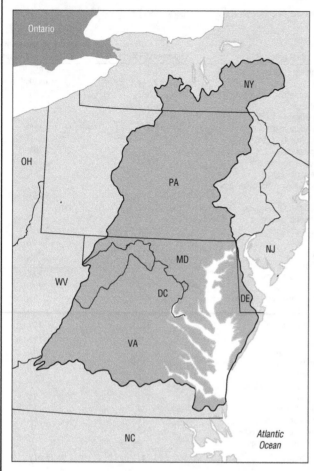

Map of Chesapeake Bay region

SOURCE: "Map," in *Fact Sheet: Chesapeake Bay Total Maximum Daily Load (TMDL)*, US Environmental Protection Agency, September 29, 2016, https://www.epa.gov/chesapeake-bay-tmdl/chesapeake-bay-tmdl-fact-sheet (accessed November 15, 2017)

- Establish a "stringent" TMDL for the entire watershed
- Expand its review of permits in the watershed
- Initiate a rulemaking to prepare new national regulations on CAFOs and urban and suburban storm water
- Establish a publicly available system for tracking and monitoring the EPA's progress toward reducing pollution in the Chesapeake Bay watershed

The EPA calls the Chesapeake Bay TMDL "the largest and most complex [TMDL] ever developed in the nation, involving pollution sources throughout a 64,000-square-mile watershed that includes six states and the District of Columbia." In December 2010 the agency (https://www.epa.gov/chesapeake-bay-tmdl) finalized the TMDL. It requires massive load reductions in nitrogen, phosphorus, and sediment to water bodies in Delaware, Maryland, New York, Pennsylvania, Virginia, West Virginia, and the District of Columbia. Full implementation of the required pollution control measures is expected by 2025.

CAFOs are operations that house large numbers of livestock. Some CAFOs are required to be permitted under the NPDES. According to the press release "CBF and EPA Reach New Agreement to Reduce Pollution from Animal Operations" (June 5, 2013, http://www.cbf.org/news-media/newsroom/2013/fed/cbf-and-epa-reach-new-agreement-to-reduce-pollution-from-animal-operations.html), the Chesapeake Bay Foundation and the EPA announced in June 2013 that they had revised the original settlement agreement to eliminate the requirement for a new national CAFO regulation. The Chesapeake Bay Foundation explains it agreed to the change because it feared that such a regulation would be subject to numerous and lengthy court challenges. Instead, the foundation agreed to allow the EPA to conduct a series of investigations and inspections related to CAFO management and then decide whether any revisions to the existing CAFO rules are warranted. Some environmental groups were extremely disappointed in the outcome and accused the Obama administration of giving in to pressure from the agricultural industry, which was staunchly opposed to tighter CAFO regulation.

.cbf.org), a nonprofit organization whose stated mission is to "Save the Bay, and Keep It Saved." The lawsuit was filed during the waning days of the administration of President George W. Bush (1946–); only weeks later Barack Obama (1961–) was sworn in as president.

The case never reached the courtroom. On May 15, 2009, President Obama issued Executive Order 13508, Chesapeake Bay Protection and Restoration (https://www.gpo.gov/fdsys/pkg/FR-2009-05-15/pdf/E9-11547.pdf), which established a committee to investigate and report on the major challenges involved in protecting and restoring the bay and outline the pollution control strategies and actions that the EPA should take in response. In May 2010 the EPA announced that it had reached a settlement agreement with the plaintiffs. In the press release "EPA Reaches Settlement in Chesapeake Bay Lawsuit" (May 11, 2010), the agency notes that it agreed to do the following:

NATIONAL WATER QUALITY SAMPLING PROGRAMS

The data collected by the states under Title III, Sections 303(d) and 305(b) of the CWA provide one perspective on the nation's overall water quality. Other perspectives can be obtained through scientifically rigorous sampling programs that are overseen by the EPA and the USGS.

EPA National Aquatic Resource Surveys

The EPA relies on probability-based studies that are conducted at various sites around the country using nationally consistent methods and designs. This approach is used in the National Aquatic Resources Surveys (NARS; https://www.epa.gov/national-aquatic-resource-surveys), which are collaborations between the EPA and other federal agencies, state agencies, and other public and private partners. The NARS assess four aquatic resources: rivers and streams; lakes, ponds, and reservoirs; coastal waters; and wetlands. As of January 2018, the most recent NARS reports on these resources were:

- Rivers and streams: *National Rivers and Streams Assessment 2008–2009: A Collaborative Survey* (March 2016, https://www.epa.gov/sites/production/files/2016-03/documents/nrsa_0809_march_2_final.pdf) with data through 2009

- Lakes, ponds, and reservoirs: *National Lakes Assessment: A Collaborative Survey of Lakes in the United States* (December 2016, https://www.epa.gov/sites/production/files/2016-12/documents/nla_report_dec_2016.pdf) with data through 2012

- Coastal waters: *National Coastal Condition Assessment 2010* (January 2016, https://www.epa.gov/sites/production/files/2016-01/documents/ncca_2010_report.pdf) with data through 2010

- Wetlands: *National Wetland Condition Assessment 2011: A Collaborative Survey of the Nation's Wetlands* (May 2016, https://www.epa.gov/sites/production/files/2016-05/documents/nwca_2011_public_report_20160510.pdf) with data through 2011

Some of the major highlights from the published NARS reports regarding noncoastal waters are presented in this section; coastal waters are addressed later in this chapter.

In *National Rivers and Streams Assessment 2008–2009* (NRSA), the EPA presents data collected at 1,924 rivers and streams of various sizes and types around the country. The results are compared with those of reference water bodies, which the agency describes as the "least-disturbed" rivers and streams in the ecological regions studied. One of the goals of the NRSA was to determine the stressors that are negatively affecting rivers and streams. The indicators that were examined during the assessment included biological indicators (e.g., aquatic life), chemical indicators (e.g., phosphorus), physical indicators (e.g., streambed sediments), and human health indicators (e.g., mercury in fish tissue). The most widespread stressors measured during the NRSA were phosphorus and nitrogen levels, riparian condition as evidenced by vegetation cover and disturbance, excess sedimentation (which can indicate erosion problems), fish habitat, salinity, and acidification. Nationally, phosphorus was found at high levels (as compared with reference water bodies) in 46% of the river and stream miles sampled. Likewise, nitrogen levels were high, when compared with least-disturbed

conditions, in 41% of river and stream miles. Other stressors that negatively affected at least 20% of river and stream miles on a national basis were riparian vegetation cover (24%) and riparian disturbance (20%). There were regional differences between the various stressors, with higher phosphorous levels found in the East and higher nitrogen levels found in the Plains and South, for example.

The EPA describes in *National Lakes Assessment: A Collaborative Survey of Lakes in the United States* the findings of its second comprehensive study of the condition of the nation's lakes. The first (baseline) study was conducted in 2007. During the 2012 study crews assessed 1,038 lakes, ponds, and reservoirs. The EPA notes, "Each field crew used consistent procedures to sample benthic macroinvertebrates (e.g., insect larvae, snails, and clams), zooplankton (small animals in the water column), algal toxins, atrazine [an herbicide], and nutrients and to observe near-shore habitat so that results could be compared across the country." Note that the study did not include the Great Lakes or the Great Salt Lake.

The results of the study are summarized in the fact sheet "National Lakes Assessment" (December 2016, https://www.epa.gov/sites/production/files/2016-12/documents/nla_fact_sheet_dec_7_2016.pdf). Overall, the EPA found widespread nutrient pollution, with 35% of lakes showing excess nitrogen and 40% showing excess phosphorus. High levels of these nutrients can make lakes prone to algal blooms (overgrowth of nontoxic or toxic algae). One algal toxin is microcystin, which is produced by cyanobacteria. (Note that microcystin is commonly referred to as an algal toxin even though the producing agent is a bacterium.) The EPA indicates that microcystin was detected in 39% of the lakes sampled; most of the concentrations, however, were below levels of concern. This was also true for concentrations of the herbicide atrazine, which was detected in 30% of the lakes. The agency found that nearly a third (31%) of all lakes had "degraded benthic macroinvertebrate communities." These conditions were mostly blamed on high levels of nutrients that are harmful to aquatic life. In general, the EPA concludes that there was little change in lake quality between the 2007 and the 2012 surveys; however, there were increases in phosphorus and some algal toxins over time.

In *National Wetland Condition Assessment 2011: A Collaborative Survey of the Nation's Wetlands*, the EPA describes a survey of 1,179 wetlands across the country that were assessed for algae, hydrology, soils, vegetation, and water chemistry. Potential stressors were also noted. The results are summarized in the fact sheet "The National Wetland Condition Assessment 2011" (March 31, 2017, https://www.epa.gov/sites/production/files/2016-05/documents/2011_nwca_fact_sheet_final.pdf). The EPA indicates that 48% of the wetlands were in "good" condition with healthy plant communities. Another 20% were in "fair" condition, and 32% were in "poor" condition. The most common problems cited were ditching, compacted soil (e.g., from road building), and removal or loss of vegetation due to forest clearing, grazing, mowing, or other activities. Approximately 19% of the wetlands were stressed by nonnative plants that harmed the biodiversity and habitat conditions for fish and wildlife.

USGS Water Quality Data Sources

The USGS (https://water.usgs.gov/owq/) collects water quality data at surface water and groundwater sampling locations around the country. The results are provided in various databases, including the National Water Information System (https://waterdata.usgs.gov/nwis/qw), the National Water Quality Network for Rivers and Streams (https://cida.usgs.gov/quality/rivers/home), and the National Water-Quality Assessment (https://water.usgs.gov/nawqa/) databases.

The USGS also publishes reports that summarize collected data on selected topics. For example, in *The Quality of Our Nation's Waters: Water Quality in Principal Aquifers of the United States, 1991–2010* (2015, https://pubs.usgs.gov/circ/1360/pdf/circ1360report.pdf), Leslie A. DeSimone, Peter B. McMahon, and Michael R. Rosen summarize the results from nine regional USGS assessments of the nation's groundwater quality. The studies focused on principal aquifers, particularly those that supply large amounts of drinking water. In total, 6,600 wells were sampled, and 1.3 million chemical analyses were performed. The researchers found that groundwater in 22% of the sampled wells contained at least one chemical constituent at levels higher than human-health benchmarks for drinking water. Most of these constituents were believed to be naturally occurring, for example, arsenic or radon that dissolved from underground rock formations into the groundwater. One troublesome constituent was linked with anthropogenic (human-based) sources. Nitrate was detected at levels above human-health benchmarks in more than 1% of the sampled wells. As noted earlier, nitrate is a nutrient associated with sewage/wastewater treatment plants, septic tanks, fertilizer, animal wastes, and certain industrial discharges.

In "The Quality of the Nation's Groundwater: Progress on a National Survey" (December 7, 2017, https://www.usgs.gov/news/quality-nation-s-groundwater-progress-a-national-survey), the USGS notes that, as of December 2017, it was approximately halfway through a second massive survey of the nation's groundwater quality. The survey is scheduled to run through 2023 and will provide detailed information about the presence of pesticides and other constituents of concern in 20 major drinking water

aquifers. As of January 2018, the USGS had published the results for nine of the aquifers. The findings from these reports reveal that organic constituents (such as pesticides) rarely exceeded concentrations considered levels of concern. There were numerous exceedances of human health benchmarks for inorganic constituents, primarily elements such as arsenic, fluoride, and manganese, that were believed to have originated from natural (geological) sources. The USGS notes that nitrate was the only constituent from anthropogenic sources that exceeded a human-health benchmark in some of the nine aquifers sampled.

COASTAL WATERS

As shown in Table 9.2, only 12.6% of the nation's coastal shoreline miles were assessed in 2014 as part of the CWA-required Section 303(d) and 305(b) analyses performed by the states. Overall, 3,325 miles (72%; 5,350 km) out of 4,615 miles (7,426 km) of coastal shoreline miles were deemed impaired. The primary causes of impairment were mercury, pathogens, and oxygen enrichment/oxygen depletion. (See Table 9.11.)

Since 2001 the EPA has published five NARS reports on the country's coastal areas. As of January 2018, the most recent report, *National Coastal Condition Assessment 2010*, was published in 2016. The EPA compiles data collected by various federal and state agencies and assesses coastal areas based on water and sediment quality, coastal habitat condition, benthic health (the condition of bottom-dwelling organisms), and fish tissue contaminants. In 2010, 1,104 sites were sampled that represented 35,400 square miles (91,686 square km) of US coastal waters along the Pacific Coast, Gulf Coast, and Atlantic Coast. The nearshore waters of the Great Lakes were also included. The results of the survey are summarized in the factsheet "The National Coastal Condition Assessment 2010" (December 2015, https://www.epa.gov/sites/production/files/2016-01/documents/ncca_2010_fact_sheet_01_26_2016.pdf) with ratings for the waters as follows:

- Biological quality—56% good, 10% fair, and 18% poor

- Water quality—36% good, 48% fair, and 14% poor

- Sediment quality—55% good, 21% fair, and 13% poor

- Ecological fish tissue quality—less than 1% good, 26% fair, and 49% poor

Hypoxic Coastal Waters

Hypoxia is a low-oxygen condition that poses a severe danger to fish, crustaceans, and other aquatic life. As described earlier, nutrient pollution—an excess of nitrogen and phosphorus that encourages excessive algal growth—is one of the primary causes of organic enrichment/oxygen depletion. Figure 9.6 shows the minimum

FIGURE 9.6

Minimum oxygen requirements for Chesapeake Bay aquatic life

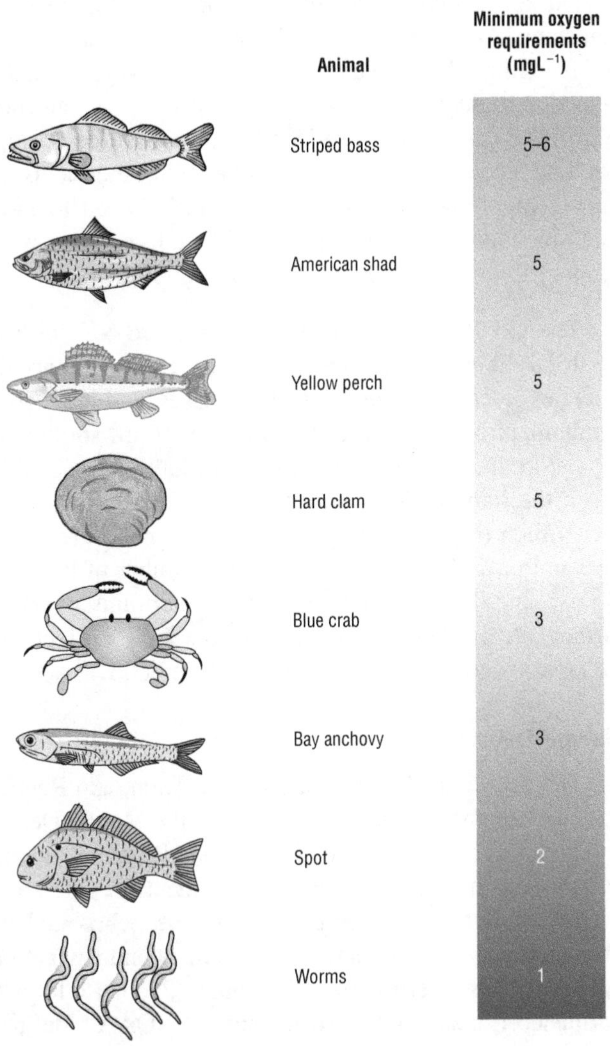

Animal	Minimum oxygen requirements (mgL⁻¹)
Striped bass	5–6
American shad	5
Yellow perch	5
Hard clam	5
Blue crab	3
Bay anchovy	3
Spot	2
Worms	1

mgL⁻¹ = Milligrams per liter.

SOURCE: Adapted from "Box 3. Hypoxia Definition," in *Scientific Assessment of Hypoxia in US Coastal Waters*, Committee on Environment and Natural Resources, Interagency Working Group on Harmful Algal Blooms, Hypoxia, and Human Health of the Joint Subcommittee on Ocean Science and Technology, September 2010, https://obamawhitehouse.archives.gov/sites/default/files/microsites/ostp/hypoxia-report.pdf (accessed November 16, 2017)

into the Gulf from the Mississippi and Atchafalaya Rivers. In "Gulf of Mexico 'Dead Zone' Is the Largest Ever Measured" (August 2, 2017, http://www.noaa.gov/media-release/gulf-of-mexico-dead-zone-is-largest-ever-measured), NOAA indicates that the dead zone measured 8,776 square miles (22,730 square km) in 2017, the largest ever recorded. The average size during the period from 2013 to 2017 was 5,806 square miles (15,037 square km).

In 1998 Congress passed the Harmful Algal Bloom and Hypoxia Research and Control Act (https://cdn.coastalscience.noaa.gov/page-attachments/research/habhrca.pdf). It established an interagency task force to examine the ecological and economic consequences of harmful algal blooms and hypoxia and to report on alternatives for reducing, mitigating, and controlling them. In 2008 the task force set a goal of reducing the dead zone by the year 2015 to 1,930 square miles (5,000 square km). This objective was not realized. In fact, the 2017 dead zone was more than four times the goal size.

The task force has been reauthorized through various amendments, including the Harmful Algal Bloom and Hypoxia Research and Control Amendments Act of 2014, which directed the EPA (through the task force) to submit a progress report biennially to Congress. *Mississippi River/Gulf of Mexico Watershed Nutrient Task Force: 2017 Report to Congress* (August 2017, https://www.epa.gov/sites/production/files/2017-11/documents/hypoxia_task_force_report_to_congress_2017_final.pdf) is the second report in the series. The task force describes nutrient monitoring data and discharge limits for the 12 affected states and notes that all of them had "draft or complete strategies to reduce nitrogen and phosphorus pollution" in the Mississippi/Atchafalaya River basin. Furthermore, 2035 is the new target date to lower the size of the dead zone to 1,930 square miles (5,000 square km).

Beaches

In 2000 Congress passed the Beaches Environmental Assessment and Coastal Health (BEACH) Act. It established a program of federal grants to state and local governments to facilitate water quality monitoring at the nation's beaches. However, funding for the program ceased in fiscal year (FY) 2013. In *FY 2013: EPA Budget in Brief* (February 2012, (https://yosemite.epa.gov/sab/sabproduct.nsf/2B686066C751F34A852579A4007023C2/$File/FY2013_BIB.pdf), the EPA notes that state and local governments have established beach monitoring programs that "can continue without federal support."

The BEACH Act requires the EPA to collect information from coastal states regarding beach closings because of environmental problems. The information is reported in the EPA's Beach Advisory and Closing Online Notification database (https://watersgeo.epa.gov/beacon2/beacon.html). The public can search the database

oxygen requirements for various sea creatures inhabiting the Chesapeake Bay, one of two US water bodies, along with the Gulf of Mexico, in which hypoxia has been extensively studied.

Each year since 1985 the National Oceanic and Atmospheric Administration (NOAA) has reported the size of the Gulf of Mexico hypoxic "dead zone." Agricultural sources, such as crop fertilization and livestock wastes, are the primary sources believed responsible for excessive nitrogen and phosphorus concentrations flowing

to learn about any current or previous warnings or closures at particular beaches. Such information is also available from state and local agencies. For example, San Diego County (http://www.sdbeachinfo.com) in California monitors environmental conditions at dozens of beaches along its coastline. As of January 2018, the Tijuana Slough Shoreline, a stretch of ocean shoreline from the US-Mexico border to the north end of the Tijuana Slough National Wildlife Refuge was closed because of contamination from sewage runoff from the Tijuana River.

OCEAN PROTECTION

Throughout history humans have used the oceans virtually as they pleased. Ocean waters have long served as highways and harvest grounds. Now, however, humankind is at a threshold. Marine debris (garbage created by humans) is a problem of global proportions and is particularly evident in countries such as the United States, where there is extensive recreational and commercial use of coastal waterways.

US ocean protection laws date back to 1972, when the Marine Protection, Research, and Sanctuaries Act was passed to regulate intentional ocean disposal of materials and to authorize research. Title 1 of the act, known as the Ocean Dumping Act, prohibits all ocean dumping, except that allowed by permits, in any ocean waters under US jurisdiction by any US vessel or by any vessel sailing to or from a US port. The act bans the dumping of radiological, chemical, and biological warfare agents, high-level radioactive waste, and medical waste. In 1997 Congress amended the act to ban the dumping of municipal sewage sludge and industrial waste.

Oil Pollution Act

In 1989 the oil freighter *Exxon Valdez* ran into a reef in Prince William Sound, Alaska, spilling more than 11 million gallons (41.6 million L) of oil into one of the richest and most ecologically pristine areas in North America. An oil slick the size of Rhode Island killed wildlife and marine species. A $5 billion damage penalty was levied against Exxon, whose ship captain was found to be at fault in the wreck. (The US Supreme Court cut the amount to $507.5 million in 2008.)

In response to the *Exxon Valdez* oil spill, Congress passed the Oil Pollution Act of 1990, which went into effect in 1993. The law requires companies that are involved in storing and transporting petroleum to have standby plans for cleaning up oil spills on land or in water. The law makes the US Coast Guard responsible for approving cleanup plans and procedures for coastal and seaport oil spills, whereas the EPA oversees cleanups on land and in inland waterways. In addition, oil tankers must be built with double hulls to better secure the oil in the event of a hull breach.

In April 2010 an explosion aboard an offshore drilling platform in the Gulf of Mexico killed 11 workers and resulted in the largest oil spill in US history. Leased by the BP oil company, the Deepwater Horizon platform was located approximately 50 miles (80 km) off the coast of Louisiana. An estimated 4.9 million barrels of oil spewed into the Gulf before the damaged well head was eventually capped. Although a massive response effort was launched to mitigate (to relieve or reduce in harshness) the ecological and economic damages of the spill, thousands of aquatic birds and other creatures were believed to have died. In addition, fishing and shellfish harvesting were temporarily banned in large areas of the Gulf.

The Oil Pollution Act of 1990 limits to $75 million the total liability of responsible parties for economic damages suffered by residents, businesses, and local governments in a spill area. Following the BP oil spill some legislators introduced bills that would have retroactively raised the liability limit under the act. These bills, however, failed to gain widespread support in Congress and were not passed. The spill spawned a number of lawsuits against and between BP and its owner and operator partners. A detailed examination of the spill's effects on the area's wetlands is presented in Chapter 11.

Marine Debris

The Marine Debris Research, Prevention, and Reduction Act became law in 2006. It created the Marine Debris Research, Prevention, and Reduction Program within NOAA and the Coast Guard to help identify, determine sources of, and reduce or prevent marine debris and its adverse impacts on the marine environment and navigation safety. In "Discover the Issue" (January 25, 2018, https://marinedebris.noaa.gov/discover-issue), NOAA defines marine debris as "any persistent solid material that is manufactured or processed and directly or indirectly, intentionally or unintentionally, disposed of or abandoned into the marine environment or the Great Lakes."

Ocean current patterns can cause marine debris to become concentrated in accumulation areas known as "garbage patches." For example, the Great Pacific Garbage Patch lies in the Pacific Ocean between Hawaii and the western coast of the United States. According to NOAA, the "garbage patch" is not one continuous large pile of marine debris. Instead, the agency (https://marinedebris .noaa.gov/info/patch.html) notes, "While higher concentrations of litter items can be found in this area, along with other debris such as derelict fishing nets, much of the debris is actually small pieces of floating plastic that are not immediately evident to the naked eye." Ingestion of these microplastics can harm marine life. The NOAA indicates that the microplastics originate from a variety of sources, including discarded plastic shopping bags and containers that break down over time.

The problem of marine debris took on added significance following the devastating earthquake and tsunami that struck Japan in March 2011. According to NOAA (https://marinedebris.noaa.gov/current-efforts/emergency-response/japan-tsunami-marine-debris), the Japanese government estimates that approximately 5 million tons (4.5 million t) of debris was swept off the land into the ocean. Although about 70% of the debris is believed to have sunk off the Japanese coast, the remainder—roughly 1.5 million tons (1.4 million t)—floated out to sea. Pieces of the debris have since washed up onto US and Canadian shores. The NOAA Marine Debris Program (http://marinedebris.noaa.gov) tracks and maps marine debris locations and advises people and government agencies on what to do with debris that washes ashore.

DRINKING WATER
Drinking Water Legislation

The Safe Drinking Water Act (SDWA) of 1974 mandated that the EPA establish and enforce minimum national drinking water standards for all public water systems—community and noncommunity—in the United States. The law also required the EPA to develop guidelines for water treatment and to set testing, monitoring, and reporting requirements. Congress intended that, after the EPA had set regulatory standards, each state or US territory would run its own drinking water program. The EPA established the Primary Drinking Water Standards by setting the maximum contamination levels for contaminants that are known to be detrimental to human health. All public water systems in the United States are required to meet primary standards. Secondary standards cover nonhealth-threatening aspects of drinking water, such as odor, taste, staining properties, and color. Secondary standards are recommended but not required.

Over the decades the SDWA has been amended numerous times. These changes are described in detail by Mary Tiemann of the Congressional Research Service in *Safe Drinking Water Act (SDWA): A Summary of the Act and Its Major Requirements* (March 1, 2017, https://fas.org/sgp/crs/misc/RL31243.pdf). For example, in 1996, the law changed the relationship between the federal government and the states in administering drinking water programs by giving states greater flexibility and more responsibility.

The EPA and state health or environmental departments regulate public water supplies. Public supplies are required to ensure that the water meets certain government-defined health standards. The SDWA governs this regulation. The law mandates that all public suppliers test their water regularly to check for the existence of contaminants and treat their water supplies constantly to take out or reduce certain pollutants to levels that will not harm human health.

Private water supplies, usually wells, are not regulated under the SDWA. System owners are solely responsible for the quality of the water that is provided from private sources. However, many states have programs that are designed to help well owners protect their water supplies. Usually, these state-run programs are not regulatory but provide safety information. This type of information is vital because private wells are often shallower than those used by public suppliers. The shallower the well, the greater the potential for contamination.

Public Health and Safety

It is difficult to know how many illnesses are caused by contaminated water. People may not know the source of many illnesses and may attribute them to food (which may also have been in contact with polluted water), chronic illness, or other causes.

The health hazards of lead (a very toxic element) in water have been understood since the mid-20th century. The EPA's "Lead and Copper Rule" (March 15, 2017, https://www.epa.gov/dwreginfo/lead-and-copper-rule) was established in 1991 and has been tightened since then to better ensure that drinking water systems control lead (and copper) concentrations. In most cases, these metals enter drinking water by leaching out of old service lines that become corroded over time. In 2015 the city of Flint, Michigan, was rocked by scandal after high lead levels were detected in some tap water samples. Analysts discovered that the city's treatment plant was not taking appropriate measures to prevent lead leaching from service lines. The city began adding corrosion control chemicals to the water supply and changed its water source to remedy the leaching problem. Meanwhile, the city also experienced in 2015 an outbreak of Legionnaires' disease (a severe respiratory infection caused by *Legionella* bacteria) that was also linked to poor water treatment practices. Dozens of people were sickened and at least 12 died. There was evidence that some water treatment plant and city and state officials knew that the city's water was unsafe but acted to hide that fact. As of January 2018, more than a dozen former state and local officials had been charged with crimes in connection with the scandal.

Since 1971 the Centers for Disease Control and Prevention (CDC) and the EPA have collected and reported data that relate to waterborne-disease outbreaks. As of January 2018, the most recent data were presented and analyzed by Katharine M. Benedict et al. in "Surveillance for Waterborne Disease Outbreaks Associated with Drinking Water—United States, 2013–2014" (*Morbidity and Mortality Weekly Report*, vol. 66, no. 44, November 10, 2017). The results indicate that there were 42 outbreaks between 2013 and 2014 in water intended for drinking. They caused 1,006 people to become ill and killed 13 people.

More than half of the outbreaks and all of the deaths were linked to *Legionella* bacteria. The microscopic parasite *Cryptosporidium* was implicated in many other cases. The parasite has a hard outer shell and is resistant to chlorine and other typical chemical treatments. In 1993 more than 400,000 residents of Milwaukee, Wisconsin, were sickened after *Cryptosporidium* flourished in the city water supply. At least 40 deaths resulted. The city incorporated new water treatment protocols to effectively kill the parasite spores.

The CDC's report for 2013–14 is notable because it marks the first occasion that the National Outbreak Reporting System has included outbreaks associated with algal toxins in drinking water. Two separate outbreaks in Ohio during September 2013 and August 2014 were blamed on cyanobacteria toxins, specifically microcystin, in community water systems. As noted earlier in this chapter, algal blooms due to high nutrient concentrations are becoming a worrisome problem for many of the nation's surface waters. Public water systems that rely on relatively warm and still surface water bodies are most prone to trouble. For example, the Ohio outbreaks occurred during warm-weather months when algal blooms are more common. Although not mentioned in the CDC report, the source of the contaminated water was Lake Erie, a large freshwater lake that receives massive inflows of nutrients and increasingly experiences harmful algal blooms.

In 2015 Congress passed an SDWA amendment called the Drinking Water Protection Act (https://www.gpo.gov/fdsys/pkg/PLAW-114publ45/pdf/PLAW-114publ45.pdf). It calls on the EPA to produce a strategic plan to assess and manage the risks associated with algal toxins in drinking water provided by public water systems. The agency responded with *Algal Toxin Risk Assessment and Management Strategic Plan for Drinking Water* (November 2015, https://www.epa.gov/sites/production/files/2015-11/documents/algal-risk-assessment-strategic-plan-2015.pdf), in which it describes the many challenges associated with preventing and treating this widespread environmental problem. In "Fourth Unregulated Contaminant Monitoring Rule" (July 11, 2017, https://www.epa.gov/dwucmr/fourth-unregulated-contaminant-monitoring-rule), the EPA notes that it published a rule in December 2016 that requires public water systems from 2018 through 2020 to monitor 30 unregulated chemical contaminants, including 10 cyanobacteria toxins, such as microcystin. The agency states, "This monitoring provides a basis for future regulatory actions to protect public health." In other words, the monitoring data may prompt the EPA to propose new regulations to deal with the growing threat posed by algal blooms to drinking water sources.

CHAPTER 10
TOXINS IN EVERYDAY LIFE

The Swiss-born chemist Paracelsus (1493?–1541) once stated that "it is the dose that makes the poison." Many of the substances naturally found in the environment or released by modern, industrialized society are poisonous at certain dosages. These substances may be found in the home, workplace, or backyard, in the food and water people eat and drink, and in medications and consumer products.

WHY ARE TOXINS TOXIC?

A toxin is a substance (bacterial, viral, chemical, metal, fibrous, or radioactive) that poisons or harms a living organism. A toxin may cause immediate, short-term symptoms such as gastroenteritis, or cause harm after long-term exposure such as living in a lead- or radon-contaminated home for many years. Some toxins can have both immediate and long-term effects: living in an environment with poor air quality may trigger an acute asthma attack, or, after many years of exposure, it may contribute to lung cancer. Although the effects of a toxin may not show up for years, these effects may, nevertheless, be serious.

Toxins are often grouped according to their most harmful effect on living creatures. These categories include carcinogens, mutagens, and teratogens:

- A carcinogen is any substance that causes cancerous growth.

- A mutagen is an agent capable of producing genetic change.

- A teratogen is a substance that produces malformations or defective development.

The risks posed by environmental contamination may not be blatantly obvious. For example, people or animals that are exposed to contaminants may suffer damage to their immune systems and have difficulty recovering from infectious diseases. However, tracing the problem to environmental pollutants can be difficult.

GOVERNMENT LEGISLATION

Toxins that can be encountered in everyday life are regulated under a variety of federal and state laws. The following are the major pieces of federal legislation.

The Pure Food and Drug Act was originally passed in 1906 and substantially strengthened in 1938 by passage of its replacement, the Federal Food, Drug, and Cosmetic Act. This act was amended during the 1950s and 1960s to tighten restrictions on pesticides (a category that includes insecticides and herbicides), food additives, and drugs. Responsibility for enforcement of the act lies with the US Food and Drug Administration (FDA) under the US Department of Health and Human Services. The FDA oversees food supplies, human and veterinary drugs, biological products (such as vaccines and blood supplies), medical devices, cosmetics, and electronic products that emit radiation.

In 1947 Congress passed the Federal Insecticide, Fungicide, and Rodenticide Act. Although it was originally enforced by the US Department of Agriculture (USDA), authority passed to the US Environmental Protection Agency (EPA) after its creation in 1970. The act was strengthened and expanded by major amendments over the next few decades, particularly in 1996. The act provides the EPA with primary control over pesticide distribution, sale, and use. States also have authority to regulate pesticides and can do so at more restrictive levels than what the EPA requires. The EPA studies the environmental and health effects of pesticide use and requires some users to register when purchasing pesticides. All pesticides that are to be marketed in the United States must first be registered with the EPA.

The Federal Hazardous Substances Labeling Act was passed in 1960. The US Consumer Product Safety

Commission (CPSC), a federal government agency that is charged with protecting US consumers from unsafe products, administers the law as it applies to household products. The CPSC has jurisdiction over thousands of consumer products that pose a fire, electrical, chemical, or mechanical hazard. Household products (such as cleaners) that contain hazardous chemicals must be labeled with consumer warnings about their potential hazards.

The Toxic Substances Control Act (TSCA) was enacted by Congress in 1976. It gives the EPA authority to track the thousands of industrial chemicals that are produced in or imported to the United States. The EPA screens the chemicals and can require that industries test chemicals that may pose a hazard to the environment or human health. The EPA can ban chemicals it deems too risky. The EPA indicates in "About the TSCA Chemical Substance Inventory" (September 14, 2016, https://www.epa.gov/tsca-inventory/about-tsca-chemical-substance-inventory) that approximately 85,000 chemicals are tracked and controlled by the agency under the TSCA. Primary responsibility for administering the TSCA lies with the EPA's Office of Pollution Prevention and Toxics.

In 1984 a deadly cloud of chemicals was released from the Union Carbide pesticide plant in Bhopal, India, following an explosion in the plant. The methyl isocyanate gas killed approximately 3,000 people and injured 200,000 others. Shortly afterward, a similar chemical release occurred in West Virginia, where a cloud of gas sent 135 people to the hospital with eye, throat, and lung irritation complaints. There were no fatalities. Such incidents fueled demands from workers and the general public for information about hazardous materials in their areas. As a result, Congress passed the Emergency Planning and Community Right-to-Know Act of 1986.

The act established, among other things, the Toxics Release Inventory (TRI; https://www.epa.gov/toxics-release-inventory-tri-program), a public database that contains information on toxic chemical releases by various facilities. More than 650 toxic chemicals are on the TRI list.

RISK MANAGEMENT

In general, the risks that are associated with toxin exposures are assessed by scientists using the following five-step approach:

1. Identify the hazard—gather and evaluate data on the hazards to human health of exposure to specific substances. This step typically involves research into the ways in which substances affect living tissues and cells; for example, tests may be conducted using laboratory animals.

2. Determine the dose response—calculate a numerical relationship between the amount of exposure (the dose) and the extent of harm. There may be many different dose responses for a single substance, depending on how the exposure occurs. The duration and pathway of exposure are key variables. Pathways include inhalation into the lungs, dermal (skin) contact, and ingestion (swallowing).

3. Assess the exposure—ascertain information about the population that has been or will likely be exposed to particular substances.

4. Characterize the risk—use data from the first three steps to determine the likelihood that harm is going to occur to a population from a particular exposure to a particular substance.

5. Manage the risk—impose regulatory or other control measures to minimize the known risks that are associated with particular exposures to toxic substances by vulnerable populations.

The science of risk management is quite complex. Table 10.1 presents some of the common terms and acronyms that the EPA uses to characterize exposure and risk data.

Sources of Public Data

The prevalence and biological effects of some chemical toxins have been studied extensively. Experts acknowledge, however, that there are many toxins for which few data are available. In general, data on the generation, usage, and levels of chemicals in the environment (air, water, soil, and so on) are much more plentiful than data on the known effects of chemicals on human health. This raises difficulties for regulatory agencies that wish to set health-based limits on particular toxins. It also makes it harder for the public to determine whether a particular exposure is harmful or not.

TOXICS RELEASE INVENTORY. In *2015 Toxics Release Inventory National Analysis* (January 2017, https://www.epa.gov/sites/production/files/2017-01/documents/tri_na_2015_complete_english.pdf), the EPA states that facilities released 3.4 billion pounds (1.5 billion kg) of TRI chemicals in 2015. Figure 8.5 in Chapter 8 shows the distribution of releases to the environment in 2015. Figure 8.7 and Figure 8.6, also in Chapter 8, show the breakdown by chemical and industry, respectively, for that year.

AMERICAN ASSOCIATION OF POISON CONTROL CENTERS. Since 1983 the American Association of Poison Control Centers has maintained a national database on poison exposure. The National Poison Data System (http://www.aapcc.org/data-system) presents information from dozens of poison control centers around the country. According to David D. Gummin et al., in *2016 Annual Report of the American Association of Poison Control Centers' National Poison Data System (NPDS): 34th Annual Report* (November 2017, https://aapcc.s3.amazon

TABLE 10.1

Exposure and risk management terms

Acronym (if any)	Term	Definition
	Acute exposure	Exposure by the oral, dermal, or inhalation route for 24 hours or less.
	Short-term exposure	Repeated exposure by the oral, dermal, or inhalation route for more than 24 hours, up to 30 days.
	Subchronic exposure	Repeated exposure by the oral, dermal, or inhalation route for more than 30 days, up to approximately 10% of the life span in humans.
	Chronic exposure	Repeated exposure by the oral, dermal, or inhalation route for more than approximately 10% of the life span in humans.
LED_{10}	Lower limit on effective dose$_{10}$	The 95% lower confidence limit of the dose of a chemical needed to produce an adverse effect in 10% of those exposed to the chemical, relative to control.
LOAEL	Lowest-observed-adverse-effect	The lowest exposure level at which there are biologically significant increases in frequency or severity of adverse effects between the exposed population and its appropriate control group.
LOEL or LEL	Lowest-observed-effect level	In a study, the lowest dose or exposure level at which a statistically or biologically significant effect is observed in the exposed population compared with an appropriate unexposed control group.
NOAEL	No-observed-adverse-effect level	The highest exposure level at which there are no biologically significant increases in the frequency or severity of adverse effect between the exposed population and its appropriate control; some effects may be produced at this level, but they are not considered adverse or precursors of adverse effects.
NOEL	No-observed-effect level	An exposure level at which there are no statistically or biologically significant increases in the frequency or severity of any effect between the exposed population and its appropriate control.
RfC	Reference concentration	An estimate (with uncertainty spanning perhaps an order of magnitude) of a continuous inhalation exposure to the human population (including sensitive subgroups) that is likely to be without an appreciable risk of deleterious effects during a lifetime.
RfD	Reference dose	An estimate (with uncertainty spanning perhaps an order of magnitude) of a daily oral exposure to the human population (including sensitive subgroups) that is likely to be without an appreciable risk of deleterious effects during a lifetime.

SOURCE: Adapted from "Integrated Risk Information System (IRIS) Glossary," in *Vocabulary Catalog*, US Environmental Protection Agency, August 23, 2017, https://iaspub.epa.gov/sor_internet/registry/termreg/searchandretrieve/glossariesandkeywordlists/search.do?details=&vocabName=IRIS%20Glossary#formTop (accessed November 16, 2017)

aws.com/pdfs/annual_reports/2016_AAPCC_NPDS_Annual _Report.pdf), US poison centers handled 2.7 million calls in 2016. The majority—2.2 million—of the calls involved human exposures. The substances most frequently involved in human exposures were painkillers, household cleaning substances, and cosmetics and personal care products.

THE NATIONAL REPORT ON HUMAN EXPOSURE TO ENVIRONMENTAL CHEMICALS. The Centers for Disease Control and Prevention (CDC) regularly provides updated information about the exposure of the US population to environmental chemicals based on biomonitoring results. Biomonitoring involves collecting and analyzing bodily samples, such as blood, urine, breast milk, and hair, to measure the concentrations of particular chemical substances. This is also known as determining the "body burden" of chemicals. The CDC defines environmental chemicals as chemicals that are present in air, water, food, soil, dust, or other environmental media (including consumer products).

As of 2017, the CDC has published the following reports:

- *First National Report on Human Exposure to Environmental Chemicals* (2001)—27 chemicals

- *Second National Report on Human Exposure to Environmental Chemicals* (2003)—116 chemicals

- *Third National Report on Human Exposure to Environmental Chemicals* (2005)—148 chemicals

- *Fourth National Report on Human Exposure to Environmental Chemicals* (2009)—all previously published data plus data for 75 previously untested environmental chemicals

Overall, the chemicals tracked by the CDC fall into the following categories:

- Metals (such as lead and mercury)

- Pesticides (including insecticides and herbicides)

- Phthalates (a class of chemicals that are used in many consumer products, including adhesives, detergents, oils, solvents, soaps, shampoos, and plastics)

- Phytoestrogens (naturally occurring plant-based chemicals with hormonal effects)

- Polycyclic aromatic hydrocarbons (chemicals resulting from incomplete combustion of fossil fuels)

- Polychlorinated compounds (chlorine-containing organic chemicals that are used in a wide variety of industrial and commercial products)

- Cotinine (a component of tobacco smoke)

The CDC (https://www.cdc.gov/exposurereport/index .html) maintains a listing of supplemental data published since 2009 that provide biomonitoring results for these and other chemicals. The CDC notes that its reports do not assess the potential harmfulness of the chemicals examined. The reports provide scientists with biomonitoring data so that research priorities can be set to determine human health effects for particular exposure levels.

OTHER BIOMONITORING STUDIES. The Minnesota Department of Health (MDH) operates a public health tracking system (http://www.health.state.mn.us/tracking) that collects data on chemical exposures and related health trends and uses the information to set public health priorities. In *Environmental Public Health Tracking and Biomonitoring: Report to the Legislature* (March 2017, http://www.health.state.mn.us/divs/hpcd/tracking/pubs/2017legreport.pdf), the MDH describes some of the major results from the program. The agency notes that its Minnesota Family Environmental Exposure Tracking project, launched in 2015, measures mercury, lead, and cadmium concentrations in the blood of pregnant women and newborns in the Twin Cities area. As of March 2017, 337 women in the program had given birth; of these, 15 were found to have elevated results for mercury. They were provided with follow-up care. The MDH has also tested small numbers of subjects for concentrations of arsenic, cotinine, and organic chemicals, such as perfluorochemicals, bisphenol A, and paraben. The results have been used to further the agency's public health programs and to justify larger biomonitoring studies devoted to environmental chemical exposures.

Biomonitoring has also become a popular tool for individuals to publicize their concerns about the widespread nature of toxins.

In 2006 *National Geographic* magazine paid laboratories to test blood and urine samples from one of its journalists, David Ewing Duncan, for more than 300 chemicals. Duncan describes the results in "The Pollution Within" (NationalGeographic.com, October 2006). He reports that scientists detected numerous toxins within his body, including dichloro-diphenyl-trichloroethane, the pesticides chlordane and heptachlor, polychlorinated biphenyls (PCBs), phthalates, perfluorinated acids, dioxins, mercury, and polybrominated diphenyl ethers (commonly used in flame retardants). Although the dosages for most of the chemicals were extremely low, Duncan notes that toxicologists know very little about the additive or combined effects of mixtures of chemical toxins in the human body.

The Commonweal Biomonitoring Resource Center collaborates with the Environmental Working Group in the Human Toxome Project. The project (https://www.ewg.org/sites/humantoxome/) provides biomonitoring results obtained from individuals of various ages and sexes for a wide variety of chemicals. It also offers information on the health effects (or concerns) that are associated with various chemical groups.

INTEGRATED RISK INFORMATION SYSTEM. The most sophisticated source of publicly available data regarding human exposure to toxins is the EPA electronic database Integrated Risk Information System (https://www.epa.gov/iris). The database contains information on the human health effects that are associated with exposure to environmental substances. There are many thousands of chemicals in use in the United States; as of January 2018, however, the database included health hazard information for only about 500 chemicals.

CHEMICAL TOXINS

Chemical toxins are the broadest and most common type of toxic substances that people are likely to encounter in their daily life. These toxins can be found in a variety of products. The following are the primary sources:

- Household cleaners, solvents, adhesives, and paints
- Fertilizers and pesticides
- Metal, fibrous, and wooden building materials
- Plastics and electronics

In addition, people can be exposed daily to chemicals that are purposely introduced to their environment. These releases may have beneficial purposes (e.g., chlorination and fluoridation of public water supplies) or they may be consequences of industrial, commercial, or residential processes.

Information on some selected chemical toxins follows.

Lead

Lead is a naturally occurring metal. Exposure to even low levels of lead can severely impact human health. Before the 1970s it was commonly used in many industries and in many products, including gasoline and paint. Although these uses have been phased out, millions of older residences around the country were painted at one time with paints containing lead. Painted surfaces pose little danger as long as the paint remains undamaged. The greatest hazard is when chips of paint flake off or when renovations are performed that involve sanding or stripping paint.

Other household products that may contain unacceptable levels of lead include ceramics and crystal ware, miniblinds, weights used for draperies, wheel balances, fishing lures, seams in stained-glass windows, linoleum, batteries, solder, ammunition, and plumbing. Test kits and laboratories that test for lead can check questionable items and locations for the presence of the heavy metal.

The CDC also warns about the lead content in toys and trinkets that are imported from other countries. Lead can be present in plastics and paints that are used in toy manufacturing. In 2003 a child died from lead poisoning after swallowing a piece of toy jewelry. Another child died in 2006 after swallowing a small charm from a toy bracelet. Both incidents prompted massive recalls of the items involved. As of January 2018, the CPSC (https://www.cpsc.gov/Recalls) listed 353 recalls that had been issued since 2001 on consumer products due to lead concerns. The majority of the recalled products were toys and toy jewelry. In 2007 millions of toys were recalled by manufacturers because of the presence of lead-containing paint that had been applied in Chinese factories.

Most of the lead in water comes from lead pipes and lead solder in plumbing systems. Overly corrosive water can cause lead to leach out of pipes into the drinking water supply. Chapter 9 describes the Safe Drinking Water Act, which was originally passed in 1974 and has been amended numerous times. Since the late 1980s it has required that new installations and systems use lead-free pipes and plumbing fittings or fixtures. However, lead pipes are still in use, because the act does not require replacement of existing pipes that might contain lead. By 1993 all large public water supply systems were required to add substances such as lime or calcium carbonate to their water lines to reduce the corrosion of older pipes.

BLOOD LEAD LEVELS. Lead is highly toxic and can harm the brain, kidneys, bone marrow, and central nervous system. Infants, children, and pregnant women can experience serious health effects with levels as low as 10 micrograms of lead per deciliter of blood. (See Figure 10.1.) At high levels of exposure (now rare in the United States), lead can cause intellectual disabilities, convulsions, and even death.

The CDC monitors blood lead levels (BLLs) of children and adults. Figure 10.2 shows the number of children aged 72 months (six years) old and younger tested between 1997 and 2015 and determined to have elevated BLLs (more than 10 micrograms per deciliter). The graph illustrates that about 0.5% of the approximately 2.5 million children tested in 2015 had elevated BLLs.

REDUCING LEAD EXPOSURE. In 1971 Congress passed the Lead-Based Poisoning Prevention Act, restricting residential use of lead paint in structures that were constructed or funded by the federal government. The phaseout of leaded fuel in automobiles began during the 1970s.

The Lead Contamination Control Act of 1988 banned the sale of lead-lined drinking water coolers and authorized the CDC to create and expand programs at the state and local levels for screening BLLs in infants and children and referring those with elevated BLLs for treatment.

In 1992 Congress amended the TSCA to add Title IV (Lead Exposure Reduction). Title IV directs the EPA to address the general public's exposure to lead-based paint through regulations, education, and other activities. A particular concern of Congress and the EPA is the potential lead exposure risk that is associated with housing renovation. The law directs the EPA to publish lead hazard information and make it available to the general public, especially to those undertaking renovations.

Also in 1992 Congress passed the Residential Lead-Based Paint Hazard Reduction Act, which is known as

FIGURE 10.1

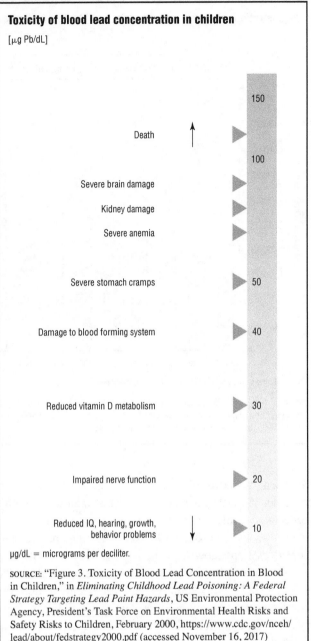

Toxicity of blood lead concentration in children

[μg Pb/dL]

- 150
- Death
- 100
- Severe brain damage
- Kidney damage
- Severe anemia
- Severe stomach cramps — 50
- Damage to blood forming system — 40
- Reduced vitamin D metabolism — 30
- Impaired nerve function — 20
- Reduced IQ, hearing, growth, behavior problems — 10

μg/dL = micrograms per deciliter.

SOURCE: "Figure 3. Toxicity of Blood Lead Concentration in Blood in Children," in *Eliminating Childhood Lead Poisoning: A Federal Strategy Targeting Lead Paint Hazards*, US Environmental Protection Agency, President's Task Force on Environmental Health Risks and Safety Risks to Children, February 2000, https://www.cdc.gov/nceh/lead/about/fedstrategy2000.pdf (accessed November 16, 2017)

Title X. The law requires sellers and landlords to disclose information about lead-based paint hazards to buyers and leasers. The law also stopped the use of lead-based paint in federal structures and set up a framework to evaluate and remove lead-based paint from buildings nationwide. In 1996 Congress once again amended the TSCA, adding Section 402a to establish and fund training programs for lead abatement and to set up training and certification requirements for technicians and lead-abatement professionals.

As noted earlier, manufacturers recalled millions of toys in 2007 because of the presence of lead paint. In 2008 Congress passed the Consumer Product Safety Improvement Act. It supplements the extensive Consumer Product Safety Act, which was enacted during the 1970s and

FIGURE 10.2

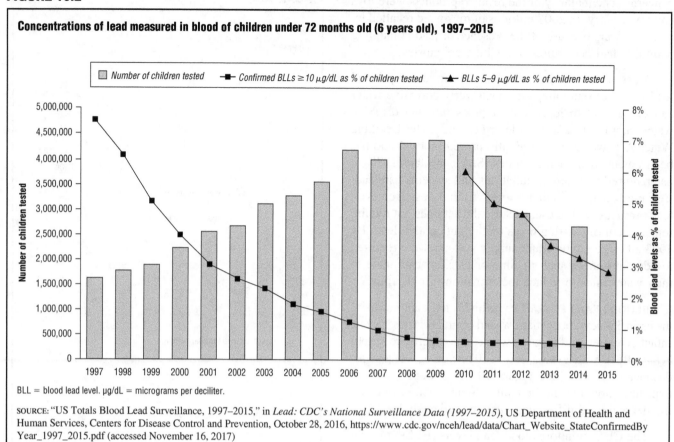

Concentrations of lead measured in blood of children under 72 months old (6 years old), 1997–2015

BLL = blood lead level. μg/dL = micrograms per deciliter.

SOURCE: "US Totals Blood Lead Surveillance, 1997–2015," in *Lead: CDC's National Surveillance Data (1997–2015)*, US Department of Health and Human Services, Centers for Disease Control and Prevention, October 28, 2016, https://www.cdc.gov/nceh/lead/data/Chart_Website_StateConfirmedBy Year_1997_2015.pdf (accessed November 16, 2017)

has been amended several times. The new law covers consumer products for both children and adults. Children's products sold after August 2011 must not contain lead in concentrations exceeding 100 parts per million. The law (https://www.cpsc.gov/Regulations-Laws--Standards/Statutes/ The-Consumer-Product-Safety-Improvement-Act) also includes lead-testing requirements for US manufacturers and importers of covered products. Complaints from business groups prompted the CPSC to delay implementation of these requirements until 2013.

RADIATION

Radiation is energy that travels in waves or particles. Radiation exposure comes from natural and human-made sources. People are exposed to natural radiation from outer space (cosmic radiation), the earth (terrestrial radiation and radon), and their own body (from naturally occurring radioactive elements). According to the US Nuclear Regulatory Commission, in "Exposure" (April 10, 2017, https://www.nrc.gov/reading-rm/basic-ref/glossary/exposure .html), these sources account for approximately half of the average person's radiation exposure. Human-made sources, such as those listed in Table 10.2, include medical devices, electromagnetic equipment, and consumer products. The Nuclear Regulatory Commission estimates that

TABLE 10.2

Human-made sources of radiation

In general, the following man-made sources expose the public to radiation (the significant radioactive isotopes are indicated in parentheses):

- Medical sources (by far, the most significant man-made source)
  - Diagnostic x-rays
  - Nuclear medicine procedures (iodine-131, cesium-137, and others)
- Consumer products
  - Building and road construction materials
  - Combustible fuels, including gas and coal
  - X-ray security systems
  - Televisions
  - Fluorescent lamp starters
  - Smoke detectors (americium)
  - Luminous watches (tritium)
  - Lantern mantles (thorium)
  - Tobacco (polonium-210)
  - Ophthalmic glass used in eyeglasses
  - Some ceramics

SOURCE: "Members of the Public," in *Man-Made Sources*, US Nuclear Regulatory Commission, October 2, 2017, https://www.nrc.gov/about-nrc/ radiation/around-us/sources/man-made-sources.html (accessed November 16, 2017)

these sources account for the other half of a person's average radiation exposure.

Radon

Radon is an invisible, odorless radioactive gas formed by the decay of uranium in rocks and soil. This gas seeps from underground rock into the basements and foundations of structures via cracks in foundations, pipes, and sometimes through the water supply. Because it is naturally occurring, it cannot be entirely eliminated from the environment. When radon is inhaled into the lungs, it undergoes radioactive decay by releasing particles that damage the deoxyribonucleic acid in the lung tissue.

In "Basic Radon Facts" (February 2013, https://www.epa.gov/sites/production/files/2016-08/documents/july_2016_radon_factsheet.pdf), the EPA recommends that people have testing done to determine the radon level in their home. The agency recommends that homes with radon levels at or above 4 picocuries per liter (pCi/L) be fixed to reduce the radon levels. The radon content in most homes can be reduced with devices such as specially designed sumps and fans that suck radon away from the foundation of a home and discharge it harmlessly above the roof. (See Figure 10.3.)

INDOOR AIR TOXINS

Indoor air pollution has become a serious problem in the United States. Although most people think of outdoor air when they think of air pollution, studies now reveal that indoor environments are not safe havens from air pollution. Modern indoor environments contain a variety of pollution sources, including building materials and consumer products. (See Table 10.3.) People and pets also contribute to indoor airborne pollution. Improvements in home and building insulation and the widespread use of central air conditioning and heating systems have largely ensured that any contaminant present indoors will not be diluted by outside air and, therefore, will become more concentrated.

FIGURE 10.3

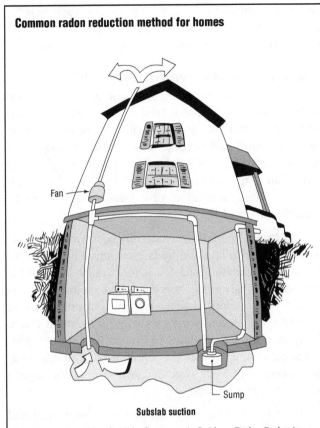

Common radon reduction method for homes

Fan

Sump

Subslab suction

SOURCE: "Subslab Suction," in *Consumer's Guide to Radon Reduction: How to Fix Your Home*, US Environmental Protection Agency, 2016, https://www.epa.gov/sites/production/files/2016-12/documents/016_consumers_guide_to_radon_reduction.pdf (accessed November 16, 2017)

TABLE 10.3

Sources and health effects of indoor air pollutants

Pollutant	Example sources	Primary health effects
Biological pollutants	Dust mites, fungi, bacteria, and pests such as cockroaches and mice	Allergic reactions (from inflammation to asthma). Infections and toxic reactions can also occur.
Volatile organic compounds (VOCs) including benzene, dichlorobenzene, ethyl benzene, chloroform, formaldehyde, methyl tertiary butyl ether, perchloroethylene, tetrachloroethene, toluene, and xylenes	Personal care products, cleaning products, paints, pesticides, building materials, and furniture	Effects vary by chemical, but include eye and respiratory irritation, rashes, headaches, nausea, vomiting, shortness of breath, and cancer.
Asbestos	Older insulation, building materials, some vinyl floor tiles, shingles, and heat-resistant fabrics	Lung cancer, mesothelioma, and (with occupational exposures) asbestosis.
Incomplete combustion products, including particulates and carbon monoxide	Solid fuels, for example, wood used for home heating	Particulate matter effects include respiratory irritation, respiratory infections, bronchitis, and lung cancer. Carbon monoxide exposure can cause low birth weight, headaches, nausea, dizziness, and death.
Polychlorinated biphenyls (PCBs)	Consumer products, including caulking in older buildings, paints, plastics, adhesives, and lubricants	PCBs have been shown to cause several adverse effects in animals, including cancer and immune, reproductive, nervous, and endocrine system effects. Human studies provide evidence supporting these effects.
Polybrominated biphenyl ethers (PBDEs), which are used as flame retardants	Consumer products, including upholstery, construction materials, and electrical appliances	Animal research suggests PBDEs can cause neurodevelopmental, kidney, thyroid, and liver toxicity and can disrupt endocrine systems.

SOURCE: Adapted from "The Sources and Effects of Indoor Pollutants Include," in *Our Built and Natural Environments: A Technical Review of the Interactions among Land Use, Transportation, and Environmental Quality, Second Edition*, US Environmental Protection Agency, June 2013, https://www.epa.gov/sites/production/files/2014-03/documents/our-built-and-natural-environments.pdf (accessed November 16, 2017)

Asbestos

Asbestos is the generic name for several fibrous minerals that are found in nature. Long and thin fibers are bundled together to make asbestos, which is an excellent thermal and electrical insulator. The physical properties that give asbestos its resistance to heat and decay have long been linked to adverse health effects in humans. Asbestos is found in mostly older homes and buildings, primarily in indoor insulation. Other sources include materials used for construction and industrial purposes, such as roof coatings and pipeline wraps.

Asbestos tends to break into microscopic fibers. These tiny fibers can remain suspended in the air for long periods and can easily penetrate body tissues when inhaled. Because of their durability, these fibers can lodge and remain in the body for many years. No safe exposure threshold for asbestos has been established, but the risk of disease generally increases with the length and amount of exposure. Diseases that are associated with asbestos inhalation include asbestosis (scarring of the lungs), lung and throat cancers, malignant mesothelioma (a tissue cancer in the chest or abdomen), and nonmalignant pleural disease (accumulation of bloody fluid around the lungs).

Asbestos was one of the first substances regulated under Section 112 of the Clean Air Act of 1970 as a hazardous air pollutant. The discovery that asbestos is a strong carcinogen has resulted in the need for its removal or encapsulation (sealing off so that residue cannot escape) from known locations, including schools and public buildings. Many hundreds of millions of dollars have been spent on such cleanups.

Under the Clean Air Act asbestos-containing materials must be removed from demolition and renovation sites without releasing asbestos fibers into the environment. Among other safeguards, workers must wet asbestos insulation before stripping the material from pipes and must seal the asbestos debris while it is still wet in leakproof containers to prevent the release of asbestos dust. The laws of most states have specific requirements for asbestos workers. A number of legal convictions have resulted from improper and illegal asbestos removal.

The Asbestos Hazard Emergency Response Act was signed into law in 1986. It requires public and private primary and secondary schools to inspect their buildings for asbestos-containing building materials. In 1989 the EPA banned the importation, production, processing, and distribution of many asbestos-containing products in the United States. The ban was challenged in court and partially overturned. As a result, only a handful of asbestos-containing products remain banned. However, the use of asbestos is banned in products that have not traditionally contained it.

TOXINS IN FOOD

The presence of environmental toxins in food has become a topic of major concern in recent years. Chemical pollutants that end up in food can come from air and wastewater emissions or from land sources, such as landfills or farms. Food can also pose a danger to human health if it is contaminated by biological organisms.

Persistent and Bioaccumulative Chemicals

The most worrisome chemical contaminants in food are those that are persistent (resistant to biodegradation) and bioaccumulative, meaning that they are absorbed by lower life forms and become concentrated as they work their way up the food chain. There are four chemical toxins found in food that are particularly noted for their persistent bioaccumulative properties: mercury, pesticides, dioxins, and PCBs.

MERCURY. Mercury is a naturally occurring inorganic element. It is also released by human activities, primarily via waste incineration and fossil fuel combustion. In the environment, inorganic mercury can convert to an organic form called methylmercury. It accumulates in fish and shellfish and works its way up the food chain. Methylmercury accumulates in human tissue when people eat contaminated fish. At certain dosages it can damage the central nervous system, cause severe neurological impairment, and be fatal.

The EPA recommends that people consult local and state fish advisories regarding the safety of fish caught in their area. It provides links to state advisories on its website (https://www.epa.gov/fish-tech). State advisories typically list major water bodies and provide consumption restrictions (if any) for fish that are caught from those waters. Although mercury is the subject of most restrictions, other contaminants are also a concern, including pesticides, dioxins, and PCBs.

PESTICIDES. Water contamination is a primary pathway for pesticides to reach food sources, particularly fish. Other foods can be affected via the use of contaminated irrigation waters. Pesticides are also spread directly on and around crops and fruit trees.

The FDA notes in *Pesticide Monitoring Program—2009 Pesticide Report* (June 7, 2013, https://wayback.archive-it.org/7993/20170723104945/https://www.fda.gov/downloads/Food/FoodborneIllnessContaminants/Pesticides/UCM352872.pdf) that the responsibility for monitoring pesticides in food is divided among three government agencies: the EPA, the USDA, and the FDA. As mentioned earlier, the EPA regulates pesticide use and sets tolerance levels for pesticides. The USDA's Agricultural Marketing Service conducts the Pesticide Data Program, in which a wide range of edible and drinkable commodities are tested for pesticide content. Testing is performed on both fresh and processed foods.

In *Pesticide Data Program—Annual Summary, Calendar Year 2015* (November 2016, https://www.ams.usda.gov/sites/default/files/media/2015PDPSummary.pdf), the USDA reports the testing results for 2015. The agency tested 10,187 samples, the vast majority (96.9%) of which were fresh or processed fruits and vegetables. The remaining 3.1% of samples were of peanut butter. In more than 99% of the samples, pesticide residues were well below EPA tolerance levels; 15% had no detectable pesticide residue. In 0.5% of the samples, residues exceeded EPA tolerance levels. Table 10.4 shows the number of pesticides detected per sample. At least one pesticide was detected in all but one of the commodities. Only frozen sweet corn had zero pesticides detected per sample.

Fear of agricultural pesticide usage has contributed to a rise in consumer interest in organic foods. The USDA's National Organic Program defines organic agriculture as that which excludes the use of synthetic fertilizers and pesticides. More importantly, it strives for low environmental impact and enlists natural biological systems (cover crops, crop rotation, and natural predators) to increase fertility and decrease the likelihood of pest infestation.

DIOXINS AND PCBS. Dioxins are a group of several hundred chlorinated organic compounds with similar chemical structures and biological effects. They are known to damage the major organs and systems of laboratory animals. The chemicals are also linked with adverse effects to the skin and liver in humans. Dioxins are classified as probable human carcinogens.

Dioxin categories include chlorinated dibenzo-p-dioxins, chlorinated dibenzofurans, and some PCBs. Dioxins are most commonly associated with the burning or combustion of other substances. Certain industrial processes, such as chlorine bleaching of pulp and paper, also produce dioxins. They are generated by natural sources, primarily forest fires, and are introduced to the environment by humans through a variety of activities.

PCBs are a group of synthetic organic chemicals that were primarily used as lubricants and coolants in electrical equipment before the 1970s. The manufacture of PCBs was halted in the United States in 1977 because of concerns about their effects on the environment and human health. PCBs are known to cause a variety of serious health

TABLE 10.4

Number of pesticides detected per sample, by food commodity, 2015

Commodity (# of samples)	\multicolumn{19}{c}{Number of pesticides* detected per sample}
	0	1	2	3	4	5	6	7	8	9	10	11	12	13	14	15	16	18	20
Fresh fruit and vegetables:									Percent										
Apples (708)	2.1	4.2	11.3	18.5	18.8	18.1	12.1	7.6	4.2	1.7	0.4	0.3	0.4	0.1	—	—	—	—	—
Cherries (232)	1.3	4.3	2.6	13.4	15.5	19.4	16.8	13.8	6.5	6.0	0.4	—	—	—	—	—	—	—	—
Cucumbers (378)	9.0	20.9	25.4	19.8	10.3	9.5	3.7	0.5	0.8	—	—	—	—	—	—	—	—	—	—
Grapefruit (177)	5.6	31.1	42.4	14.7	6.2	—	—	—	—	—	—	—	—	—	—	—	—	—	—
Grapes (708)	4.2	5.2	9.0	14.1	14.4	12.3	11.2	10.0	8.8	5.8	3.5	0.7	0.6	0.1	—	—	—	—	—
Green beans (754)	27.9	21.1	22.9	16.3	6.9	2.8	0.9	0.5	0.4	0.3	—	—	—	—	—	—	—	—	—
Lettuce (378)	19.0	28.8	18.8	10.8	5.8	5.3	4.2	1.6	2.4	2.1	0.3	0.5	—	—	—	0.3	—	—	—
Nectarines (578)	0.3	5.7	10.4	10.9	17.6	13.5	13.0	10.4	7.6	4.2	1.7	1.6	1.2	—	0.3	—	—	—	—
Oranges (707)	6.9	20.7	67.5	4.5	0.4	—	—	—	—	—	—	—	—	—	—	—	—	—	—
Peaches (362)	1.7	11.6	18.8	16.3	15.7	12.7	11.9	5.5	3.0	2.2	0.3	0.3	—	—	—	—	—	—	—
Pears (705)	11.9	6.2	7.1	8.5	15.7	13.6	14.3	10.1	6.4	3.3	2.0	0.6	0.3	—	—	—	—	—	—
Potatoes (707)	0.1	17.0	39.5	24.0	14.7	3.0	1.1	0.6	—	—	—	—	—	—	—	—	—	—	—
Spinach (708)	3.4	6.1	4.8	7.1	9.9	13.4	14.3	12.1	7.9	7.5	5.4	2.4	3.5	0.7	1.3	0.3	—	—	—
Strawberries (706)	4.4	2.0	1.4	4.5	6.8	7.8	11.6	14.7	12.7	11.0	7.9	5.2	3.5	2.7	2.0	0.7	0.4	0.3	0.1
Sweet corn (468)	98.1	1.7	0.2	—	—	—	—	—	—	—	—	—	—	—	—	—	—	—	—
Tomatoes (708)	8.6	9.9	14.5	16.9	16.7	12.0	9.5	4.0	3.0	2.4	1.3	0.3	0.4	0.1	0.3	0.1	—	—	—
Watermelon (370)	29.2	38.6	23.0	6.2	2.2	0.5	0.3	—	—	—	—	—	—	—	—	—	—	—	—
Processed fruit and vegetables:																			
Cherries, frozen (453)	—	5.5	3.5	9.7	15.5	13.0	10.8	15.5	9.1	7.3	6.4	2.2	0.9	0.4	0.2	—	—	—	—
Sweet corn, frozen (65)	100	—	—	—	—	—	—	—	—	—	—	—	—	—	—	—	—	—	—
Percent of total samples	12.8	11.8	17.7	12.0	11.0	8.9	7.8	6.2	4.4	3.2	1.9	0.9	0.8	0.4	0.3	0.1	0.03	0.02	0.01
Actual number of samples	1,264	1,167	1,748	1,180	1,086	874	768	612	430	313	187	89	75	36	2.6	11	3	2	1
Total number of fruit & vegetable samples = 9,872																			
Nut product:																			
Peanut butter (315)	99.0	1.0	—	—	—	—	—	—	—	—	—	—	—	—	—	—	—	—	—
Actual number of samples	312	3	—	—	—	—	—	—	—	—	—	—	—	—	—	—	—	—	—

*Environmental contaminants have been excluded from the count of pesticides.
Note: Parent compounds and their metabolites are combined to report the number of "pesticides" rather than the number of "residues."

SOURCE: "Appendix H. Number of Pesticides Detected per Sample," in *Pesticide Data Program Annual Summary, Calendar Year 2015*, US Department of Agriculture, Agricultural Marketing Service, November 2016, https://www.ams.usda.gov/sites/default/files/media/2015PDPSummary.pdf (accessed November 16, 2017)

problems, such as liver cancer, in laboratory animals. They are classified as possible carcinogens in humans.

Since the mid-1990s the USDA has conducted occasional sampling studies to determine the levels of dioxins and dioxin-like compounds in the US domestic meat supply. As of January 2018, the most recent study was *Dioxin FY2013 Survey: Dioxins and Dioxin-Like Compounds in the U.S. Domestic Meat and Poultry Supply* (May 2015, https://www.fsis.usda.gov/wps/wcm/connect/da1d623d-3005-4116-bef7-2a61d1ebd543/Dioxin-Report-FY2013.pdf?MOD=AJPERES), which was conducted in 2012–13. In this report, the USDA indicates that its survey during the mid-1990s found "low levels of dioxin" in samples taken from the carcasses of cattle, hogs, chickens, turkeys, and miscellaneous livestock. The levels generally declined in subsequent surveys conducted in 2002–03, 2007–08, and 2012–13. The USDA concludes that dioxin levels in hogs, chickens, and turkeys decreased 20% to 80% between the mid-1990s and 2012–13. However, the levels in cattle either remained flat or declined only slightly.

Biological Contaminants

According to federal officials, foodborne illnesses due to pathogens (disease-causing biological organisms) pose a substantial health burden in the United States. Although the US food supply is among the safest in the world, episodes of food poisoning and disease do regularly occur.

Foodborne illnesses became the object of intense public scrutiny following an outbreak of *Escherichia coli* (*E. coli*) in 1993 that killed four people and sickened hundreds. The illness was attributed to undercooked hamburgers from fast-food restaurants. The FDA responded by raising the recommended internal temperature for cooked hamburgers to 155 degrees Fahrenheit (68.3 degrees C). It also launched a sampling program to test for *E. coli* in raw ground beef and required that consumer packages of raw meats and poultry be labeled with food-handling instructions.

Since then, there have been other serious outbreaks of foodborne illnesses that have sickened and killed victims in the United States. These include outbreaks caused by *E. coli* in spinach in 2006, *Salmonella* in peanut products in 2009, and *Listeria* in ice cream in 2015.

Federal and state agencies operate a surveillance program called FoodNet to monitor laboratory-confirmed foodborne illnesses that are related to pathogens. FoodNet data for 2016 are presented in Table 10.5. In total, 19,412 cases of foodborne illnesses were related to monitored pathogens in 2016. The most common pathogens were *Salmonella* (7,554 cases), *Campylobacter* (5,782), and *Shigella* (2,256). Overall, foodborne illnesses resulted in 4,622 hospitalizations and 81 deaths in 2016.

TABLE 10.5

Number of cases of foodborne pathogens causing infection, hospitalizations, and death, by pathogen, 2016

Pathogen	Confirmed			Confirmed or CIDT positive–only		
		Hospitalizations	Deaths		Hospitalizations	Deaths
	No. cases	No. (%)	No. (%)	No. cases	No. (%)	No. (%)
Bacteria						
Campylobacter	5,782	1,082 (19)	10 (0.2)	8,547	1,697 (20)	26 (0.3)
Listeria[a, b]	127	123 (97)	17 (13.4)	127	123 (97)	17 (13.4)
Salmonella	7,554	2,163 (29)	39 (0.5)	8,172	2,255 (28)	40 (0.5)
Shigella	2,256	519 (23)	2 (0.1)	2,913	579 (20)	2 (0.1)
STEC[c]	1,399	326 (23)	3 (0.2)	1,845	408 (22)	3 (0.2)
Vibrio	218	61 (28)	4 (1.8)	252	73 (29)	4 (1.6)
Yersinia	205	54 (27)	3 (1.5)	302	83 (28)	3 (1.0)
Parasite						
Cryptosporidium[b]	1,816	291 (16)	3 (0.2)	1,816	291 (16)	3 (0.2)
Cyclospora[b]	55	3 (5)	0 (—)	55	3 (5)	0 (—)
Total	**19,412**	**4,622**	**81**	**24,029**	**5,512**	**98**

CIDT = culture-independent diagnostic test. FoodNet = CDC's Foodborne Diseases Active Surveillance Network. STEC = Shiga toxin-producing *Escherichia coli*.

[a]*Listeria* cases are defined as isolation of *L. monocytogenes* from a normally sterile site or, in the setting of miscarriage or stillbirth, isolation of *L. monocytogenes* from placental or fetal tissue.

[b]All *Listeria*, *Cryptosporidium*, and *Cyclospora* infections were confirmed, so confirmed numbers are displayed in both columns.

[c]For STEC, all serogroups were combined as it is not possible to distinguish between serogroups using CIDTs. Shiga toxin—positive reports from clinical laboratories that were Shiga toxin–negative at a state public health laboratory were excluded (population = 568).

Notes: CIDT positive-only is defined as detection of the bacterial pathogen, or for STEC, Shiga toxin, or the genes that encode a Shiga toxin, in a stool specimen or enrichment broth using a CIDT. Any positive CIDT result that was confirmed by culture is counted only among the confirmed infections. For STEC, only CIDT reports that were positive at a state public health laboratory were counted. Connecticut, Georgia, Maryland, Minnesota, New Mexico, Oregon, Tennessee, and selected counties in California, Colorado, and New York. Data for 2016 are preliminary.

SOURCE: Ellyn P. Marder et al., "Table 1. Number of Confirmed and CIDT Positive-Only Bacterial and Confirmed Parasitic Infections, Hospitalizations, and Deaths, by Pathogen—FoodNet, 10 US Sites, 2016," in *Morbidity and Mortality Weekly Report*, vol. 66, no. 15, April 21, 2017, https://www.cdc.gov/mmwr/volumes/66/wr/pdfs/mm6615a1.pdf (accessed November 16, 2017)

CHAPTER 11
DEPLETION AND CONSERVATION OF NATURAL RESOURCES

Throughout history humans have relied on the world's natural resources for survival. Early civilizations were dependent on sources of clean water, fertile soils, and wild animals that could be hunted for meat, skins, and fur. As time passed, societies learned to harvest and use other natural resources, primarily wood, metals, minerals, and fossil fuels. For centuries, little thought was given to the consequences of depleting these resources. The supply appeared to be never-ending.

Despite many technological advances, humans in the 21st century are still dependent on some of the same natural resources that sustained the first civilizations. In addition, there is enormous demand for wood, metals, minerals, and other natural materials from which goods are manufactured. Finally, fossil fuels (coal, natural gas, and oil) provide the bulk of the world's power. Since the latter half of the 20th century, scientists have been aware that these natural resources are limited in terms of quantity and quality.

Natural resources are important not only for their practical value and economic worth but also for their contribution to environmental health. For example, forests and wetlands provide habitat for a wide variety of plant and animal life. These ecosystems are also appreciated by humans for their aesthetic appeal and recreational purposes. Developers and industrial entities, however, have an interest in using these lands for different purposes. To balance competing interests, the government has created a number of agencies with responsibility for overseeing the management of natural resources. A list of federal agencies is provided in Table 11.1.

FORESTS

Forests are one of the world's most important natural resources. They not only offer a source of wood but they also perform a wide range of social and ecological functions. They provide livelihoods for forest workers, protect and enrich soils, regulate the hydrologic cycle, affect local and regional climate through evaporation, and help stabilize the global climate. Through the process of photosynthesis, they absorb carbon dioxide and release the oxygen that humans and animals breathe. They provide habitat for many plant and animal species, are the main source of wood for industrial and domestic heating, and are widely used for recreation.

Status of US Forests

As shown in Table 11.2, forested lands are prevalent in many regions of the United States and covered 766.2 million acres (310.1 million ha) in 2012. The vast majority of the forestland—521.2 million acres (210.9 million ha), or 68%—was used or was capable of being used for commercial timber production. (See Table 11.3.) Another 73.5 million acres (29.8 million ha) was reserved. According to Daniel P. Bigelow and Allison Borchers of the Economic Research Service, in *Major Uses of Land in the United States, 2012* (August 2017, https://www.ers.usda.gov/webdocs/publications/84880/eib-178.pdf?v=42972), this means the forest is "withdrawn from timber use through statute, administrative regulation, or designation without regard to productive status." This acreage includes forested wilderness areas and parks that are off-limits to timber harvesting. The remaining 171.6 million acres (69.4 million ha) of total forestland in 2012 was devoted to other purposes.

The US Forest Service (FS) regularly publishes reports describing the value and condition of US forests. As of January 2018, the most recent comprehensive report in the series was *National Report on Sustainable Forests—2010* (https://www.fs.fed.us/research/sustain/docs/national-reports/2010/2010-sustainability-report.pdf), which was published in June 2011. An updated report that includes

TABLE 11.1

Federal agencies that oversee natural resources

Federal agency	Founded	Description
US Army Corps of Engineers	1802	Grants permits for dredging and filling in certain waterways, including many wetlands.
US Department of Agriculture		
Forest Service	1905	Manages more than 193 million acres of public lands in national forests and grasslands.
Natural Resources Conservation Service	1935*	Helps private land owners/managers conserve their natural resources. Participation is voluntary.
US Department of the Interior		
Bureau of Indian Affairs	1824	Manages 55 million acres of land held in trust for American Indians, Indian tribes, and Alaska Natives.
Bureau of Land Management	1812*	Manages 245 million acres of public lands (mostly in the West) and 300 acres of subsurface mineral resources.
Bureau of Reclamation	1902	Provides water and energy to more than 31 million people via hundreds of dams, reservoirs, canals, and power plants it has constructed in 17 western states.
Fish and Wildlife Service	1871*	Conserves, protects and enhances fish, wildlife, plants and their habitats for the benefit of the public.
Bureau of Ocean Energy Management, Regulation and Enforcement	1982	Manages the nation's natural gas, oil and other mineral resources on the outer continental shelf.
National Park Service	1916	Preserves the resources of more than 80 million acres comprising the national park system.
Office of Surface Mining	1977	Oversees surface mining on federal lands and some tribal and state lands.
US Geological Survey	1879	Provides data related to Earth sciences, natural disasters, and management of natural resources.
US Environmental Protection Agency	1970	Develops and enforces regulations that implement environmental laws enacted by Congress.

*Date of founding of predecessor agency that evolved into current agency.

SOURCE: Created by Kim Masters Evans for Gale, © 2017

TABLE 11.2

Forested land, by region, 2012

Region	Grazed forest	Ungrazed forest-use land	Total forest-use land	Forested land in other uses*	Total forestland
			Thousand acres		
Northeast	464	65,206	65,670	7,022	72,692
Lake States	1,750	50,168	51,918	2,560	54,478
Corn Belt	5,277	30,160	35,437	815	36,252
Northern Plains	2,869	3,309	6,178	545	6,723
Appalachia	2,745	67,884	70,629	2,435	73,064
Southeast	2,529	73,475	76,004	2,222	78,226
Delta States	3,374	49,310	52,684	325	53,009
Southern Plains	11,457	10,556	22,013	30,561	52,574
Mountain	71,481	27,364	98,845	25,770	124,615
Pacific	27,837	31,351	59,188	25,091	84,279
Far West	30	93,086	93,116	37,209	130,325
United States	**129,813**	**501,869**	**631,682**	**134,555**	**766,237**

*Forested land not included in "forest-use" was reclassified for the purposes of the Major Land Uses series. Much of this land was determined to fit under the special-uses category, which includes forested parks and wilderness areas. However, in some States (e.g., Texas and Oklahoma), grassland pasture and range appeared to be the best fit. In Alaska, much of the other forested land is contained in the "miscellaneous" use category.

SOURCE: Daniel P. Bigelow and Allison Borchers, "Table 8. Total Forested Land by Region, 2012," in *Major Uses of Land in the United States, 2012*, US Department of Agriculture, Economic Research Service, August 2017, https://www.ers.usda.gov/webdocs/publications/84880/eib-178.pdf?v=42972 (accessed November 17, 2017)

TABLE 11.3

Forested land, by class and region, 2012

	Forestland			
	Timberland	Reserved	Other	Total forestland
		Thousand acres		
Northeast	67,962	4,323	407	72,692
Lake States	52,118	1,468	892	54,478
Corn Belt	35,438	527	288	36,252
Northern Plains	6,180	63	482	6,723
Appalachia	71,121	1,689	252	73,064
Southeast	76,093	1,680	452	78,226
Delta States	52,684	230	95	53,009
Southern Plains	22,012	276	30,285	52,574
Mountain	64,844	17,425	42,345	124,615
Pacific	59,189	11,908	13,183	84,279
48 states*	507,641	39,589	88,681	635,912
Alaska	12,817	33,735	82,025	128,577
Hawaii	700	196	853	1,748
United States*	**521,158**	**73,520**	**171,559**	**766,237**

*Distributions may not add due to rounding.

SOURCE: Daniel P. Bigelow and Allison Borchers, "Table 9. Total Forestland and Woodland by Class and Region, 2012," in *Major Uses of Land in the United States, 2012*, US Department of Agriculture, Economic Research Service, August 2017, https://www.ers.usda.gov/webdocs/publications/84880/eib-178.pdf?v=42972 (accessed November 17, 2017)

---

data collected through 2015 was expected to be published sometime in 2018. Overall, the FS focuses its analysis on three forest issues:

- The loss of forestlands and working forests

- The relationship between forests, climate change, and bioenergy development

- Changing forest health and disturbance patterns

Forest Losses

The FS notes in *National Report on Sustainable Forests* that forests covered an estimated 1 billion acres (404.7 million ha) at the time of European colonization. Widespread deforestation occurred in the eastern United States during the 19th century, when forestland was converted to agricultural land. Most of this conversion was completed by the early 1900s. Since that time US forest acreage has remained relatively constant. The FS indicates, however, that the overall statistics on forest acreage do not show the whole picture. US forests have become increasingly fragmented and perforated by human developments via subdivisions, recreational areas, and vacation and retirement homes. The FS explains that this is problematic because "large, contiguous tracts of forest" are optimal for ecosystem health.

Another challenge cited by the FS is the loss of working forests (forests that are actively managed by landowners). Forestlands owned by government entities and the forest industry are typically managed to optimize forest health, particularly for timber production. These owners may regularly monitor for diseases or other problems and take corrective actions as needed. According to the FS, other forest owners more often "live farther away from the parcels they own" than in the past and are less likely to actively manage their lands. The FS notes, "With the loss of an active management focus and the revenue streams that often accompany it, the survival of these forests and their associated ecosystem services is in question."

Climate Change and Bioenergy Development

Climate and forests are inextricably linked in that climate affects forests, and forests impact climate. The mechanisms and challenges associated with global warming and associated climate change are described in Chapter 3. In brief, increasing concentrations of carbon in the atmosphere due to anthropogenic (human-caused) sources (particularly the combustion of fossil fuels) are believed to be warming the planet and inducing climatic changes. The chief culprit is carbon dioxide, which is emitted in voluminous amounts by power plants, transportation vehicles, and industrial facilities. Carbon dioxide and other atmosphere-warming gases are called greenhouse gases.

Carbon dioxide is a fertilizing agent for vegetation, including trees. Thus, in *National Report on Sustainable Forests*, the FS indicates that increasing atmospheric carbon dioxide concentrations will likely boost forest growth in some areas. A warming climate will certainly change forest composition in terms of tree and vegetation types. For example, warm-weather species will probably spread into areas that were once too cool to sustain them. In addition, climate change may aggravate three major forest health stressors: drought, wildfires, and insect infestations. The linkage, however, is not known with certainty. Although the FS indicates that some of these impacts "may already be occurring," more data are needed to ascertain their exact relationships.

Vegetation mitigates the effect of carbon buildup in the atmosphere by absorbing and storing carbon. This is an example of natural carbon sequestration. As is described in Chapter 3 and shown in Figure 3.7 in Chapter 3, land use, land-use change, and forestry serve as a net greenhouse gas sink for the United States. In other words, they absorb more greenhouse gases than they emit. The EPA notes in *Inventory of U.S. Greenhouse Gas Emissions and Sinks, 1990–2015* (April 2017, https://www.epa.gov/sites/production/files/2017-02/documents/2017_complete_report.pdf) that the land use, land-use change, and forestry sector offset approximately 11.8% of the United States' total (gross) greenhouse gas emissions in 2015. The vast majority of this sink effect was attributed to the nation's forests.

Deforestation (clearing existing forest) has a twofold effect on the carbon cycle. First, it reduces the amount of natural carbon sequestration that can be achieved. Second, it releases carbon stored in the trees and other vegetation into the environment. This release may occur slowly, for example, as felled trees decay, or it can occur rapidly, as during a forest fire. Losing large areas of forests to purposeful deforestation or natural wildfires releases massive amounts of greenhouse gases into the atmosphere.

BIOENERGY CONSIDERATIONS. Forest vegetation (or biomass) is combustible and can be purposely burned as a fuel to produce electricity or for other purposes. In *Monthly Energy Review: January 2018* (January 26, 2018, https://www.eia.gov/totalenergy/data/monthly/pdf/mer.pdf), the US Department of Energy reports that 2 quadrillion British thermal units of wood-derived energy were consumed in the United States in 2016. This was about 2% of the nation's total energy consumption of 97.4 quadrillion British thermal units.

The FS explains in *National Report on Sustainable Forests* that over the long term, forest biomass combustion is considered carbon-neutral because the carbon released during combustion is assumed equal to that sequestered by subsequent forest regrowth.

Forest Health

In *National Report on Sustainable Forests*, the FS focuses on four major forest stressors: fragmentation (which is addressed earlier in this chapter), droughts, wildfires, and pests. The agency indicates that these factors are interrelated, and the effects of the latter three stressors may be aggravated by global warming and associated climate change.

DROUGHTS. Drought trends can be tracked using the Palmer Drought Severity Index (PDSI), which is compiled by the National Climatic Data Center (NCDC) and uses temperature and precipitation data to estimate relative dryness. The standardized index ranges from -10 (driest) to +10 (wettest). According to the NCDC (https://www.ncdc.noaa.gov/temp-and-precip/drought/historical-palmers/), index values correspond to drought severity classes as follows:

- PDSI -4 and below—extreme drought
- PDSI -3 to -3.99—severe drought
- PDSI -2 to -2.99—moderate drought

Figure 11.1 compares changes in PDSI drought severity classes for western and eastern forestlands between 1960–86 and 1987–2013. Western forests spent a markedly higher percentage of months in drought during the latter period compared with the earlier period. The change over time was much less pronounced for eastern forests, which have historically experienced higher precipitation rates than western forests. Nevertheless, even eastern forests experienced more intense drought conditions during 1987–2013 than they did during 1960–86. Prolonged dryness in combination with above-normal temperatures stresses trees, making them more susceptible to wildfires and insect and disease infestation.

WILDFIRES. Before pioneers settled the West, fires occurred frequently, keeping the forest clear of undergrowth. Fuels seldom accumulated, and the fires were generally of low intensity, consuming undergrowth but not igniting the tops of large trees. Disrupting this normal cycle of fire has produced an accumulation of hazardous fuels, which are capable of feeding an increasing number of large, uncontrollable, and catastrophic wildfires. In addition, the threat of wildfires is aggravated by global warming and drought.

The National Interagency Coordination Center at the National Interagency Fire Center compiles wildland fire statistics. Table 11.4 shows the number of wildland fires

FIGURE 11.1

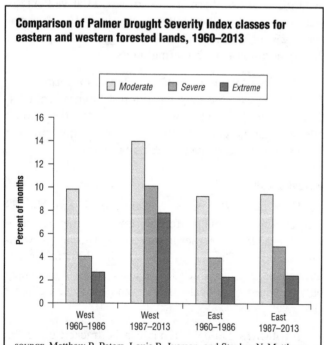

Comparison of Palmer Drought Severity Index classes for eastern and western forested lands, 1960–2013

SOURCE: Matthew P. Peters, Louis R. Iverson, and Stephen N. Matthews, "Figure 2. Comparison of Palmer Drought Severity Index Classes among Eastern and Western US Forested Land for the Period 1960–2013," in *Spatio-temporal Drought Trends by Forest Type in the Conterminous United States, 1960–2013*, US Department of Agriculture, Forest Service, December 2014, https://www.fs.fed.us/nrs/pubs/rmap/rmap_nrs7.pdf (accessed November 17, 2017)

TABLE 11.4

Total number of wildland fires and acreage burned, 1960–2016

Year	Fires	Acres
2016	67,743	5,509,995
2015	68,151	10,125,149
2014	63,312	3,595,613
2013	47,579	4,319,546
2012	67,774	9,326,238
2011	74,126	8,711,367
2010	71,971	3,422,724
2009	78,792	5,921,786
2008	78,979	5,292,468
2007	85,705	9,328,045
2006	96,385	9,873,745
2005	66,753	8,689,389
2004	65,461	*8,097,880
2003	63,629	3,960,842
2002	73,457	7,184,712
2001	84,079	3,570,911
2000	92,250	7,393,493
1999	92,487	5,626,093
1998	81,043	1,329,704
1997	66,196	2,856,959
1996	96,363	6,065,998
1995	82,234	1,840,546
1994	79,107	4,073,579
1993	58,810	1,797,574
1992	87,394	2,069,929
1991	75,754	2,953,578
1990	66,481	4,621,621
1989	48,949	1,827,310
1988	72,750	5,009,290
1987	71,300	2,447,296
1986	85,907	2,719,162
1985	82,591	2,896,147
1984	20,493	1,148,409
1983	18,229	1,323,666
1982	174,755	2,382,036
1981	249,370	4,814,206
1980	234,892	5,260,825
1979	163,196	2,986,826
1978	218,842	3,910,913
1977	173,998	3,152,644
1976	241,699	5,109,926
1975	134,872	1,791,327
1974	145,868	2,879,095
1973	117,957	1,915,273
1972	124,554	2,641,166
1971	108,398	4,278,472
1970	121,736	3,278,565
1969	113,351	6,689,081
1968	125,371	4,231,996
1967	125,025	4,658,586
1966	122,500	4,574,389
1965	113,684	2,652,112
1964	116,358	4,197,309
1963	164,183	7,120,768
1962	115,345	4,078,894
1961	98,517	3,036,219
1960	103,387	4,478,188

*2004 fires and acres do not include state lands for North Carolina.

SOURCE: "Total Wildland Fires and Acres (1960–2016)," in *Statistics: Historical Wildland Fire Information*, National Interagency Fire Center, 2017, https://www.nifc.gov/fireInfo/fireInfo_stats_totalFires.html (accessed November 17, 2017)

and the acreage burned annually between 1960 and 2016. In 2016, 67,743 wildland fires burned 5.5 million acres (2.2 million ha). The number of fires and the affected acreage increased dramatically during the 21st century compared with earlier years. Following the 2000 fire season, the FS collaborated with other agencies to develop a national fire plan. As of January 2018, the most recent plan was published in April 2014. In *The National Strategy* (https://www.forestsandrangelands.gov/strategy/documents/strategy/CSPhaseIIINationalStrategyApr2014.pdf), the Wildland Fire Leadership Council addresses three factors that are considered key to dealing with future wildfires:

- Restoring and maintaining resilient landscapes such as by reducing excessive undergrowth in forests

- Creating fire-adapted communities so that humans and their infrastructure can better withstand wildfires without loss of life or property

- Responding to wildfires with a coordinated management plan that takes into account all stakeholders

PESTS. Pests, such as insects and pathogens, can infest huge areas of forests and kill thousands of trees. This is damaging by itself, but it also exaggerates other threats to forests, such as wildfires. Wildfires are more likely to spread quickly and burn hotter when forests contain large numbers of trees that have been weakened or killed by insect damage. Scientists fear that global warming and climate change will result in increased populations of native and nonnative (or exotic) insects that prey on vegetation, thus further stressing forests.

The FS estimates in *National Report on Sustainable Forests* the acreage of forest mortality caused by biotic processes and agents (i.e., insects, diseases, and invasive alien species) from 2003 to 2007 compared with the reference period 1997 to 2002. The acreage afflicted with mortality more than tripled from 12 million acres (4.9 million ha) to 37 million acres (15 million ha). The agency notes that insects of concern in US forests include bark beetles and engraver beetles (also known as ips beetles), which are native species, and gypsy moths, which are nonnative species. Nonnative species can be harmful because they do not have natural predators in their new environment. This allows them to "invade" their new territory and spread quickly.

The FS employs a variety of measures to combat abiotic processes and agents, including the application of insecticides and the release of biological control agents. These agents include insects and pathogens that prey on the nonnative invasive pests.

WETLANDS: FRAGILE ECOSYSTEMS

Marshes, swamps, bogs, estuaries, and bottomlands are specific biosystems with sometimes distinctive characteristics; however, they are commonly grouped together under the term *wetlands*. Wetlands are always or often saturated by enough surface or groundwater to sustain vegetation that is typically adapted to saturated soil conditions, such as cattails, bulrushes, red maples, wild rice, blackberries, cranberries, and peat moss. The Florida Everglades and the coastal Alaskan salt marshes are examples of wetlands, as are the sphagnum-heath bogs of Maine. Because some varieties of wetlands are rich in minerals and nutrients and provide many of the advantages of both land and water environments, they are often dynamic systems that teem with a diversity of species, including many insects, which are a basic link in the food chain.

Wetlands were once regarded as useless swamps, good only for breeding mosquitoes and taking up otherwise valuable space. As a result, much wetland acreage has been lost to development. The US Fish and Wildlife Service (FWS) tracks wetlands status and trends as part of its National Wetlands Inventory (https://www.fws.gov/wetlands/Status-and-Trends/index.html). As of January 2018, the most recent national report from the National Wetlands Inventory program was published in September 2011. In *Status and Trends of Wetlands in the Conterminous United States 2004 to 2009: Report to Congress* (https://www.fws.gov/wetlands/documents/Status-and-Trends-of-Wetlands-in-the-Conterminous-United-States-2004-to-2009.pdf), Thomas E. Dahl of the FWS estimates that between the 1950s and 1970s, 458,000 acres (185,300 ha) of wetlands were lost annually in the conterminous (the lower 48 states) United States. (See Figure 11.2.) Wetlands continued to be lost annually from the 1970s through the 1990s, but the losses declined over the decades. Between 1998 and 2004 there was a gain of 32,000 acres (12,900 ha) per year. This trend reversed itself, however, between 2004 and 2009, when 13,800 acres (5,600 ha) of wetlands were lost annually.

Chapter 9 describes the water quality data collected by the states and compiled by the US Environmental Protection Agency (EPA) under the Clean Water Act into a national database. Most of the assessments were performed in 2014. As shown in Table 9.2 in Chapter 9, 665,494 acres (269,316 ha) of the total 1.1 million acres (445,700 ha) of assessed wetlands were rated as impaired. The probable causes and sources of impairment are listed in Table 9.11 and Table 9.12, respectively, in Chapter 9. Organic enrichment/oxygen depletion due to natural causes/wildlife were blamed for impairing the largest acreage of wetlands.

The Many Roles of Wetlands

Productive wetlands are rich ecosystems that support diverse forms of plants and wildlife. They provide food and habitat for many animals and breeding and nesting

FIGURE 11.2

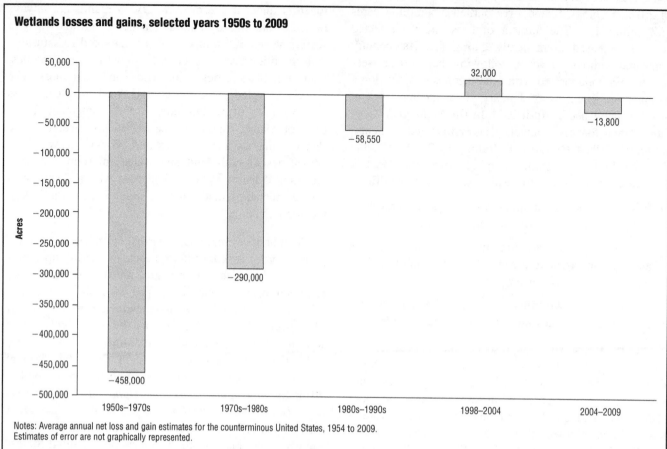

Wetlands losses and gains, selected years 1950s to 2009

Notes: Average annual net loss and gain estimates for the conterminous United States, 1954 to 2009. Estimates of error are not graphically represented.

SOURCE: Thomas E. Dahl, "Figure 19. Average Annual Net Loss and Gain Estimates for the Conterminous United States, 1954 to 2009," in *Status and Trends of Wetlands in the Conterminous United States 2004 to 2009: Report to Congress*, US Department of the Interior, US Fish and Wildlife Service, September 2011, https://www.fws.gov/wetlands/Documents/Status-and-Trends-of-Wetlands-in-the-Conterminous-United-States-2004-to-2009.pdf (accessed November 17, 2017)

areas for aquatic life. They also serve as way stations for migrating birds. Wetlands can temporarily or permanently trap pollutants such as excess nutrients, toxic chemicals, suspended materials, and disease-causing microorganisms—thus cleansing the water that flows over and through them. Some pollutants that become trapped in wetlands are biochemically converted to less harmful forms; other pollutants remain buried there; still others are absorbed by wetland plants and are either recycled through the wetland or carried away from it. (See Figure 11.3.) Wetlands support commercial fishing and are useful for floodwater reduction, shoreline stabilization, and recreational activities.

Wetlands Regulation

Wetlands are affected by two major pieces of federal legislation: the Clean Water Act (CWA) and the Rivers and Harbors Appropriation (RHA) Act of 1899. Regulations carrying out the intent of these acts are promulgated by the EPA and the US Army Corps of Engineers (ACE).

Sections of the CWA regulate activities that affect wetlands, particularly discharges to them of dredged or fill material. These discharges are subject to the requirements of Sections 401 and 404 of the CWA. They are also regulated under many state regulations. The RHA Act regulates activities that could obstruct navigation of the country's waterways. For example, the building of dams, bridges, wharves, and piers is regulated, as are excavation and fill activities. The creation of any obstruction requires the approval of the ACE. The restrictions of the RHA Act apply only to wetlands that are navigable. The federal government defines navigable as a body of water that is subject to tides and/or has been, is, or could likely be used to transport interstate or foreign commerce.

There are other federal laws and programs that are designed to protect wetlands through the use of incentives (e.g., grants) or disincentives (e.g., denial of federal funding for certain projects that affect wetlands). In addition, wetlands are regulated by a host of state and local agencies. Overall, there is no one federal program that oversees all aspects of wetland protection. Furthermore, the existing federal legislation regulates the filling of wetlands but not other activities that could damage them. Critics complain that these policies do not provide

FIGURE 11.3

Wetlands' contribution to improving water quality and reducing storm water runoff

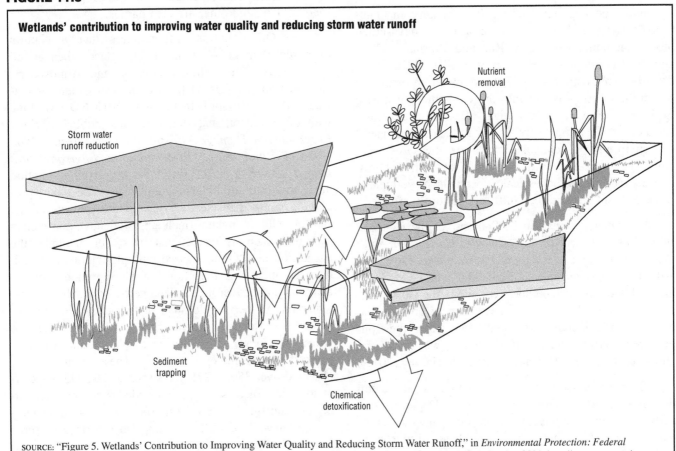

SOURCE: "Figure 5. Wetlands' Contribution to Improving Water Quality and Reducing Storm Water Runoff," in *Environmental Protection: Federal Incentives Could Help Promote Land Use That Protects Air and Water Quality*, US General Accounting Office, October 2001, http://www.gao.gov/new .items/d0212.pdf (accessed November 17, 2017)

adequate protection for wetlands. Nevertheless, many private landowners, farmers, and developers believe that existing legislation is too restrictive.

During the late 1980s President George H. W. Bush (1924–) set a national goal for eliminating wetland losses in the short term and achieving net gains in wetlands over the long term. The concept was called no-net-loss. Land developers were encouraged to offset wetland losses by developing or buying shares in wetland mitigation banks. For example, a utility company that wanted to destroy wetlands in one location to build a power plant could develop a larger acreage of wetlands in another suitable location. Wetland banking has become a common means through which wetland losses are offset.

FEDERAL JURISDICTION CONTROVERSY. The wetland restrictions of the CWA are a source of controversy because of confusion over which types of wetlands are subject to the law. The original law did not specifically mention wetlands, but gave the EPA jurisdiction over "waters of the United States." As is discussed in Chapter 9, in June 2015 the EPA and the ACE published the Clean Water Rule (*Federal Register*, vol. 80, no. 124) to clarify

which water bodies (including wetlands) are subject to federal jurisdiction. The new rule extended coverage to small wetlands that "impact downstream waters" and other wetlands that were not previously covered. As such, the Clean Water Rule aroused much controversy and triggered numerous lawsuits. Dozens of states and private parties sued the EPA, arguing the new rule was too sweeping in scope.

In October 2015 a federal appeals court stayed (temporarily postponed) enforcement of the Clean Water Rule. As a result, it had not gone into effect when President Donald Trump (1946–) took office in January 2017. As a Republican, he shares the Republican Party's general viewpoint that environmental regulation is too burdensome. Trump has made it a priority to diminish the power and regulatory reach of the EPA and to roll back regulations that were established during the administration of his predecessor, President Barack Obama (1961–), a Democrat. In June 2017 the EPA and the ACE published an official proposal to rescind the Clean Water Rule. As of January 2018, the rescission had not become final. It is expected to face fierce opposition from some conservation and environmental groups that desire stricter federal regulation of the nation's wetlands.

The Gulf Coast's Wetlands

Since the beginning of the 21st century the Gulf Coast's wetlands have suffered a series of devastating blows, including Hurricanes Rita and Katrina in 2005 and the BP Deepwater Horizon oil spill in 2010. As is described in Chapter 9, the latter dumped an estimated 4.9 million barrels of oil into the Gulf after an oil rig exploded approximately 50 miles (80 km) off the Louisiana coast. To mitigate (relieve or reduce in harshness) the environmental damage, numerous measures were employed after the spill, including controlled burns, floating barriers, and chemical dispersants. Nevertheless, some wetland areas in the Gulf were seriously affected.

According to Jonathan L. Ramseur of the Congressional Research Service, in *Deepwater Horizon Oil Spill: Recent Activities and Ongoing Developments* (April 17, 2015, https://fas.org/sgp/crs/misc/R42942.pdf), nearly 1,100 miles (1,800 km) of shoreline were oiled. The Gulf's wetlands were already stressed by development, erosion, and organic enrichment/oxygen depletion when the spill occurred. Further damage after the spill was caused by Hurricanes Lee (2011), Isaac (2012), and Harvey (2017).

BP faced numerous fines and penalties for its role in the oil spill. In November 2012 the US Department of Justice reached a settlement with the company over criminal charges. The company agreed to plead guilty to more than a dozen charges and pay $4 billion in fines. More than half of the money ($2.4 billion) was slated to go to the National Fish and Wildlife Foundation (NFWF) "to support restoration efforts in the Gulf states." The NFWF is a private nonprofit organization created by Congress during the 1980s. It works with government and private partners to award grants for conservation projects. Another $100 million of the BP fine was earmarked for the North American Wetlands Conservation Fund. The remainder was apportioned to various federal programs and funds.

Andy Tully indicates in "BP Settles with US Gov for $20.8 billion" (OilPrice.com, October 6, 2015) that in October 2015 BP reached a $20.8 billion settlement with the Department of Justice and the five Gulf Coast states (Alabama, Florida, Louisiana, Mississippi, and Texas). The amount includes a $5.5 billion fine for violating the Clean Water Act and $7.1 billion in damage claims under the Oil Pollution Act. The details of the settlement are contained in the legal document *Consent Decree among Defendant BP Exploration & Production Inc., the United States of America, and the States of Alabama, Florida, Louisiana, Mississippi, and Texas* (April 2016, https://www.justice.gov/enrd/file/838066/download). In "BP's Deepwater Horizon Costs Total $62B" (USAToday.com, July 14, 2016), Nathan Bomey notes that as of July 2016 the company estimated its total pretax costs for the spill at $62 billion. This includes the government settlements and additional settlements reached with property owners, shareholders, and other affected parties.

The Oil Pollution Act requires that a Natural Resource Damage Assessment take place when an oil spill occurs. The National Oceanic and Atmospheric Administration (NOAA) headed the assessment associated with the BP spill. In February 2016 NOAA, along with other federal and state agencies, published *Final Programmatic Damage Assessment and Restoration Plan (PDARP) and Final Programmatic Environmental Impact Statement (PEIS)* (http://www.gulfspillrestoration.noaa.gov/restoration-planning/gulf-plan). The report provides a comprehensive overview of the impacts of the spill on wildlife, habitat (including wetlands), and human activities, such as recreational uses. For example, the agencies state, "Oiling caused multiple injuries to marsh habitats, including reductions in aboveground biomass and total plant cover in mainland herbaceous salt marshes, reductions in periwinkle snail abundance, reductions in shrimp and flounder growth rates, reduced reproductive success in forage fish, reduced amphipod survival, and reduced nearshore oyster cover. These injuries were observed over 350 to 721 miles (563 to 1,160 kilometers) of shoreline. Increased erosion of oiled shorelines has also been documented over at least 108 miles (174 kilometers) of coastal wetlands." The report also describes the proposed restoration plan for the ecosystems affected by the oil spill. According to the agencies, implementation of the plan will cost about $8.8 billion, which will be paid by BP under the consent decree.

BIODIVERSITY

Biological diversity, or biodiversity, refers to the full range of plant, animal, and microbial life and the ecosystems that house them. The loss of biodiversity leads to problems beyond the simple loss of animal and plant variety. When local populations of a species are wiped out, the genetic diversity within that species that enables it to adapt to environmental change is diminished, resulting in a situation of biotic impoverishment. The loss of habitats, the contamination of water and food supplies, poaching, and indiscriminate hunting and fishing have depleted the population of many species. Most scientists agree that prospects for the survival of many species of wildlife, and hence biodiversity, are getting worse.

Worldwide, species loss is monitored by the International Union for Conservation of Nature (IUCN), which is based in Switzerland. Since 1960 the IUCN has evaluated thousands of plant and animal species for its annual *Red List of Threatened Species* (http://www.iucnredlist.org). The IUCN categorizes species based on their level of risk of extinction in the wild. According to the IUCN (December 5, 2017, http://cmsdocs.s3.amazonaws.com/summarystats/2017-3_Summary_Stats_Page_Documents/

2017_3_RL_Stats_Table_1.pdf), 25,821 species were "threatened with extinction" in 2017. The IUCN examined 91,523 species for the report. This constituted only 5% of the 1.7 million species that the IUCN considers "described species." Thus, many more species may be classified as threatened as more species are evaluated in the future.

In the United States species loss is tracked at the national level through programs established under the Endangered Species Act (ESA), which was passed in 1973. As of November 2017, 1,661 animal and plant species in the United States were listed as endangered or threatened under the law. (See Table 11.5.)

The ESA has become one of the most controversial laws ever passed by Congress. Like other environmental laws, the ESA mandates protection requirements that have economic costs and other consequences. In particular, it impacts the rights of landowners and how they manage their properties if endangered species are present. Critics complain the act overly restricts land and water development projects on public and private properties. They contend the ESA protects wildlife regardless of the economic burden to human beings. There are also substantial litigation costs associated with the ESA, given that states and private groups frequently sue the federal government over its species protection measures (or lack thereof). ESA advocates believe the law should be more fully implemented and supported by greater funding to help ensure the survival of imperiled species and promote biodiversity.

In general, Republicans are the harshest critics of the ESA and the most desirous for significant changes in the law to reduce its economic impact on industry and landowners. Following the November 2016 elections, Republicans achieved majority control of both the US House of Representatives and the US Senate and controlled the executive branch through President Trump. Matthew Daly reports in "GOP Targets Endangered Species Act as Protections Lifted" (Associated Press, July 19, 2017) that during the summer of 2017 Republican-led congressional committees were considering bills "to revise the law and limit lengthy and costly litigation associated with it." As of January 2018, no substantial bills related to this effort had been passed by Congress.

THE SPOTTED OWL CONTROVERSY. Environmentalists have long argued with government and industry over the question of logging in the Pacific Northwest. Timber production has economic benefits to society, but environmentalists want to limit logging to aid the health of the ecosystem.

The argument came to a head in 1990, when the spotted owl—which lives only in this particular region—was added to the list of endangered species. The owl's presence halted logging there (following protests by environmental groups) at considerable economic loss to communities and families in the area. Numerous lawsuits followed while the federal government tried to come up with a compromise that was satisfactory to all the stakeholders involved. The result in 1994 was the Northwest Forest Plan (NWFP), which allowed logging to resume with restrictions on the size, number, and distribution of trees to be cut. The NWFP is implemented by a variety of federal agencies through the Regional Ecosystem Office (REO). In "Northwest Forest Plan" (2018, https://www.fs.fed.us/r6/reo/nwfp/), the REO notes that the NWFP covers 24.5 million acres (9.9 million ha) in Oregon, Washington, and Northern California.

In 2015 the FS (https://www.fs.fed.us/r6/reo/monitoring/reports/20-year/) published a series of reports that present NWFP data collected since the early 1990s. In *Status and Trends of Northern Spotted Owl Habitat Monitoring (20yr)* (June 2015, https://www.fs.fed.us/r6/reo/monitoring/reports/20-year/5_%20NSO%20habitat%20%20Davis%20060915.pdf), Raymond J. Davis et al. estimate that northern spotted owl nesting and roosting habitat areas declined 1.5% between 1993 and 2012 on federal lands covered by the NWFP. Wildfire was the primary cause of habitat loss. The 1.5% rate of habitat

TABLE 11.5

Number of threatened and endangered US species, as of November 17, 2017

Group	United States* Endangered	Threatened	Total listings
Amphibians	20	15	35
Annelid worms	0	0	0
Arachnids	12	0	12
Birds	81	21	102
Clams	75	14	89
Corals	0	6	6
Crustaceans	24	4	28
Fishes	92	73	165
Flatworms and roundworms	0	0	0
Hydroids	0	0	0
Insects	74	11	85
Mammals	68	27	95
Millipedes	0	0	0
Reptiles	17	28	45
Snails	40	12	52
Sponges	0	0	0
Animal totals	**503**	**211**	**714**
Conifers and cycads	1	3	4
Ferns and allies	36	2	38
Flowering plants	737	166	903
Lichens	2	0	2
Plant totals	**776**	**171**	**947**

*United States listings include those populations in which the United States shares jurisdiction with another nation.

SOURCE: Adapted from "Listed Species Summary (Boxscore): Summary of Listed Species Listed Populations and Recovery Plans as of Fri., 17 Nov 2017 16:23:43 GMT," in *Species Reports*, US Fish and Wildlife Service, November 17, 2017, https://ecos.fws.gov/ecp0/reports/box-score-report (accessed November 17, 2017)

loss over two decades is lower than the rate of 5% per decade that was expected when the NWFP was implemented. Davis et al. do not include spotted owl population data in their report; however, estimates are available from previous reports. In *Status and Trends of Northern Spotted Owl Populations and Habitats* (October 2011, https://www.fs.fed.us/pnw/pubs/pnw_gtr850.pdf), Davis et al. estimate that spotted owl populations declined between 0.4% and 7.1% annually across the federal study areas between 1994 and 2008.

Fisheries and Aquaculture

Every two years the Food and Agriculture Organization (FAO) of the United Nations publishes an assessment of the world's fish populations. It estimates in *State of World Fisheries and Aquaculture, 2016* (2016, http://www.fao.org/3/a-i5555e.pdf) that 184.3 million tons (167.2 million t) of fish were captured in the wild or farmed (via aquaculture) worldwide for consumption and other purposes in 2014. Just over half (56%) of the haul was wild-caught fish. The remainder was produced by the aquaculture industry.

The FAO also estimates the status of the world's marine (oceanic) fish stocks as of 2013:

- Fully fished—58.1%, meaning that catches were at or very close to their maximum sustainable yield. This means that there is "no room for further expansion" of the catch of them.

- Overfished—31.4%, meaning that they need "strict management plans to rebuild stock abundance to full and biologically sustainable productivity"

- Underfished—10.5%, meaning that the stocks "have been exposed to relatively low fishing pressure and may have some potential to increase their production"

Fisheries exploitation is important not only for its human effects (i.e., economic and food consumption impacts) but also for its negative impacts on ocean ecology and ecosystems. The aquaculture industry has its own negative environmental impacts, primarily the discharge of biological wastes into water bodies and the transmission of disease from farmed stocks to wild populations. These problems are rooted in the nature of coastal aquaculture, which commonly features heavily concentrated populations of cultivated fish in cages or other facilities. Escapees and circulation of aquaculture water with the ocean at large pose the greatest hazards to natural ecosystems.

MINERALS AND OIL

Materials extracted from the earth are needed to provide humans with food, clothing, and housing and to continually upgrade their standard of living. Some of the materials needed are renewable resources, such as agricultural and forestry products, whereas others are nonrenewable, such as minerals and fossil fuels.

The Clean Air Act, the CWA, and the Resource Conservation and Recovery Act of 1976 regulate certain aspects of mining but, in general, the states are primarily responsible for regulation, which varies widely from state to state. In addition, coastal states wield control over oil and gas recovery within their legally defined offshore waters; jurisdiction varies by state, but in some cases it extends out as far as 10 miles (16.1 km). The federal government has jurisdiction over the waters outside state jurisdiction and extending to the boundary of US territorial waters. State and then federal jurisdiction extend to the edge of the outer continental shelf, which is a gently sloping and relatively shallow underwater plain that extends from the US land mass to the edge of the open sea.

Offshore Drilling

Offshore drilling for oil or gas is accomplished through resource leases that are granted by the state or federal government, depending on the location of the drilling site. This practice has been controversial for decades. In 1969 an oil rig in federal waters off the coast of California suffered a leak that sent hundreds of thousands of gallons of oil into the sea, soiling beaches and harbors near Santa Barbara, California. The resulting negative publicity greatly chilled public and political support for offshore drilling. The *Exxon Valdez* oil spill in 1989 further inflamed public opinion against offshore drilling. As a result, offshore areas along the Atlantic and Pacific Coasts have been off limits for new leases for decades. However, there have been some leases granted in the waters around Alaska, and prolific offshore drilling occurs in the Gulf of Mexico.

During the first decade of the 21st century public and political opinions against offshore drilling began to change in light of historically high gasoline prices and fears about US dependence on foreign oil. At the federal level, offshore oil and gas leases are administered by the Bureau of Ocean Energy Management (BOEM), which sets five-year plans for lease activities. The agency (https://www.boem.gov/National-OCS-Program/) divides the nation's coastlines into dozens of planning areas that are contained within four main regions: Alaska, Atlantic, Gulf of Mexico, and Pacific.

According to the BOEM, in "Proposed Outer Continental Shelf Oil and Gas Leasing Program for 2012–2017" (November 8, 2011, https://www.boem.gov/uploadedfiles/5-year_program_factsheet.pdf), in 2009, as the agency began formulating a proposed lease plan for 2012 to 2017, it was considering allowing new leases in previously untapped areas. John M. Broder reports in "Obama to Open Offshore Areas to Oil Drilling for First Time" (NYTimes.com, March 31, 2010) that the Obama administration was preparing to allow drilling in previously banned areas along the coasts of the Northeast, the Gulf of Mexico, and northern Alaska. After, however, the massive BP oil spill occurred in the Gulf of Mexico in April 2010, Obama reversed his decision.

Even so, in January 2015 the BOEM issued *2017–2022 Outer Continental Shelf Oil and Gas Leasing Draft Proposed Program* (https://www.boem.gov/2017-2022-DPP/), which proposed a lease sale in 2021 for areas in the south and mid-Atlantic Ocean. In "What's behind U.S. Plan to Open Atlantic to Offshore Drilling?" (NationalGeographic.com, January 28, 2015), Wendy Koch asserts that President Obama's decision to open the Atlantic Ocean to drilling was driven by a political desire to compromise with Republican leaders wanting expanded drilling. As is explained in Chapter 1, public opinion polling reveals that Republicans strongly support the development of US energy supplies over environmental protection. Koch states, "Environmentalists oppose opening the Atlantic [Ocean] to oil and gas drilling, citing the ecological risks of spills and climate dangers of expanding fossil fuel use."

In March 2016 the BOEM indicated in *2017–2022 Outer Continental Shelf Oil and Gas Leasing Proposed Program* (https://www.boem.gov/2017-2022-Proposed-Program-Decision/) that Atlantic Ocean drilling was off the table, explaining that "after a robust public comment process, the Mid- and South Atlantic Program Area lease sale proposed for 2021 in the DPP has been removed from the Proposed Program for a number of reasons, including strong local opposition, conflicts with other ocean uses, and current market dynamics. The decision to remove the Atlantic from the 2017–2022 Program was also based on careful consideration of the comments received from Governors of affected states." Furthermore, the BOEM notes in "2017–2022 OCS Oil and Gas Leasing Program" (2018, https://www.boem.gov/Five-Year-Program-2017-2022/) that when the final schedule was published in November 2016, it included only areas in the Gulf of Mexico and the Cook Inlet of the Gulf of Alaska.

In April 2017 President Trump issued Executive Order 13795 (http://www.presidency.ucsb.edu/ws/index.php?pid=123867), which implemented his "America-First Offshore Energy Strategy." He ordered the US secretary of the interior to consider revising the schedule of proposed oil and gas lease sales to encompass all offshore regions. As of January 2018, the BOEM (https://www.boem.gov/National-OCS-Program/) indicated it was working to develop a new lease program for 2019–24 that would replace the 2017–22 program. The possibility of offshore drilling along the Atlantic coastline and other coastlines that have long been off-limits worried some residents and politicians in these areas. For example, the private group Oceana indicates in "Grassroots Opposition to Offshore Drilling and Exploration in the Atlantic Ocean and Eastern Gulf of Mexico" (http://usa.oceana.org/climate-and-energy/grassroots-opposition-offshore-drilling-and-exploration-atlantic-ocean-and#toc-municipalities-) that as of January 2018, 144 municipalities along the East Coast had passed resolutions that oppose offshore drilling in the Atlantic Ocean.

Focus on Alaska

Alaska contains vast oil reserves beneath its land and coastal seas. The federal government owns huge tracts of land in the state, particularly the northernmost portion that lies next to the Beaufort and Chukchi Seas of the Arctic Ocean. (See Figure 11.4.) Much of this land is undeveloped wilderness; oil drilling, however, has taken place since the late 1960s in the Prudhoe Bay oil field. According to the Alaska Department of Environmental Conservation, in the fact sheet "Prudhoe Bay" (March 2006, https://dec.alaska.gov/spar/ppr/response/sum_fy06/060302301/factsheets/060302301_factsheet_PB.pdf), the oil field covers more than 213,500 acres (86,400 ha). The Trans-Alaska Pipeline System carries oil southward from the field to the southern Alaska port of Valdez.

NATIONAL PETROLEUM RESERVE IN ALASKA. West of Prudhoe Bay is the enormous National Petroleum Reserve in Alaska (NPRA), which is federally owned. (See Figure 11.4.) The US Geological Survey (USGS) notes in the fact sheet "U.S. Geological Survey 2002 Petroleum Resource Assessment of the National Petroleum Reserve in Alaska" (May 17, 2005, https://pubs.usgs.gov/fs/2002/fs045-02/index.html) that the NPRA encompasses 23 million acres (9.3 million ha). In October 2010 the agency released a report estimating the volumes of oil and natural gas that are potentially available in the NPRA. In the fact sheet "2010 Updated Assessment of Undiscovered Oil and Gas Resources of the National Petroleum Reserve in Alaska" (http://pubs.usgs.gov/fs/2010/3102/pdf/FS10-3102.pdf), the USGS provides estimates of 896 million barrels of oil and 52.8 trillion cubic feet (1.5 trillion m^3) of natural gas in "conventional undiscovered accumulations." Development of the natural gas would require a new pipeline or other means to transport it southward.

The US Department of the Interior's Bureau of Land Management notes in the press release "BLM Approves Greater Mooses Tooth Unit Oil and Gas Development Project in Alaska" (February 13, 2015, https://www.blm.gov/press-release/blm-approves-greater-mooses-tooth-unit-oil-and-gas-development-project-alaska) that the federal government first approved a request to drill on federally owned land within the NPRA in 2015. ConocoPhillips established exploratory wells in the far northeastern corner of the NPRA, near the adjacent Alpine oil field. (See

FIGURE 11.4

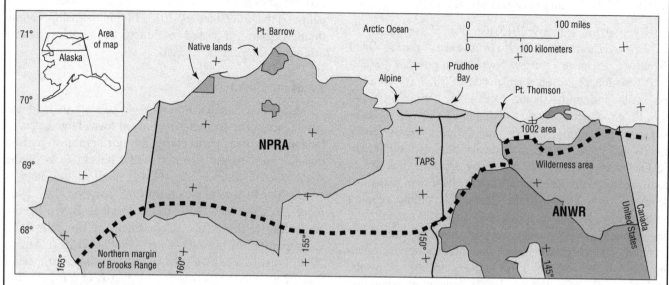

Northern Alaska, showing locations and relative sizes of the National Petroleum Reserve in Alaska and the Arctic National Wildlife Refuge

TAPS = Trans-Alaska Pipeline System.
NPRA = National Petroleum Reserve in Alaska.
ANWR = Arctic National Wildlife Refuge.

SOURCE: Kenneth J. Bird and David W. Houseknecht, "Figure 1. Map of Northern Alaska Showing Locations and Relative Sizes of the National Petroleum Reserve in Alaska (NPRA) and the Arctic National Wildlife Refuge (ANWR)," in *US Geological Survey 2002 Petroleum Resource Assessment of the National Petroleum Reserve in Alaska (NPRA)*, US Department of the Interior, 2002, https://pubs.usgs.gov/fs/2002/fs045-02/fs045-02.pdf (accessed November 17, 2017)

Figure 11.4.) In January 2017 the company announced it had discovered a large pool of oil. Over subsequent months the Trump administration decided to significantly expand leasing options across the NPRA. In December 2017, 10 million acres (4 million ha) of land were offered for lease—the largest-ever allotment. However, according to Tim Bradner in "State Pleased at Results of Its North Slope Lease Sale, but Bids in Federal NPR-A Sale Were Skimpy" (AnchoragePress .com, December 15, 2017), the federal sale attracted few bidders. Only 79,000 acres (32,000 ha) were leased on the federal lands. Bradner indicates that the oil industry is much more interested in NPRA lands along the Beaufort Sea. Those lands were not part of the sale because they were put off-limits during the Obama administration under a land management plan for the reserve. It was expected that the Trump administration would eventually rescind the plan.

ARCTIC NATIONAL WILDLIFE REFUGE. Along the US-Canadian border is the Arctic National Wildlife Refuge (ANWR), also a federal holding, that covers 19 million acres (7.7 million ha). (See Figure 11.4.) The refuge was established in 1980, and much of it has long been protected from development. However, there has been substantial industry interest in a coastal chunk called the 1002 area. According to the USGS, in "Assessment of

the Arctic National Wildlife Refuge (ANWR) 1002 Area" (June 1, 2017, https://energy.usgs.gov/Regional Studies/Alaska/ANWR1002.aspx), the 1002 area covers 1.5 million acres (607,000 ha). Importantly, the FWS notes in "Management of the 1002 Area within the Arctic Refuge Coastal Plain" (February 12, 2014, https:// www.fws.gov/refuge/arctic/1002man.html) that the 1002 area was not deemed a "wilderness area" when the ANWR was originally established. Geologists believe it holds large stores of oil and natural gas. As a result, environmental groups fear that oil and gas development will seriously harm the Arctic ecosystems.

In 2002, following heated debate, the Senate killed a proposal by the administration of President George W. Bush (1946–) to allow oil companies to drill in the ANWR. The proposal was raised again in subsequent years, particularly during times of high gasoline prices, but was defeated. The Obama administration did not support drilling in the ANWR, and no federal legislation was passed during President Obama's time in office that allowed the practice. President Trump, however, has vigorously championed such drilling, as have many Republican lawmakers. In December 2017 Congress passed a massive tax reform bill that was subsequently signed into law by Trump. One of its provisions allows the federal government to sell drilling leases in the 1002 area, a move staunchly opposed by many environmentalists. The Congressional Budget Office estimates in "A Legislative Proposal Related to the Arctic National Wildlife Refuge" (November 8, 2017, https://www.energy.senate.gov/public/index.cfm/files/serve?File_id=3454269F-6DC5-4E6C-9F23-99D1E3E64698) that these sales could generate around $2.2 billion in revenues between 2018 and 2027, with half going to the state of Alaska and half to the federal government.

Hydraulic Fracturing

Environmental advocates are becoming increasingly concerned about a drilling method called hydraulic fracturing (or fracking). This method involves the injection of large volumes (up to 1 million gallons [3.8 million L]) of water, sand, and chemicals deep into the earth. (See Figure 11.5.) The high-pressure mixture opens fissures (fractures or cracks) throughout rock formations that harbor oil or natural gas in their pores. Hydraulic fracturing has been in use for decades, but recent technological advancements and high prices for fossil fuels have made the process extremely popular in the oil and gas industry.

Environmental advocates complain that hydraulic fracturing is poorly regulated by the EPA and endangers the quality of groundwater, particularly drinking water wells. The latter claim has been supported by some studies. For example, in "Methane Contamination of Drinking Water Accompanying Gas-Well Drilling and Hydraulic Fracturing" (*Proceedings of the National Academy of Sciences*, vol. 108, no. 20, May 17, 2011),

FIGURE 11.5

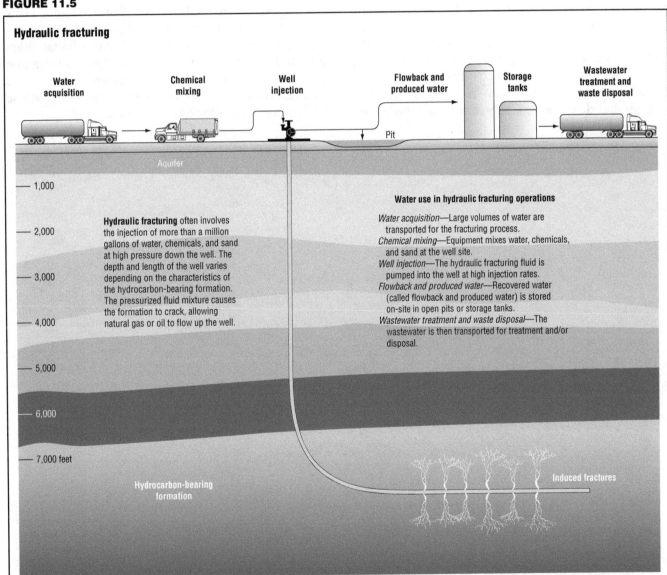

SOURCE: "Figure 6a. Illustration of a Horizontal Well Showing the Water Lifecycle in Hydraulic Fracturing," in *Draft Plan to Study the Potential Impacts of Hydraulic Fracturing on Drinking Water Resources*, US Environmental Protection Agency, Office of Research and Development, February 2011, https://yosemite.epa.gov/sab/sabproduct.nsf/0/D3483AB445AE61418525775900603E79/$File/Draft+Plan+to+Study+the+Potential+Impacts+of+Hydraulic+Fracturing+on+Drinking+Water+Resources-February+2011.pdf (accessed November 17, 2017)

Stephen G. Osborn et al. of Duke University found abnormally high methane concentrations in drinking water wells located within 0.6 of a mile (1 km) of active hydraulic fracturing operations.

In 2010 the EPA began its own comprehensive study regarding the impacts of hydraulic fracturing on drinking water and groundwater. In December 2016 the agency released its final report, *Hydraulic Fracturing for Oil and Gas: Impacts from the Hydraulic Fracturing Water Cycle on Drinking Water Resources in the United States* (https://ofmpub.epa.gov/eims/eimscomm.getfile?p_download_id=530159). It presents substantial scientific information and data on the fracking process and its environmental impacts. The EPA states, "Impacts can range in frequency and severity, depending on the combination of hydraulic fracturing water cycle activities and local- or regional-scale factors." In particular, the agency concludes that certain scenarios are linked with more frequent or more severe impacts. They include water withdrawals in times or areas with low water availability; spills of hydraulic fracturing fluids, chemicals, and associated water into groundwater resources; the use of wells that are not mechanically sound; fracturing directly into underground drinking water resources; and inadequate treatment and discharge of wastewater to either surface water or groundwater resources.

Although the EPA does not take a stance on the risk-benefit trade-off of fracking, some jurisdictions have rejected the practice. For example, as of January 2018, Maryland, New York, and Vermont had banned fracking statewide. The bans in Maryland and New York are particularly noteworthy because portions of the states sit atop the Marcellus basin, a geological formation believed to be especially rich in natural gas deposits. In "Maryland Governor Signs Fracking Ban into Law" (TheHill.com, April 4, 2017), Devin Henry quotes Larry Hogan (1956–), the governor of Maryland, as saying, "The possible environmental risks of fracking simply outweigh any potential benefits." By contrast, Pennsylvania, another Marcellus basin state, has heartily embraced fracking. President Trump is also an advocate for the process. According to Daly, in "Trump Admin Halts Obama-Era Rule on Fracking on Public Land" (Associated Press, March 15, 2017), the Trump administration announced in March 2017 its intention to rescind a rule created during the Obama administration that would require fracking operators on federal lands to disclose information about their chemical usage.

IMPORTANT NAMES
AND ADDRESSES

American Lung Association
55 W. Wacker Drive, Ste. 1150
Chicago, IL 60601
1-800-586-4872
Email: info@lung.org
URL: http://www.lung.org/

Bureau of Land Management
1849 C St. NW, Rm. 5665
Washington, DC 20240
(202) 208-3801
FAX: (202) 208-5242
URL: https://www.blm.gov/

Bureau of Ocean Energy Management
1849 C St. NW
Washington, DC 20240
(202) 208-6474
URL: https://www.boem.gov/

Centers for Disease Control and Prevention
1600 Clifton Rd.
Atlanta, GA 30329-4027
1-800-232-4636
URL: https://www.cdc.gov/

Environmental Defense Fund
257 Park Ave. South
New York, NY 10010
(212) 505-2100
FAX: (212) 505-2375
URL: https://www.edf.org/

Idaho National Laboratory
1955 N. Fremont Ave.
Idaho Falls, ID 83415
1-866-495-7440
URL: https://www.inl.gov/

National Aeronautics and Space Administration
300 E. St. SW, Ste. 5R30
Washington, DC 20546
(202) 358-0001
FAX: (202) 358-4338
URL: https://www.nasa.gov/

National Atmospheric Deposition Program
Illinois State Water Survey
2204 Griffith Dr.
Champaign, IL 61820-7495
(217) 333-7871
URL: http://nadp.sws.uiuc.edu/

National Audubon Society
225 Varick St., Seventh Floor
New York, NY 10014
(212) 979-3196
URL: http://www.audubon.org/

National Environmental Education Foundation
4301 Connecticut Ave. NW, Ste. 160
Washington, DC 20008-2326
(202) 833-2933
FAX: (202) 261-6464
URL: https://www.neefusa.org/

National Interagency Fire Center
3833 Development Ave.
Boise, ID 83705-5354
(208) 387-5512
Email: BLM_FA_NIFC_Comments@blm.gov
URL: https://www.nifc.gov/

National Oceanic and Atmospheric Administration
1401 Constitution Ave. NW, Rm. 5128
Washington, DC 20230
(202) 482-3436
URL: http://www.noaa.gov/

National Safety Council
1121 Spring Lake Dr.
Itasca, IL 60143-3201
(630) 285-1121
1-800-621-7615
FAX: (630) 285-1434
Email: customerservice@nsc.org
URL: http://www.nsc.org/pages/home.aspx/

National Weather Service Climate Prediction Center
5830 University Research Ct.
College Park, MD 20740
(301) 683-3419
URL: http://www.cpc.ncep.noaa.gov/

Natural Resources Defense Council
40 W. 20th St., 11th Floor
New York, NY 10011
(212) 727-2700
Email: nrdcinfo@nrdc.org
URL: https://www.nrdc.org/

Oak Ridge National Laboratory
Bethel Valley Rd.
Oak Ridge, TN 37830
(865) 576-7658
URL: https://www.ornl.gov/

Sierra Club
2101 Webster St., Ste. 1300
Oakland, CA 94612
(415) 977-5500
FAX: (510) 208-3140
Email: information@sierraclub.org
URL: https://www.sierraclub.org/

Union of Concerned Scientists
Two Brattle Sq.
Cambridge, MA 02138-3780
(617) 547-5552
FAX: (617) 864-9405
URL: https://www.ucsusa.org/

United Nations Environment Programme
PO Box 30552, 00100
Nairobi, Kenya
(011-254-20) 7621234
Email: unepinfo@unep.org
URL: https://www.unenvironment.org/

US Bureau of Reclamation
1849 C St. NW
Washington, DC 20240-0001
(202) 513-0501
FAX: (202) 513-0309
URL: https://www.usbr.gov/

US Department of Agriculture
1400 Independence Ave. SW
Washington, DC 20250
(202) 720-2791
URL: https://www.usda.gov/

US Department of Energy
1000 Independence Ave. SW
Washington, DC 20585
(202) 586-5000
URL: https://www.energy.gov/

US Environmental Protection Agency
1200 Pennsylvania Ave. NW
Washington, DC 20460
(202) 564-4700
URL: https://www.epa.gov/

US Fish and Wildlife Service
1849 C St NW
Washington, DC 20240
1-800-344-9453
URL: https://www.fws.gov/

US Food and Drug Administration
10903 New Hampshire Ave.
Silver Spring, MD 20993
1-888-463-6332
URL: https://www.fda.gov/

US Forest Service
Sidney R. Yates Federal Bldg.
201 14th St. SW
Washington, DC 20024
1-800-832-1355
URL: https://www.fs.fed.us/

US Geological Survey
12201 Sunrise Valley Dr.
Reston, VA 20192
(703) 648-5953
1-888-275-8747
URL: https://www.usgs.gov/

US Global Change Research Program
1800 G St. NW, Ste. 9100
Washington, DC 20006

(202) 223-6262
FAX: (202) 223-3065
URL: https://www.globalchange.gov/

US Government Accountability Office
441 G St. NW
Washington, DC 20548
(202) 512-3000
Email: contact@gao.gov
URL: https://www.gao.gov/

US Nuclear Regulatory Commission
Washington, DC 20555-0001
(301) 415-7000
1-800-368-5642
URL: https://www.nrc.gov/

Wilderness Society
1615 M St. NW
Washington, DC 20036
(202) 833-2300
Email: action@tws.org
URL: https://wilderness.org/

RESOURCES

The US Environmental Protection Agency monitors the status of the nation's environment and publishes a variety of materials on environmental issues. Numerous other US government agencies provided reports and data that were used in the preparation of this book. They included the Bureau of Ocean Energy Management; the Centers for Disease Control and Prevention; the Congressional Budget Office; the Congressional Research Service; the National Aeronautics and Space Administration; Oak Ridge National Laboratory; the US Census Bureau; the US Commission on Civil Rights; the US Consumer Product Safety Commission; the US Department of Agriculture; the US Department of Agriculture, Agricultural Marketing Service; the US Department of Commerce, the National Oceanic and Atmospheric Administration; the US Department of Education; the US Department of Energy; the US Department of Transportation, National Highway Traffic Safety Administration; the US Fish and Wildlife Service; the US Food and Drug Administration; the US Forest Service; the US Geological Survey; the US Global Change Research Program; the US Government Accountability Office; and the US Nuclear Regulatory Commission. The California Air Resources Board provided information about that state's air quality and climate change initiatives and legislation.

Useful international organizations included the Food and Agriculture Organization of the United Nations, the International Union for Conservation of Nature, and the United Nations Environment Programme.

Public opinion surveys that were conducted by Gallup, Inc., were extremely useful. Also helpful were the American Association of Poison Control Centers, the American Cancer Society, the American Lung Association, the Environmental Defense Fund, and the Center for Climate and Energy Solutions.

Various news organizations and journals were helpful for providing timely stories related to the environment, particularly *Chicago Tribune*, *Environmental Health Perspectives*, *Geophysical Research Letters*, *Journal of the American Society of Nephrology*, *Los Angeles Times*, *Morbidity and Mortality Weekly Report*, *National Geographic*, *Nature*, *Nature Communications*, *Nature Geoscience*, *New York Times*, *Proceedings of the National Academy of Sciences*, *Science*, and *USA Today*.

INDEX

Page references in italics refer to photographs. References with the letter t *following them indicate the presence of a table. The letter* f *indicates a figure. If more than one table or figure appears on a particular page, the exact item number for the table or figure being referenced is provided.*

A

Abandoned mines, 122, 123*f*

Accidents
    nuclear power plants, 125–126
    Union Carbide chemical release, 156
    Waste Isolation Pilot Plant, 131–132, 133*f*
    See also Oil spills

ACE (US Army Corps of Engineers), 138, 170, 171

Acid rain
    Acid Rain Program sulfur dioxide allowances, 84(*t*5.3)
    air quality, by regions, 86(*t*5.6)
    ecosystems, recovery of, 84–88
    emissions from power plants affected by federal acid rain regulations, 85*t*
    measurement, 79
    power plants affected by federal acid rain regulations, 84(*t*5.2)
    regional trends in sulfur and nitrogen deposition, 86(*t*5.7)
    sources, 79–80, 80(*f*5.1)
    water quality, 145–146

Acid Rain Program (ARP), 4, 83–84, 84(*t*5.2), 84(*t*5.3)

Adaptation, climate change, 62

Adirondack Mountains, 86

Adopt Your Watershed program, 140

Advanced technology vehicles, 37

Advancing Sustainable Materials Management (EPA), 101

Aerobic bacteria, 97, 144

Aerosols, 69, 72

Afforestation, 65

Africa, 9

African Americans, 12

Agricultural Marketing Service, USDA, 162

Agriculture
    climate change effects, 62
    nitrogen oxides emissions, 45
    nonhazardous waste, 90
    toxins in food, 163
    water quality impairment, 145

Air Pollution Control Act, 15

Air quality
    acid rain, 86(*t*5.6)
    Acid Rain Program, 4
    alternative fuel sites, 36*t*
    alternative fuel vehicles, 34–37, 35*t*, 37*t*
    carbon monoxide, 16–17, 18*f*
    Clean Air Act and amendments costs and benefits, 37–38
    cross-state air pollution, 28–30
    diesel emissions scandals, 32–33
    environmental revolution, 1–2
    hazardous air pollutants, 30–31
    health effects of hazardous air pollutants, 31*t*
    indoor air toxins, 161–162, 161*t*
    lead, 17–19, 20*f*
    legislation, 15–16
    motor vehicles exhaust emissions limits, 31–32
    NAAQS, people living in counties with air quality above, 19*f*
    nitrogen dioxide, 19–21, 21*f*
    ozone, 21–24, 24*t*
    particulate matter, 24–26, 25*f*, 26*f*
    priority pollutant emissions, 17*t*
    progress in emissions reduction, 27–28
    radon, 161*f*
    sulfur dioxide, 26–27, 27*f*
    unhealthy Air Quality Index, days of, 28(*f*2.9)
    waste-to-energy process, 102–103

Air Quality Index (AQI), 23, 28(*f*2.9)

Alaska, 152, 169, 175–177, 176*f*

ALF (Animal Liberation Front), 3

Algal blooms, 149, 154

Alternative fuel vehicles, 34–37, 35*t*, 36*t*, 37*t*

Amazon rain forest, 65

American Association of Poison Control Centers, 156–157

American Clean Energy and Security Act, 59

American Trucking Association Inc., Whitman v., 22

Anaerobic digestion, 103

Animal Liberation Front (ALF), 3

Animals
    acid rain, 81–82, 82*f*
    biodiversity, 172–174, 173*t*
    Chesapeake Bay watershed quality, 148
    climate change effects, 54
    hypoxic waters, 151*f*
    marine debris, 152
    methane, 41
    nonhazardous waste, 90
    ozone depletion consequences, 71
    pesticide effects, 2
    water quality impairment, 144, 145
    wetlands, role of, 169–170

Animas River watershed, 122

Antarctica, 69–70, 74, 75

Anti-coal Energy Law (MN), 65

Antiglobalism movement, 4–5

ANWR (Arctic National Wildlife Refuge), 176–177

Appalachian Mountains, 87, 88

AQI (Air Quality Index), 23, 28(*f*2.9)

Aquaculture, 174

Aquatic ecosystems
    acid rain, 81, 82*f*, 86–88
    hypoxia, 150–151
    National Aquatic Resource Surveys, 149–150

Aquifers, 137, 150

Arctic National Wildlife Refuge (ANWR), 176–177

Arizona, 23, 25

ARP (Acid Rain Program), 4, 83–84, 84(t5.2), 84(t5.3)

Arson, 3

Asbestos, 162

Asbestos Hazard Emergency Response Act, 162

Asia Pacific region, 76

Atlanta Journal-Constitution (newspaper), 106

Atlantic Ocean, 175

Atmospheric deposition. *See* Acid rain

Atmospheric ozone. *See* Ozone depletion

Augusta, GA, 126

Automobiles. *See* Motor vehicles

Aviation gasoline, 18

B

Backyard composting. *See* Composting

Bacteria

    decomposition, 97

    eutrophication, 144

    nitrification and denitrification, 45

    waterborne diseases, 154–155

Bays and estuaries, 142, 143(t9.5)

BEACH (Beaches Environmental Assessment and Coastal Health) Act, 151

Beaches, 151–152

Beaches Environmental Assessment and Coastal Health (BEACH) Act, 151

Beaufort Sea, 175

Beijing Amendment, 72

Berlin Mandate, 55

Beverage container deposit systems, 111

Bhopal, India, 156

Bioaccumulation, 143, 144, 162–164

Biodegradable materials, 97, 103

Biodiversity, 172–174

Bioenergy, 166, 167

Biomonitoring, 157–158

Biosolids, 106, 107t

Birds and acid rain, 81–82

Black ducks, 81–82

Black market trade in ozone-depleting chemicals, 75–77

BLM (Bureau of Land Management), 122, 123f, 175–176

Blood lead levels, 159, 159f, 160f

Blue Ribbon Commission on America's Nuclear Future, 133

Blueprint for a Secure Energy Future (Obama administration), 126

BMW, 36, 37

BOEM (Bureau of Ocean Energy Management), 174–175

BP oil spill, 152, 172

Bromine, 69, 72

Budgets, agency. *See* Funding and budget issues

Building materials and acid rain, 82

Bullard, Robert D., 13

Bureau of Ocean Energy Management (BOEM), 174–175

Bush, George H. W., 56, 58, 171

Bush, George W.

    alternative fuel vehicles, 35

    Arctic National Wildlife Refuge, oil drilling in the, 176

    Chesapeake Bay watershed, 148

    climate change policies, 58

    environmental policies, 9

    Kyoto Protocol, 56

    Yucca Mountain nuclear waste site, 132

Buy-back centers, 111

By-product synergy, 105

C

C & A Carbone Inc. v. Clarkstown, 103

CAFE (Corporate Average Fuel Economy) standards, 33–34

CAFOs (concentrated animal feeding operations), 145, 148

CAIR (Clean Air Interstate Rule), 29, 83

California

    abandoned mine sites, 122

    alternative fuel sites, 35

    beaches, 152

    climate change initiatives, 65

    coastal water quality, 152

    environmental revolution, 1–2

    landfill gas-to-energy projects, 99

    medical waste, 92

    motor vehicle emissions standards, 32

    nonpoint source water pollution management, 139

    nuclear weapons sites cleanup, 128

    oil spills, 174

    ozone, 22, 23

    particulate matter, 25

California Department of Public Health, 92

California Environmental Protection Agency, 65

Canada, 56, 65, 82, 83, 114

Cancer and carcinogens, 30, 126, 155, 162, 163, 164

Cap-and-trade programs

    Acid Rain Program, 4, 5f

    carbon emissions, 58

    greenhouse gases, 65

Carbon cycle, 41

Carbon dioxide

    atmospheric concentrations of, 48, 50(f3.9)

    cap-and-trade programs, 58

    carbon sequestration, 66

    cars and light-duty trucks emissions, 61f

    environmental movement history, 5–6

    fossil fuel combustion emissions, 59t

    as greenhouse gas, 41

    greenhouse gas emissions regulations, 60–62

    international emissions, 46–47, 49f, 49t

    Kyoto Protocol, 56

    motor vehicle exhaust emissions standards, 33t, 34t

    transportation sector emissions, 60f

Carbon monoxide, 16–17, 18f

Carbon sequestration, 65–66, 167

Carbon tetrachloride, 75–76

Carbon trading, 4, 5f, 56, 58, 60, 64–65

Carcinogens. *See* Cancer and carcinogens

Carlsbad, NM, 131

Carson, Rachel, 2

CASAC (Clean Air Scientific Advisory Committee), 16, 22

Catskills Mountains, 86

CDC. *See* Centers for Disease Control and Prevention

Cement kiln dust, 92

Centers for Disease Control and Prevention (CDC)

    blood lead levels, 159

    DDT, 9

    drinking water quality, 153–154

    National Report on Human Exposure to Environmental Chemicals, 157

CERCLA (Comprehensive Environmental Response, Compensation, and Liability Act), 120–123

Certification, zero waste, 106

CFCs (chlorofluorocarbons), 45, 69, 71–72, 75, 76

Chemical toxins. *See* Hazardous waste; Toxins

Chemical Waste Management v. Hunt, 100

Chernobyl accident, 125–126

Chesapeake Bay Foundation, 147–148

Chesapeake Bay watershed, 148f, 151, 151f

Chevrolet, 37

Children and toxins, 158–160

China, 159

Chlorine, 69, 72

Chlorofluorocarbons (CFCs), 45, 69, 71–72, 75, 76

Chukchi Sea, 175

Citizen lawsuits, 2–3

Clams, 81

Clarkstown, C & A Carbone Inc. v., 103

Clean Air Act and amendments

    acid rain, 83

    air quality assessments, 17

    asbestos, 162

    costs and benefits, 37–38

    cross-state air pollution, 28

    gasoline formulations, 33

    goals of, 9

hazardous air pollutants, 30
history, 15–16
minerals and oil extraction, 174
motor vehicle emissions, 31–32
municipal solid waste management, 103
political partisanship, 4
priority air pollutants, 27
refrigerants, 76–77
science and the scientific community, 8
Clean Air Interstate Rule (CAIR), 29, 83
Clean Air Mercury Rule, 31
Clean Air Scientific Advisory Committee
(CASAC), 16, 22
Clean Power Plan, 10, 60
Clean Water Act (CWA)
BP oil spill, 172
concentrated animal feeding operations,
145
environmental *vs.* economic interests, 4
jurisdiction, 137–138
total maximum daily loads, 146–148
water quality assessments, 140–146,
141(*t*9.2)
wetlands, 169, 170
Clean Water Rule, 138, 171
Cleanup
Comprehensive Environmental
Response, Compensation, and Liability
Act, 120–123
nuclear weapons facilities, 128–129
oil spills, 152
Cleveland, OH, 2, 137
Climate Action Team, 65
Climate change
carbon dioxide, 41, 50(*f*3.9)
carbon dioxide emissions for cars and
light-duty trucks, 61*f*
carbon dioxide emissions from fossil
fuel combustion, 59*t*
carbon dioxide emissions from
transportation sector, 60*f*
carbon monoxide emissions, 17
climate effects of global warming,
40(*f*3.2)
defining climate and climate change, 39
engineered gases, 45
environmental movement history, 5–6
as global problem, 39–40
global sea surface temperatures, 52*f*
global temperature trends, 51–54, 53*f*
global warming potential of various
chemicals, 71*t*
greenhouse effect, 40(*f*3.1)
greenhouse gas emissions, annual
percentage change in, 45*f*
greenhouse gas emissions, by economic
sector, 46*f*
greenhouse gas emissions, by gas, 42*f*
greenhouse gas emissions, by gas and
source, 43*t*–44*t*

greenhouse gas emissions, by source,
45–46, 48*f*
greenhouse gases, 48–49, 51
indirect greenhouse gases, 45
international agreements, 55–58
international carbon dioxide emissions,
49*f*, 49*t*
international greenhouse gas emissions,
46–47
IPCC assessment reports, 52–55
local and state government initiatives,
63–65
methane, 41, 43–44, 50(*f*3.10)
mitigation, 65–66
nitrogen oxides, 44–45
ozone, 44
ozone-depleting substances, 77
presidential policies, 9–10, 58–62
public opinion, 66–67, 66*t*, 67*t*
regional temperature changes, 62*t*
scientific community, 8
sea surface temperatures, 63*t*
skeptics, 66
synthetic gases, 45
US reports on climate science, 62–63
water vapor, 40–41
The Climate Change Action Plan, 58
*Climate Change Impacts in the United
States*, 62
Climate Change in the United States, 63
Climatic Research Unit, 51
Clinton, Bill, 13, 56, 58
Coal combustion residuals, 92–93, 93*t*, 106
Coal-fired power plants
acid rain, 79, 83
carbon sequestration, 66
coal combustion residuals, 92–93
greenhouse gas emissions regulations,
59, 60
hazardous air pollutants, 30–31
state climate change initiatives, 65
Coastal waters. *See* Oceans and coastal
waters
Colorado, 122
Columbia River, 128
Combustion with energy recovery. *See*
Waste-to-energy process
Commonweal Biomonitoring Resource
Center, 158
Community-based compostable waste
programs, 110
Composting, 96, 110, 112(*t*7.4), 112(*t*7.5),
112(*t*7.6)
Comprehensive Environmental Response,
Compensation, and Liability Act
(CERCLA), 120–123
Comprehensive Procurement Guidelines, 113
Concentrated animal feeding operations
(CAFOs), 145, 148
Connecticut, 63, 65
ConocoPhillips, 175–176

Conservation, 172
Conservation organizations, 3
Construction and demolition debris, 90–91,
90*t*, 90(*t*6.2), 91*f*, 91*t*, 106
Consumer electronics waste, 94, 109–110, 114
Consumer Product Safety Commission
(CPSC), 155–156, 158–159
Consumer Product Safety Improvement Act,
159–160
Consumer products, 155–156, 158–160
Consumerism, 6
Convention for the Protection of the Ozone
Layer, 72
Convention on Long-Range Transboundary
Air Pollution, 83
Cool Counties Initiative, 63
Copenhagen Accord, 56
Copenhagen Amendment, 72
Corporate Average Fuel Economy (CAFE)
standards, 33–34
Cost-benefit analysis. *See* Risk-benefit
analysis
Council on Environmental Quality, 83
Court cases
C & A Carbone Inc. v. Clarkstown, 103
Chemical Waste Management v. Hunt, 100
*Environmental Protection Agency v.
EME Homer City Generation*, 29, 83
Fowler v. EPA, 147–148
*Michigan v. Environmental Protection
Agency*, 31
North Carolina v. EPA, 29
Rapanos v. United States, 137
*Solid Waste Agency of Northern Cook
County v. US Army Corps of
Engineers*, 137
*United Haulers Association, Inc. v.
Oneida-Herkimer Solid Waste
Management Authority*, 103
*United States v. Riverside Bayview
Homes, Inc.*, 137
*Whitman v. American Trucking
Association Inc.*, 22
Cox Enterprises, 106
CPSC (Consumer Product Safety
Commission), 155–156, 158–159
Cross-State Air Pollution Rule (CSAPR),
29–30, 29*t*, 83–84, 84(*t*5.2)
Cross-state pollution, 28–30, 29*t*, 83
Cryptosporidium in drinking water, 154
CSAPR (Cross-State Air Pollution Rule),
29–30, 29*t*, 83–84, 84(*t*5.2)
Curbside recycling programs, 111
Cuyahoga River, 2, 137
CWA. *See* Clean Water Act
Cyanobacteria, 149, 154

D

Daimler AG, 36
The Day after Tomorrow (movie), 5
DDT, 2, 3, 8–9

Dead zones, 151

Decomposition of waste matter, 97

Deepwater Horizon, 152, 172

Deforestation, 65, 166–167

Delaware, 63, 148

Democratic Party. *See* Political affiliation

Demolition debris. *See* Construction and demolition debris

Denitrification, 45

Deposit systems of materials recovery, 111

Developed countries
greenhouse gas emissions, 47
international climate change agreements, 55
international response to environmental problems, 11–12
Montreal Protocol, 73
Vienna Convention, 72

Developing countries
greenhouse gas emissions, 47
international climate change agreements, 55
Montreal Protocol, 72
Vienna Convention, 72

Development, land, 171

Dibee, Joseph Mahmoud, 3

Dichloromethane, 76

Diesel emissions scandals, 32–33

Dioxins, 163–164

District of Columbia, 148

Dobson, Gordon M. B., 69

Dobson units, 69–70

DOE. *See* US Department of Energy

Drinking water
hydraulic fracturing, 177–178
pathogens, 144
toxins, 159
USGS water quality data sources, 150
water quality, 153–154

Drinking Water Protection Act, 154

Drop-off recycling centers, 111

Droughts, 167–168, 168*f*

Duncan, David Ewing, 158

Durban Platform, 57

E

E. coli, 144, 164

Earth, 2*f*

Earth Day, 3

Earth Liberation Front (ELF), 3

Earth System Research laboratory, 74

Earthwatch, 11

Eastern United States, 83, 166–167, 175

Economic issues
Clean Air Act and amendments, 16, 37–38
emissions compared with measures of economic growth, 28(*f*2.10)
environmental movement, 4

environmentalism, effect on, 1

EPA budget, 10, 11*f*, 12*t*

green consumerism, 6

greenhouse gas emissions and sources, 46

international greenhouse gas emissions, 47

international response to environmental problems, 11–12

Kyoto Protocol, 5, 56

market-based emissions reduction mechanisms, 4, 16, 56, 57, 63–64, 65

ozone standards compliance costs, 22

presidential environmental policies, 9–10

public opinion on the environment *vs.* the economy as a priority, 7–8, 7(*t*1.2)

risk-benefit analysis, 8

Ecosystems
acid rain, 81, 81*t*, 84–88
biodiversity, 172–174
climate change, 62
National Aquatic Resource Surveys, 149–150
ozone depletion consequences, 71
ozone effects, 23–24
pesticide effects, 2
wetlands, 169–172

Ecoterrorism, 3

Education, environmental, 13

EIA (US Energy Information Administration), 46–47

Electric vehicles, 35, 37, 37*t*

Electronics TakeBack Coalition, 114

ELF (Earth Liberation Front), 3

EME Homer City Generation, Environmental Protection Agency v., 29, 83

Emergency Planning and Community Right-to-Know Act, 117–118, 156

Emissions
acid rain, 79–80, 83–84
Acid Rain Program, 4
alternative fuel vehicles, 35, 37
annual percentage change in US greenhouse gas emissions, 45*f*
carbon dioxide, 41
carbon dioxide emissions from fossil fuel combustion, 59*f*
carbon dioxide emissions from transportation sector, 60*f*
carbon monoxide, 16–17
carbon sequestration, 66
diesel emissions scandals, 32–33
engineered gases, 45
forests and natural carbon sequestration, 167
international carbon dioxide emissions, 49*f*, 49*t*
international greenhouse gas emissions, 46–47

lead, 17–18

measures of economic growth compared with, 28(*f*2.10)

methane, 41, 43–44

motor vehicle exhaust emissions limits, 31–32, 33*t*, 34*t*

nitrogen oxides, 20, 45

ozone, 22, 44

particulate matter, 24

power plants affected by federal acid rain regulations, 85*t*

progress in emissions reduction, 27–28

sulfur dioxide, 26–27

synthetic gases, 45

US greenhouse gas emissions, by economic sector, 46*f*, 47*f*

US greenhouse gas emissions, by source, 48*f*

waste-to-energy process, 102–103

See also Greenhouse gases

Emissions Trading System, 56

Endangered and threatened species, 4, 54, 172–173, 173*t*

Endangered Species Act, 4, 173

Energy
alternative fuel vehicles, 34–37
Clean Power Plan, 10
greenhouse gas emissions, 46, 47
landfill gas-to-energy projects, 99
waste-to-energy process, 94, 101–103, 101*f*

Energy Independence and Security Act, 35

Energy Policy Act of 2005, 35

Energy Recovery Council, 101–102

Energy Security Act, 83

Engineered gases, 45

Enteric fermentation, 41

Environmental education, 13

Environmental Equity (EPA), 12

Environmental Investigation Agency, 75–76

Environmental justice, 12–13

Environmental movement and organizations
Arctic National Wildlife Refuge, 177
Chesapeake Bay watershed quality, 148
Clean Water Act jurisdiction, 138
history, 1–6
nonpoint source water pollution management, 139
offshore drilling, 17
public opinion, 6

Environmental Protection Agency (EPA)
acid rain, 83–84, 85, 87–88
backyard composting, 112(*t*7.5), 112(*t*7.6)
Beach Advisory and Closing Online Notification database, 151–152
budget, 10, 11*f*, 12*t*
Chesapeake Bay watershed quality, 147–148

Clean Air Act and amendments costs and benefits, 37–38
Clean Water Act jurisdiction, 137–138
Climate Change in the United States, 63
coal combustion residuals, 92–93
coastal water quality assessment data, 150
composting, 110
Comprehensive Environmental Response, Compensation, and Liability Act, 120–123
construction and demolition debris, 90–91
creation of, 2
cross-state air pollution, 28–30
drinking water quality, 153
environmental justice, 12–13
greenhouse gas emissions regulations, 59, 60, 61–62
hazardous air pollutants, 30–31
hazardous waste, 115, 116–117
hydraulic fracturing, 178
hydrocarbon substitutes for HFCs, 77
Integrated Risk Information System, 158
landfill design, 100
landfills, 97, 99
materials recovery facilities, 111
medical waste, 92
mercury in water, 143
Montreal Protocol, 73
motor vehicle emissions standards, 31–32
municipal solid waste composition, 93–94
municipal solid waste recycling and recovery, 106–110, 113
National Aquatic Resource Surveys, 148–150
oil spills, 152
ozone depletion effects, 71
pesticides, 162
presidential policies, 9–10
radioactive waste, 124
Resource Conservation and Recovery Act, 89–90, 119
science and the scientific community, 8
Significant New Alternative Policy program, 77
special wastes, 92
Sustainable Materials Management Electronics Challenge program, 109
total maximum daily loads, 147
Toxics Release Inventory, 117–119
toxins, 155, 156
toxins in food, 163
universal wastes, 124
waste-to-energy process, 101
water body uses, state-designated, 142
watershed management, 139–140
wetlands, 169, 170
See also Priority pollutants

Environmental Protection Agency, Michigan v., 31
Environmental Protection Agency v. EME Homer City Generation, 29, 83
Environmental Working Group, 158
EPA. *See* Environmental Protection Agency
EPA, Fowler v., 147–148
EPA, North Carolina v., 29
Escherichia coli (E. coli), 144, 164
Estuaries. *See* Bays and estuaries
Ethanol, 34–35
Europe, 82, 83
European Union, 56, 78, 114
Eutrophication, 144
Executive Order 12898, 13
Executive Order 13508, 148
Executive Order 13795, 175
Exhaust emissions limits, 31–32
Extended producer responsibility, 114
Extreme weather and natural disasters, 54–55, 62, 65, 172
Exxon Valdez oil spill, 152, 174

F

FBI (Federal Bureau of Investigation), 3
FDA (US Food and Drug Administration), 155, 162, 164
Federal Actions to Address Environmental Justice in Minority Populations and Low-Income Populations, 13
Federal Agency Hazardous Waste Compliance Docket, 122
Federal Bureau of Investigation (FBI), 3
Federal Food, Drug, and Cosmetic Act, 155
Federal funding. *See* Funding and budget issues
Federal Hazardous Substances Labeling Act, 155–156
Federal Insecticide, Fungicide, and Rodenticide Act, 155
Federal lands, 122, 123*f*, 175–176, 178
Federal Register, 122
Federal regulations. *See* Government regulations
Federal Water Pollution Control Act. *See* Clean Water Act
Fertilizers, 45, 145
Fiat Chrysler Automobiles, 32–33
First International Symposium on Acid Precipitation and the Forest Ecosystem, 82
Fish
acid rain effects, 81
fisheries and aquaculture, 174
mercury, 143
oil spills, 172
ozone depletion effects, 71
PCBs, 144
Flex-fuel vehicles, 35
Flint, MI, 153
Florida, 35, 128, 169

Flow-control laws, 103
Food
fisheries and aquaculture, 174
pathogens, 164, 164*t*
toxins, 162–164, 163*t*
Food and Agriculture Organization (FAO), 174
Food chain, 2, 71
Food waste, 10, 112(*t*7.4), 112(*t*7.5), 112(*t*7.6)
FoodNet, 164
Forests
acid rain, 81, 85–86
drought, 167–168, 168*f*
ground-level ozone, 23–24
pests, 169
purposeful carbon capture, 65
status of, 165–169, 166*t*
wildfires, 168–169, 168*t*
Fort St. Vrain, CO, 129
Fossil fuels
acid rain, 79, 80
carbon dioxide emissions, 59*t*
carbon monoxide emissions, 16–17
climate change, 5
greenhouse gases, 41, 46, 59
mercury, 30
methane, 43–44
special wastes, 92
state and local climate change initiatives, 65
sulfur dioxide emissions, 26
Foundry sand, 106
Fowler, C. Bernard, 147
Fowler v. EPA, 147–148
Fracking, 177–178, 177*f*
Freon, 72, 76
Frogs, 81
FS (US Forest Service), 122, 165–166, 169, 173–174
Fuel cell vehicles, 35–37
Fuel economy standards, 33–34, 33*t*, 34*t*, 61–62
Fukushima Daiichi nuclear power plant accident, 126
Funding and budget issues
BEACH Act, 151
environmental education, 13
environmental justice programs, 13
EPA, 10, 11*f*, 12*t*
Montreal Protocol implementation, 73
nuclear weapons facilities cleanup, 128, 129
Superfund, 121–122

G

Gasoline
ethanol, 34–35
government regulations, 33
lead emissions, 17–18

Gas-to-energy projects, 99
General Motors, 33, 36
Geologic repositories for radioactive waste, 130–134, 130f–133f
Geological carbon sequestration, 65–66
Georgia, 35
Glacier melt, 52, 54
Glass recycling and recovery, 108
Global Change Research Act, 58
Global temperatures, 66, 67t
Global warming. *See* Climate change
Global warming potential (GWP), 41, 45, 77
Global Warming Solutions Act (CA), 65
Global Warming Solutions Act (CT), 65
Goddard Institute for Space Studies, 51
Gold King mine, 122
Gore, Albert, Jr., 5, 54, 56
Government funding. *See* Funding and budget issues
Government regulations
    acid rain, 83–84, 84(t5.2), 84(t5.3)
    agencies that oversee natural resources, 166(t11.1)
    biodiversity, 173–174
    Clean Water Act jurisdiction, 137–138
    Corporate Average Fuel Economy standards, 33–34
    cross-state air pollution, 28–30
    environmental movement history, 2–3
    fuel economy and carbon dioxide emissions standards, 33t, 34t
    gasoline standards regulations, 33
    greenhouse gas emissions regulations, 58–62
    hazardous air pollutants, 30–31
    hazardous waste, 115, 117–123
    minerals and oil, 174–178
    Montreal Protocol, 73
    motor vehicle emissions, 31–32
    municipal solid waste management, 103
    municipal solid waste recycling and recovery, 113
    nonhazardous waste, 89–90
    ozone standards, 22
    political partisanship, 4
    power plants and acid rain regulations, 85t
    presidential policies, 9–10
    public opinion, 8(t1.5)
    scientific risk assessment, 8
    special wastes, 92–93
    toxins, 155–156
    wetlands, 170–172
Great Lakes, 142, 144t
Great Pacific Garbage Patch, 152
Great Recession
    environmentalism, effect on, 1, 6
    greenhouse gas emissions and sources, 46
    Kyoto Protocol, 56
    Obama's environmental policies, 10

Green Business Certification Inc., 106
Green consumerism, 6
Greenhouse effect, 39, 40(f3.1)
Greenhouse gases
    annual percentage change in US greenhouse gas emissions, 45f
    atmospheric concentrations, 48–49, 51
    atmospheric concentrations of carbon dioxide, 50(f3.9)
    atmospheric concentrations of methane, 50(f3.10)
    carbon dioxide emissions for cars and light-duty trucks, 61f
    carbon dioxide emissions from fossil fuel combustion, 59t
    carbon dioxide emissions from transportation sector, 60f
    Clean Power Plan, 10
    emissions, by gas, 42f
    emissions, by gas and source, 43t–44t
    engineered gases, 45
    environmental movement history, 5–6
    indirect greenhouse gases, 45
    international carbon dioxide emissions, 49f, 49t
    international emissions, 46–47
    methane, 41, 43–44
    nitrogen oxides, 44–45
    ozone, 44
    ozone-depleting substances, 77
    presidential policies on emissions of, 58–62
    synthetic gases, 45
    US greenhouse gas emissions, by economic sector, 46f, 47f
    US greenhouse gas emissions, by source, 45–46, 48f
    water vapor, 40–41
Groundwater
    hydraulic fracturing, 177–178
    hydrologic cycle, 137f
    usage, 137
    USGS water quality data sources, 150
Guinn, Kenny, 132
Gulf Coast states, 115
Gulf of Mexico, 151, 152, 172
GWP (global warming potential), 41, 45, 77

H

Habitat loss, 173–174
Hadley Centre, 51
Halon, 73
Hanford Site, 128–129
Harmful Algal Bloom and Hypoxia Research and Control Act, 151
Harriman, TN, 92
Harrisburg, PA, 125
Hazardous air pollutants, 30–31, 31t
Hazardous waste
    consumer electronics, 94, 109–110, 114

    environmental justice, 12
    generation, by state, 116t
    industrial hazardous waste, 115–116
    management of, 116–117, 118f, 118(t8.2)
    National Priorities List, 120–121, 121t
    small businesses, 123–124
    Toxics Release Inventory, 117–119, 118f, 118t, 119f, 120f
    types, 116f
    universal wastes, 124
    See also Radioactive waste; Toxins
HCFCs (hydrochlorofluorocarbons), 72, 73, 75, 76–77
Health issues
    acid rain effects, 81t, 82
    air quality, 15
    asbestos exposure, 162
    carbon monoxide emissions, 17
    Clean Air Act and amendments, 38
    climate change, 54, 62
    DDT, 2, 9
    drinking water quality, 153–154
    hazardous air pollutants, 30–31, 31t
    hazardous waste, 115
    lead, 18, 19, 158–159, 159f
    nitrogen dioxide emissions, 21
    nuclear power plant accidents, 125–126
    ozone depletion, 71
    ozone emissions, 23
    particulate matter, 25–26
    pesticides, 2
    radiation, 124, 124f
    radon, 161
    sulfur dioxide emissions, 27
    toxins, 155, 158
    toxins in food, 162–164, 164t
    unhealthy Air Quality Index, days of, 28(f2.9)
    Union Carbide chemical release, 156
    water quality, 144
HFCs (hydrofluorocarbons), 45, 77–78
HFI (Hydrogen Fuel Initiative), 35
High GWP gases. *See* Engineered gases
High-level radioactive waste (HLW), 129, 130, 132, 133
High-volume, low-toxicity waste. *See* Special wastes
HLW (high-level radioactive waste), 129, 130, 132, 133
Hogan, Larry, 178
Honda Motor Company, 36
Household hazardous waste, 124
Household products, 156, 158
Human Toxome Project, 158
Hunt, Chemical Waste Management v., 100
Hurricanes, 172
Hybrid vehicles, 37, 37t
Hydraulic fracturing, 177–178, 177f

Hydrochlorofluorocarbons (HCFCs), 72, 73, 75, 76–77
Hydrofluorocarbons (HFCs), 45, 77–78
Hydrogen Fuel Initiative (HFI), 35
Hydrogen-fueled vehicles, 35–37
Hydrologic cycle, 135, 136f, 137f
Hypoxia, 150–151, 151f
Hyundai, 36, 37

I

Ice melt, 52, 54
Idaho, 128
Idaho National Laboratory, 128, 129
Incentives, recycling, 113, 114
Incineration, waste, 94, 101–103
An Inconvenient Truth (Gore), 5, 54
Indigenous peoples, 62
Indirect greenhouse gases, 45
Indoor air toxins, 161–162, 161t
Industrial Resources Council, 105
Industrial Revolution, 1, 41
Industrialized countries. *See* Developed countries
Industry and manufacturing
    carbon offsetting, 5–6
    Comprehensive Environmental Response, Compensation, and Liability Act, 121–123
    extended producer responsibility, 114
    hazardous waste sources, 115–116
    nonhazardous waste regulations, 90
    ozone depleting chemicals, 72
    presidential environmental policies, 10
    Resource Conservation and Recovery Act, 119
    Superfund tax, 121–122
    Toxic Substances Control Act, 156
    Toxics Release Inventory, 117–119, 120f
    waste recovery, 105–106, 105t, 107f
Infrastructure, effects of climate change on, 62
Injection wells, 117
Insecticides. *See* Pesticides
Integrated Compliance Information System, 138
Integrated Risk Information System, 158
Intergovernmental Panel on Climate Change (IPCC), 39–40, 52–55
International agreements. *See* Treaties and international agreements
International issues
    acid rain, 82–83
    biodiversity, 172–173
    carbon dioxide emissions, 49f, 49t
    climate change, 39–40
    endangered species, 172–173
    environmental crimes, 75–76
    fisheries and aquaculture, 174
    greenhouse gas emissions, 46–47

history of response to environmental problems, 10–12
    See also Treaties and international agreements
International Mother Earth Day, 3
International Union for Conservation of Nature (IUCN), 172–173
Interstate air pollution. *See* Cross-state air pollution
Interstate commerce clause, 103
Interstate municipal solid waste imports and exports, 100
Iowa, 139
IPCC (Intergovernmental Panel on Climate Change), 39–40, 52–55
Irrigation, 136

J

Japan, 56, 114, 153
Japanese Meteorological Agency, 51
Jarboe, James F., 3
Jenkinsville, SC, 127
Jurisdictional issues, 137–138, 171

K

Kansas, 147
Kentucky, 128
Kigali Amendment, 77–78
Kyoto Protocol, 5, 55–57, 58, 63

L

Labeling
    food handling instructions, 164
    toxic substances, 155–156
Lakes, reservoirs, and ponds, 80, 81, 142, 142(t9.3), 149
Land development, 171
Landfill Methane Outreach Program, 99
Landfills
    decomposition of biodegradable matter, 97
    design, 99–100, 100f
    environmental justice, 12
    hazardous waste, 116, 117
    interstate municipal solid waste imports and exports, 100
    materials in, 98t, 99f
    methane, 41, 97, 99
    municipal solid waste management methods, 96
    Resource Conservation and Recovery Act, 89
    trends in development of, 100–101
Las Vegas, NV, 132–134
Lawsuits
    acid rain, 83
    Chesapeake Bay watershed quality, 147–148
    citizen-suit provisions, 2–3
    Clean Water Act jurisdiction, 138

oil spills, 152, 172
ozone standards, 22
state climate change initiatives, 65
Lead
    air quality, 17–19, 20f
    chemical toxins, 158–160, 159f, 160f
    drinking water quality, 153
Lead Contamination Control Act, 159
Lead-Based Poisoning Prevention Act, 159
Legionnaires' disease, 153, 154
Legislation
    Acid Precipitation Act, 84
    Air Pollution Control Act, 15
    American Clean Energy and Security Act, 59
    Anti-coal Energy Law (MN), 65
    Asbestos Hazard Emergency Response Act, 162
    Beaches Environmental Assessment and Coastal Health Act, 151
    Comprehensive Environmental Response, Compensation, and Liability Act, 120–123
    Consumer Product Safety Improvement Act, 159–160
    Cross-State Air Pollution Rule, 29t
    Drinking Water Protection Act, 154
    Emergency Planning and Community Right-to-Know Act, 117–118, 156
    Endangered Species Act, 173
    Energy Independence and Security Act, 35
    Energy Policy Act, 35
    Energy Security Act, 83
    Federal Food, Drug, and Cosmetic Act, 155
    Federal Hazardous Substances Labeling Act, 155–156
    Federal Insecticide, Fungicide, and Rodenticide Act, 155
    Global Change Research Act, 58
    Global Warming Solutions Act (CA), 65
    Global Warming Solutions Act (CT), 65
    Harmful Algal Bloom and Hypoxia Research and Control Act, 151
    Lead Contamination Control Act, 159
    Lead-Based Poisoning Prevention Act, 159
    Marine Debris Research, Prevention, and Reduction Act, 152
    Medical Waste Management Act, 92
    Next Generation Energy Act (MN), 65
    Nuclear Waste Policy Act, 132
    Ocean Dumping Act, 152
    Oil Pollution Act, 152, 172
    Pollution Prevention Act, 116, 118
    Pure Food and Drug Act, 155
    Recycling Opportunity Act (OR), 112
    Residential Lead-Based Paint Hazard Reduction Act, 159
    Revenue Reconciliation Act, 76

Rivers and Harbors Appropriation Act, 170
Safe Drinking Water Act, 153, 159
Solid Waste Disposal Act, 89
Toxic Substances Control Act, 156
Waste Isolation Pilot Plant Land Withdrawal Act, 132
Water Infrastructure Improvements for the Nation Act, 93
See also Clean Air Act and amendments; Clean Water Act; Resource Conservation and Recovery Act
Less developed countries
  black market trade in ozone-depleting chemicals, 76
  international response to environmental problems, 11–12
Listeria, 164
Livestock, 90, 144, 145, 148
Local government initiatives, 63, 112–113
Logging, 173–174
London, 15
London Amendment, 72, 73
Los Alamos National Laboratory, 128, 132
Los Angeles, 1–2, 15
Louisiana, 115
Low-income people and environmental justice, 13
Low-level radioactive waste, 129, 131f

M

Maine, 63, 169
Maintenance areas, 16, 17, 21
Malaria and DDT use, 9
Manure, 90, 145
Marine debris, 152
Marine Debris Research, Prevention, and Reduction Act, 152
Market-based emissions reduction mechanisms, 4, 16, 56, 57, 63–64, 65
Maryland, 63, 147–148, 178
Massachusetts, 63
Materials and acid rain, 82
Materials Marketplace, 105
Materials recovery facilities (MRFs), 111
Mauna Loa, HI, 75
McConnell, John, 3
Meat contamination, 164
Medical waste, 91–92
Medical Waste Management Act, 92
Mercury, 30–31, 143, 162
Mercury and Air Toxics Standards rule, 30–31, 31t
Met office, 51
Metal slags, 106
Metals recycling and recovery, 108
Methane
  atmospheric concentrations, 48–49, 50(f3.10), 51
  greenhouse gases, 41, 43–44

hydraulic fracturing, 177–178
  landfills, 97, 99
Methylene chloride, 76
Methylmercury, 162
Michigan, 99, 128, 153
Michigan v. Environmental Protection Agency, 31
Microcystin, 149, 154
Mill tailings, uranium, 129
Milwaukee, WI, 154
Mineral processing wastes, 92, 92t
Mining
  abandoned mine sites, 122
  Comprehensive Environmental Response, Compensation, and Liability Act, 123
  regulations, 174
  uranium mill tailings, 129
Minnesota, 65
Minnesota Family Environmental Exposure Tracking project, 158
Minorities and environmental justice, 12–13
Mississippi, 115
Mississippi River, 151
Mitigation, climate change, 55, 62, 65–66
Molina, Mario J., 69
Montreal Amendment, 72
Montreal Protocol, 72–75, 73t, 74t, 77–78
Motor vehicles
  alternative fuel vehicles, 34–37, 35t, 37t
  California climate change initiatives, 65
  diesel emissions scandals, 32–33
  exhaust emissions limits, 31–32
  fuel economy and carbon dioxide emissions standards, 33t, 34t
  fuel economy and emissions standards, 33–35
  greenhouse gas emissions, 59, 60–62, 60f, 61f
Mozambique, 73
MRFs (materials recovery facilities), 111
Multilateral Fund for the Implementation of the Montreal Protocol, 73
Municipal solid waste
  backyard composting, 112(t7.5), 112(t7.6)
  breakdown of generation and disposition, 102(t6.15)
  combustion with energy recovery, 101–103
  composition of, 93–94, 95t, 96f, 96t, 97t
  disposition of, 113f
  federal regulations, 103
  generation, recovery, and discard amounts for, 99t
  generation and disposition of, 111t
  generation of, total and per capita, 94f, 96–97
  government role in recycling, 112–113
  landfills, 97, 98t, 99–101, 99f

management methods, 94, 96–97, 97f
  recycling, history and current strength of, 113–114
  recycling and composting, by material, 112(t7.4)
  recycling and recovery, by material, 108–110, 109f, 110f
  recycling and recovery rates, 106–107, 108f
  recycling programs, 110–113
  Resource Conservation and Recovery Act, 89–90
  waste-to-energy process, 102(t6.14)
Mutagens, 155

N

NAAQS (National Ambient Air Quality Standards), 15–16, 19f
NARS (National Aquatic Resource Surveys), 148–150
NASA (National Aeronautics and Space Administration), 51, 70–71, 76
National Acid Precipitation Assessment Program, 83
National Aeronautics and Space Administration (NASA), 51, 70–71, 76
National Air Toxics Assessments, 30
National Ambient Air Quality Standards (NAAQS), 15–16, 19f
  See also Priority pollutants
National Aquatic Resource Surveys (NARS), 148–150
National Carbon Capture Center, 66
National Climatic Data Center, 51, 167–168
National Coastal Condition Assessment (EPA), 150
National Emissions Inventory. See Priority pollutants
National Emissions Standards for Hazardous Air Pollutants, 16
National Energy Technology Laboratory, 66
National Fish and Wildlife Foundation, 172
National Geographic magazine, 158
National Highway Traffic Safety Administration (NHTSA), 32, 33–34, 61–62
National Interagency Fire Center, 168–169
National Low Emission Vehicle program, 32
National Oceanic and Atmospheric Administration (NOAA), 51, 74–75, 151, 152, 153
National Outbreak Reporting System, 154
National Petroleum Reserve, 175–176
National Poison Data System, 156–157
National Pollutant Discharge Elimination System (NPDES), 138, 145, 148
National Priorities List, 120–121, 121t
National Report on Human Exposure to Environmental Chemicals (CDC), 157
National Report on Sustainable Forests (US Forest Service), 165–166, 169

National Research Council (NRC), 51

National Water Information System, 150

National Water-Quality Assessment databases, 150

National Wetlands Inventory, 169

Natural acid rain factors, 79

Natural carbon sinks, 65

Natural disasters. *See* Extreme weather and natural disasters

Natural resources
  biodiversity, 172–174, 173*t*
  drought, 168*f*
  federal oversight agencies, 166(*t*11.1)
  fisheries and aquaculture, 174
  forests, 165–166, 166(*t*11.2), 166(*t*11.3)
  oil and gas extraction, 174–178, 176*f*, 177*f*
  wetlands, 169–172, 170*f*
  wildfires, 168–169, 168*t*

Near coastal waters. *See* Oceans and coastal waters

Nelson, Gaylord, 3

Nevada, 23, 122, 128, 132–134

New Hampshire, 63, 147

New Mexico, 128, 131

New Source Performance Standards, 16

New Trends in ODS Smuggling (Environmental Investigation Agency), 75, 76

New York (state), 63, 128, 148, 178

New York State Department of Environmental Conservation, 114

Newspapers, 106, 113

Next Generation Energy Act (MN), 65

NHTSA (National Highway Traffic Safety Administration), 32, 33–34, 61–62

Nitrate, 150

Nitrification, 45

Nitrogen oxides
  acid rain, 79–80, 83–84, 85
  air quality, 19–21, 21*f*
  greenhouse gases, 44–45
  regional trends in deposition of, 86(*t*5.7)
  water quality, 87(*t*5.8), 149

Niwot Ridge, CO, 75

Nixon, Richard M., 2

NOAA (National Oceanic and Atmospheric Administration), 51, 74–75, 151, 152, 153

Nobel Peace Prize, 54

Nonattainment areas
  carbon monoxide, 17
  gasoline formulations, 33
  lead, 19
  ozone, 22
  particulate matter, 25
  sulfur dioxide, 27
  upgrading of, 16

No-net-loss land development, 171

Nonhazardous waste
  agricultural wastes, 90
  construction and demolition debris, 90–91, 90*t*, 90(*t*6.2), 91*f*, 91*t*
  industrial waste, 90
  industrial waste recovery, 105–106, 105*t*
  legislation, 89–90
  medical waste, 91–92
  Resource Conservation and Recovery Act, 90(*t*6.1)
  special wastes, 92–93, 93*t*
  See also Municipal solid waste

Non-OECD countries. *See* Developing countries

Nonpoint Source Pollution Control Program (CA), 139

Nonpoint source water pollution management, 138–139, 139*f*

North American black ducks, 81–82

North American Wetlands Conservation Fund, 172

North Carolina, 147

North Carolina v. EPA, 29

Northwest Forest Plan (NWFP), 173

NPDES (National Pollutant Discharge Elimination System), 138, 145, 148

NRC (National Research Council), 51

NRC (US Nuclear Regulatory Commission), 124, 127, 133, 160

Nuclear power plants, 124–128, 125*f*–126*f*, 127*f*

Nuclear Waste Policy Act, 132

Nuclear weapons, 128–129

Nutrient and water quality impairment, 144

NWFP (Northwest Forest Plan), 173

Nye County, NV, 132

O

Obama, Barack
  Arctic National Wildlife Refuge, 176
  Chesapeake Bay watershed quality, 148
  Clean Water Rule, 171
  climate change, 58–61
  Comprehensive Environmental Response, Compensation, and Liability Act, 123
  environmental policies, 9–10
  Kyoto Protocol, 56
  nuclear power plants, 126
  offshore drilling, 174–175
  ozone standards, 22
  Paris Agreement, 57
  power plant emissions regulations, 31
  Yucca Mountain nuclear waste site, 133–134

Ocean Dumping Act, 152

Ocean warming, 51, 52*f*

Oceana, 175

Oceans and coastal waters
  Clean Water Act, 142, 143(*t*9.t6)
  climate change effects, 62

coastal water quality, 150–152
  hypoxia, 150–151
  natural sinks, 65
  offshore drilling, 174–175
  sea level rises, 54
  sea surface temperatures, 63, 63*t*
  water quality, 142, 143(*t*9.7), 152–153

ODS (ozone-depleting substances), 72–77, 77*t*

Office of Environmental Justice, EPA, 13

Office of Environmental Management, DOE, 128

Office of Pollution Prevention and Toxics, EPA, 156

Offshore drilling, 174–175

Ohio, 128, 137, 154

Ohio River valley, 83

Oil and gas extraction, 174–175, 177*f*

Oil Pollution Act, 152, 172

Oil spills, 152, 172, 174

Oneida-Herkimer Solid Waste Management Authority, United Haulers Association, Inc. v., 103

Operation Backfire, 3

Oregon, 112

Organic by-products, 106, 107*t*

Organic enrichment/oxygen depletion, 144

Organic food, 163

Organisation for Economic Co-operation and Development countries. *See* Developed countries

Our Nation's Air (EPA), 17, 19

Overaker, Josephine Sunshine, 3

Overfishing, 174

OzonAction, 74

Ozone, 21–24, 24*t*, 44

Ozone depletion
  altitude profile and distribution of ozone, 70*f*
  black market trade in ozone-depleting chemicals, 75–77
  chemical sources, 71–72
  consequences of, 71
  global warming potential of various chemicals, 71*t*
  Montreal Protocol, 72–75, 74*t*
  ozone-depleting substances and their alternatives, 77, 77*t*
  scientific evidence, 69–71
  Southern Hemisphere, 70*t*
  trends in atmospheric concentrations of ozone-depleting chemicals, 75*f*, 78*f*

Ozone-depleting substances (ODS), 72–77, 77*t*

P

Pacific Northwest Plan, 173

Pacific Ocean marine debris, 152

Packaging, recoverability of, 114

Paint, lead-based, 158, 159–160

Palmer Drought Severity Index (PDSI), 167–168

Paper waste, 93, 96, 101, 108, 111

Paris Agreement, 57–58

Particulate matter
acid rain, 82, 83
air quality, 24–26, 25f, 26f
nitrogen dioxide, 21

Partisanship, political. *See* Political affiliation

Pathogens, 144, 164, 164t

Pathway21, 105

PCBs (polychlorinated biphenyls), 144–145, 163–164

PDSI (Palmer Drought Severity Index), 167–168

Pennsylvania, 99, 147, 148, 178

Perfluorocarbons (PFCs), 45

Permafrost thawing, 52

Permit Compliance System, 138

Persistent chemicals, 162–164

Pesticide Data Program, 162

Pesticides, 2, 3, 8–9, 162–163, 163t

Pests, forest, 169

Petroleum industry, 66, 92, 174–178, 177f

PFCs (perfluorocarbons), 45

pH and acid rain, 79, 80(f5.2), 81, 82f

Phosphorus, 149

Photosynthesis, 71, 165

Phytoplankton, 71

Plant Vogtle nuclear power plant, 126, 127–128

Plasma gasification, 103

Plastics, 71, 108–109, 152

Point Barrow, AK, 75

Point source water pollution management, 138, 139f

Poison control centers, 156–157

Polar regions, 70, 71

Political affiliation
Arctic National Wildlife Refuge, 176–177
endangered species, 173
environmental regulations, 4
greenhouse gas emissions regulations, 60
offshore drilling, 175
presidential environmental policies, 9–10
public opinion on climate change, 66–67
public opinion on environmental issues, 6–8

Pollutants, priority. *See* Priority pollutants

Pollution Prevention Act, 116, 118

Polychlorinated biphenyls (PCBs), 144–145, 163–164

Ponds. *See* Lakes, reservoirs, and ponds

Poverty, 13

Power plants
acid rain, 79, 80, 83, 85t
carbon sequestration, 66
Clean Power Plan, 10
coal combustion residuals, 92–93

cross-state air pollution, 29–30
greenhouse gas emissions, 46, 47, 59, 60
hazardous air pollutants, 30–31
nuclear power plants, 124–128, 125f–126f, 127f
state climate change initiatives, 64–65
thermoelectric power, 135

Precipitation, 52

The President's Climate Action Plan (Obama administration), 59

Prevention of Significant Deterioration program, 16

Primary Drinking Water Standards, 153

Prince William Sound, AK, 152

Priority pollutants
carbon monoxide, 16–17, 18f
change in emissions of, 17t
concentrations of, change in, 18t
cross-state air pollution, 29–30
lead, 20f
NAAQS, people living in counties with air quality above, 19f
nitrogen dioxide, 19–21, 21f
ozone, 21–24, 24t
particulate matter, 24–26, 25f, 26f
progress in emissions reduction, 27–28
sulfur dioxide, 26–27, 27f

Private property rights, 4

Project Skyhole Patching, 76

Property rights, 4

Pruitt, Scott, 10, 34, 123

Public lands, 122, 123f, 175–176, 178

Public opinion
climate change, 66–67, 66t, 67t
the economy *vs.* the environment as a priority, 7(t1.2)
energy production *vs.* environmental concerns, 7(t1.3)
environmental quality, 8(t1.4)
federal environmental protection, 8(t1.5)
political partisanship, 6–8
status of the environment, 6t

Public water supply, 136, 144, 153–154, 159

Pulp and paper processing residuals, 106

Pure Food and Drug Act, 155

Purposeful carbon capture, 65–66

Pyrolysis, 103

Q

The Quality of Our Nation's Waters (USGS), 150

Quebec, Canada, 65

R

Race and environmental justice, 12–13

Radiation
greenhouse effect, 39, 40(f3.1)
ozone depletion, 44, 71
toxins, 160–161, 160t

Radical environmentalism, 3

Radioactive waste
classes of, 129
geologic repositories, 130–134, 130f–133f
low-level radioactive waste disposal facility, 131f
military and defense sources, 128–129
nuclear power plants, 124–128
ocean dumping, 152

Radon, 160–161, 161f

Rapanos v. United States, 137

RCPs (representative concentration pathways), 63

RCRA. *See* Resource Conservation and Recovery Act

Recalls, consumer product, 158–159

Recovered Materials Advisory Notices, 113

Recycling and recovery
backyard composting, 112(t7.5), 112(t7.6)
biosolids, 106, 107t
collection methods, 111
components in the recycling process, 110–111
government role in, 112–113
green consumerism, 6
industrial waste recovery, 105–106, 105t, 107f
municipal solid waste, by material, 109f, 110f, 112(t7.4)
municipal solid waste management methods, 96
municipal solid waste recovery rates, 106–107
municipal solid waste recycling history and status, 113–114
municipal solid waste recycling rates, 108f
waste-to-energy process, 101–102

Recycling Opportunity Act (OR), 112

Red List of Threatened Species (International Union for Conservation of Nature), 172–173

Refrigerants, 72, 73, 76, 77–78

Regional Greenhouse Gas Initiative, 63–64

Regulations. *See* Government regulations

Renewable Fuels Association, 35

Representative concentration pathways (RCPs), 63

Republican Party. *See* Political affiliation

Reservoirs. *See* Lakes, reservoirs, and ponds

Residential Lead-Based Paint Hazard Reduction Act, 159

Resource Conservation and Recovery Act (RCRA)
consumer electronics disposal, 109
hazardous waste, 115, 118
industrial hazardous waste, 119
landfill design, 100
landfills and methane gas, 97
mineral processing wastes, 92t

mining, 174

municipal solid waste management, 103

outline of, 90(t6.1)

purpose of, 89

recycling and recovery, 113

small business and household waste, 124

special wastes, 92–93

Revenue Reconciliation Act, 76

Reverse supply chain waste reduction
methods, 109

Rhode Island, 64

Risk-benefit analysis, 8–9, 37–38

Rivers and Harbors Appropriation Act, 170

Rivers and streams, 81, 142, 142(t9.3), 149,
150

*Riverside Bayview Homes, Inc., United
States v.*, 137

Rock mining rule, 123

Rowland, F. Sherwood, 69

Runoff, 145

Russia, 56, 57, 76

S

Safe Drinking Water Act (SDWA), 153,
154, 159

Safety, nuclear power plant, 127

Salmonella, 164

San Diego County, CA, 152

Santa Barbara, CA, 174

Savannah River Site, 128, 129

Scandinavian countries, 82

Schools, asbestos in, 162

Schwarzenegger, Arnold, 65

Science and the scientific community
acid rain, 82–83
climate science reports, 62–63
global warming skeptics, 66
ozone depletion, 69–71
public opinion on the belief in global
warming by scientists, 66t
risk-benefit analysis, 8–9

Scrap tires, 106

Scripps Institute of Oceanography, 48

SDWA (Safe Drinking Water Act), 153,
154, 159

Sea level rise, 54, 62

Sea surface temperatures, 51, 52f, 63, 63t

Settlements, 32, 172

Shigella, 164

Sierra Club, 63, 139

Significant New Alternative Policy (SNAP)
program, 77

Silent Spring (Carson), 2, 8–9

*Siting of Hazardous Waste Landfills and
Their Correlation with Racial and
Economic Status of Surrounding
Communities* (congressional study), 12

Skeptics, global warming, 66

Small business hazardous waste, 123–124

Smith, Robert Angus, 79

Smog, 1–2, 15, 21, 22–23

Smuggling of ozone-depleting chemicals,
75–77

Snails, 81

Social activism, 4–5

Software, emission control, 32–33

Soils, 44–45, 65, 81, 86

Solid waste. *See* Hazardous waste;
Municipal solid waste; Nonhazardous
waste

*Solid Waste Agency of Northern Cook County
v. US Army Corps of Engineers*, 137

Solid Waste Disposal Act, 89

Source reduction practices, 114t

Sources, pollutant. *See* specific pollutants

South Carolina, 127–128, 129

Southeast Asia, 76

Southern Hemisphere ozone depletion, 70t

Soviet Union, 125–126

Special wastes, 92–93, 92t, 93t

Species loss. *See* Endangered and threatened
species

Spent nuclear fuel, 129, 130f

Spotted owl controversy, 173–174

States
acid rain, 83–84
alternative fuel sites, 35, 36t
Clean Water Act jurisdiction, 138
climate change initiatives, 63–65
consumer electronics waste, 94, 109, 114
cross-state air pollution, 28–30
Cross-State Air Pollution Rule, 29t
environmental agencies, 3
environmental education, 13
gasoline standards regulations, 33
geologic repositories for radioactive
waste, 130f
greenhouse gas emissions regulations, 60
Gulf Coast wetlands, 172
hazardous waste, 115, 116t
hydraulic fracturing, 178
landfill gas-to-energy projects, 99
landfills regulations, 89
medical waste, 92
motor vehicle emissions standards, 32
municipal solid waste imports and
exports, 100
municipal solid waste management, 103
National Ambient Air Quality Standards,
16
nonpoint source water pollution
management, 139
nuclear power plants, 125f–126f, 128
recycling and recovery, 101–102, 112–113
surface water quality assessments, 141
total maximum daily loads, 147
water body uses, 142

Statistical information
Acid Rain Program sulfur dioxide
allowances, 84(t5.3)

air pollutant concentrations, 18t

air pollutant emissions, 17t

alternative fuel sites, 36t

alternative fuel vehicles, 35t

blood lead levels in children, 159f

carbon dioxide, atmospheric
concentrations of, 50(f3.9)

carbon dioxide emissions for cars and
light-duty trucks, 61f

carbon dioxide emissions from fossil
fuel combustion, 59t

carbon dioxide emissions from
transportation sector, 60f

carbon monoxide air quality, 18f

construction and demolition debris, 91f,
91t

drought, 168f

emissions compared with measures of
economic growth, 28(f2.10)

Environmental Protection Agency
budget, 11f, 12t

forested land, 166(t11.2), 166(t11.3)

fuel economy and carbon dioxide
emissions standards, 33t, 34t

greenhouse gas emissions, annual
percentage change in, 45f

greenhouse gas emissions, by gas, 42f

greenhouse gas emissions, by gas and
source, 43t–44t

hazardous waste generation, by state, 116t

health effects of hazardous air pollutants,
31t

international carbon dioxide emissions,
49f, 49t

landfills, materials in, 98t, 99f

lead air quality, 20f

methane, atmospheric concentrations of,
50(f3.10)

municipal solid waste, breakdown of
generation and disposition, 102(t6.15)

municipal solid waste, composition of,
95t, 96f, 96t, 97t

municipal solid waste, disposition of, 113f

municipal solid waste, generation,
recovery, and discard amounts for, 99t

municipal solid waste, total and per
capita generation of, 94f

municipal solid waste management
methods, 97f

NAAQS, people living in counties with
air quality above, 19f

nitrogen dioxide air quality, 21f

nitrogen oxide emissions from power
plants, 85(t5.5)

ozone air quality, 24t

ozone depletion, 70t

ozone depletion potential and global
warming potential of various
chemicals, 71t

ozone-depleting chemicals, trends in
atmospheric concentrations of, 75f, 78f

particulate matter air quality, 25f, 26f

pesticides in food, 163t

power plants affected by federal acid rain regulations, 84(t5.2)

public opinion on climate change, 66t

public opinion on energy production vs. environmental concerns, 7(t1.3)

public opinion on environmental quality, 8(t1.4)

public opinion on federal environmental protection, 8(t1.5)

public opinion on the environment vs. the economy as a priority, 7(t1.2)

public opinion on the status of the environment, 6t

recovery and recycling of municipal solid waste, by material, 109f

recycling rates for municipal solid waste, 108f

regional trends in air quality, 86(t5.6)

regional trends in sulfur and nitrogen deposition, 86(t5.7)

sea surface temperatures, 63t

sulfur dioxide air quality, 27f

sulfur dioxide emissions from power plants, 85(t5.4)

total maximum daily loads, 147t

Toxics Release Inventory production-related waste management, by method, 118f, 118(t8.2)

Toxics Release Inventory wastes, management of, 119f, 120f

unhealthy AQI, days of, 28(f2.9)

US greenhouse gas emissions, by economic sector, 46f, 47f

US greenhouse gas emissions, by source, 48f

US regional temperature changes, 62t

waste-to-energy process, 102(t6.14)

water bodies assessed for water quality, 141(t9.2)

water bodies with exceedances of critical loads for nitrogen and sulfur, 87(t5.9)

water chemistry, regional trends in, 87(t5.8)

wetlands losses and gains, 170f

wildfires, 168t

Stratospheric ozone. See Ozone depletion

Streams. See Rivers and streams

Sulfur dioxide

acid rain, 79–80, 83–84, 84–85, 85(t5.4)

Acid Rain Program allowances, 84(t5.3)

air quality, 26–27, 27f

cross-state air pollution, 30

regional trends in deposition of, 86(t5.7)

water bodies with exceedances of critical loads for, 87(t5.9)

Sulfur hexafluoride, 45

Summer power plant, 127–128

Superfund, 120–123, 121t

Surface water

acid rain, 80, 81, 86–88

National Aquatic Resource Surveys, 148–150

nitrogen and sulfur exceedances, 87(t5.9)

usage, 135–136

water quality, 142t, 143t, 144t, 146t

water quality assessment results, 141–146

Sustainability and green consumerism, 6

Sustainable Materials Management Electronics Challenge program, 109

Synthetic gases. See Engineered gases

T

Taxes and the Superfund program, 121–122

Temperatures

changes in US temperatures, 62–63

global temperatures, 51–54, 52f, 53f, 66, 67t

global warming skeptics, 66

public opinion on climate change, 67t

sea surface temperatures, 63t

Tennessee, 128

Teratogens, 155

Tesla Motors, 37

Texas, 35, 115, 128, 129

Thermoelectric power plants, 135

Thirty Percent Club, 83

Three Mile Island accident, 125

Tijuana River, 152

Tijuana Slough Shoreline, 152

Tires, scrap, 106

Title X, 159

TMDLs (total maximum daily loads), 138, 146–148, 147t

Total maximum daily loads (TMDLs), 138, 146–148, 147t

Toxic Substances Control Act (TSCA), 156

Toxic Waste and Race in the United States (United Church of Christ), 12

Toxic Wastes and Race at Twenty (Bullard), 13

Toxics Release Inventory (TRI), 117–119, 118f, 118t, 119f, 120f, 156

Toxins

asbestos, 162

environmental movement history, 2, 3

food, 163t

in food, 162–164

government legislation, 155–156

indoor air toxins, 161–162, 161t

lead, 158–160, 159f, 160f

radiation sources, 160t

radon, 160–161

risk management, 156–158

See also Hazardous air pollutants; Hazardous waste

Toyota, 36

Toys, 158–159

Transboundary pollution, 28–30, 29t, 82–83

Transuranic (TRU) waste, 129, 130, 131–132

Treaties and international agreements

Convention for the Protection of the Ozone Layer, 72

Kyoto Protocol, 5, 55–57

Montreal Protocol, 72–75, 73t

Paris Agreement, 57–58

UN Framework Convention on Climate Change, 55

UNECE Convention on Long-Range Transboundary Air Pollution, 83

Trees. See Forests

TRI (Toxics Release Inventory), 117–119, 118f, 118t, 119f, 120f, 156

Tropospheric ozone. See Ozone depletion

TRU (transuranic) waste, 129, 130, 131–132

TRUE Zero Waste certification, 106

Trump, Donald

Arctic National Wildlife Refuge, 176–177

Clean Water Rule, 171

climate change, 60, 61, 67, 78

Comprehensive Environmental Response, Compensation, and Liability Act, 123

endangered species, 173

environmental policies, 10

hazardous air pollutants regulations, 31

hydraulic fracturing, 178

motor vehicle exhaust emissions standards, 34

offshore drilling, 175

ozone standards, 22

Paris Agreement, 57–58

Superfund funding, 122

Yucca Mountain nuclear waste site, 134

TSCA (Toxic Substances Control Act), 156

U

Ultraviolet (UV) light, 21, 44, 69, 71

UN. See United Nations

Underground nuclear waste storage. See Geologic repositories for radioactive waste

UNECE (United Nations Economic Commission for Europe), 83

UNECE Convention on Long-Range Transboundary Air Pollution, 83

UNEP (United Nations Environment Programme), 11, 39–40, 72, 73, 74, 76

UNFCCC (United Nations Framework Convention on Climate Change), 55

Union Carbide, 156

United Church of Christ, 12

United Haulers Association, Inc. v. Oneida-Herkimer Solid Waste Management Authority, 103

United Nations (UN)

Earth Day, 3

environmental conference of 1972, 10–11

Food and Agriculture Organization (FAO), 174

Paris Agreement, 57

United Nations Economic Commission for Europe (UNECE), 83

United Nations Environment Programme (UNEP), 11, 39–40, 72, 73, 74, 76

United Nations Framework Convention on Climate Change (UNFCCC), 55

United States
  acid rain and the recovery of ecosystems, 85–88
  air quality, by regions, 86(t5.6)
  biodiversity, 173–174, 173t
  black market trade in ozone-depleting chemicals, 76–77
  climate science reports, 62–63
  forests, status of, 165–169
  greenhouse gas emissions, 45–46
  greenhouse gas emissions, by economic sector, 46f, 47f
  greenhouse gas emissions, by source, 48f
  Kigali Amendment, 78
  Kyoto Protocol, 55–56
  materials recovery facilities, 111
  Montreal Protocol, 74t
  municipal solid waste generation, 96–97
  presidential climate change policies, 58–62
  temperature changes, 62t

United States, Rapanos v., 137

United States v. Riverside Bayview Homes, Inc., 137

Universal wastes, 124

Upper Animas River watershed, 122

Uranium mill tailings, 129

US Army Corps of Engineers (ACE), 138, 170, 171

US Army Corps of Engineers, Solid Waste Agency of Northern Cook County v., 137

US Bureau of Land Management (BLM), 122, 123f, 175–176

US Business Council for Sustainable Development, 105

US Climate Change Research Initiative, 58

US Climate Change Science Program, 58

US Coast Guard, 152

US Consumer Product Safety Commission (CPSC), 155–156

US Department of Agriculture (USDA), 122, 162, 163

US Department of Energy (DOE)
  carbon sequestration, 66
  Office of Environmental Management, 128
  radioactive waste, 124, 131–132
  waste treatment plants, 129
  Yucca Mountain nuclear waste site, 133–134

US Department of Justice, 32–33

US Department of the Interior, 122

US Energy Information Administration (EIA), 46–47

US Food and Drug Administration (FDA), 155, 162, 164

US Forest Service (FS), 122, 165–166, 169, 173–174

US Geological Survey (USGS), 150, 175, 176

US Global Change Research Program (USGCRP), 58, 62

US Government Accountability Office, 122

US Nuclear Regulatory Commission (NRC), 124, 127, 133, 160

USDA (US Department of Agriculture), 122, 162, 163

USGCRP (US Global Change Research Program), 58, 62

USGS (US Geological Survey), 150, 175, 176

Utah, 122, 128, 129

UV (ultraviolet) light, 21, 44, 69, 71

V

Vail, CO, 3

Vegetation and acid rain, 81

Vermont, 64, 178

Vienna Convention, 72

Virgil C. Summer power plant, 127–128

Virginia, 128, 148

VOCs (volatile organic compounds), 16, 27

Volatile organic compounds (VOCs), 16, 27

Volkswagen Group, 32

W

Warren County, NC, 12

Washington (state), 35, 129

Waste. See Hazardous waste; Municipal solid waste; Nonhazardous waste; Radioactive waste

Waste Isolation Pilot Plant (WIPP), 128, 129, 130–132, 132f, 133f

Waste Isolation Pilot Plant Land Withdrawal Act, 132

Waste treatment plants, 129

Waste-to-energy process, 94, 101–103, 101f, 102(t6.14)

Wastewater treatment biosolids recycling, 106

Water availability and usage, 135–137

Water Infrastructure Improvements for the Nation Act, 93

Water quality
  abandoned mines, 122
  acid rain, 80, 81, 86–88, 87t
  Clean Water Act jurisdiction, 137–138
  Clean Water Act–required assessments, 140–141
  climate change effects, 62
  coal combustion residuals, 92–93
  coastal waters, 150–152
  drinking water, 153–154
  environmental movement, 2
  hydraulic fracturing, 177–178
  lead, 159
  National Aquatic Resource Surveys, 148–150
  nonpoint source management, 138–139

ocean protection, 152–153
  pesticides, 162
  point source management, 138
  point sources and nonpoint sources, examples of, 139f
  pollution controls, 146–148
  rivers and streams, 142(t9.3)
  surface water, 142t, 143t, 144t, 146t
  surface water quality assessment results, 141–146
  total maximum daily loads, 147t
  US Geological Survey data sources, 150
  water bodies assessed for, 141(t9.2)
  watershed management, 139–140, 140f, 141(t9.1)
  wetlands, 169–172, 171f

Water treatment, drinking, 153, 154

Water vapor, 40–41

Waterborne diseases, 153–154

Watersheds, 139–140, 140f, 141(t9.1), 147–148
  See also Chesapeake Bay watershed

Weather, extreme. See Extreme weather

Weather and natural sinks, 65

Well water, 150

West Valley Demonstration Project, 128, 129

West Virginia, 147, 148, 156

Western Climate Initiative, 63

Westinghouse Electric Company, 127–128

Wetlands
  coal combustion residuals, 92
  contribution to improving water quality and reducing runoff, 171f
  losses and gains, 170f
  National Aquatic Resource Surveys, 149–150
  roles of, 169–170
  water quality, 142, 143(t9.8), 144

Whitman v. American Trucking Association Inc., 22

WHO (World Health Organization), 9, 126

Wildfires, 168–169, 168t

WIPP (Waste Isolation Pilot Plant), 128, 129, 130–132, 132f, 133f

WMO (World Meteorological Organization), 39, 71

World Health Organization (WHO), 9, 126

World Meteorological Organization (WMO), 39, 71

World Trade Organization summit, 4–5

Y

Yard trimmings, 110, 112(t7.4), 112(t7.5), 112(t7.6)

Yucca Mountain nuclear waste site, 132–134

Z

Zero waste, 106